The Vampire BRAT

and other tales of Supernatural Law
by Batton Lash

EXHIBIT A PRESS

SAN DIEGO, CALIFORNIA

Acknowledgments

"The Vampire Brat' originally appeared in *Mavis* issue 2, *Wolff & Byrd, Counselors of the Macabre* issue 23, and *Supernatural Law* issue 24. "Fashionably Late" originally appeared in *Supernatural Law* issue 25; "Black Market Souls" originally appeared in *Supernatural Law* issue 26; "Courting Disaster" originally appeared in *Supernatural Law* issues 28 and 29.

All art is by Batton Lash. All lettering is by Jackie Estrada and Batton Lash.

Dedicated to Nancy Roberts and S. S. Wilson

Writer/artist: Batton Lash
Editor: Jackie Estrada
Technical consultant: Mitch Berger, Esq.
Art assists: Derek Ozawa, Melissa Uran
Cover colors: Gary Sassaman
Staff 'n stuff: S. Derma

First printing, November 2001

Printed in the United States of America

ISBN #0-9633954-7-5
Library of Congress Control Number: 2001 131742

Contents

Introduction

The straight-faced adventures of a couple of lawyers practicing in defense of super-natural creatures is more than unique: It is an idea whose time has come. We are now in an era that has seen the probability of the impossible. The magic of genetics and the incredible visitation to other planets are only a few of the unbelievable things with which we live day to day. All of which, by the way, was once in the realm of the supernatural. It is therefore hardly surprising that today's readers find Batton Lash's world of the macabre so acceptable and engaging.

With hysterically funny situations and smart, fluid dialogue, Wolff and Byrd, a really cool team of lawyers, defend vampires, monsters, and creatures from the nether world. They take on cases that range from the question of the equity of a soul to the problems of a vampire brat shnook who can't even hypnotize Mavis, the law firm's cute secretary. And the stories are cunningly set in an ambience of no-kidding realism.

As a practitioner, I have always adhered to stories of reality. Only occasionally did I ever have the courage to attempt anything other than a candid separation between reality and supernatural. That is probably why I recognize in Batton's work the genius of wedding the two so seamlessly. There is something uncanny about the lingering residue of reality that remains at the end of any of Lash's stories. In stories like "Black Market Souls" with its Vincent Price/Peter Lorre B-movie characters and "You'll Never Suck Blood in This Town Again," the outrageous situation is leavened by the slick, funny, real-people conversation. In the end, readers are left with a nagging sympathy for the bizarre clients and an acceptance of the incredible premise that monsters, vampires, and other-world creatures are in desperate need of legal defense. Too long have they been an abused and ignored minority.

I say hooray for Wolff and Byrd and bravo for this assembly of the best of their stories.

Here is a collection to keep, read, and reread.

There is a personal addition I must make. I know of no greater reward for teach-ing than the success of one's students. I've been following with shameless pride the burgeoning career of Batton Lash since he graduated from my class at the School of Visual Arts in New York. I remember him as a dedicated student who took seriously the subject of sequential art. At the time I knew he had a visceral interest in the law, so it is hardly surprising to me that he now uses that interest so effectively in this unique series.

Batton's command of the narrative power of sequentially arranged imagery is what makes *Supernatural Law* so readable; his keen sense of humor is what makes his work so good and so enduring.

Will Eisner
Florida 2001

SUPERNATURAL LAW

In our *litigious society,* everyone has need of legal representation--and the *paranormal* are no exception! Attorneys *Alanna Wolff* and *Jeff Byrd* have established their practice to service the strange and unusual *requirements* of a most *particular* clientele . . .

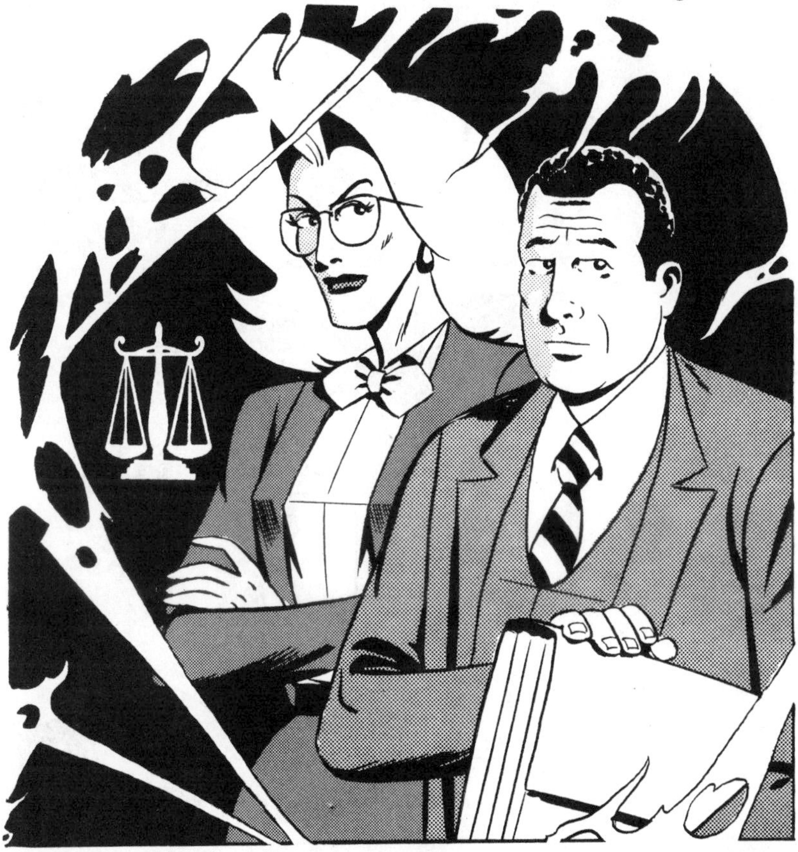

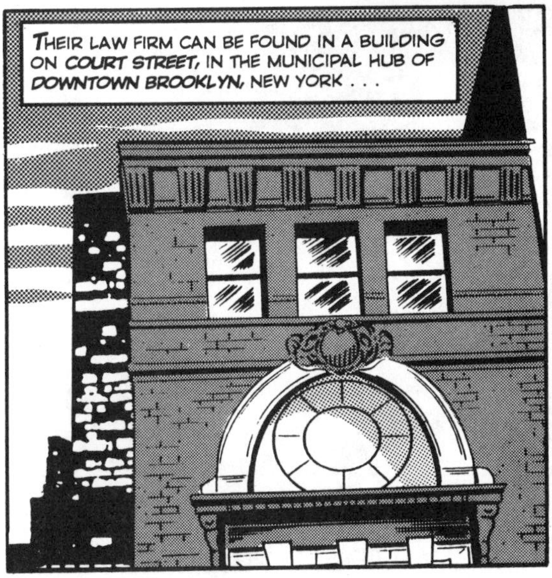
THEIR LAW FIRM CAN BE FOUND IN A BUILDING ON COURT STREET, IN THE MUNICIPAL HUB OF DOWNTOWN BROOKLYN, NEW YORK . . .

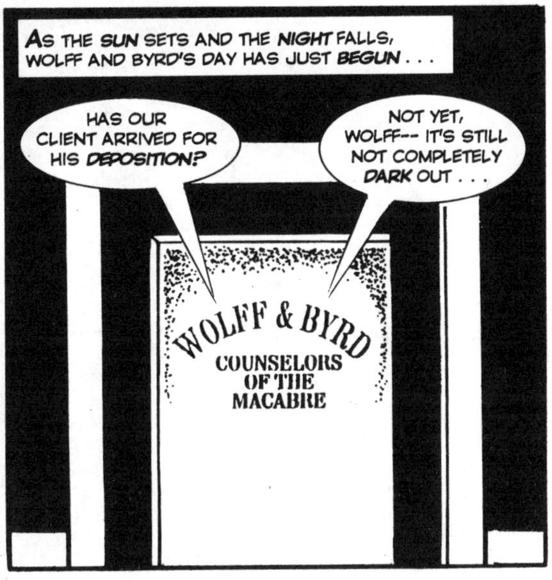
AS THE SUN SETS AND THE NIGHT FALLS, WOLFF AND BYRD'S DAY HAS JUST BEGUN . . .
HAS OUR CLIENT ARRIVED FOR HIS DEPOSITION?
NOT YET, WOLFF-- IT'S STILL NOT COMPLETELY DARK OUT . . .
WOLFF & BYRD
COUNSELORS OF THE MACABRE

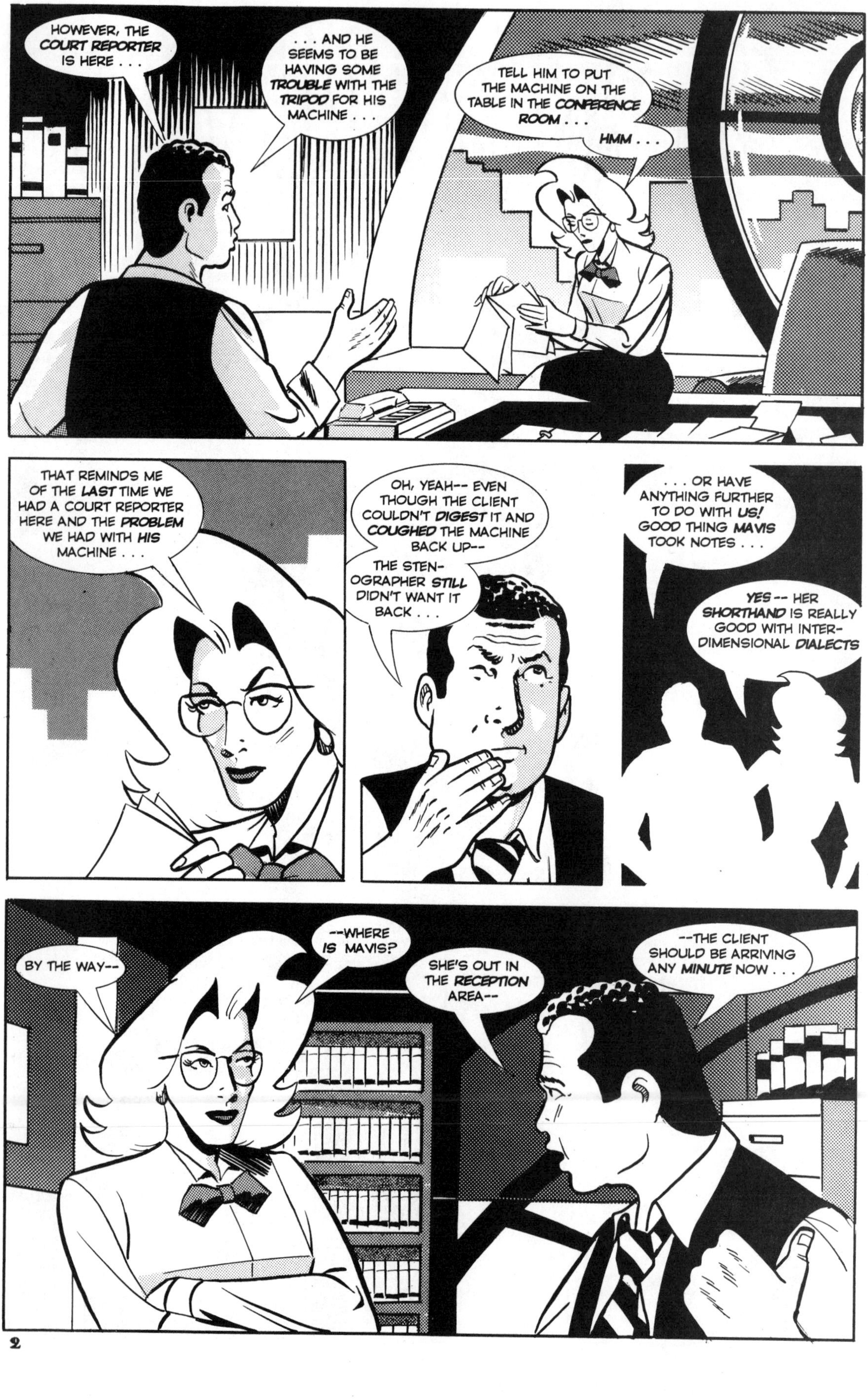
HOWEVER, THE COURT REPORTER IS HERE . . .
. . . AND HE SEEMS TO BE HAVING SOME TROUBLE WITH THE TRIPOD FOR HIS MACHINE . . .
TELL HIM TO PUT THE MACHINE ON THE TABLE IN THE CONFERENCE ROOM . . .
HMM . . .
THAT REMINDS ME OF THE LAST TIME WE HAD A COURT REPORTER HERE AND THE PROBLEM WE HAD WITH HIS MACHINE . . .
OH, YEAH-- EVEN THOUGH THE CLIENT COULDN'T DIGEST IT AND COUGHED THE MACHINE BACK UP--
THE STEN-OGRAPHER STILL DIDN'T WANT IT BACK . . .
. . . OR HAVE ANYTHING FURTHER TO DO WITH US! GOOD THING MAVIS TOOK NOTES . . .
YES -- HER SHORTHAND IS REALLY GOOD WITH INTER-DIMENSIONAL DIALECTS
BY THE WAY--
--WHERE IS MAVIS?
SHE'S OUT IN THE RECEPTION AREA--
--THE CLIENT SHOULD BE ARRIVING ANY MINUTE NOW . . .

The Vampire BRAT!
HMM . . . I THOUGHT HE'D BE ARRIVING BY WINDOW . . . !
KNOCK KNOCK
WOLFF & BYRD
COUNSELORS OF THE MACABRE

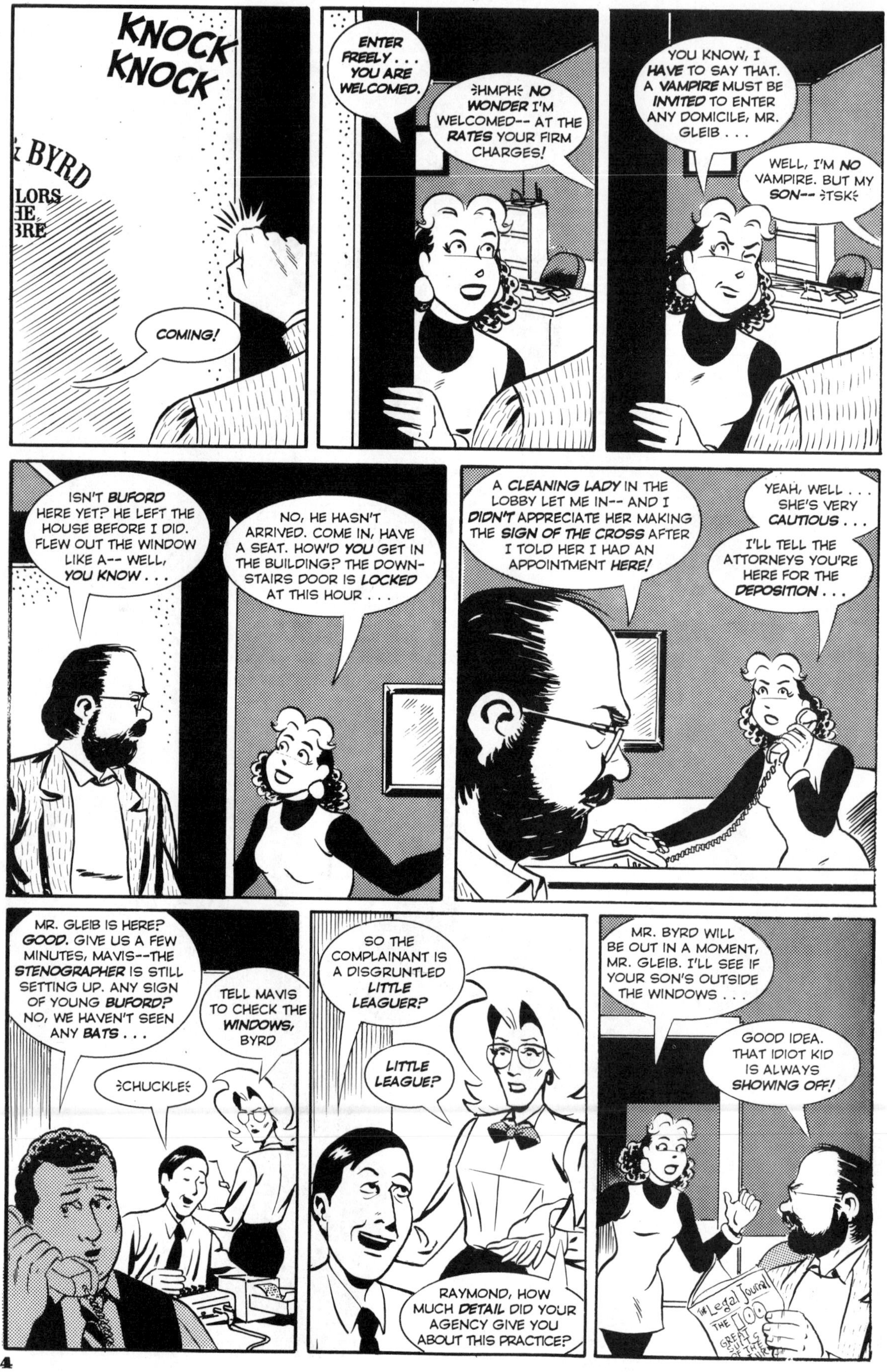
KNOCK KNOCK
& BYRD
LORS
HE
BRE
COMING!
ENTER FREELY . . . YOU ARE WELCOMED.
HMPH NO WONDER I'M WELCOMED-- AT THE RATES YOUR FIRM CHARGES!
YOU KNOW, I HAVE TO SAY THAT. A VAMPIRE MUST BE INVITED TO ENTER ANY DOMICILE, MR. GLEIB . . .
WELL, I'M NO VAMPIRE. BUT MY SON-- TSK
ISN'T BUFORD HERE YET? HE LEFT THE HOUSE BEFORE I DID. FLEW OUT THE WINDOW LIKE A-- WELL, YOU KNOW . . .
NO, HE HASN'T ARRIVED. COME IN, HAVE A SEAT. HOW'D YOU GET IN THE BUILDING? THE DOWN-STAIRS DOOR IS LOCKED AT THIS HOUR . . .
A CLEANING LADY IN THE LOBBY LET ME IN-- AND I DIDN'T APPRECIATE HER MAKING THE SIGN OF THE CROSS AFTER I TOLD HER I HAD AN APPOINTMENT HERE!
YEAH, WELL . . . SHE'S VERY CAUTIOUS . . .
I'LL TELL THE ATTORNEYS YOU'RE HERE FOR THE DEPOSITION . . .
MR. GLEIB IS HERE? GOOD. GIVE US A FEW MINUTES, MAVIS--THE STENOGRAPHER IS STILL SETTING UP. ANY SIGN OF YOUNG BUFORD? NO, WE HAVEN'T SEEN ANY BATS . . .
TELL MAVIS TO CHECK THE WINDOWS, BYRD
CHUCKLE
SO THE COMPLAINANT IS A DISGRUNTLED LITTLE LEAGUER?
LITTLE LEAGUE?
RAYMOND, HOW MUCH DETAIL DID YOUR AGENCY GIVE YOU ABOUT THIS PRACTICE?
MR. BYRD WILL BE OUT IN A MOMENT, MR. GLEIB. I'LL SEE IF YOUR SON'S OUTSIDE THE WINDOWS . . .
GOOD IDEA. THAT IDIOT KID IS ALWAYS SHOWING OFF!
The Legal Journal
THE 100

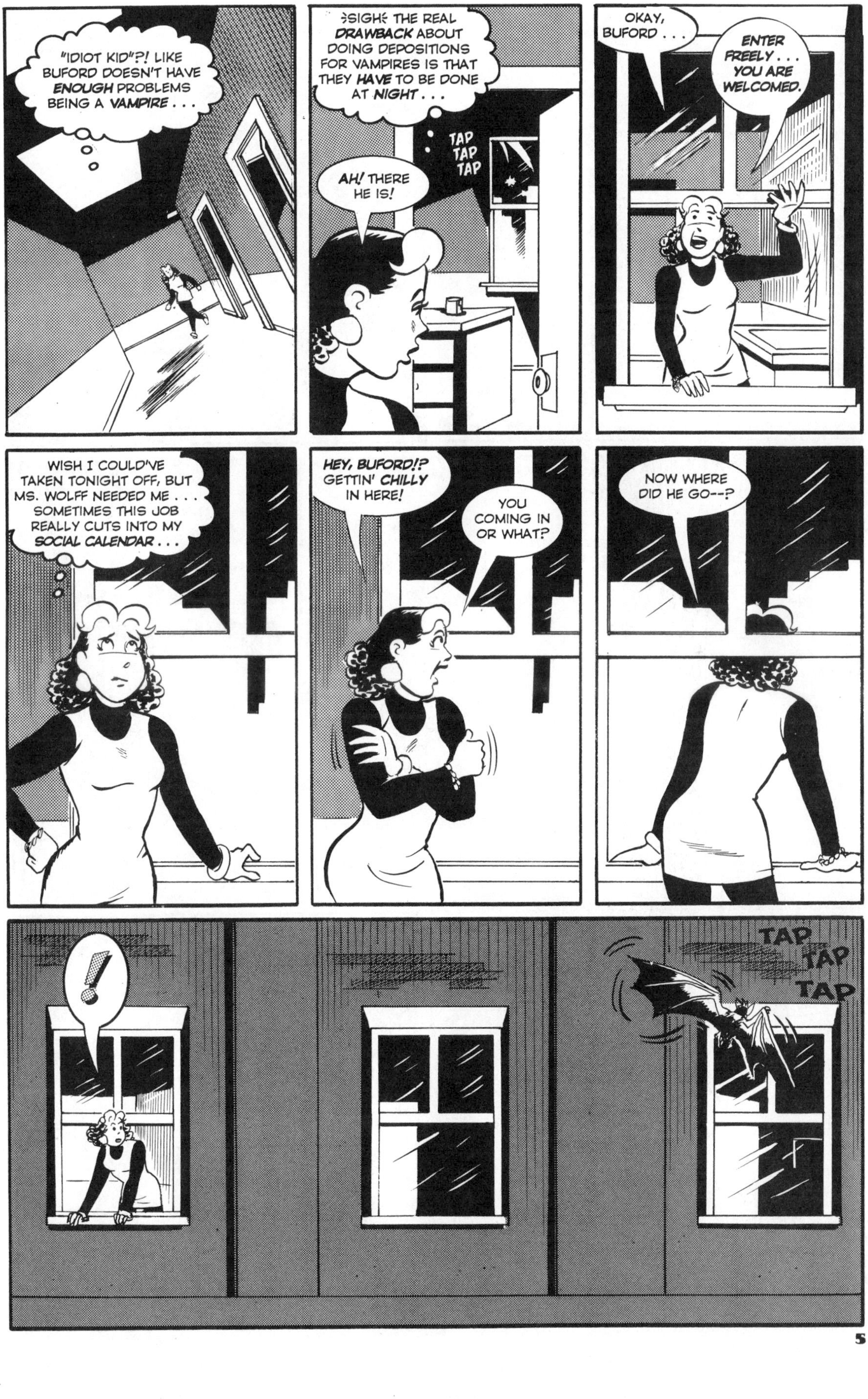
"IDIOT KID"?! LIKE BUFORD DOESN'T HAVE ENOUGH PROBLEMS BEING A VAMPIRE . . .
⊰SIGH⊱ THE REAL DRAWBACK ABOUT DOING DEPOSITIONS FOR VAMPIRES IS THAT THEY HAVE TO BE DONE AT NIGHT . . .
TAP TAP TAP
AH! THERE HE IS!
OKAY, BUFORD . . .
ENTER FREELY . . . YOU ARE WELCOMED.
WISH I COULD'VE TAKEN TONIGHT OFF, BUT MS. WOLFF NEEDED ME . . . SOMETIMES THIS JOB REALLY CUTS INTO MY SOCIAL CALENDAR . . .
HEY, BUFORD!? GETTIN' CHILLY IN HERE!
YOU COMING IN OR WHAT?
NOW WHERE DID HE GO--?
!
TAP TAP TAP

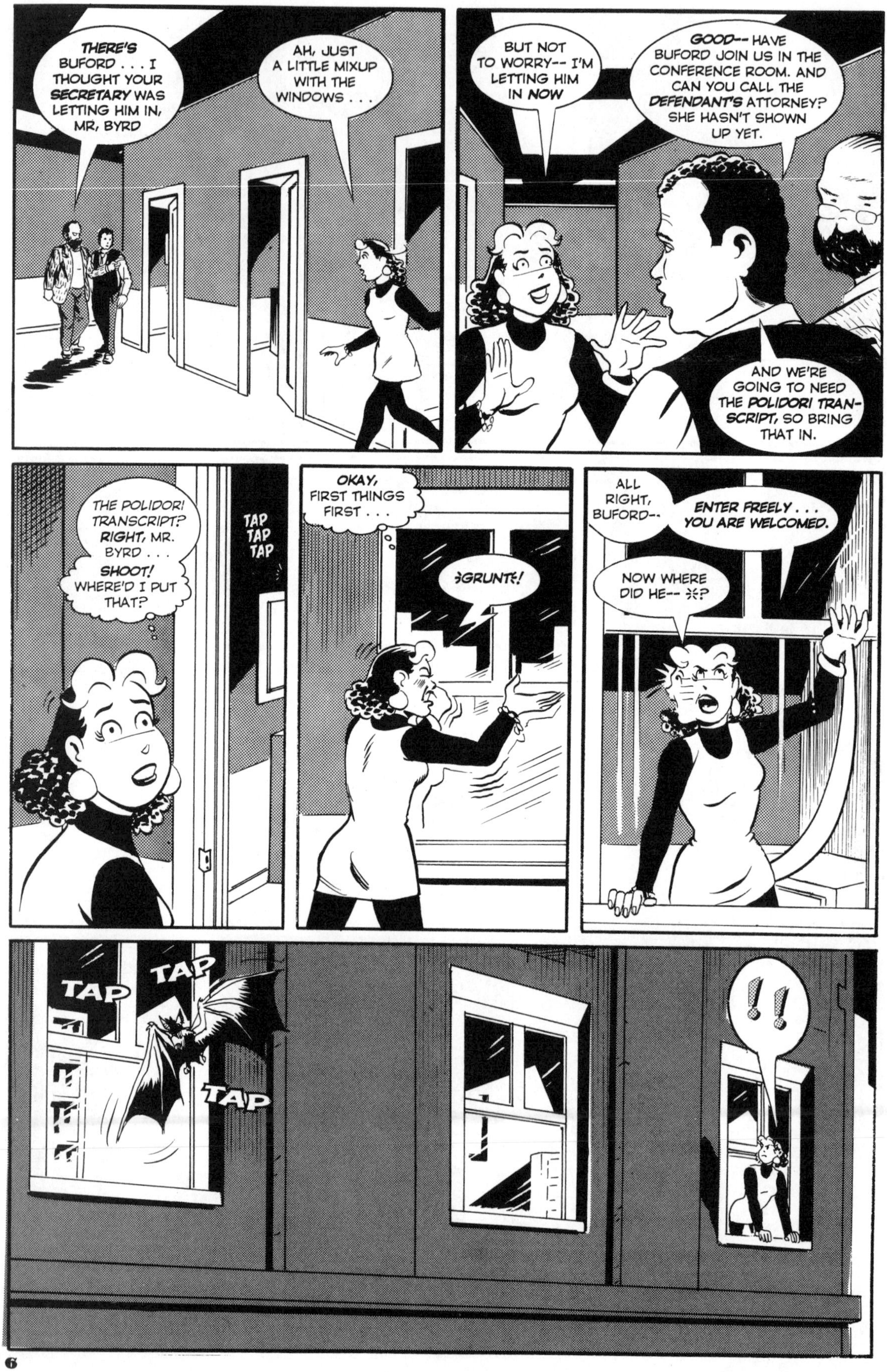
THERE'S BUFORD . . . I THOUGHT YOUR SECRETARY WAS LETTING HIM IN, MR. BYRD
AH, JUST A LITTLE MIXUP WITH THE WINDOWS . . .
BUT NOT TO WORRY-- I'M LETTING HIM IN NOW
GOOD-- HAVE BUFORD JOIN US IN THE CONFERENCE ROOM. AND CAN YOU CALL THE DEFENDANT'S ATTORNEY? SHE HASN'T SHOWN UP YET.
AND WE'RE GOING TO NEED THE POLIDORI TRANSCRIPT, SO BRING THAT IN.
THE POLIDORI TRANSCRIPT? RIGHT, MR. BYRD . . . SHOOT! WHERE'D I PUT THAT?
TAP TAP TAP
OKAY, FIRST THINGS FIRST . . .
GRUNT!
ALL RIGHT, BUFORD--
ENTER FREELY . . . YOU ARE WELCOMED.
NOW WHERE DID HE-- ?
TAP
TAP
TAP
!!

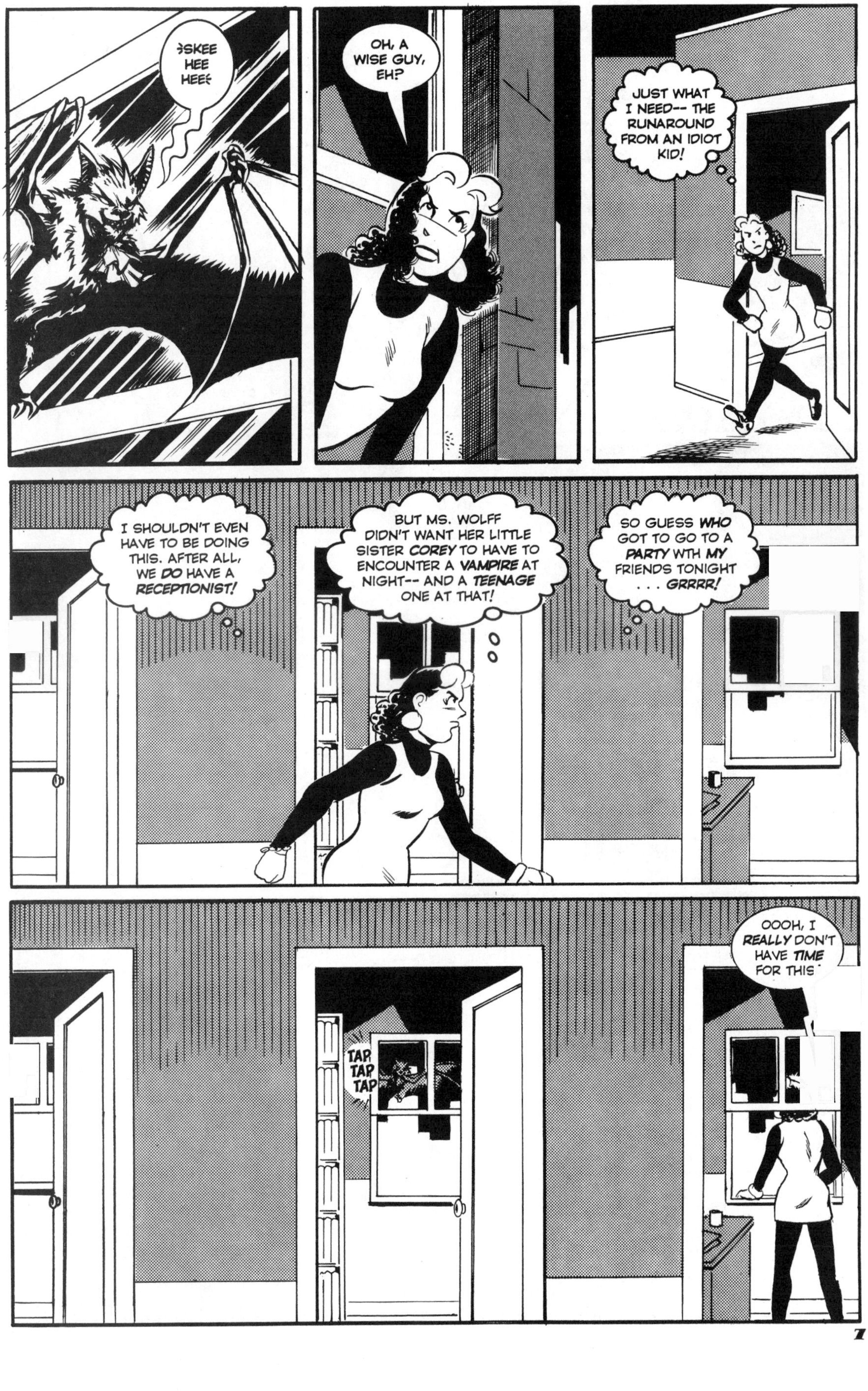
SKEE HEE HEE
OH, A WISE GUY, EH?
JUST WHAT I NEED-- THE RUNAROUND FROM AN IDIOT KID!
I SHOULDN'T EVEN HAVE TO BE DOING THIS. AFTER ALL, WE DO HAVE A RECEPTIONIST!
BUT MS. WOLFF DIDN'T WANT HER LITTLE SISTER COREY TO HAVE TO ENCOUNTER A VAMPIRE AT NIGHT-- AND A TEENAGE ONE AT THAT!
SO GUESS WHO GOT TO GO TO A PARTY WTH MY FRIENDS TONIGHT . . . GRRRR!
OOOH, I REALLY DON'T HAVE TIME FOR THIS
TAP TAP TAP

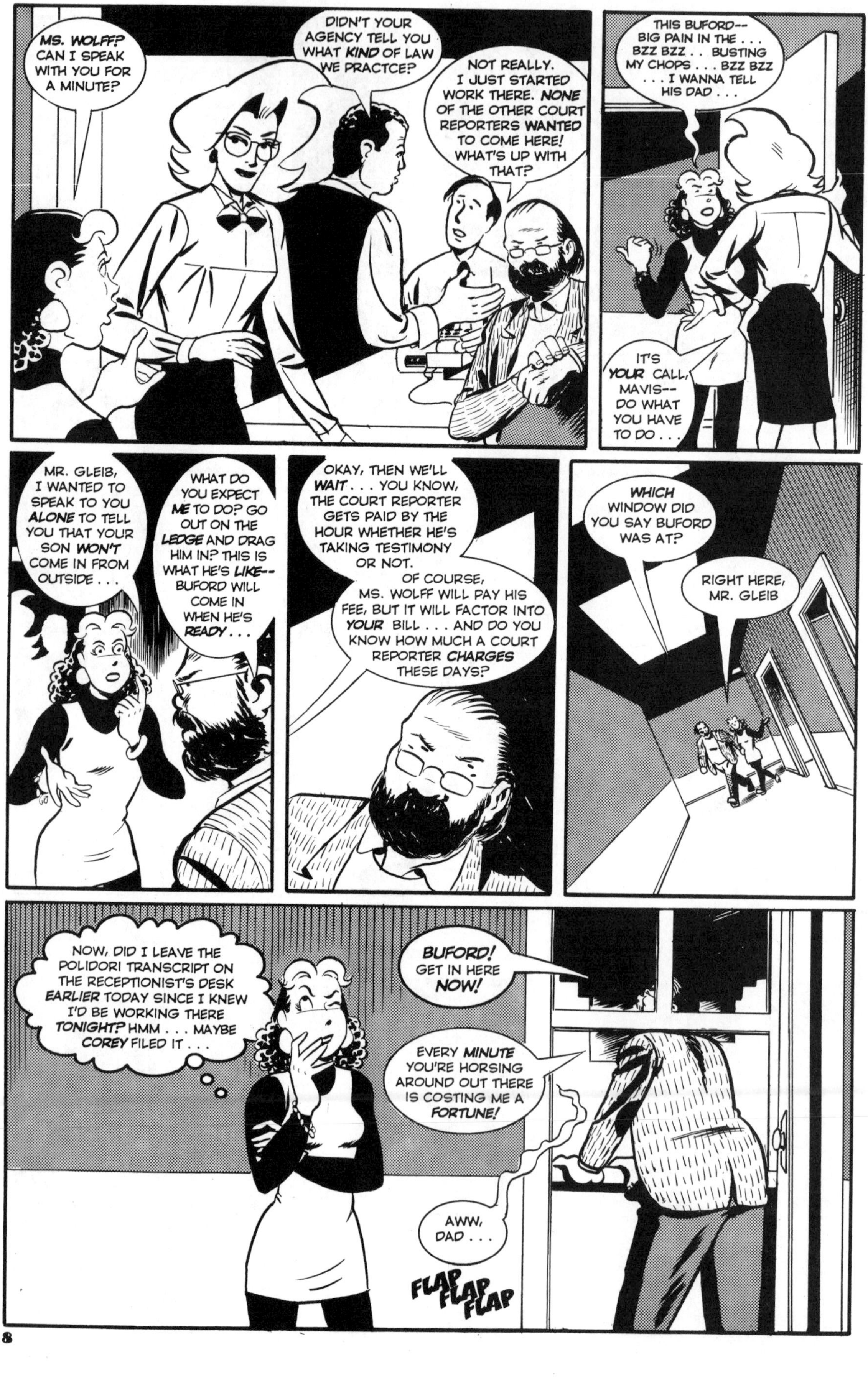
MS. WOLFF? CAN I SPEAK WITH YOU FOR A MINUTE?
DIDN'T YOUR AGENCY TELL YOU WHAT KIND OF LAW WE PRACTCE?
NOT REALLY. I JUST STARTED WORK THERE. NONE OF THE OTHER COURT REPORTERS WANTED TO COME HERE! WHAT'S UP WITH THAT?
THIS BUFORD-- BIG PAIN IN THE . . . BZZ BZZ . . BUSTING MY CHOPS . . . BZZ BZZ . . . I WANNA TELL HIS DAD . . .
IT'S YOUR CALL, MAVIS-- DO WHAT YOU HAVE TO DO . . .
MR. GLEIB, I WANTED TO SPEAK TO YOU ALONE TO TELL YOU THAT YOUR SON WON'T COME IN FROM OUTSIDE . . .
WHAT DO YOU EXPECT ME TO DO? GO OUT ON THE LEDGE AND DRAG HIM IN? THIS IS WHAT HE'S LIKE-- BUFORD WILL COME IN WHEN HE'S READY . . .
OKAY, THEN WE'LL WAIT . . . YOU KNOW, THE COURT REPORTER GETS PAID BY THE HOUR WHETHER HE'S TAKING TESTIMONY OR NOT.
OF COURSE, MS. WOLFF WILL PAY HIS FEE, BUT IT WILL FACTOR INTO YOUR BILL . . . AND DO YOU KNOW HOW MUCH A COURT REPORTER CHARGES THESE DAYS?
WHICH WINDOW DID YOU SAY BUFORD WAS AT?
RIGHT HERE, MR. GLEIB
NOW, DID I LEAVE THE POLIDORI TRANSCRIPT ON THE RECEPTIONIST'S DESK EARLIER TODAY SINCE I KNEW I'D BE WORKING THERE TONIGHT? HMM . . . MAYBE COREY FILED IT . . .
BUFORD! GET IN HERE NOW!
EVERY MINUTE YOU'RE HORSING AROUND OUT THERE IS COSTING ME A FORTUNE!
AWW, DAD . . .
FLAP FLAP FLAP

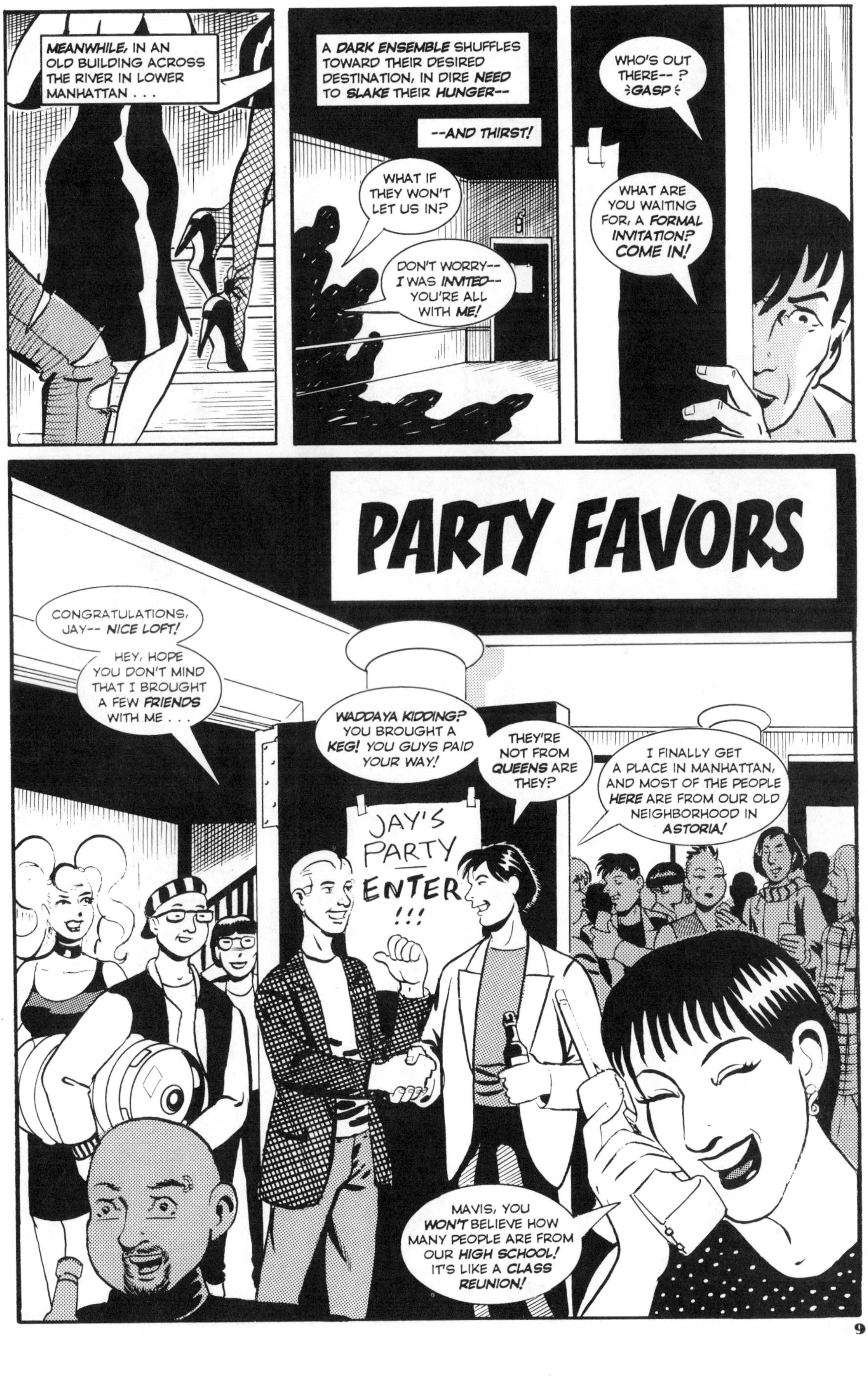
MEANWHILE, IN AN OLD BUILDING ACROSS THE RIVER IN LOWER MANHATTAN . . .
A DARK ENSEMBLE SHUFFLES TOWARD THEIR DESIRED DESTINATION, IN DIRE NEED TO SLAKE THEIR HUNGER--
--AND THIRST!
WHAT IF THEY WON'T LET US IN?
DON'T WORRY-- I WAS INVITED-- YOU'RE ALL WITH ME!
WHO'S OUT THERE-- ? GASP
WHAT ARE YOU WAITING FOR, A FORMAL INVITATION? COME IN!
PARTY FAVORS
CONGRATULATIONS, JAY-- NICE LOFT!
HEY, HOPE YOU DON'T MIND THAT I BROUGHT A FEW FRIENDS WITH ME . . .
WADDAYA KIDDING? YOU BROUGHT A KEG! YOU GUYS PAID YOUR WAY!
THEY'RE NOT FROM QUEENS ARE THEY?
I FINALLY GET A PLACE IN MANHATTAN, AND MOST OF THE PEOPLE HERE ARE FROM OUR OLD NEIGHBORHOOD IN ASTORIA!
JAY'S PARTY ENTER !!!
MAVIS, YOU WON'T BELIEVE HOW MANY PEOPLE ARE FROM OUR HIGH SCHOOL! IT'S LIKE A CLASS REUNION!

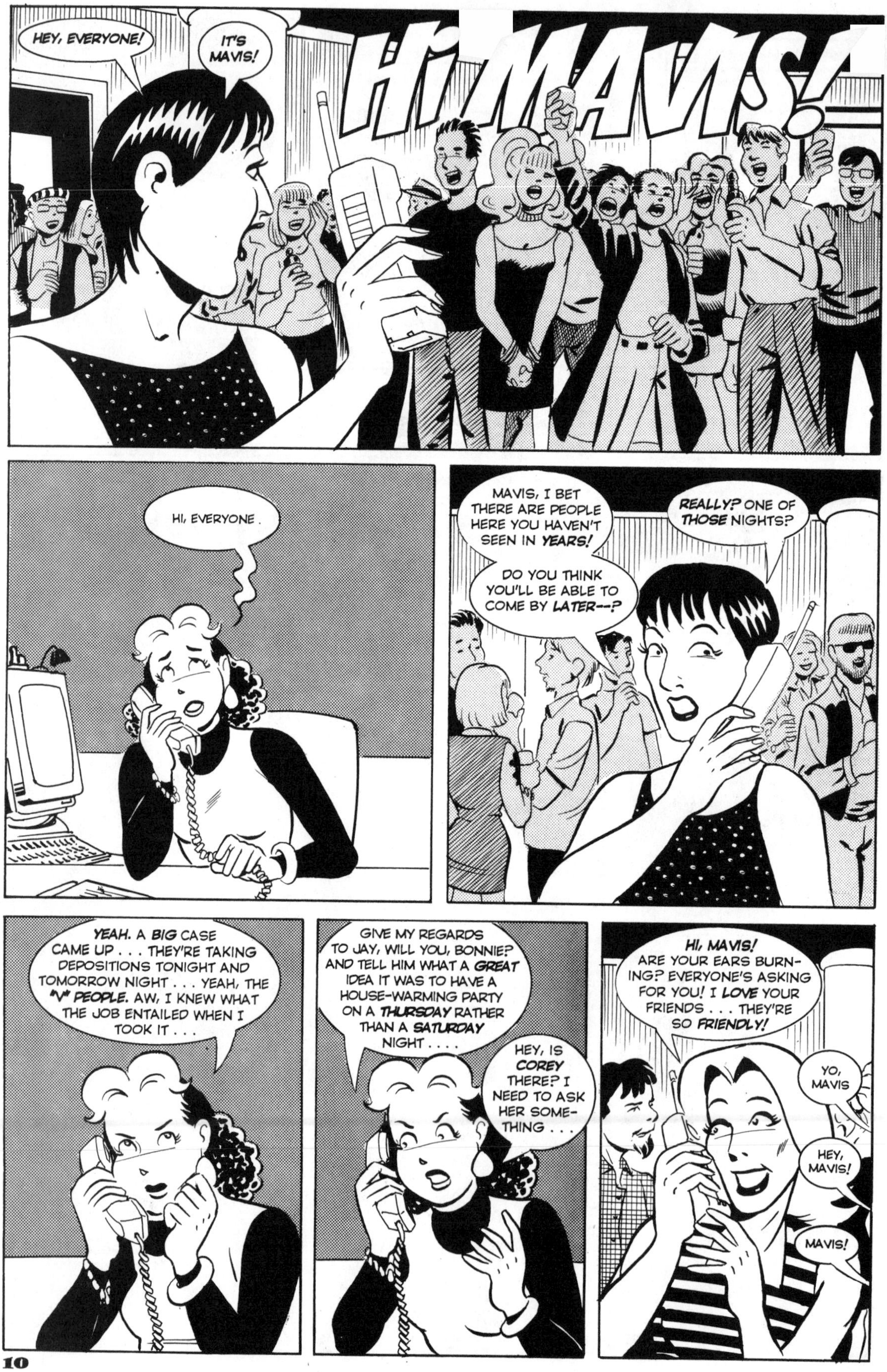
HEY, EVERYONE!
IT'S MAVIS!
HI, MAVIS!
HI, EVERYONE.
MAVIS, I BET THERE ARE PEOPLE HERE YOU HAVEN'T SEEN IN YEARS!
DO YOU THINK YOU'LL BE ABLE TO COME BY LATER--?
REALLY? ONE OF THOSE NIGHTS?
YEAH. A BIG CASE CAME UP . . . THEY'RE TAKING DEPOSITIONS TONIGHT AND TOMORROW NIGHT . . . YEAH, THE "V" PEOPLE. AW, I KNEW WHAT THE JOB ENTAILED WHEN I TOOK IT . . .
GIVE MY REGARDS TO JAY, WILL YOU, BONNIE? AND TELL HIM WHAT A GREAT IDEA IT WAS TO HAVE A HOUSE-WARMING PARTY ON A THURSDAY RATHER THAN A SATURDAY NIGHT . . . .
HEY, IS COREY THERE? I NEED TO ASK HER SOME-THING . . .
HI, MAVIS! ARE YOUR EARS BURN-ING? EVERYONE'S ASKING FOR YOU! I LOVE YOUR FRIENDS . . . THEY'RE SO FRIENDLY!
YO, MAVIS
HEY, MAVIS!
MAVIS!

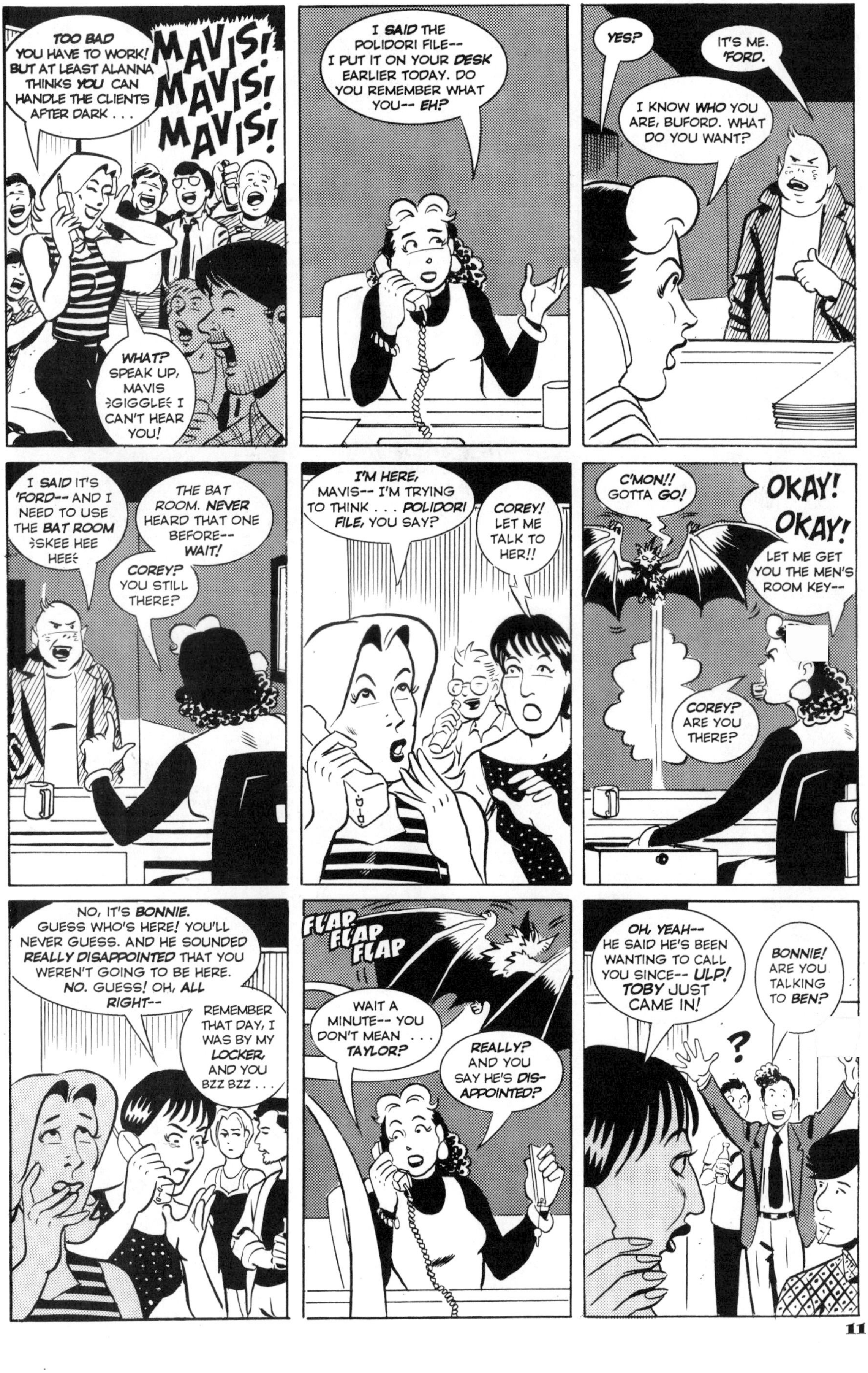
TOO BAD YOU HAVE TO WORK! BUT AT LEAST ALANNA THINKS YOU CAN HANDLE THE CLIENTS AFTER DARK . . .
MAVIS! MAVIS! MAVIS!
WHAT? SPEAK UP, MAVIS ≷GIGGLE≶ I CAN'T HEAR YOU!
I SAID THE POLIDORI FILE-- I PUT IT ON YOUR DESK EARLIER TODAY. DO YOU REMEMBER WHAT YOU-- EH?
YES?
IT'S ME. 'FORD.
I KNOW WHO YOU ARE, BUFORD. WHAT DO YOU WANT?
I SAID IT'S 'FORD-- AND I NEED TO USE THE BAT ROOM ≷SKEE HEE HEE≶
THE BAT ROOM. NEVER HEARD THAT ONE BEFORE-- WAIT!
COREY? YOU STILL THERE?
I'M HERE, MAVIS-- I'M TRYING TO THINK . . . POLIDORI FILE, YOU SAY?
COREY! LET ME TALK TO HER!!
C'MON!! GOTTA GO!
OKAY! OKAY!
LET ME GET YOU THE MEN'S ROOM KEY--
COREY? ARE YOU THERE?
NO, IT'S BONNIE. GUESS WHO'S HERE! YOU'LL NEVER GUESS. AND HE SOUNDED REALLY DISAPPOINTED THAT YOU WEREN'T GOING TO BE HERE. NO. GUESS! OH, ALL RIGHT--
REMEMBER THAT DAY, I WAS BY MY LOCKER, AND YOU BZZ BZZ . . .
FLAP FLAP FLAP
WAIT A MINUTE-- YOU DON'T MEAN . . . TAYLOR?
REALLY? AND YOU SAY HE'S DIS-APPOINTED?
OH, YEAH-- HE SAID HE'S BEEN WANTING TO CALL YOU SINCE-- ULP! TOBY JUST CAME IN!
BONNIE! ARE YOU TALKING TO BEN?
?

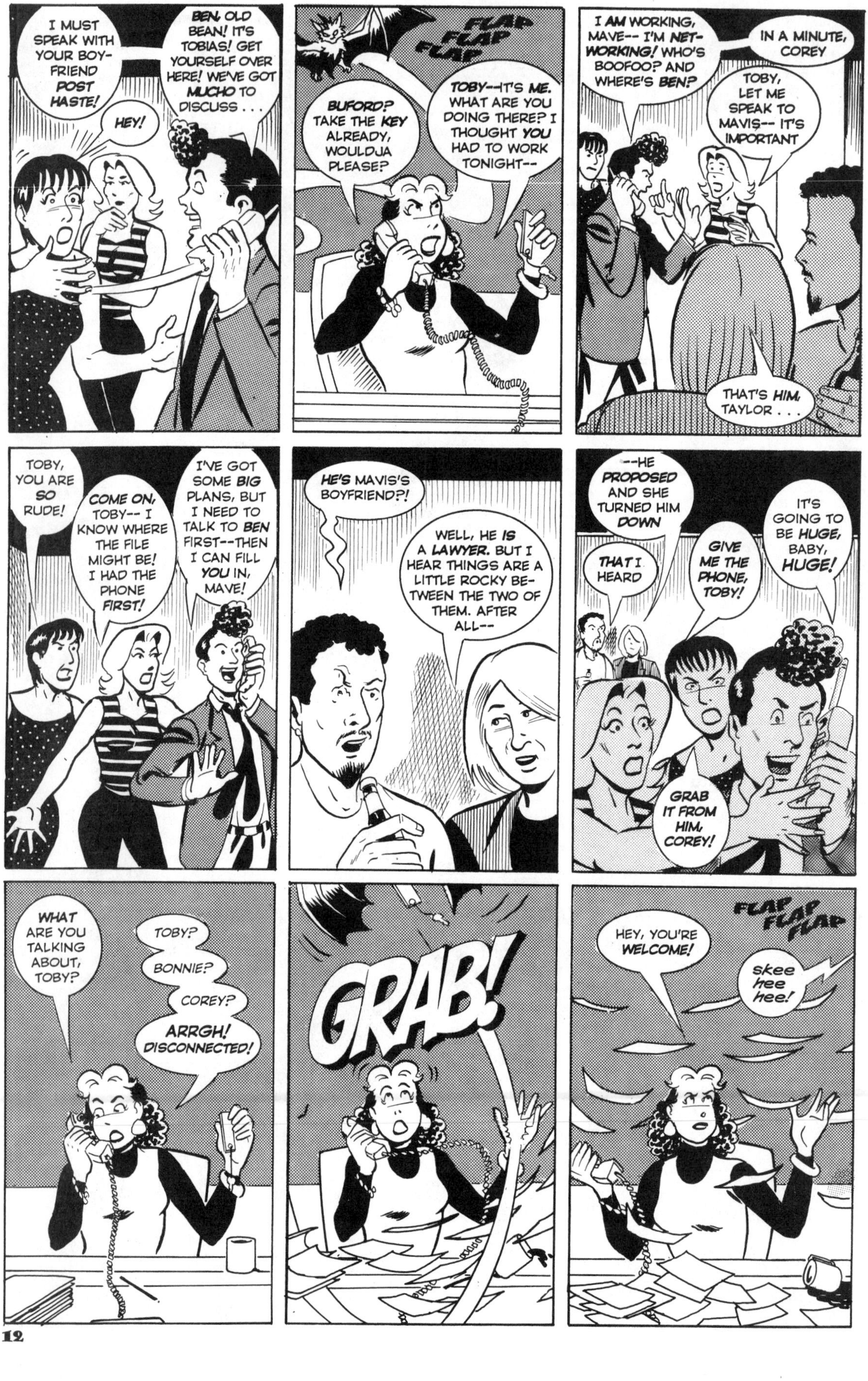
I MUST SPEAK WITH YOUR BOY-FRIEND POST HASTE!
BEN, OLD BEAN! IT'S TOBIAS! GET YOURSELF OVER HERE! WE'VE GOT MUCHO TO DISCUSS . . .
HEY!
FLAP FLAP FLAP
BUFORD? TAKE THE KEY ALREADY, WOULDJA PLEASE?
TOBY--IT'S ME. WHAT ARE YOU DOING THERE? I THOUGHT YOU HAD TO WORK TONIGHT--
I AM WORKING, MAVE-- I'M NET-WORKING! WHO'S BOOFOO? AND WHERE'S BEN?
IN A MINUTE, COREY
TOBY, LET ME SPEAK TO MAVIS-- IT'S IMPORTANT
THAT'S HIM, TAYLOR . . .
TOBY, YOU ARE SO RUDE!
COME ON, TOBY-- I KNOW WHERE THE FILE MIGHT BE! I HAD THE PHONE FIRST!
I'VE GOT SOME BIG PLANS, BUT I NEED TO TALK TO BEN FIRST--THEN I CAN FILL YOU IN, MAVE!
HE'S MAVIS'S BOYFRIEND?!
WELL, HE IS A LAWYER. BUT I HEAR THINGS ARE A LITTLE ROCKY BE-TWEEN THE TWO OF THEM. AFTER ALL--
--HE PROPOSED AND SHE TURNED HIM DOWN
THAT I HEARD
GIVE ME THE PHONE, TOBY!
IT'S GOING TO BE HUGE, BABY, HUGE!
GRAB IT FROM HIM, COREY!
WHAT ARE YOU TALKING ABOUT, TOBY?
TOBY?
BONNIE?
COREY?
ARRGH! DISCONNECTED!
GRAB!
FLAP FLAP FLAP
HEY, YOU'RE WELCOME!
skee hee hee!

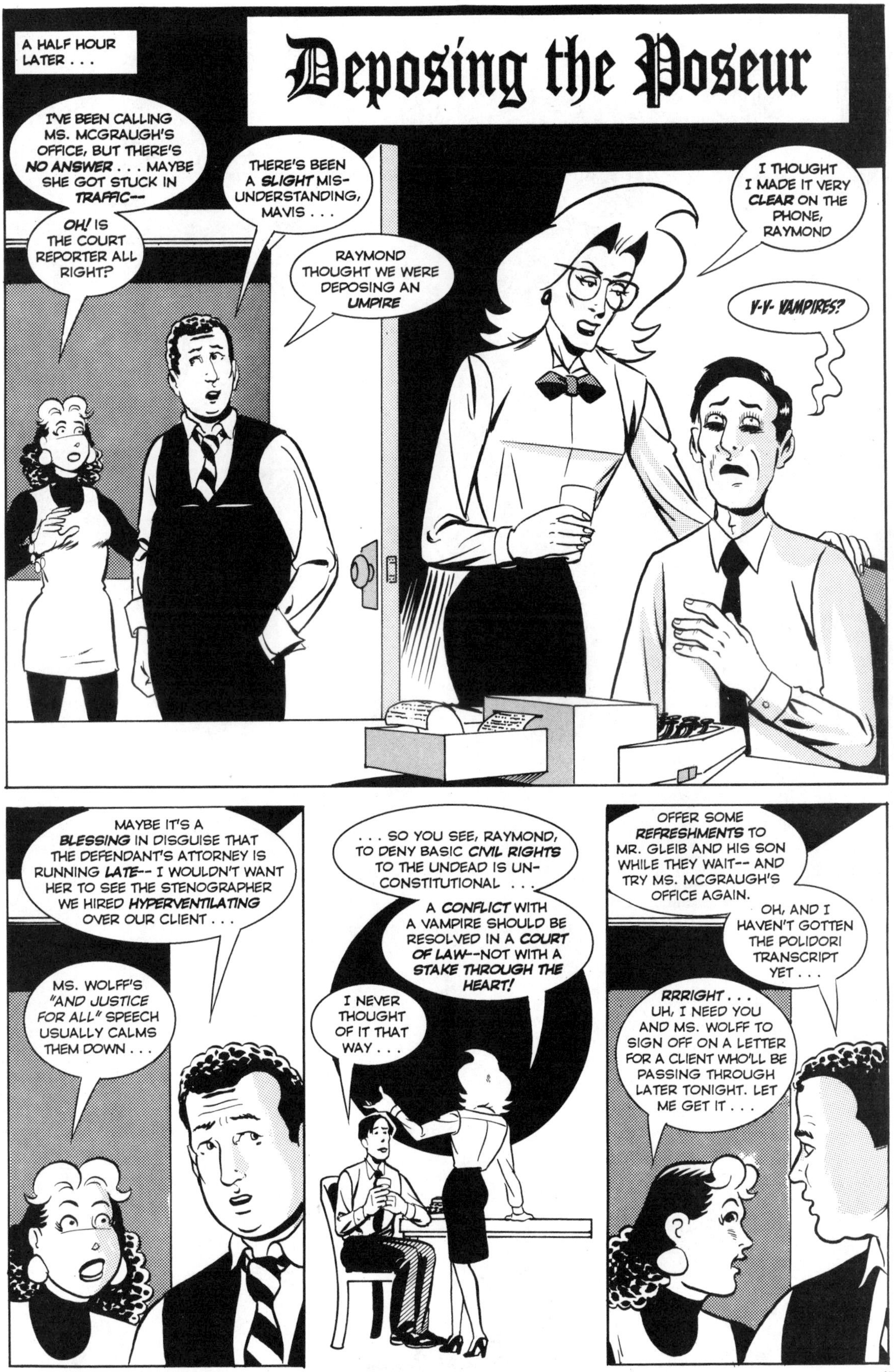
A HALF HOUR LATER . . .
Deposing the Poseur
I'VE BEEN CALLING MS. MCGRAUGH'S OFFICE, BUT THERE'S NO ANSWER . . . MAYBE SHE GOT STUCK IN TRAFFIC--
OH! IS THE COURT REPORTER ALL RIGHT?
THERE'S BEEN A SLIGHT MIS-UNDERSTANDING, MAVIS . . .
RAYMOND THOUGHT WE WERE DEPOSING AN UMPIRE
I THOUGHT I MADE IT VERY CLEAR ON THE PHONE, RAYMOND
V-V- VAMPIRES?
MAYBE IT'S A BLESSING IN DISGUISE THAT THE DEFENDANT'S ATTORNEY IS RUNNING LATE-- I WOULDN'T WANT HER TO SEE THE STENOGRAPHER WE HIRED HYPERVENTILATING OVER OUR CLIENT . . .
MS. WOLFF'S "AND JUSTICE FOR ALL" SPEECH USUALLY CALMS THEM DOWN . . .
. . . SO YOU SEE, RAYMOND, TO DENY BASIC CIVIL RIGHTS TO THE UNDEAD IS UN-CONSTITUTIONAL . . .
A CONFLICT WITH A VAMPIRE SHOULD BE RESOLVED IN A COURT OF LAW--NOT WITH A STAKE THROUGH THE HEART!
I NEVER THOUGHT OF IT THAT WAY . . .
OFFER SOME REFRESHMENTS TO MR. GLEIB AND HIS SON WHILE THEY WAIT-- AND TRY MS. MCGRAUGH'S OFFICE AGAIN.
OH, AND I HAVEN'T GOTTEN THE POLIDORI TRANSCRIPT YET . . .
RRRIGHT . . . UH, I NEED YOU AND MS. WOLFF TO SIGN OFF ON A LETTER FOR A CLIENT WHO'LL BE PASSING THROUGH LATER TONIGHT. LET ME GET IT . . .

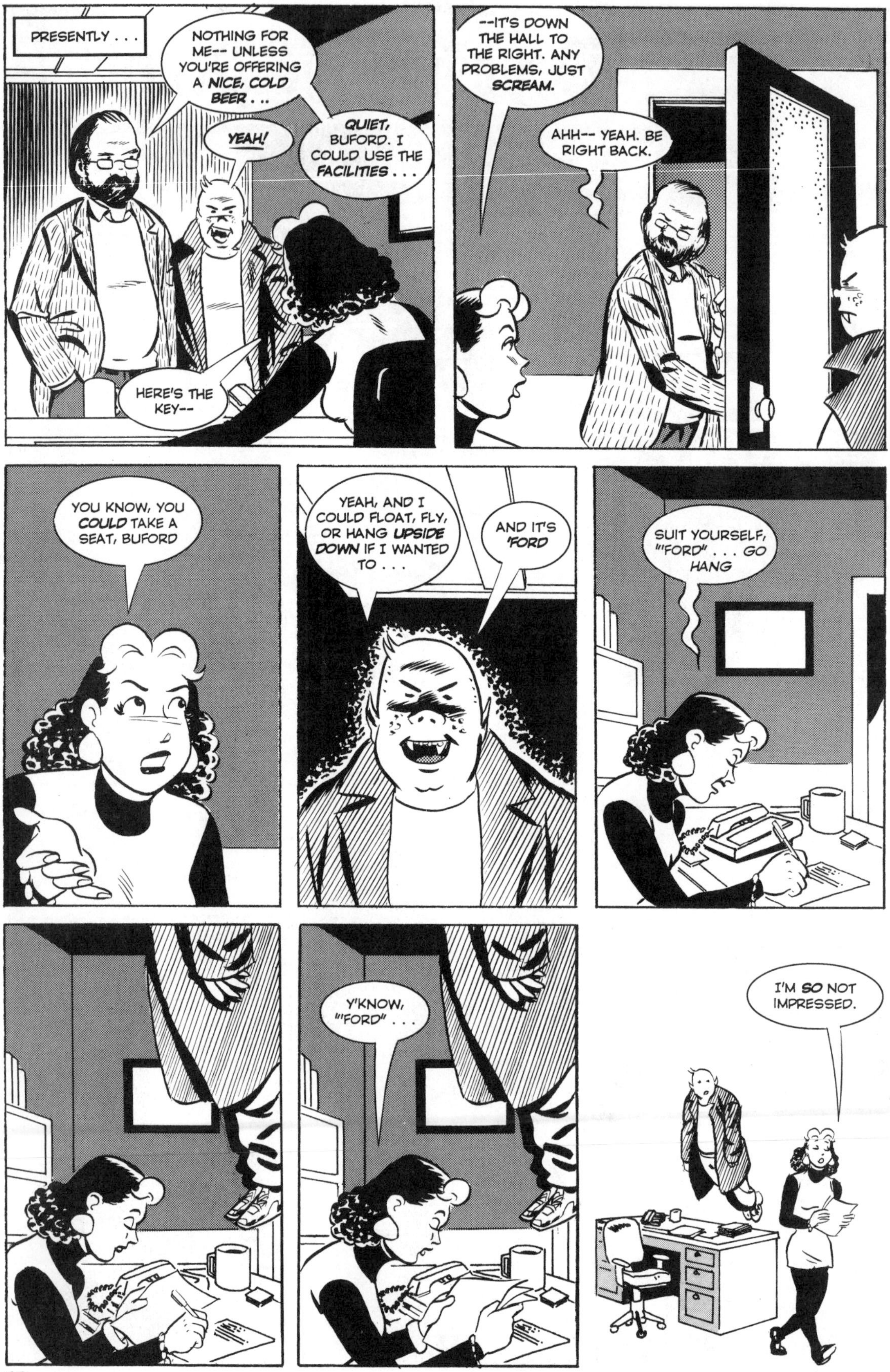
PRESENTLY . . .
NOTHING FOR ME-- UNLESS YOU'RE OFFERING A NICE, COLD BEER . . .
YEAH!
QUIET, BUFORD. I COULD USE THE FACILITIES . . .
HERE'S THE KEY--
--IT'S DOWN THE HALL TO THE RIGHT. ANY PROBLEMS, JUST SCREAM.
AHH-- YEAH. BE RIGHT BACK.
YOU KNOW, YOU COULD TAKE A SEAT, BUFORD
YEAH, AND I COULD FLOAT, FLY, OR HANG UPSIDE DOWN IF I WANTED TO . . .
AND IT'S 'FORD
SUIT YOURSELF, "FORD" . . . GO HANG
Y'KNOW, "FORD" . . .
I'M SO NOT IMPRESSED.

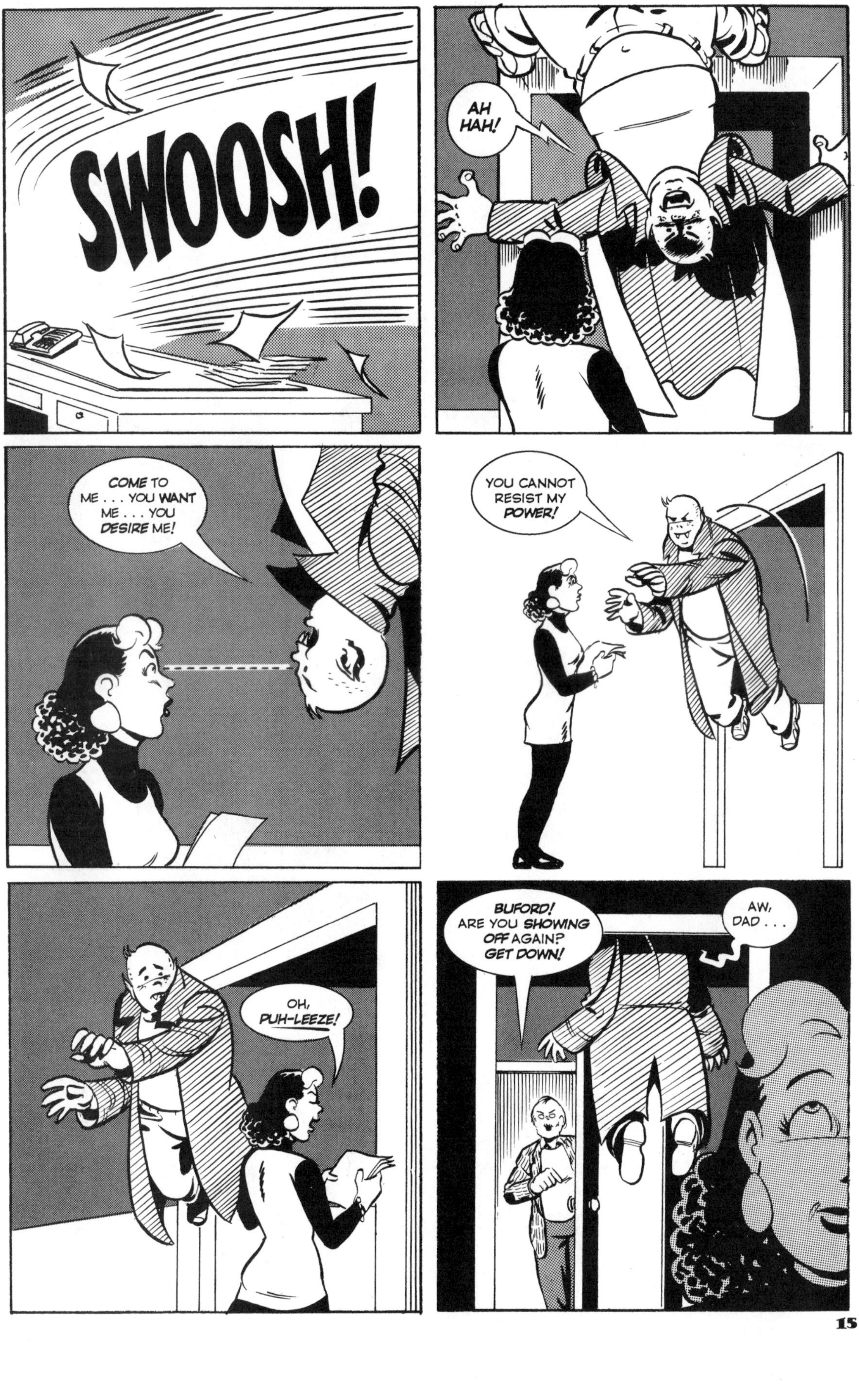
SWOOSH!
AH HAH!
COME TO ME . . . YOU WANT ME . . . YOU DESIRE ME!
YOU CANNOT RESIST MY POWER!
OH, PUH-LEEZE!
BUFORD! ARE YOU SHOWING OFF AGAIN? GET DOWN!
AW, DAD . . .

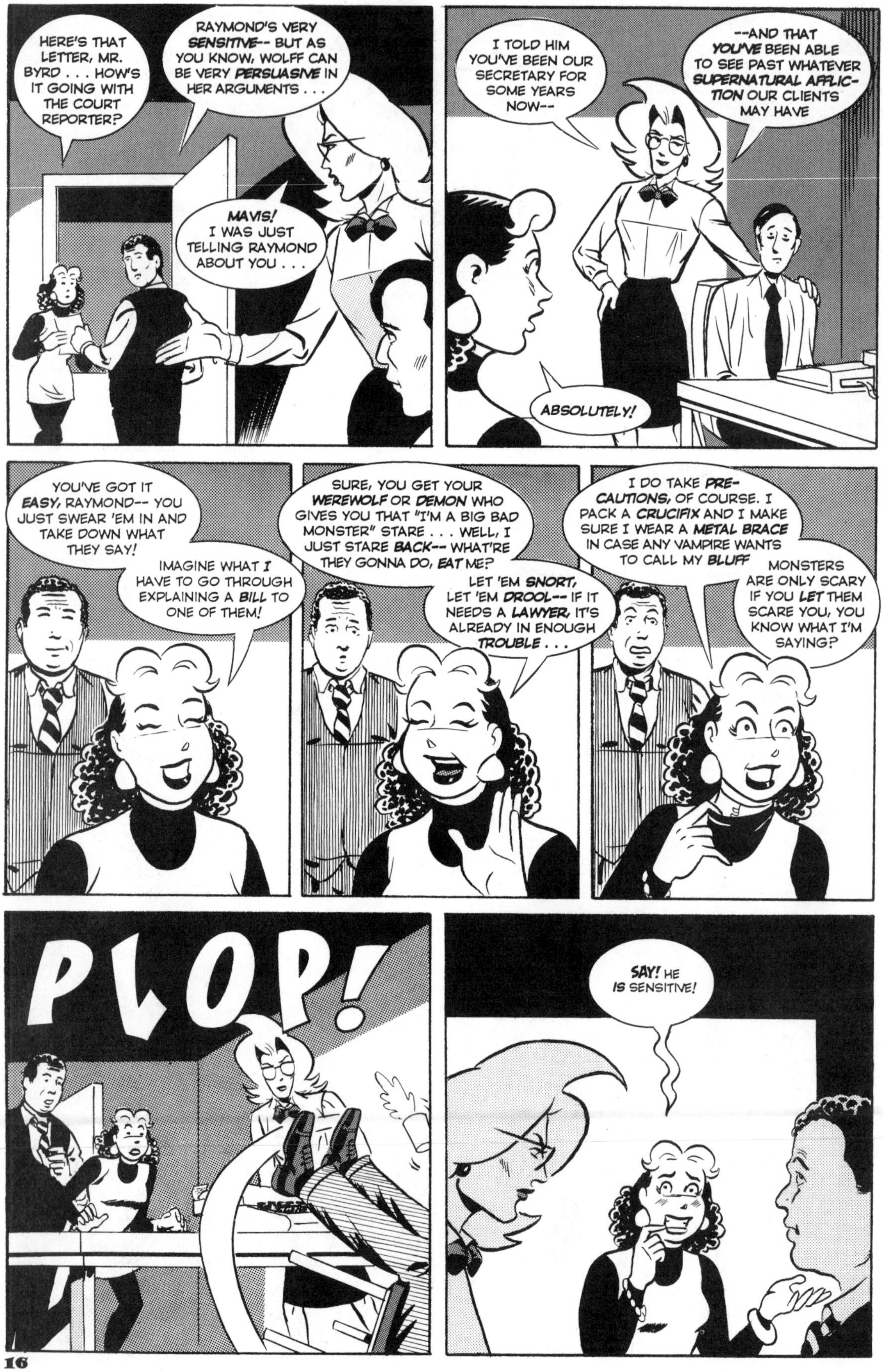
HERE'S THAT LETTER, MR. BYRD . . . HOW'S IT GOING WITH THE COURT REPORTER?
RAYMOND'S VERY SENSITIVE-- BUT AS YOU KNOW, WOLFF CAN BE VERY PERSUASIVE IN HER ARGUMENTS . . .
MAVIS! I WAS JUST TELLING RAYMOND ABOUT YOU . . .
I TOLD HIM YOU'VE BEEN OUR SECRETARY FOR SOME YEARS NOW--
--AND THAT YOU'VE BEEN ABLE TO SEE PAST WHATEVER SUPERNATURAL AFFLICTION OUR CLIENTS MAY HAVE
ABSOLUTELY!
YOU'VE GOT IT EASY, RAYMOND-- YOU JUST SWEAR 'EM IN AND TAKE DOWN WHAT THEY SAY!
IMAGINE WHAT I HAVE TO GO THROUGH EXPLAINING A BILL TO ONE OF THEM!
SURE, YOU GET YOUR WEREWOLF OR DEMON WHO GIVES YOU THAT "I'M A BIG BAD MONSTER" STARE . . . WELL, I JUST STARE BACK-- WHAT'RE THEY GONNA DO, EAT ME?
LET 'EM SNORT, LET 'EM DROOL-- IF IT NEEDS A LAWYER, IT'S ALREADY IN ENOUGH TROUBLE . . .
I DO TAKE PRECAUTIONS, OF COURSE. I PACK A CRUCIFIX AND I MAKE SURE I WEAR A METAL BRACE IN CASE ANY VAMPIRE WANTS TO CALL MY BLUFF
MONSTERS ARE ONLY SCARY IF YOU LET THEM SCARE YOU, YOU KNOW WHAT I'M SAYING?
PLOP!
SAY! HE IS SENSITIVE!

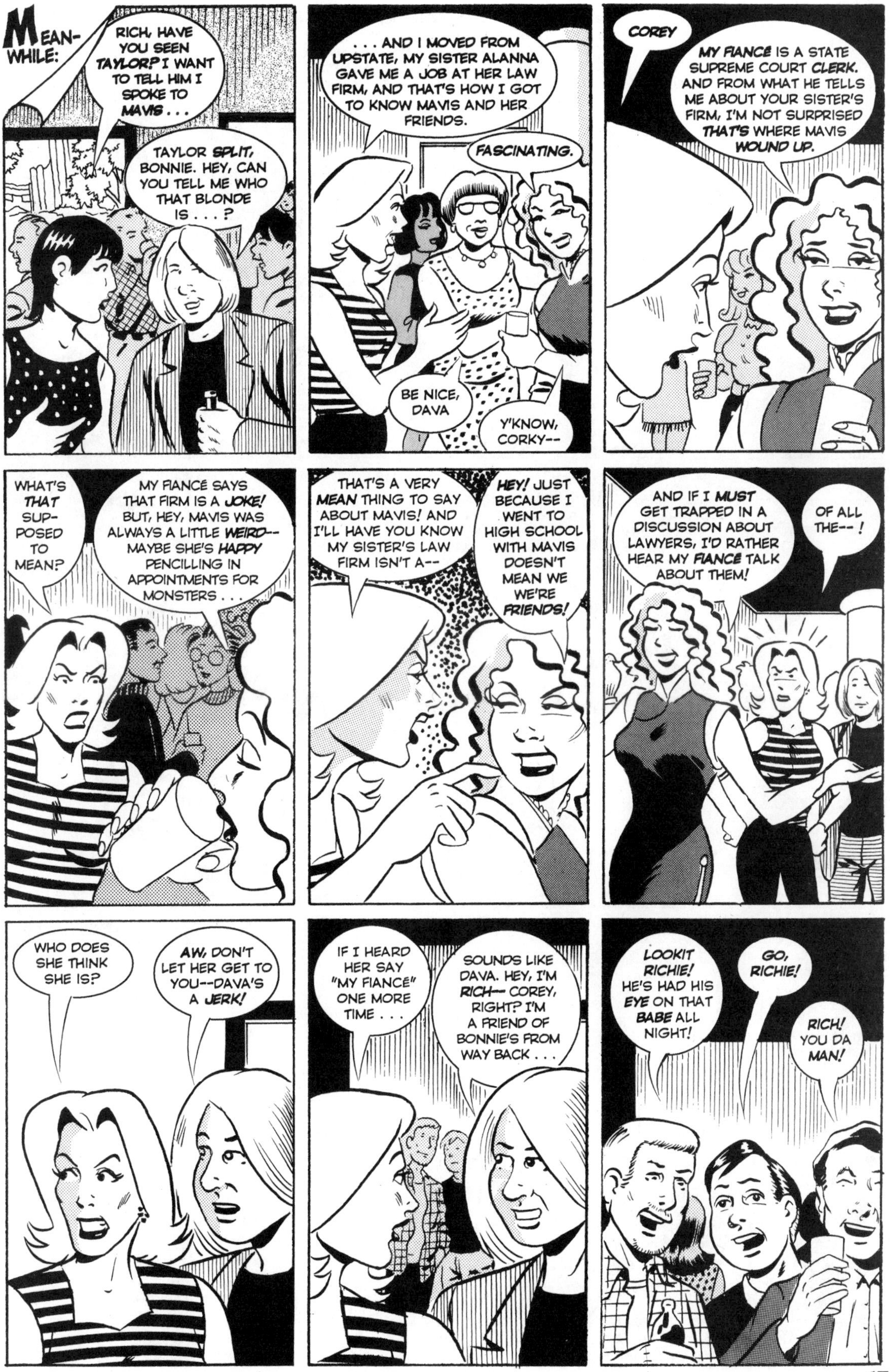
MEANWHILE:
RICH, HAVE YOU SEEN TAYLOR? I WANT TO TELL HIM I SPOKE TO MAVIS . . .
TAYLOR SPLIT, BONNIE. HEY, CAN YOU TELL ME WHO THAT BLONDE IS . . . ?
. . . AND I MOVED FROM UPSTATE, MY SISTER ALANNA GAVE ME A JOB AT HER LAW FIRM, AND THAT'S HOW I GOT TO KNOW MAVIS AND HER FRIENDS.
FASCINATING.
BE NICE, DAVA
Y'KNOW, CORKY--
COREY
MY FIANCÉ IS A STATE SUPREME COURT CLERK. AND FROM WHAT HE TELLS ME ABOUT YOUR SISTER'S FIRM, I'M NOT SURPRISED THAT'S WHERE MAVIS WOUND UP.
WHAT'S THAT SUP-POSED TO MEAN?
MY FIANCÉ SAYS THAT FIRM IS A JOKE! BUT, HEY, MAVIS WAS ALWAYS A LITTLE WEIRD-- MAYBE SHE'S HAPPY PENCILLING IN APPOINTMENTS FOR MONSTERS . . .
THAT'S A VERY MEAN THING TO SAY ABOUT MAVIS! AND I'LL HAVE YOU KNOW MY SISTER'S LAW FIRM ISN'T A--
HEY! JUST BECAUSE I WENT TO HIGH SCHOOL WITH MAVIS DOESN'T MEAN WE WE'RE FRIENDS!
AND IF I MUST GET TRAPPED IN A DISCUSSION ABOUT LAWYERS, I'D RATHER HEAR MY FIANCÉ TALK ABOUT THEM!
OF ALL THE-- !
WHO DOES SHE THINK SHE IS?
AW, DON'T LET HER GET TO YOU--DAVA'S A JERK!
IF I HEARD HER SAY "MY FIANCÉ" ONE MORE TIME . . .
SOUNDS LIKE DAVA. HEY, I'M RICH-- COREY, RIGHT? I'M A FRIEND OF BONNIE'S FROM WAY BACK . . .
LOOKIT RICHIE! HE'S HAD HIS EYE ON THAT BABE ALL NIGHT!
GO, RICHIE!
RICH! YOU DA MAN!

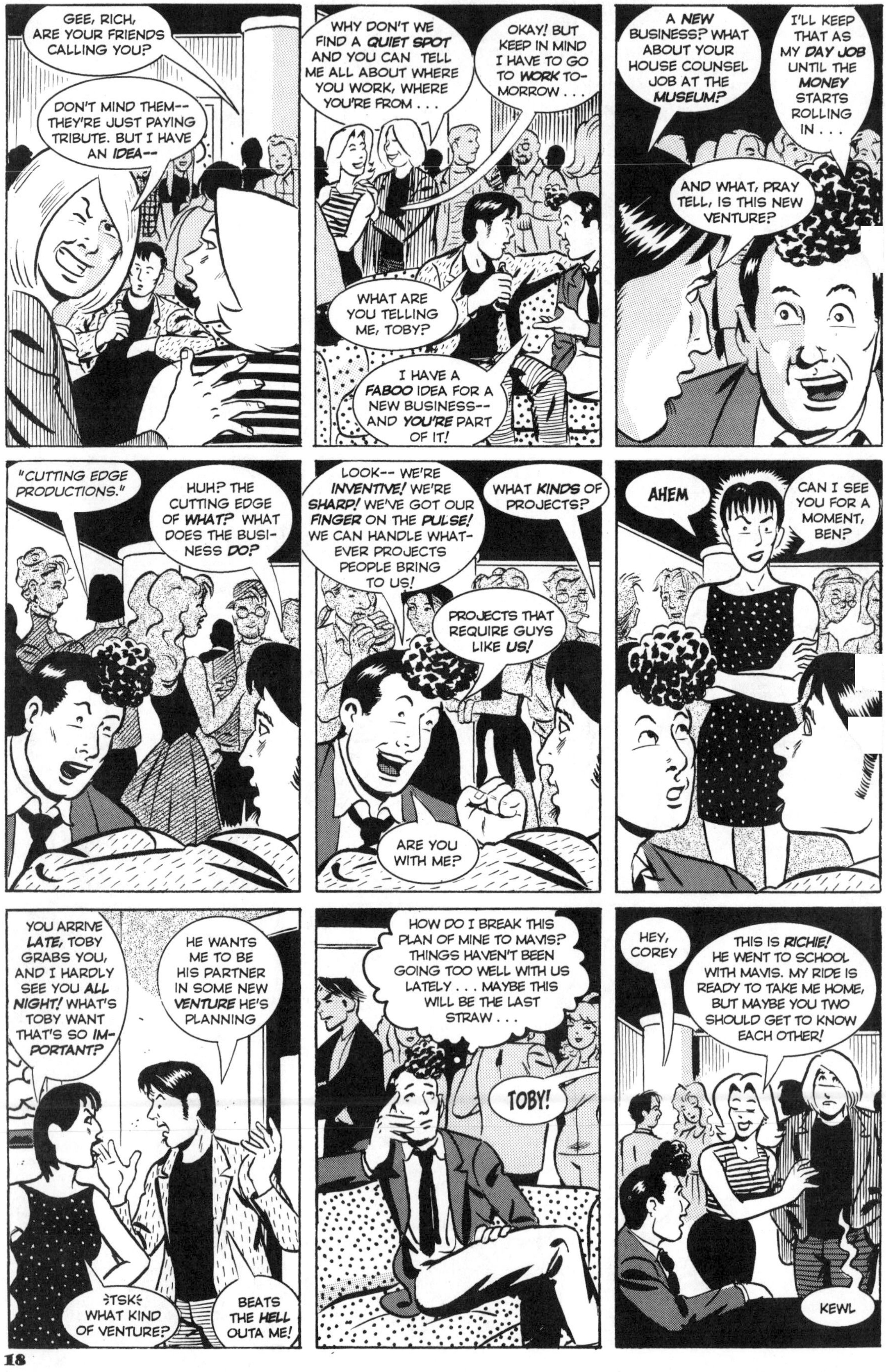
GEE, RICH, ARE YOUR FRIENDS CALLING YOU?
DON'T MIND THEM-- THEY'RE JUST PAYING TRIBUTE. BUT I HAVE AN IDEA--
WHY DON'T WE FIND A QUIET SPOT AND YOU CAN TELL ME ALL ABOUT WHERE YOU WORK, WHERE YOU'RE FROM . . .
OKAY! BUT KEEP IN MIND I HAVE TO GO TO WORK TOMORROW . . .
WHAT ARE YOU TELLING ME, TOBY?
I HAVE A FABOO IDEA FOR A NEW BUSINESS-- AND YOU'RE PART OF IT!
A NEW BUSINESS? WHAT ABOUT YOUR HOUSE COUNSEL JOB AT THE MUSEUM?
I'LL KEEP THAT AS MY DAY JOB UNTIL THE MONEY STARTS ROLLING IN . . .
AND WHAT, PRAY TELL, IS THIS NEW VENTURE?
"CUTTING EDGE PRODUCTIONS."
HUH? THE CUTTING EDGE OF WHAT? WHAT DOES THE BUSINESS DO?
LOOK-- WE'RE INVENTIVE! WE'RE SHARP! WE'VE GOT OUR FINGER ON THE PULSE! WE CAN HANDLE WHATEVER PROJECTS PEOPLE BRING TO US!
WHAT KINDS OF PROJECTS?
PROJECTS THAT REQUIRE GUYS LIKE US!
ARE YOU WITH ME?
AHEM
CAN I SEE YOU FOR A MOMENT, BEN?
YOU ARRIVE LATE, TOBY GRABS YOU, AND I HARDLY SEE YOU ALL NIGHT! WHAT'S TOBY WANT THAT'S SO IMPORTANT?
HE WANTS ME TO BE HIS PARTNER IN SOME NEW VENTURE HE'S PLANNING
TSK WHAT KIND OF VENTURE?
BEATS THE HELL OUTA ME!
HOW DO I BREAK THIS PLAN OF MINE TO MAVIS? THINGS HAVEN'T BEEN GOING TOO WELL WITH US LATELY . . . MAYBE THIS WILL BE THE LAST STRAW . . .
TOBY!
HEY, COREY
THIS IS RICHIE! HE WENT TO SCHOOL WITH MAVIS. MY RIDE IS READY TO TAKE ME HOME, BUT MAYBE YOU TWO SHOULD GET TO KNOW EACH OTHER!
KEWL

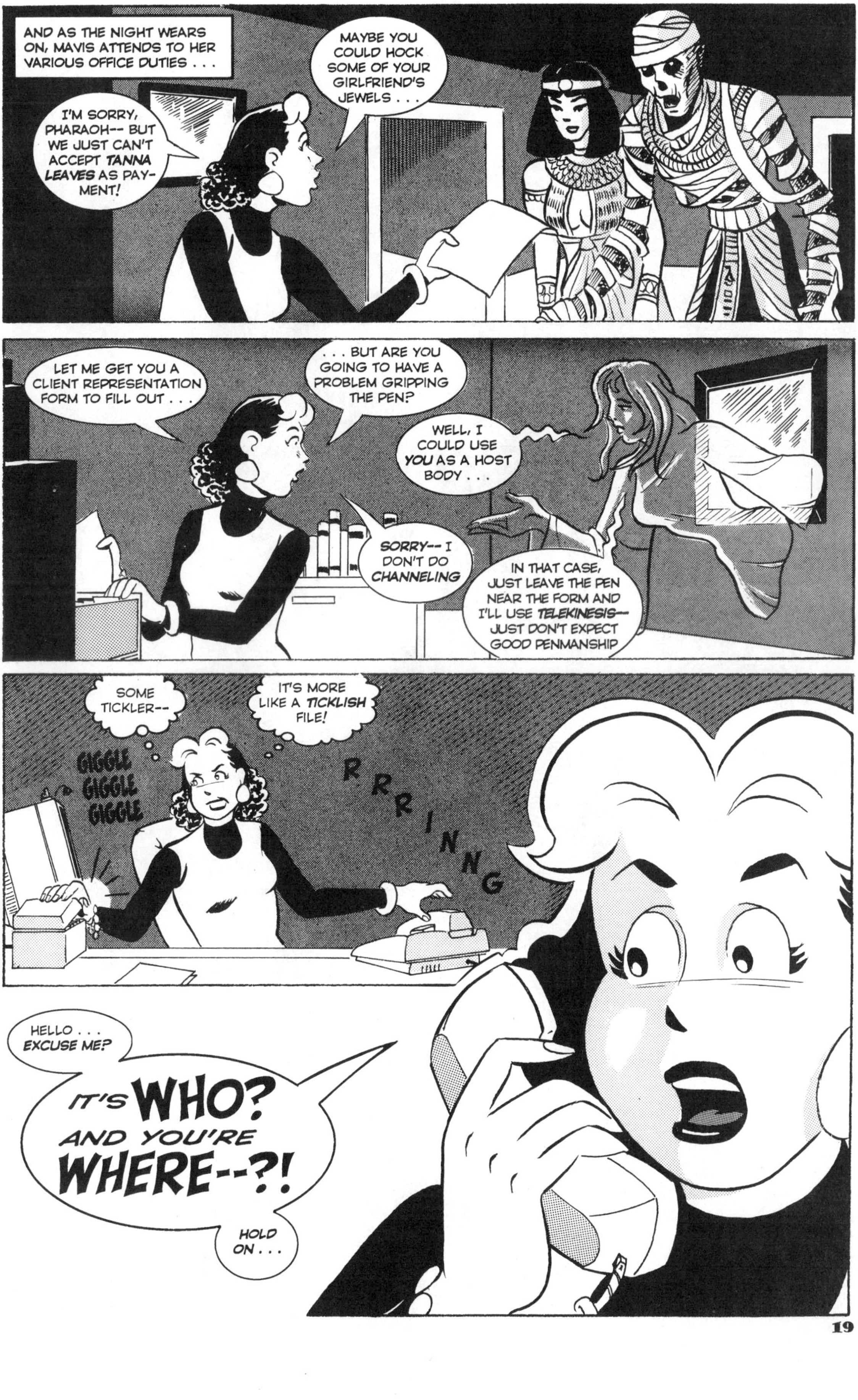
AND AS THE NIGHT WEARS ON, MAVIS ATTENDS TO HER VARIOUS OFFICE DUTIES . . .
I'M SORRY, PHARAOH-- BUT WE JUST CAN'T ACCEPT TANNA LEAVES AS PAYMENT!
MAYBE YOU COULD HOCK SOME OF YOUR GIRLFRIEND'S JEWELS . . .
LET ME GET YOU A CLIENT REPRESENTATION FORM TO FILL OUT . . .
. . . BUT ARE YOU GOING TO HAVE A PROBLEM GRIPPING THE PEN?
WELL, I COULD USE YOU AS A HOST BODY . . .
SORRY-- I DON'T DO CHANNELING
IN THAT CASE, JUST LEAVE THE PEN NEAR THE FORM AND I'LL USE TELEKINESIS-- JUST DON'T EXPECT GOOD PENMANSHIP
SOME TICKLER--
IT'S MORE LIKE A TICKLISH FILE!
GIGGLE GIGGLE GIGGLE
RRRINNNG
HELLO . . . EXCUSE ME?
IT'S WHO? AND YOU'RE WHERE--?!
HOLD ON . . .

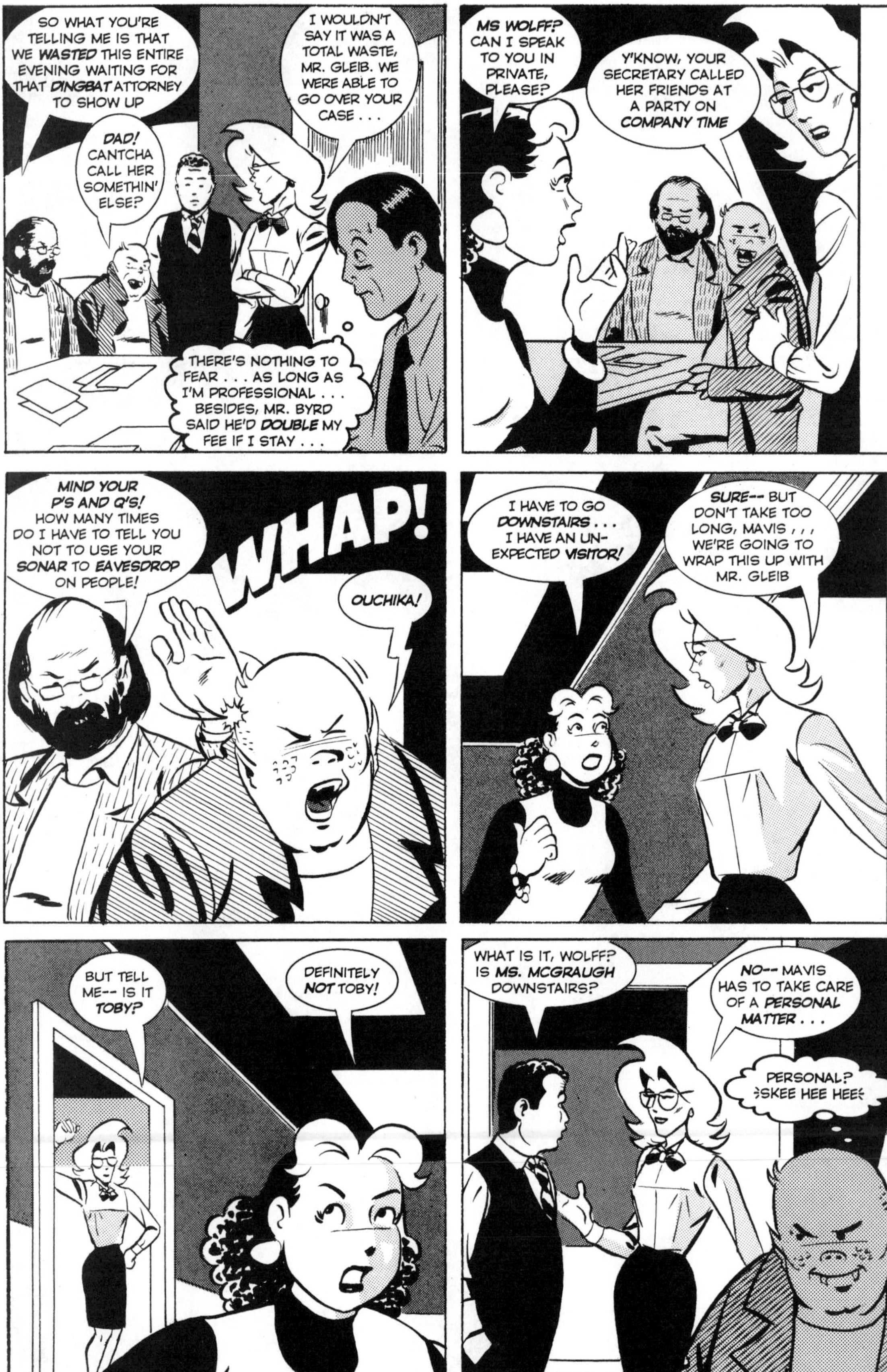
SO WHAT YOU'RE TELLING ME IS THAT WE WASTED THIS ENTIRE EVENING WAITING FOR THAT DINGBAT ATTORNEY TO SHOW UP
I WOULDN'T SAY IT WAS A TOTAL WASTE, MR. GLEIB. WE WERE ABLE TO GO OVER YOUR CASE . . .
DAD! CANTCHA CALL HER SOMETHIN' ELSE?
THERE'S NOTHING TO FEAR . . . AS LONG AS I'M PROFESSIONAL . . . BESIDES, MR. BYRD SAID HE'D DOUBLE MY FEE IF I STAY . . .
MS WOLFF? CAN I SPEAK TO YOU IN PRIVATE, PLEASE?
Y'KNOW, YOUR SECRETARY CALLED HER FRIENDS AT A PARTY ON COMPANY TIME
MIND YOUR P'S AND Q'S! HOW MANY TIMES DO I HAVE TO TELL YOU NOT TO USE YOUR SONAR TO EAVESDROP ON PEOPLE!
WHAP!
OUCHIKA!
I HAVE TO GO DOWNSTAIRS . . . I HAVE AN UN-EXPECTED VISITOR!
SURE-- BUT DON'T TAKE TOO LONG, MAVIS , , , WE'RE GOING TO WRAP THIS UP WITH MR. GLEIB
BUT TELL ME-- IS IT TOBY?
DEFINITELY NOT TOBY!
WHAT IS IT, WOLFF? IS MS. MCGRAUGH DOWNSTAIRS?
NO-- MAVIS HAS TO TAKE CARE OF A PERSONAL MATTER . . .
PERSONAL? SKEE HEE HEE

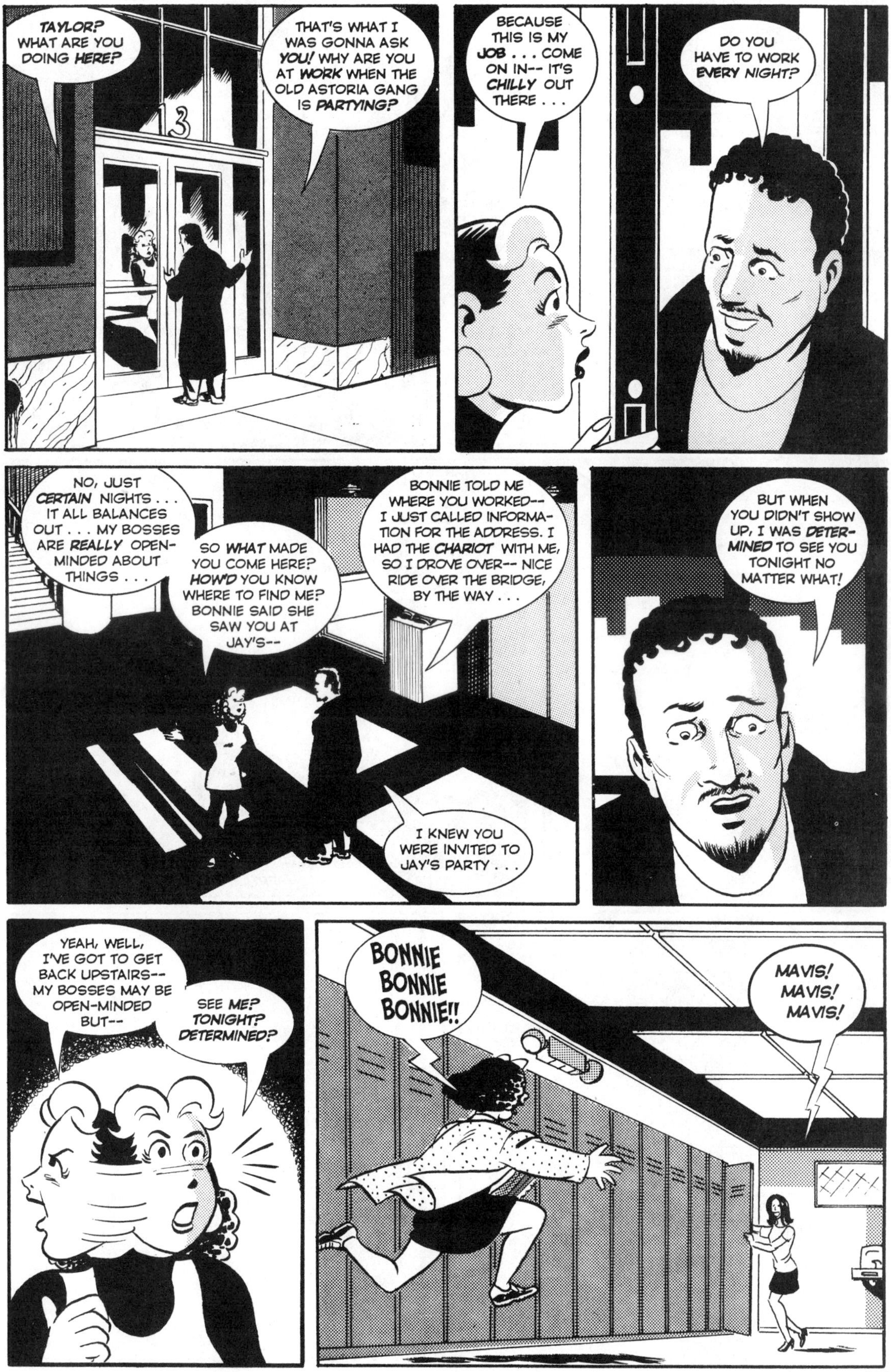
TAYLOR? WHAT ARE YOU DOING HERE?
THAT'S WHAT I WAS GONNA ASK YOU! WHY ARE YOU AT WORK WHEN THE OLD ASTORIA GANG IS PARTYING?
BECAUSE THIS IS MY JOB . . . COME ON IN-- IT'S CHILLY OUT THERE . . .
DO YOU HAVE TO WORK EVERY NIGHT?
NO, JUST CERTAIN NIGHTS . . . IT ALL BALANCES OUT . . . MY BOSSES ARE REALLY OPEN-MINDED ABOUT THINGS . . .
SO WHAT MADE YOU COME HERE? HOW'D YOU KNOW WHERE TO FIND ME? BONNIE SAID SHE SAW YOU AT JAY'S--
BONNIE TOLD ME WHERE YOU WORKED-- I JUST CALLED INFORMATION FOR THE ADDRESS. I HAD THE CHARIOT WITH ME, SO I DROVE OVER-- NICE RIDE OVER THE BRIDGE, BY THE WAY . . .
I KNEW YOU WERE INVITED TO JAY'S PARTY . . .
BUT WHEN YOU DIDN'T SHOW UP, I WAS DETERMINED TO SEE YOU TONIGHT NO MATTER WHAT!
YEAH, WELL, I'VE GOT TO GET BACK UPSTAIRS-- MY BOSSES MAY BE OPEN-MINDED BUT--
SEE ME? TONIGHT? DETERMINED?
BONNIE BONNIE BONNIE!!
MAVIS! MAVIS! MAVIS!

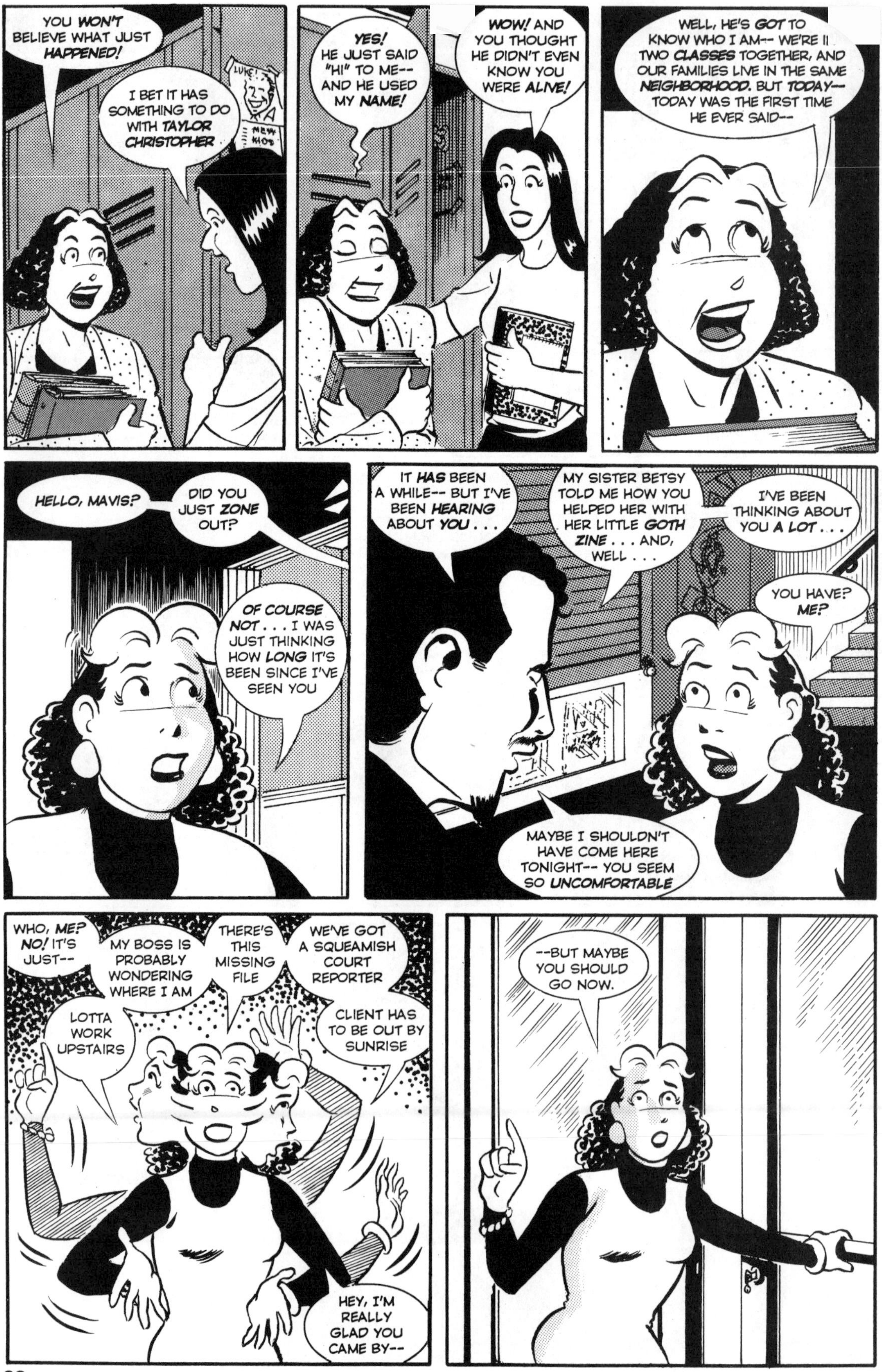
YOU WON'T BELIEVE WHAT JUST HAPPENED!
I BET IT HAS SOMETHING TO DO WITH TAYLOR CHRISTOPHER
YES! HE JUST SAID "HI" TO ME-- AND HE USED MY NAME!
WOW! AND YOU THOUGHT HE DIDN'T EVEN KNOW YOU WERE ALIVE!
WELL, HE'S GOT TO KNOW WHO I AM-- WE'RE IN TWO CLASSES TOGETHER, AND OUR FAMILIES LIVE IN THE SAME NEIGHBORHOOD. BUT TODAY-- TODAY WAS THE FIRST TIME HE EVER SAID--
HELLO, MAVIS?
DID YOU JUST ZONE OUT?
OF COURSE NOT . . . I WAS JUST THINKING HOW LONG IT'S BEEN SINCE I'VE SEEN YOU
IT HAS BEEN A WHILE-- BUT I'VE BEEN HEARING ABOUT YOU . . .
MY SISTER BETSY TOLD ME HOW YOU HELPED HER WITH HER LITTLE GOTH ZINE . . . AND, WELL . . .
I'VE BEEN THINKING ABOUT YOU A LOT . . .
YOU HAVE? ME?
MAYBE I SHOULDN'T HAVE COME HERE TONIGHT-- YOU SEEM SO UNCOMFORTABLE
WHO, ME? NO! IT'S JUST--
MY BOSS IS PROBABLY WONDERING WHERE I AM
THERE'S THIS MISSING FILE
WE'VE GOT A SQUEAMISH COURT REPORTER
LOTTA WORK UPSTAIRS
CLIENT HAS TO BE OUT BY SUNRISE
HEY, I'M REALLY GLAD YOU CAME BY--
--BUT MAYBE YOU SHOULD GO NOW.

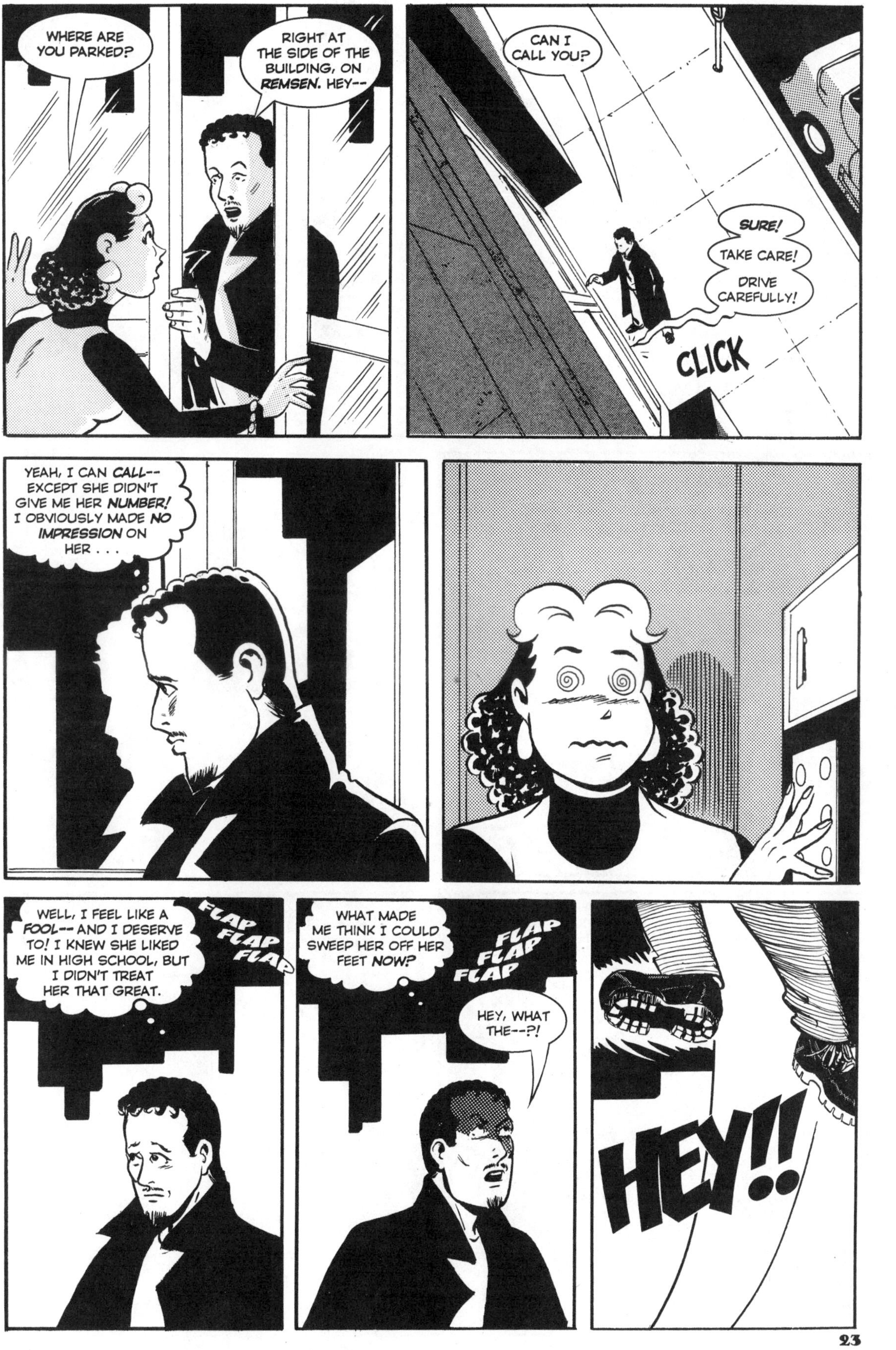
WHERE ARE YOU PARKED?
RIGHT AT THE SIDE OF THE BUILDING, ON REMSEN. HEY--
CAN I CALL YOU?
SURE!
TAKE CARE!
DRIVE CAREFULLY!
CLICK
YEAH, I CAN CALL-- EXCEPT SHE DIDN'T GIVE ME HER NUMBER! I OBVIOUSLY MADE NO IMPRESSION ON HER . . .
WELL, I FEEL LIKE A FOOL-- AND I DESERVE TO! I KNEW SHE LIKED ME IN HIGH SCHOOL, BUT I DIDN'T TREAT HER THAT GREAT.
FLAP FLAP FLAP
WHAT MADE ME THINK I COULD SWEEP HER OFF HER FEET NOW?
FLAP FLAP FLAP
HEY, WHAT THE--?!
HEY!!

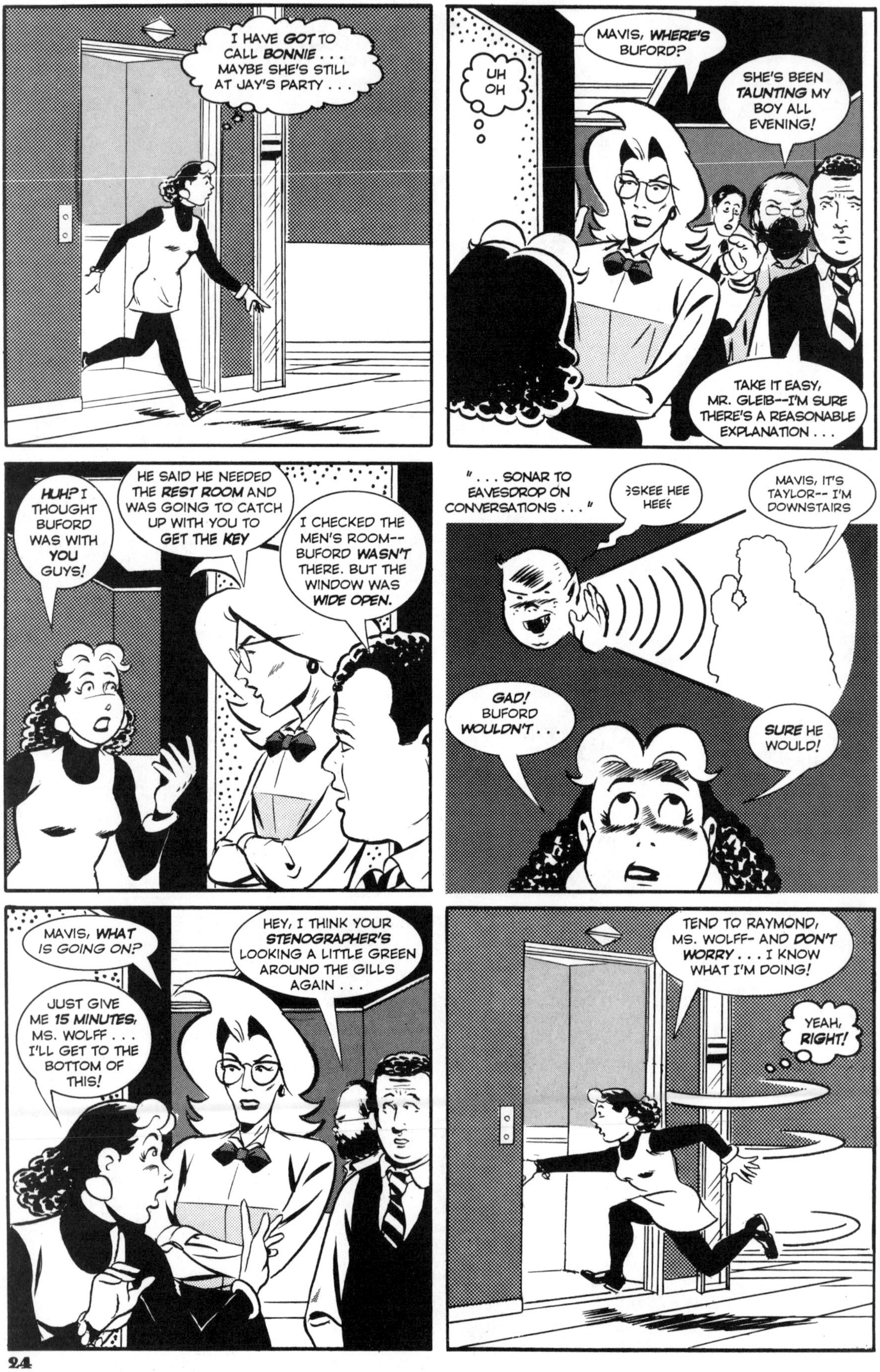
I HAVE GOT TO CALL BONNIE . . . MAYBE SHE'S STILL AT JAY'S PARTY . . .
MAVIS, WHERE'S BUFORD?
UH OH
SHE'S BEEN TAUNTING MY BOY ALL EVENING!
TAKE IT EASY, MR. GLEIB--I'M SURE THERE'S A REASONABLE EXPLANATION . . .
HUH? I THOUGHT BUFORD WAS WITH YOU GUYS!
HE SAID HE NEEDED THE REST ROOM AND WAS GOING TO CATCH UP WITH YOU TO GET THE KEY
I CHECKED THE MEN'S ROOM-- BUFORD WASN'T THERE. BUT THE WINDOW WAS WIDE OPEN.
" . . . SONAR TO EAVESDROP ON CONVERSATIONS . . . "
SKEE HEE HEE
MAVIS, IT'S TAYLOR-- I'M DOWNSTAIRS
GAD! BUFORD WOULDN'T . . .
SURE HE WOULD!
MAVIS, WHAT IS GOING ON?
HEY, I THINK YOUR STENOGRAPHER'S LOOKING A LITTLE GREEN AROUND THE GILLS AGAIN . . .
JUST GIVE ME 15 MINUTES, MS. WOLFF . . . I'LL GET TO THE BOTTOM OF THIS!
TEND TO RAYMOND, MS. WOLFF- AND DON'T WORRY . . . I KNOW WHAT I'M DOING!
YEAH, RIGHT!

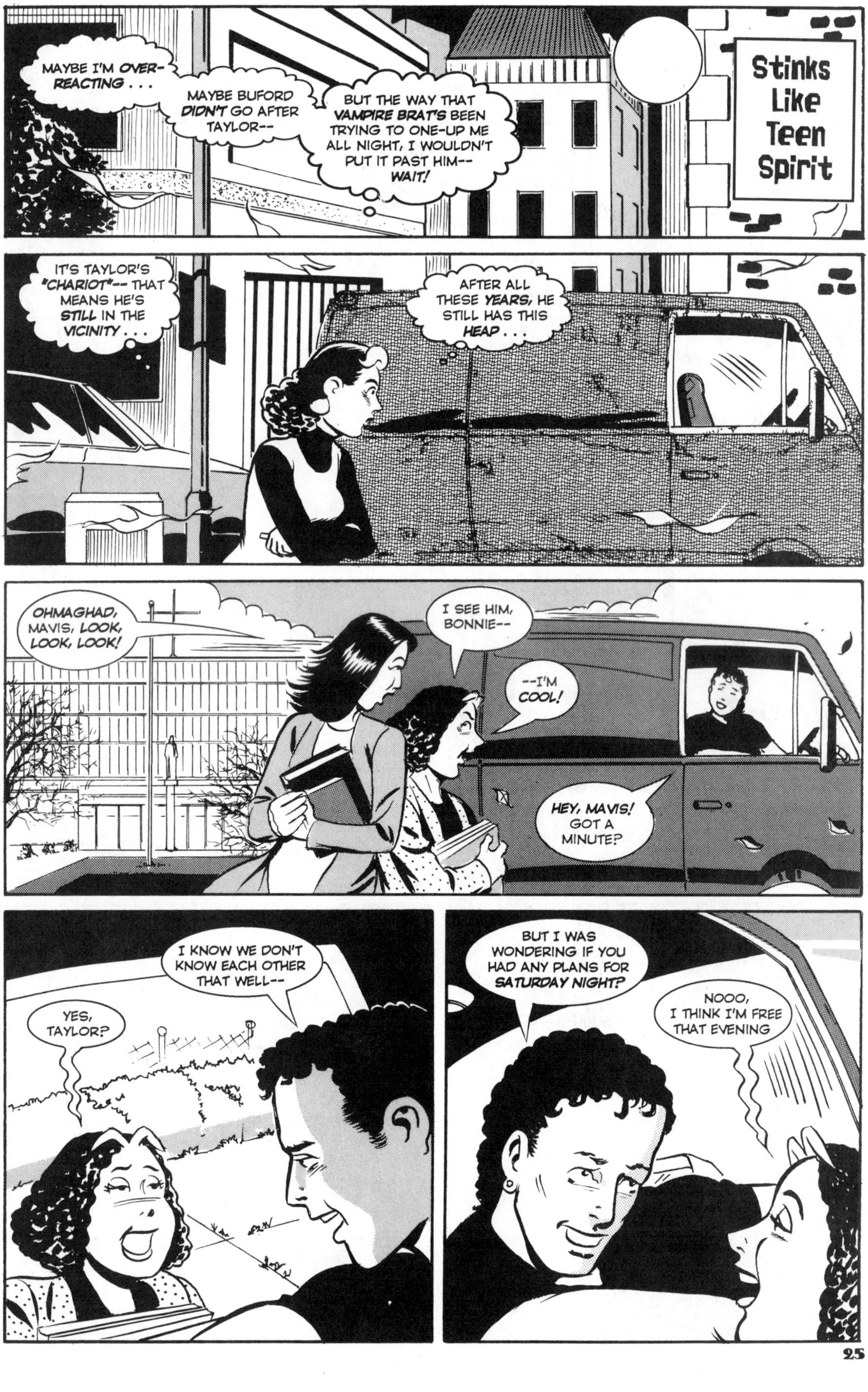
MAYBE I'M OVER-REACTING . . .
MAYBE BUFORD DIDN'T GO AFTER TAYLOR--
BUT THE WAY THAT VAMPIRE BRAT'S BEEN TRYING TO ONE-UP ME ALL NIGHT, I WOULDN'T PUT IT PAST HIM-- WAIT!
Stinks Like Teen Spirit
IT'S TAYLOR'S "CHARIOT"-- THAT MEANS HE'S STILL IN THE VICINITY . . .
AFTER ALL THESE YEARS, HE STILL HAS THIS HEAP . . .
OHMAGHAD, MAVIS, LOOK, LOOK, LOOK!
I SEE HIM, BONNIE--
--I'M COOL!
HEY, MAVIS! GOT A MINUTE?
YES, TAYLOR?
I KNOW WE DON'T KNOW EACH OTHER THAT WELL--
BUT I WAS WONDERING IF YOU HAD ANY PLANS FOR SATURDAY NIGHT?
NOOO, I THINK I'M FREE THAT EVENING

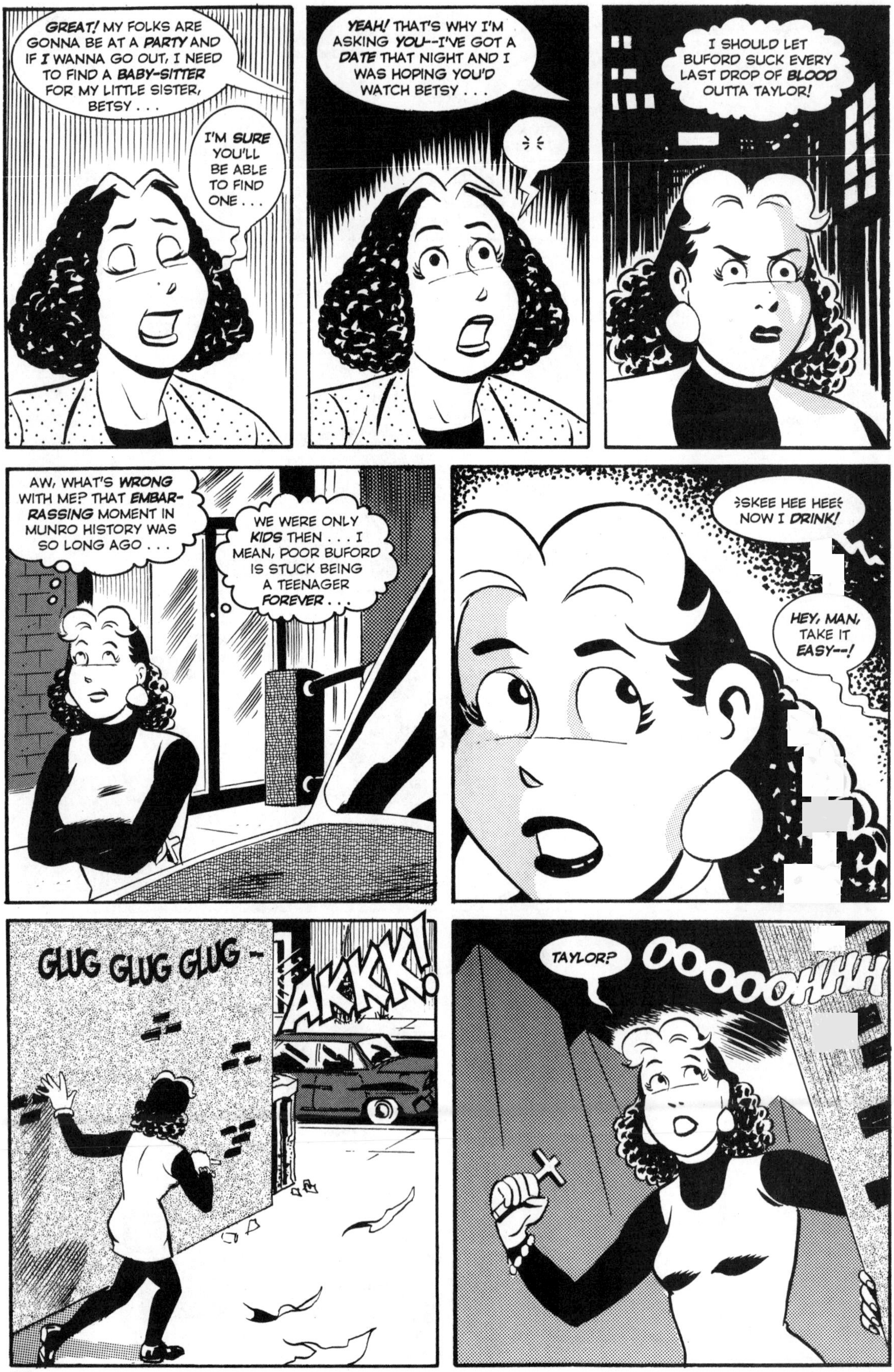
GREAT! MY FOLKS ARE GONNA BE AT A PARTY AND IF I WANNA GO OUT, I NEED TO FIND A BABY-SITTER FOR MY LITTLE SISTER, BETSY . . .
I'M SURE YOU'LL BE ABLE TO FIND ONE . . .
YEAH! THAT'S WHY I'M ASKING YOU--I'VE GOT A DATE THAT NIGHT AND I WAS HOPING YOU'D WATCH BETSY . . .
I SHOULD LET BUFORD SUCK EVERY LAST DROP OF BLOOD OUTTA TAYLOR!
AW, WHAT'S WRONG WITH ME? THAT EMBARRASSING MOMENT IN MUNRO HISTORY WAS SO LONG AGO . . .
WE WERE ONLY KIDS THEN . . . I MEAN, POOR BUFORD IS STUCK BEING A TEENAGER FOREVER . . .
SKEE HEE HEE NOW I DRINK!
HEY, MAN, TAKE IT EASY--!
GLUG GLUG GLUG --
AKKK!
TAYLOR?
OOOOOOHHHH

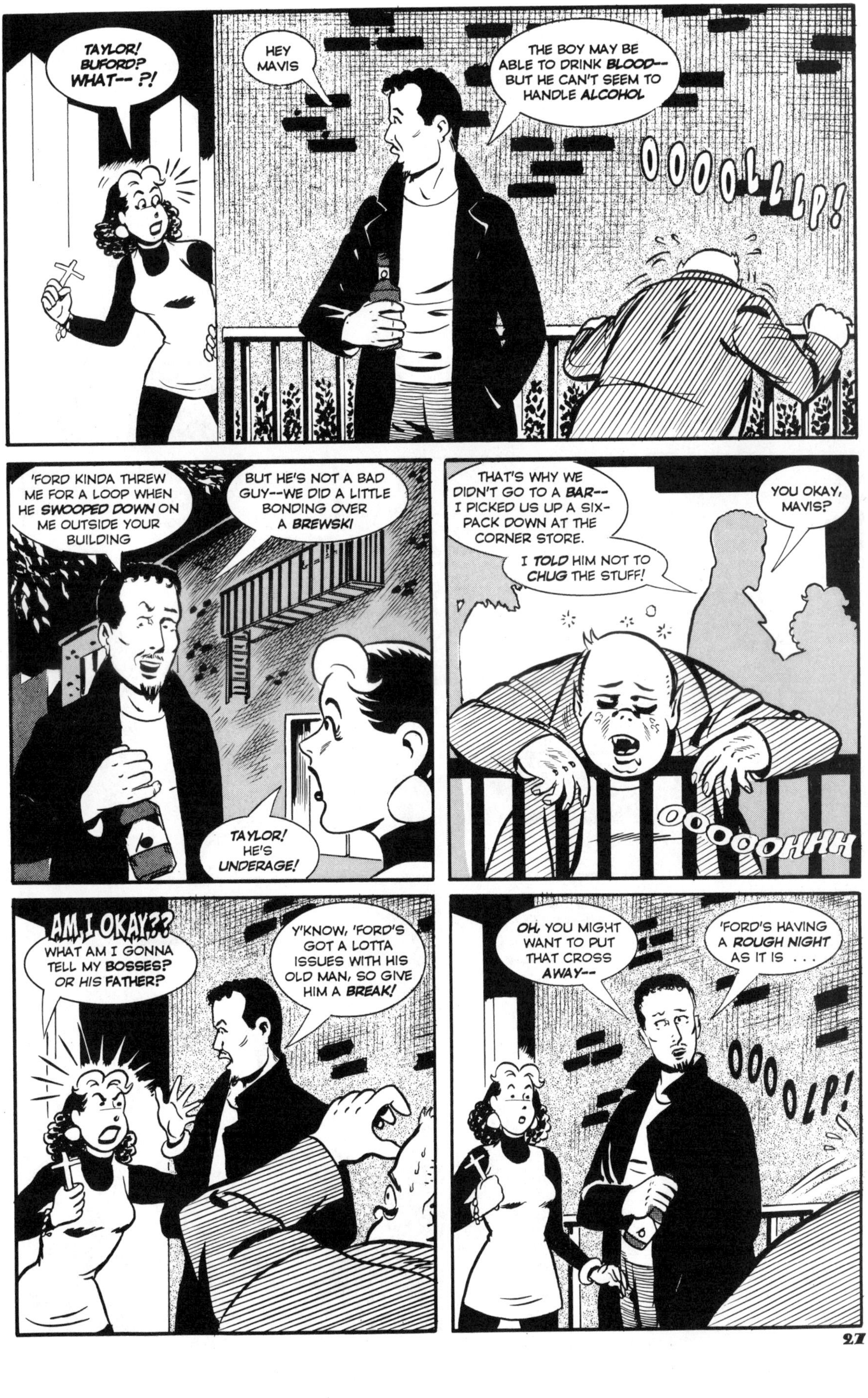
TAYLOR! BUFORD? WHAT-- ?!
HEY MAVIS
THE BOY MAY BE ABLE TO DRINK BLOOD-- BUT HE CAN'T SEEM TO HANDLE ALCOHOL
OOOOLLLP!
'FORD KINDA THREW ME FOR A LOOP WHEN HE SWOOPED DOWN ON ME OUTSIDE YOUR BUILDING
BUT HE'S NOT A BAD GUY--WE DID A LITTLE BONDING OVER A BREWSKI
TAYLOR! HE'S UNDERAGE!
THAT'S WHY WE DIDN'T GO TO A BAR-- I PICKED US UP A SIX-PACK DOWN AT THE CORNER STORE.
I TOLD HIM NOT TO CHUG THE STUFF!
YOU OKAY, MAVIS?
OOOOOOHHH
AM, I OKAY??
WHAT AM I GONNA TELL MY BOSSES? OR HIS FATHER?
Y'KNOW, 'FORD'S GOT A LOTTA ISSUES WITH HIS OLD MAN, SO GIVE HIM A BREAK!
OH, YOU MIGHT WANT TO PUT THAT CROSS AWAY--
'FORD'S HAVING A ROUGH NIGHT AS IT IS . . .
OOOOLP!

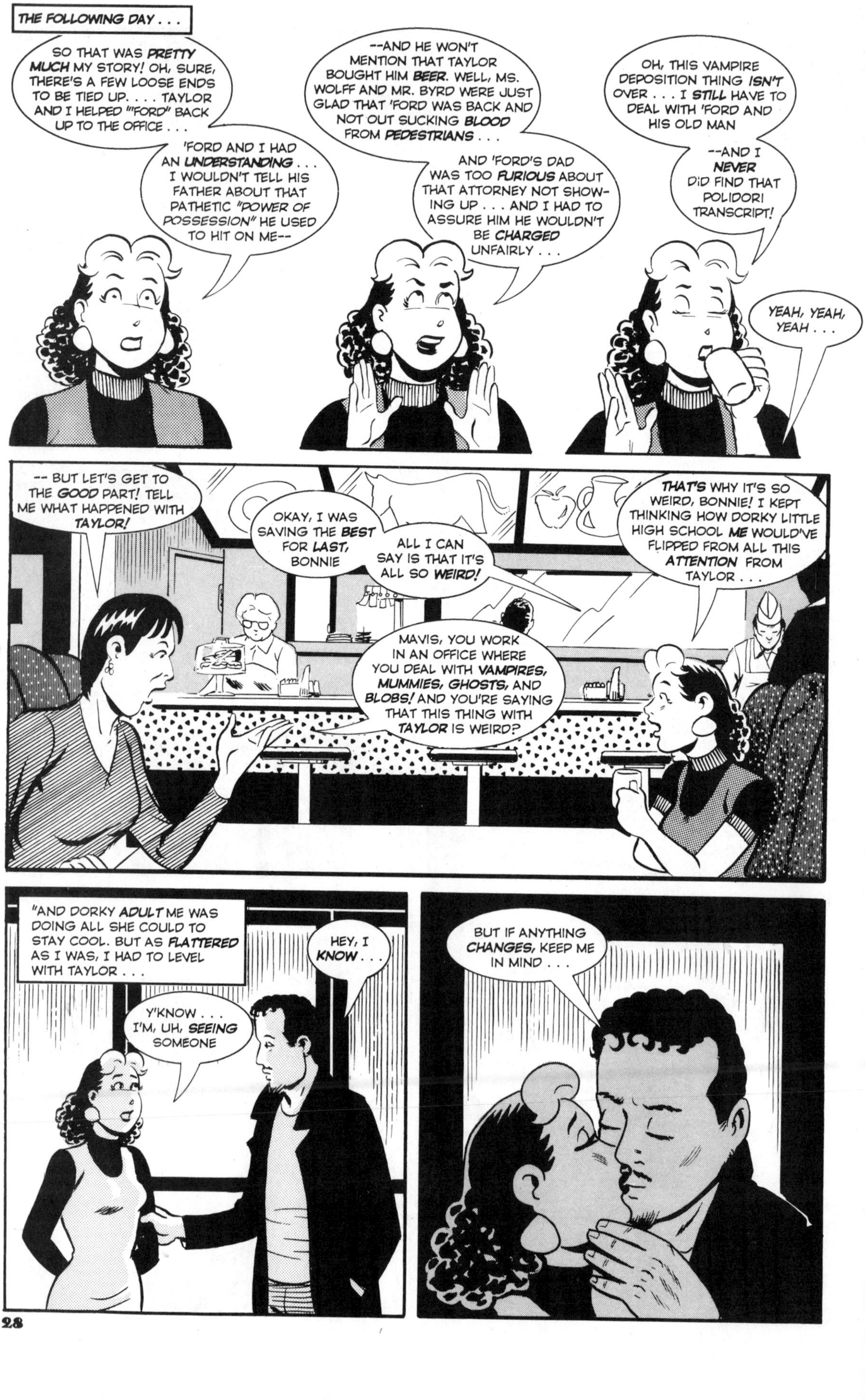
THE FOLLOWING DAY . . .
SO THAT WAS PRETTY MUCH MY STORY! OH, SURE, THERE'S A FEW LOOSE ENDS TO BE TIED UP. . . . TAYLOR AND I HELPED "'FORD" BACK UP TO THE OFFICE . . .
'FORD AND I HAD AN UNDERSTANDING . . . I WOULDN'T TELL HIS FATHER ABOUT THAT PATHETIC "POWER OF POSSESSION" HE USED TO HIT ON ME--
--AND HE WON'T MENTION THAT TAYLOR BOUGHT HIM BEER. WELL, MS. WOLFF AND MR. BYRD WERE JUST GLAD THAT 'FORD WAS BACK AND NOT OUT SUCKING BLOOD FROM PEDESTRIANS . . .
AND 'FORD'S DAD WAS TOO FURIOUS ABOUT THAT ATTORNEY NOT SHOWING UP . . . AND I HAD TO ASSURE HIM HE WOULDN'T BE CHARGED UNFAIRLY . . .
OH, THIS VAMPIRE DEPOSITION THING ISN'T OVER . . . I STILL HAVE TO DEAL WITH 'FORD AND HIS OLD MAN
--AND I NEVER DID FIND THAT POLIDORI TRANSCRIPT!
YEAH, YEAH, YEAH . . .
-- BUT LET'S GET TO THE GOOD PART! TELL ME WHAT HAPPENED WITH TAYLOR!
OKAY, I WAS SAVING THE BEST FOR LAST, BONNIE
ALL I CAN SAY IS THAT IT'S ALL SO WEIRD!
MAVIS, YOU WORK IN AN OFFICE WHERE YOU DEAL WITH VAMPIRES, MUMMIES, GHOSTS, AND BLOBS! AND YOU'RE SAYING THAT THIS THING WITH TAYLOR IS WEIRD?
THAT'S WHY IT'S SO WEIRD, BONNIE! I KEPT THINKING HOW DORKY LITTLE HIGH SCHOOL ME WOULD'VE FLIPPED FROM ALL THIS ATTENTION FROM TAYLOR . . .
"AND DORKY ADULT ME WAS DOING ALL SHE COULD TO STAY COOL. BUT AS FLATTERED AS I WAS, I HAD TO LEVEL WITH TAYLOR . . .
Y'KNOW . . . I'M, UH, SEEING SOMEONE
HEY, I KNOW . . .
BUT IF ANYTHING CHANGES, KEEP ME IN MIND . . .

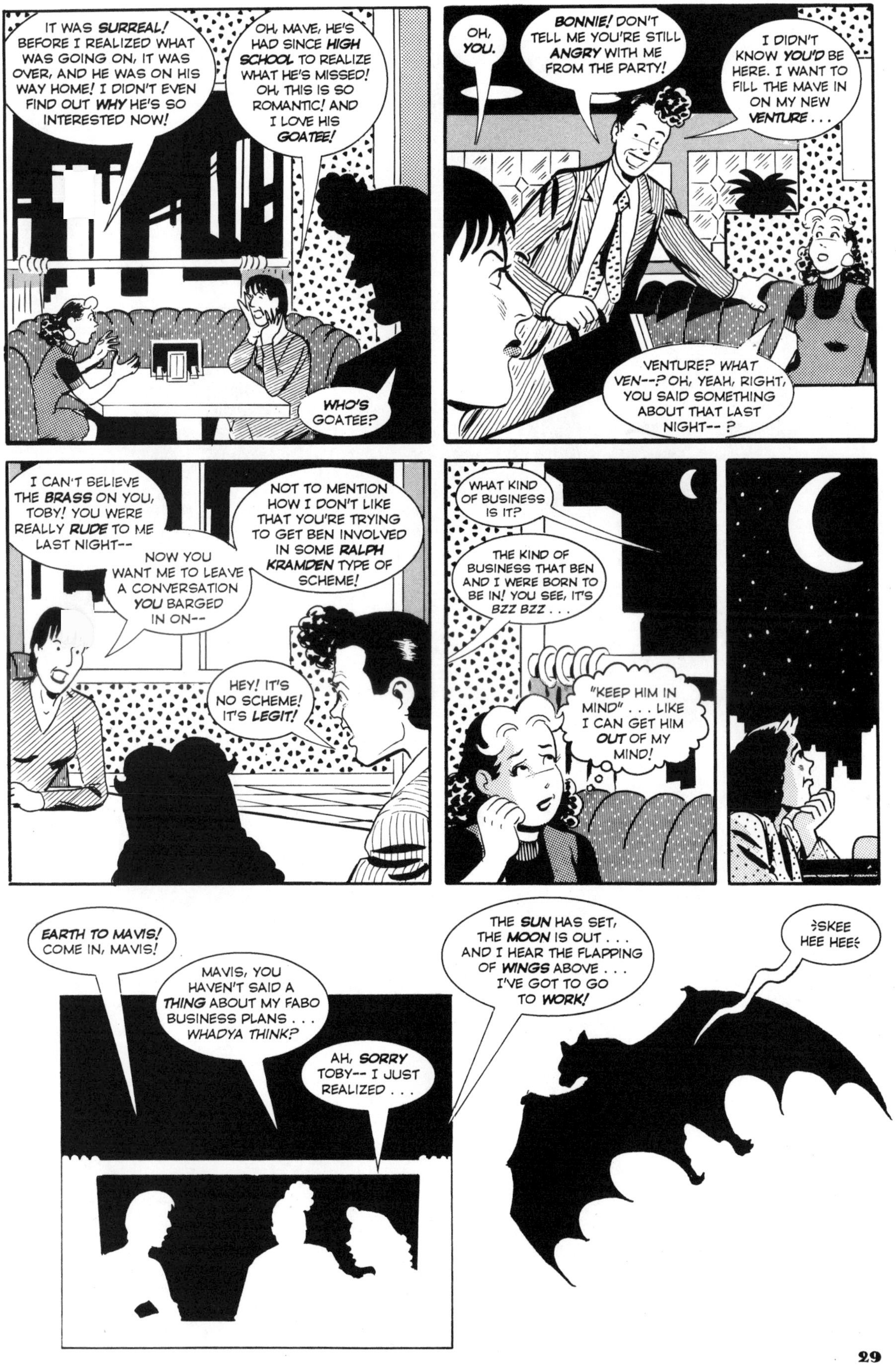
IT WAS SURREAL! BEFORE I REALIZED WHAT WAS GOING ON, IT WAS OVER, AND HE WAS ON HIS WAY HOME! I DIDN'T EVEN FIND OUT WHY HE'S SO INTERESTED NOW!
OH, MAVE, HE'S HAD SINCE HIGH SCHOOL TO REALIZE WHAT HE'S MISSED! OH, THIS IS SO ROMANTIC! AND I LOVE HIS GOATEE!
WHO'S GOATEE?
OH, YOU.
BONNIE! DON'T TELL ME YOU'RE STILL ANGRY WITH ME FROM THE PARTY!
I DIDN'T KNOW YOU'D BE HERE. I WANT TO FILL THE MAVE IN ON MY NEW VENTURE . . .
VENTURE? WHAT VEN--? OH, YEAH, RIGHT, YOU SAID SOMETHING ABOUT THAT LAST NIGHT-- ?
I CAN'T BELIEVE THE BRASS ON YOU, TOBY! YOU WERE REALLY RUDE TO ME LAST NIGHT--
NOW YOU WANT ME TO LEAVE A CONVERSATION YOU BARGED IN ON--
NOT TO MENTION HOW I DON'T LIKE THAT YOU'RE TRYING TO GET BEN INVOLVED IN SOME RALPH KRAMDEN TYPE OF SCHEME!
HEY! IT'S NO SCHEME! IT'S LEGIT!
WHAT KIND OF BUSINESS IS IT?
THE KIND OF BUSINESS THAT BEN AND I WERE BORN TO BE IN! YOU SEE, IT'S BZZ BZZ . . .
"KEEP HIM IN MIND" . . . LIKE I CAN GET HIM OUT OF MY MIND!
EARTH TO MAVIS! COME IN, MAVIS!
MAVIS, YOU HAVEN'T SAID A THING ABOUT MY FABO BUSINESS PLANS . . . WHADYA THINK?
AH, SORRY TOBY-- I JUST REALIZED . . .
THE SUN HAS SET, THE MOON IS OUT . . . AND I HEAR THE FLAPPING OF WINGS ABOVE . . . I'VE GOT TO GO TO WORK!
SKEE HEE HEE

The Vampire Brat
Part 2

MYRTLE THE VAMPIRE HATER

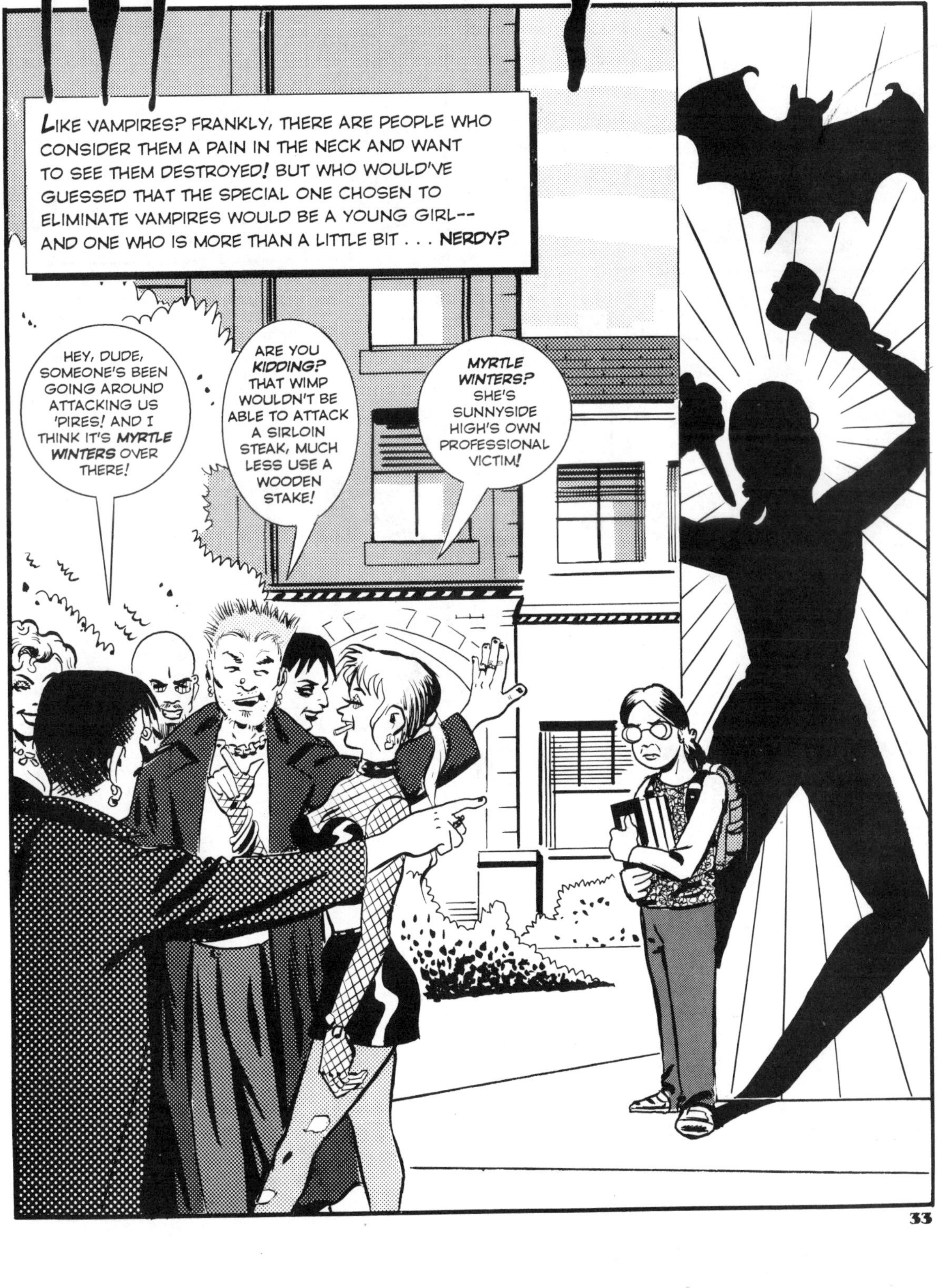
LIKE VAMPIRES? FRANKLY, THERE ARE PEOPLE WHO CONSIDER THEM A PAIN IN THE NECK AND WANT TO SEE THEM DESTROYED! BUT WHO WOULD'VE GUESSED THAT THE SPECIAL ONE CHOSEN TO ELIMINATE VAMPIRES WOULD BE A YOUNG GIRL-- AND ONE WHO IS MORE THAN A LITTLE BIT . . . NERDY?
HEY, DUDE, SOMEONE'S BEEN GOING AROUND ATTACKING US 'PIRES! AND I THINK IT'S MYRTLE WINTERS OVER THERE!
ARE YOU KIDDING? THAT WIMP WOULDN'T BE ABLE TO ATTACK A SIRLOIN STEAK, MUCH LESS USE A WOODEN STAKE!
MYRTLE WINTERS? SHE'S SUNNYSIDE HIGH'S OWN PROFESSIONAL VICTIM!

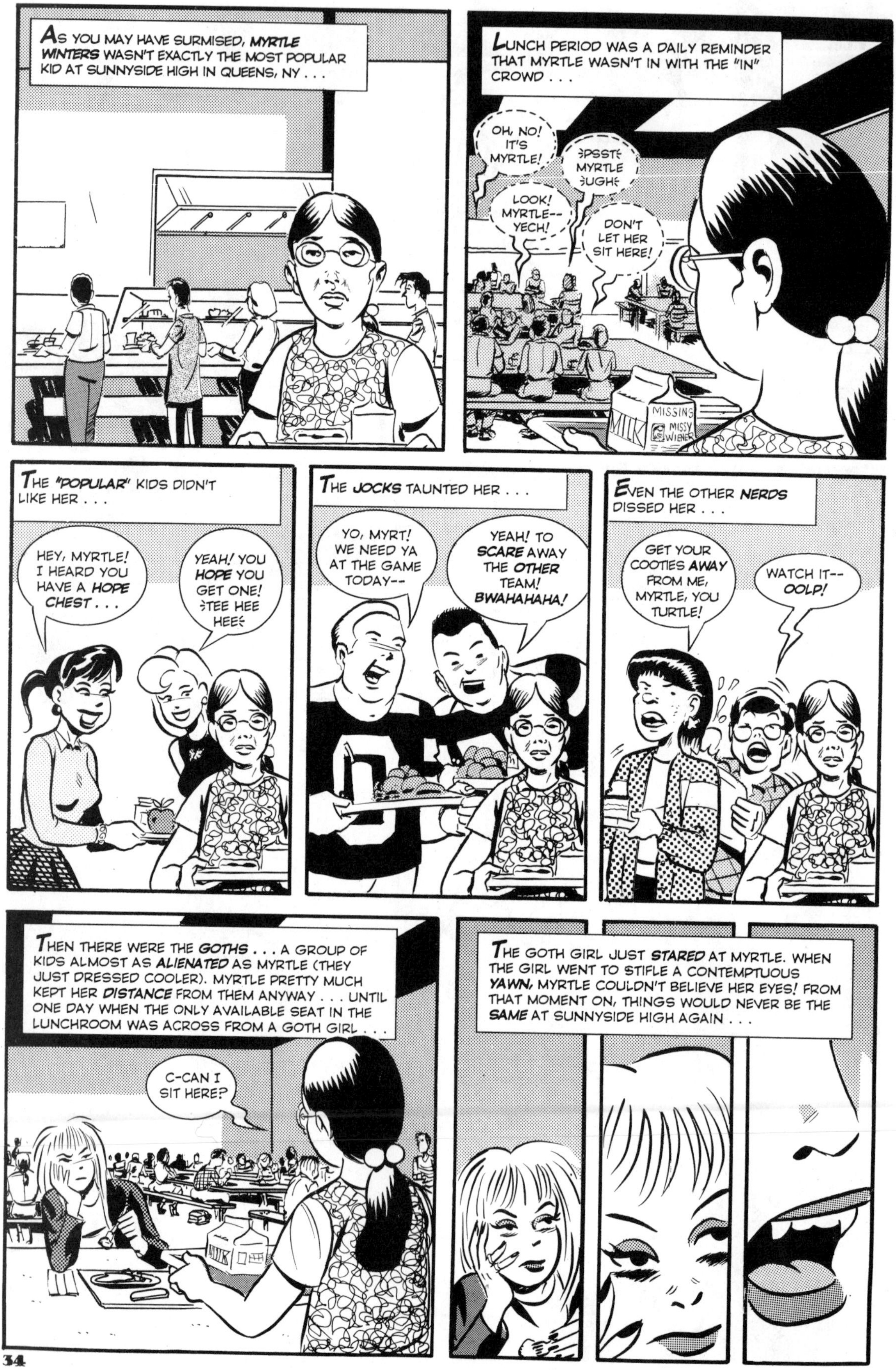

AS YOU MAY HAVE SURMISED, MYRTLE WINTERS WASN'T EXACTLY THE MOST POPULAR KID AT SUNNYSIDE HIGH IN QUEENS, NY . . .
LUNCH PERIOD WAS A DAILY REMINDER THAT MYRTLE WASN'T IN WITH THE "IN" CROWD . . .
OH, NO! IT'S MYRTLE!
PSST! MYRTLE UGH
LOOK! MYRTLE-- YECH!
DON'T LET HER SIT HERE!
MISSING MISSY WIENER
MILK
THE "POPULAR" KIDS DIDN'T LIKE HER . . .
HEY, MYRTLE! I HEARD YOU HAVE A HOPE CHEST . . .
YEAH! YOU HOPE YOU GET ONE! TEE HEE HEE
THE JOCKS TAUNTED HER . . .
YO, MYRT! WE NEED YA AT THE GAME TODAY--
YEAH! TO SCARE AWAY THE OTHER TEAM! BWAHAHAHA!
EVEN THE OTHER NERDS DISSED HER . . .
GET YOUR COOTIES AWAY FROM ME, MYRTLE, YOU TURTLE!
WATCH IT-- OOLP!
THEN THERE WERE THE GOTHS . . . A GROUP OF KIDS ALMOST AS ALIENATED AS MYRTLE (THEY JUST DRESSED COOLER). MYRTLE PRETTY MUCH KEPT HER DISTANCE FROM THEM ANYWAY . . . UNTIL ONE DAY WHEN THE ONLY AVAILABLE SEAT IN THE LUNCHROOM WAS ACROSS FROM A GOTH GIRL . . .
C-CAN I SIT HERE?
THE GOTH GIRL JUST STARED AT MYRTLE. WHEN THE GIRL WENT TO STIFLE A CONTEMPTUOUS YAWN, MYRTLE COULDN'T BELIEVE HER EYES! FROM THAT MOMENT ON, THINGS WOULD NEVER BE THE SAME AT SUNNYSIDE HIGH AGAIN . . .

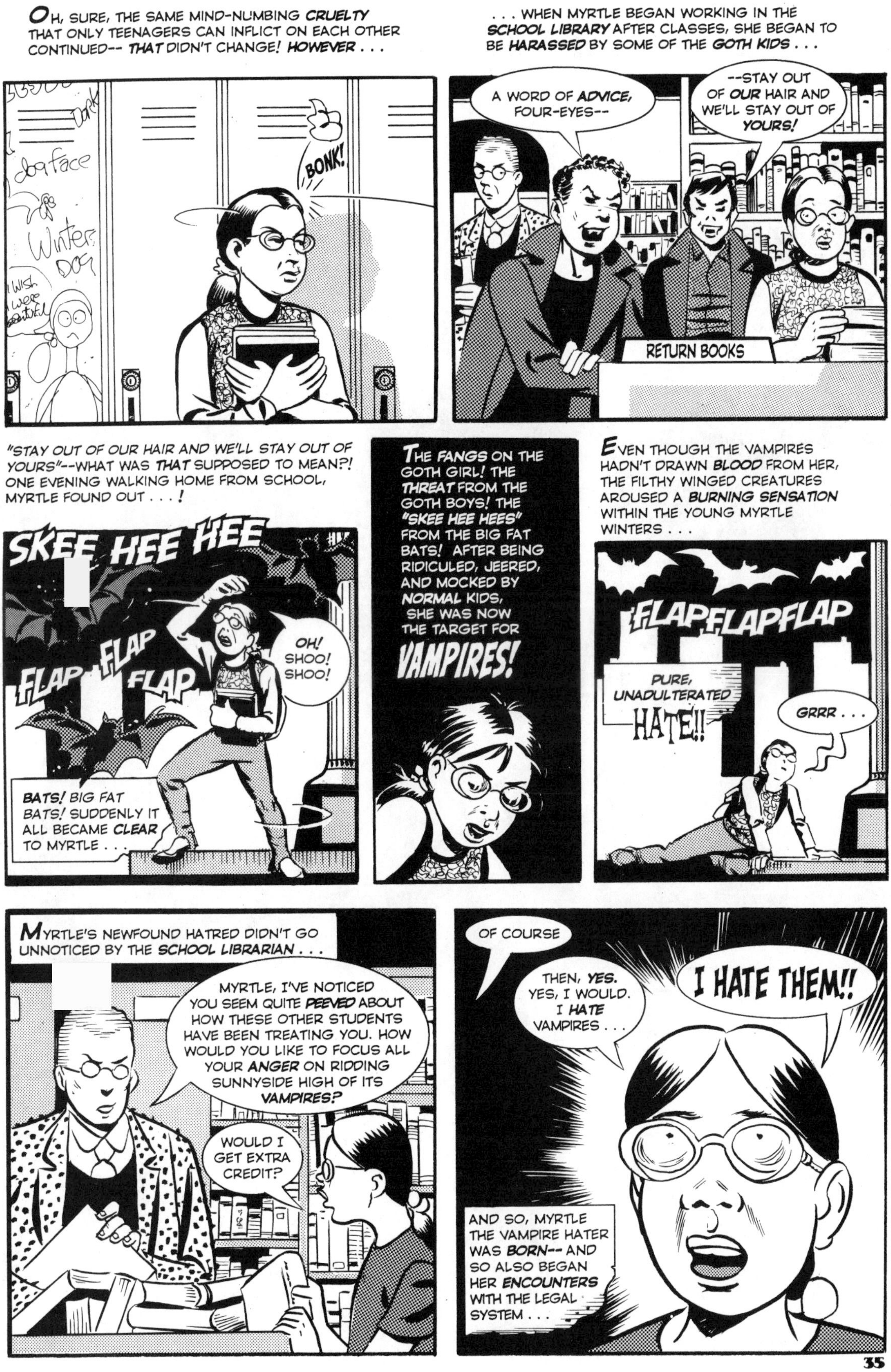
OH, SURE, THE SAME MIND-NUMBING CRUELTY THAT ONLY TEENAGERS CAN INFLICT ON EACH OTHER CONTINUED-- THAT DIDN'T CHANGE! HOWEVER . . .
Dork
dog face
Winters DOG
I wish I were
BONK!
. . . WHEN MYRTLE BEGAN WORKING IN THE SCHOOL LIBRARY AFTER CLASSES, SHE BEGAN TO BE HARASSED BY SOME OF THE GOTH KIDS . . .
A WORD OF ADVICE, FOUR-EYES--
--STAY OUT OF OUR HAIR AND WE'LL STAY OUT OF YOURS!
RETURN BOOKS
"STAY OUT OF OUR HAIR AND WE'LL STAY OUT OF YOURS"--WHAT WAS THAT SUPPOSED TO MEAN?! ONE EVENING WALKING HOME FROM SCHOOL, MYRTLE FOUND OUT . . . !
SKEE HEE HEE
FLAP FLAP FLAP
OH! SHOO! SHOO!
BATS! BIG FAT BATS! SUDDENLY IT ALL BECAME CLEAR TO MYRTLE . . .
THE FANGS ON THE GOTH GIRL! THE THREAT FROM THE GOTH BOYS! THE "SKEE HEE HEES" FROM THE BIG FAT BATS! AFTER BEING RIDICULED, JEERED, AND MOCKED BY NORMAL KIDS, SHE WAS NOW THE TARGET FOR VAMPIRES!
EVEN THOUGH THE VAMPIRES HADN'T DRAWN BLOOD FROM HER, THE FILTHY WINGED CREATURES AROUSED A BURNING SENSATION WITHIN THE YOUNG MYRTLE WINTERS . . .
FLAPFLAPFLAP
PURE, UNADULTERATED HATE!!
GRRR . . .
MYRTLE'S NEWFOUND HATRED DIDN'T GO UNNOTICED BY THE SCHOOL LIBRARIAN . . .
MYRTLE, I'VE NOTICED YOU SEEM QUITE PEEVED ABOUT HOW THESE OTHER STUDENTS HAVE BEEN TREATING YOU. HOW WOULD YOU LIKE TO FOCUS ALL YOUR ANGER ON RIDDING SUNNYSIDE HIGH OF ITS VAMPIRES?
WOULD I GET EXTRA CREDIT?
OF COURSE
THEN, YES. YES, I WOULD. I HATE VAMPIRES . . .
I HATE THEM!!
AND SO, MYRTLE THE VAMPIRE HATER WAS BORN-- AND SO ALSO BEGAN HER ENCOUNTERS WITH THE LEGAL SYSTEM . . .

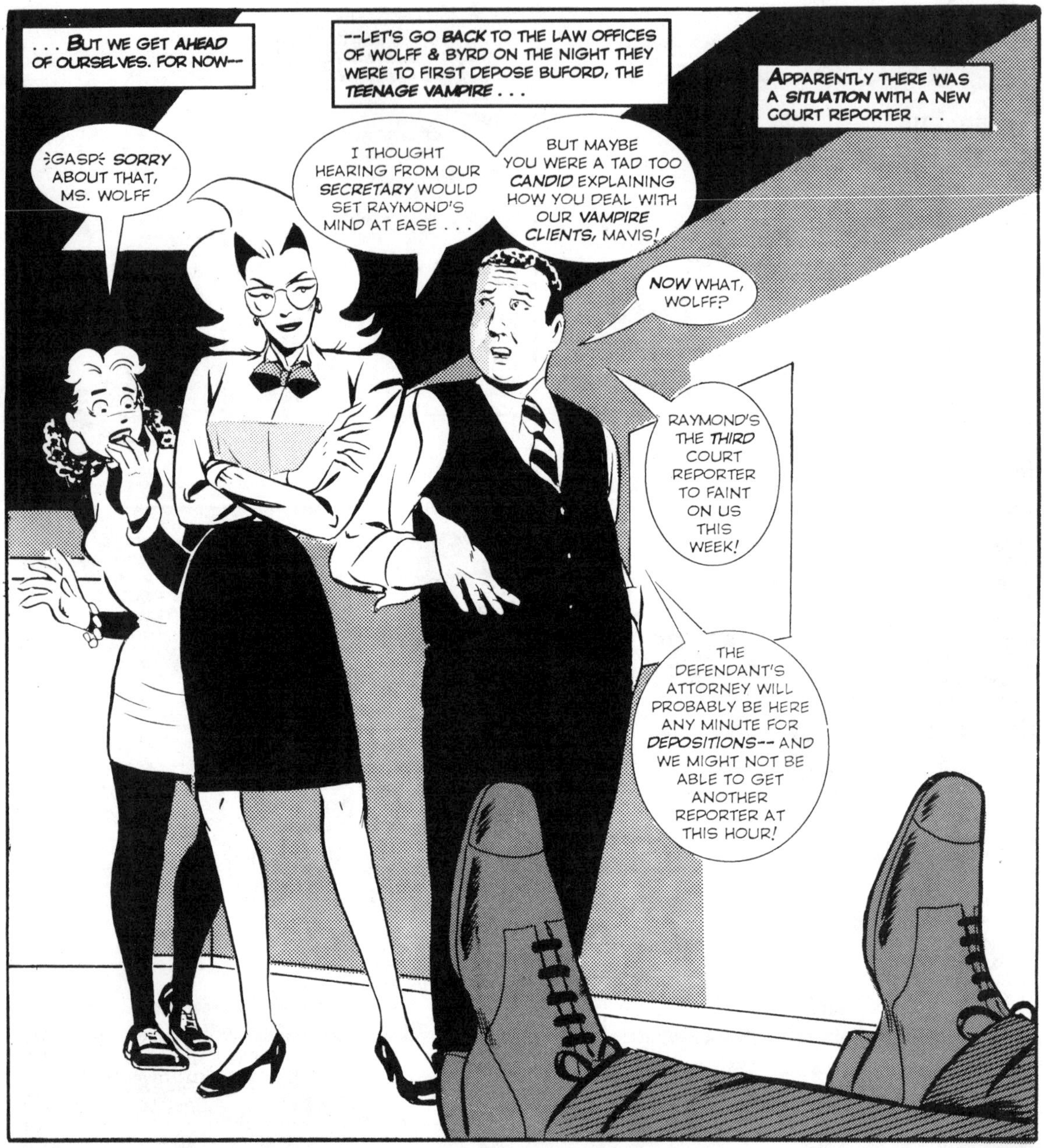
. . . BUT WE GET AHEAD OF OURSELVES. FOR NOW--
--LET'S GO BACK TO THE LAW OFFICES OF WOLFF & BYRD ON THE NIGHT THEY WERE TO FIRST DEPOSE BUFORD, THE TEENAGE VAMPIRE . . .
APPARENTLY THERE WAS A SITUATION WITH A NEW COURT REPORTER . . .
GASP SORRY ABOUT THAT, MS. WOLFF
I THOUGHT HEARING FROM OUR SECRETARY WOULD SET RAYMOND'S MIND AT EASE . . .
BUT MAYBE YOU WERE A TAD TOO CANDID EXPLAINING HOW YOU DEAL WITH OUR VAMPIRE CLIENTS, MAVIS!
NOW WHAT, WOLFF?
RAYMOND'S THE THIRD COURT REPORTER TO FAINT ON US THIS WEEK!
THE DEFENDANT'S ATTORNEY WILL PROBABLY BE HERE ANY MINUTE FOR DEPOSITIONS-- AND WE MIGHT NOT BE ABLE TO GET ANOTHER REPORTER AT THIS HOUR!

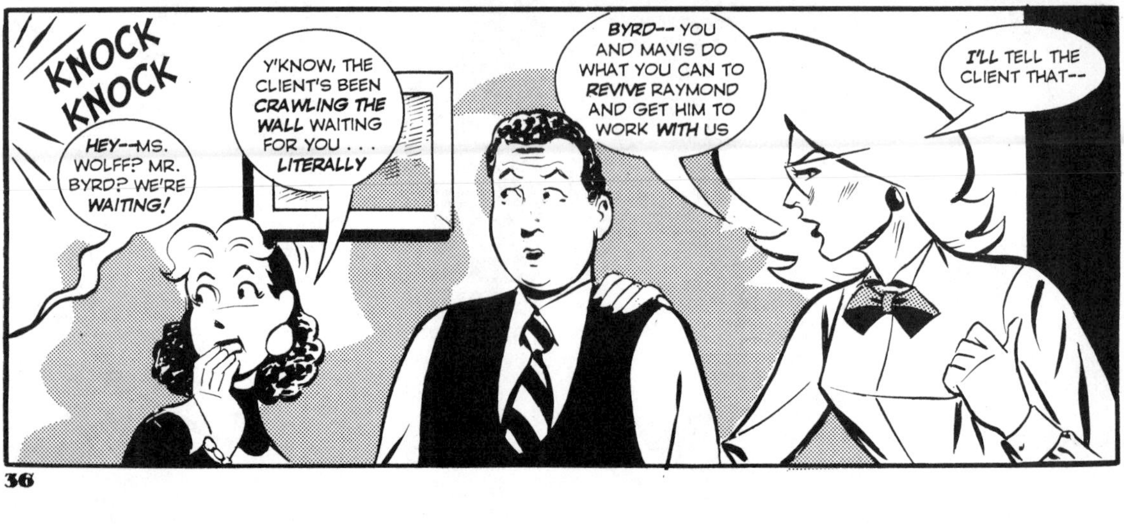
KNOCK KNOCK
HEY--MS. WOLFF? MR. BYRD? WE'RE WAITING!
Y'KNOW, THE CLIENT'S BEEN CRAWLING THE WALL WAITING FOR YOU . . . LITERALLY
BYRD-- YOU AND MAVIS DO WHAT YOU CAN TO REVIVE RAYMOND AND GET HIM TO WORK WITH US
I'LL TELL THE CLIENT THAT--

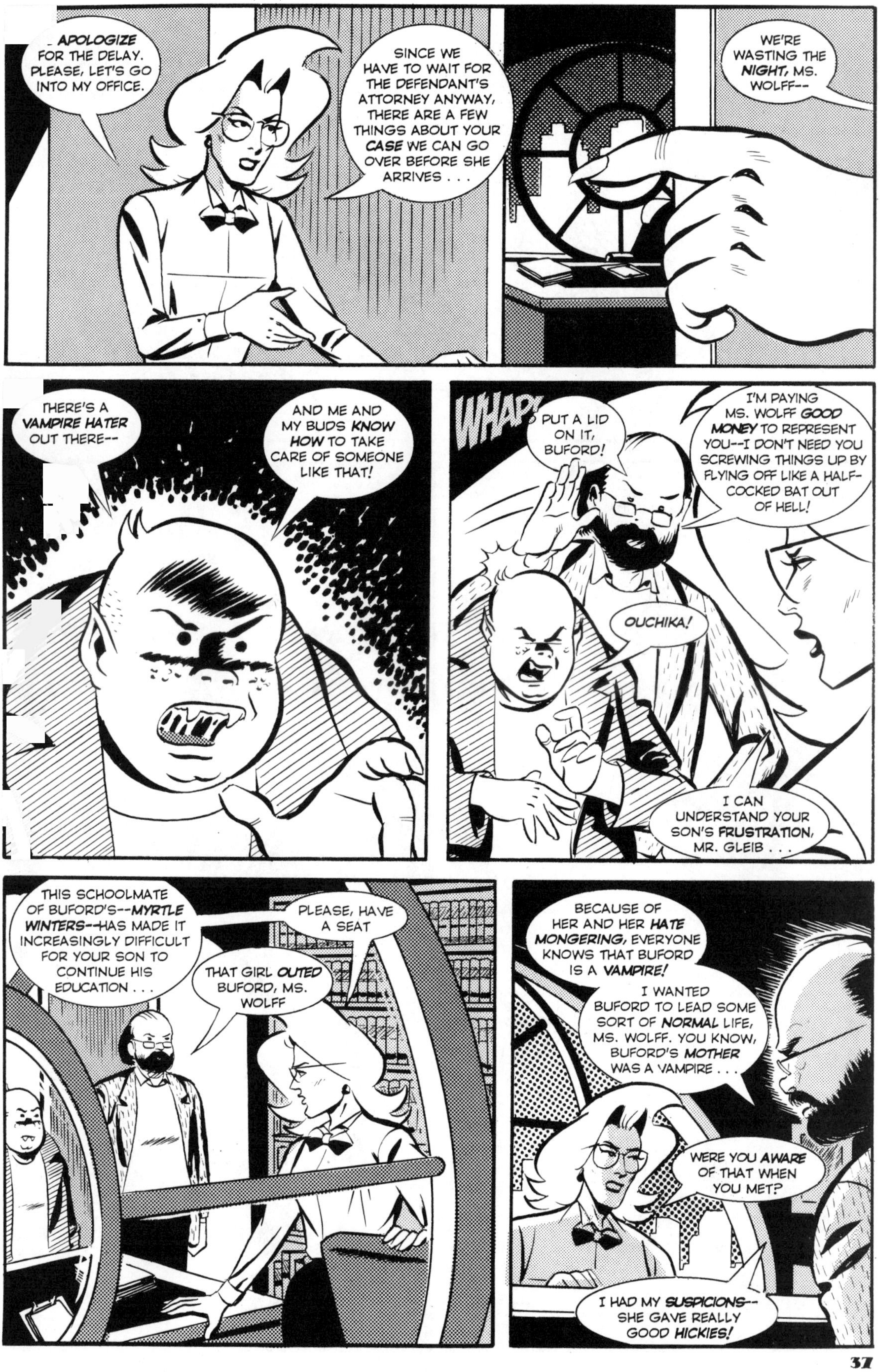

APOLOGIZE FOR THE DELAY. PLEASE, LET'S GO INTO MY OFFICE.
SINCE WE HAVE TO WAIT FOR THE DEFENDANT'S ATTORNEY ANYWAY, THERE ARE A FEW THINGS ABOUT YOUR CASE WE CAN GO OVER BEFORE SHE ARRIVES . . .
WE'RE WASTING THE NIGHT, MS. WOLFF--
THERE'S A VAMPIRE HATER OUT THERE--
AND ME AND MY BUDS KNOW HOW TO TAKE CARE OF SOMEONE LIKE THAT!
WHAP!
PUT A LID ON IT, BUFORD!
I'M PAYING MS. WOLFF GOOD MONEY TO REPRESENT YOU--I DON'T NEED YOU SCREWING THINGS UP BY FLYING OFF LIKE A HALF-COCKED BAT OUT OF HELL!
OUCHIKA!
I CAN UNDERSTAND YOUR SON'S FRUSTRATION, MR. GLEIB . . .
THIS SCHOOLMATE OF BUFORD'S--MYRTLE WINTERS--HAS MADE IT INCREASINGLY DIFFICULT FOR YOUR SON TO CONTINUE HIS EDUCATION . . .
PLEASE, HAVE A SEAT
THAT GIRL OUTED BUFORD, MS. WOLFF
BECAUSE OF HER AND HER HATE MONGERING, EVERYONE KNOWS THAT BUFORD IS A VAMPIRE!
I WANTED BUFORD TO LEAD SOME SORT OF NORMAL LIFE, MS. WOLFF. YOU KNOW, BUFORD'S MOTHER WAS A VAMPIRE . . .
WERE YOU AWARE OF THAT WHEN YOU MET?
I HAD MY SUSPICIONS--SHE GAVE REALLY GOOD HICKIES!

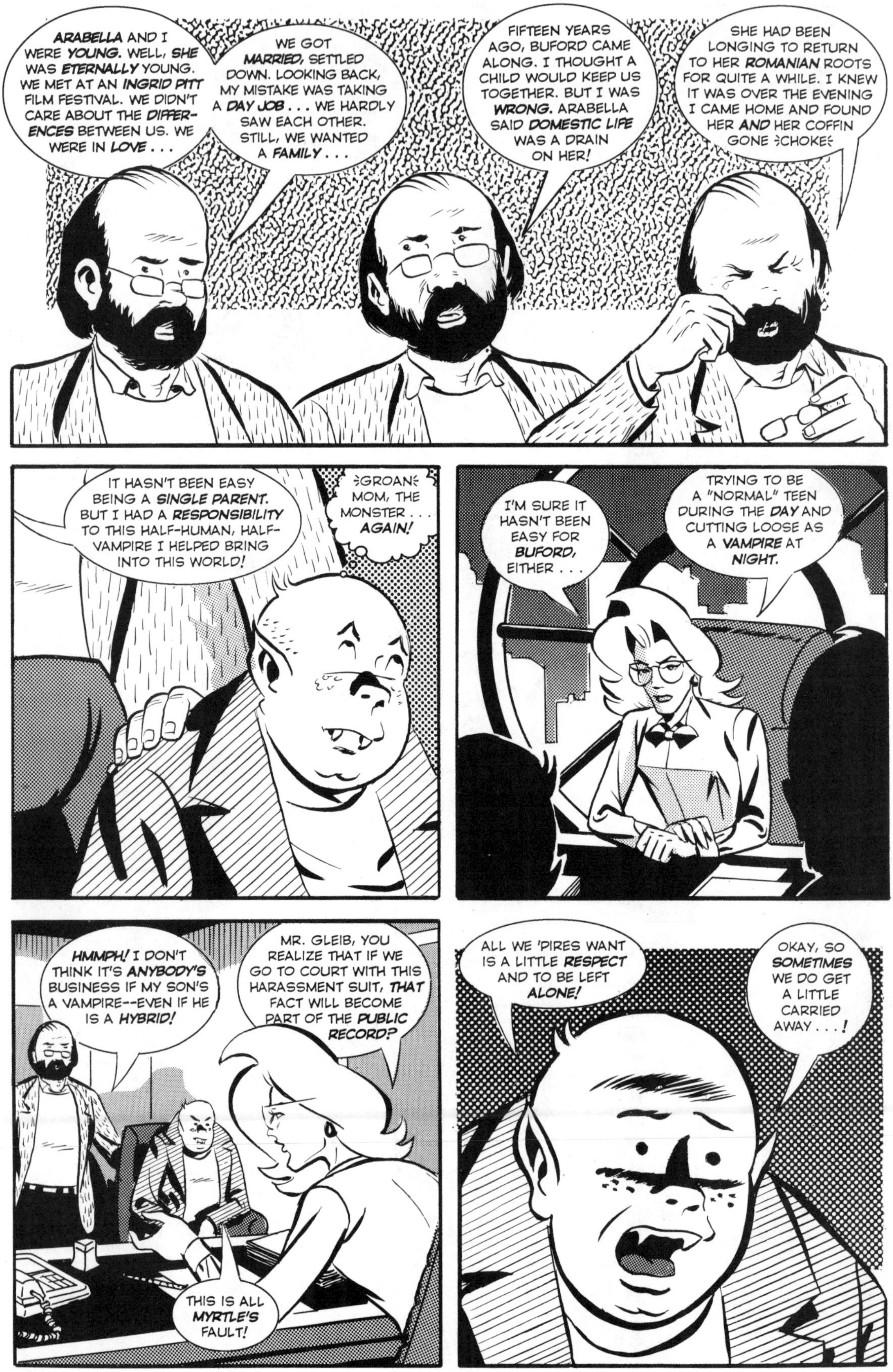
ARABELLA AND I WERE YOUNG. WELL, SHE WAS ETERNALLY YOUNG. WE MET AT AN INGRID PITT FILM FESTIVAL. WE DIDN'T CARE ABOUT THE DIFFERENCES BETWEEN US. WE WERE IN LOVE . . .
WE GOT MARRIED, SETTLED DOWN. LOOKING BACK, MY MISTAKE WAS TAKING A DAY JOB . . . WE HARDLY SAW EACH OTHER. STILL, WE WANTED A FAMILY . . .
FIFTEEN YEARS AGO, BUFORD CAME ALONG. I THOUGHT A CHILD WOULD KEEP US TOGETHER. BUT I WAS WRONG. ARABELLA SAID DOMESTIC LIFE WAS A DRAIN ON HER!
SHE HAD BEEN LONGING TO RETURN TO HER ROMANIAN ROOTS FOR QUITE A WHILE. I KNEW IT WAS OVER THE EVENING I CAME HOME AND FOUND HER AND HER COFFIN GONE ✲CHOKE✲
IT HASN'T BEEN EASY BEING A SINGLE PARENT. BUT I HAD A RESPONSIBILITY TO THIS HALF-HUMAN, HALF-VAMPIRE I HELPED BRING INTO THIS WORLD!
✲GROAN✲ MOM, THE MONSTER . . . AGAIN!
I'M SURE IT HASN'T BEEN EASY FOR BUFORD, EITHER . . .
TRYING TO BE A "NORMAL" TEEN DURING THE DAY AND CUTTING LOOSE AS A VAMPIRE AT NIGHT.
HMMPH! I DON'T THINK IT'S ANYBODY'S BUSINESS IF MY SON'S A VAMPIRE--EVEN IF HE IS A HYBRID!
MR. GLEIB, YOU REALIZE THAT IF WE GO TO COURT WITH THIS HARASSMENT SUIT, THAT FACT WILL BECOME PART OF THE PUBLIC RECORD?
THIS IS ALL MYRTLE'S FAULT!
ALL WE 'PIRES WANT IS A LITTLE RESPECT AND TO BE LEFT ALONE!
OKAY, SO SOMETIMES WE DO GET A LITTLE CARRIED AWAY . . . !

"THERE'S THIS 'PIRE CHICK, ***MALIA,*** WHO STARTED GOOFIN' ON MYRTLE. SHE DIDN'T WANNA SUCK MYRTLE'S BLOOD OR ANYTHING, SHE JUST WANTED TO ***SCARE*** HER. GUESS WHAT? MALIA ***NEVER CAME BACK*** TO SCHOOL AFTER THAT DAY . . .

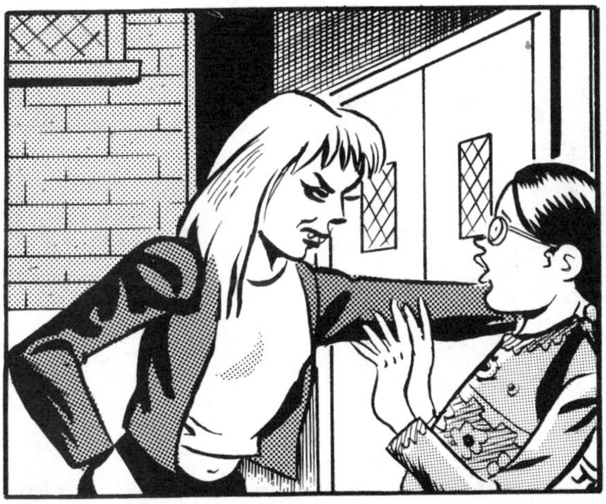

"I THOUGHT MALIA HAD DROPPED OUT--BUT WORD UP WITH THE 'PIRES I HANG WITH WAS, THERE WAS SOME ***BAD MOJO*** IN THE AIR--SOMEONE HAD IT IN FOR 'PIRES--SOMEONE WHO WANTED TO TAKE US ***DOWN!***

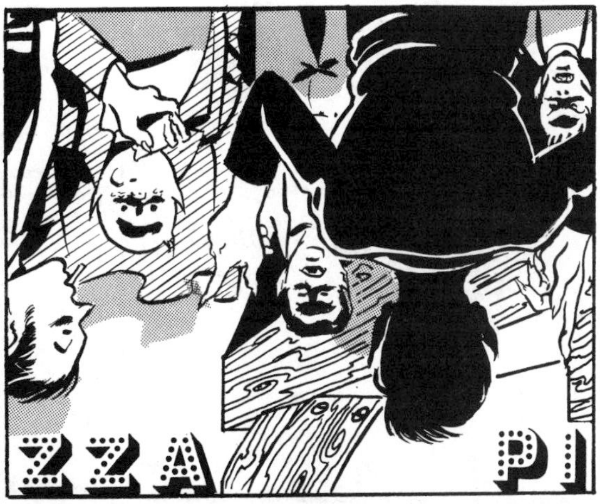
ZZA
PI

"I DIDN'T THINK ANYONE WOULD MESS WITH A 'PIRE, UNTIL THE NEXT DAY WHEN I FOUND AN UNPLEASANT SURPRISE IN MY LOCKER . . . ***!***

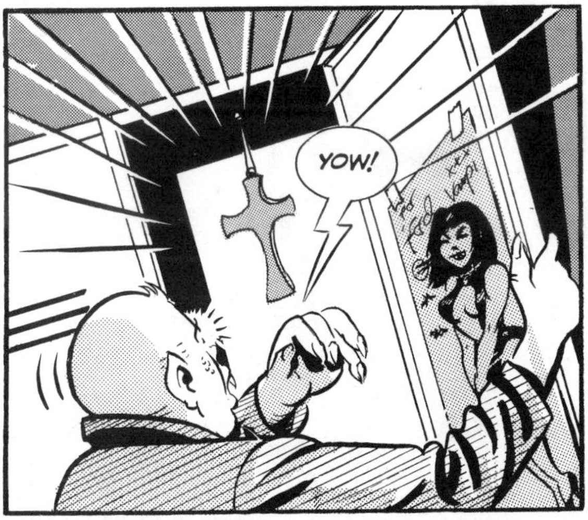
YOW!

"I WAS SO THROWN I DIDN'T NOTICE THAT SOMEONE HAD BEEN ***WATCHING*** ME. SHE RAN OFF BEFORE I COULD GET A GOOD LOOK AT HER . . .

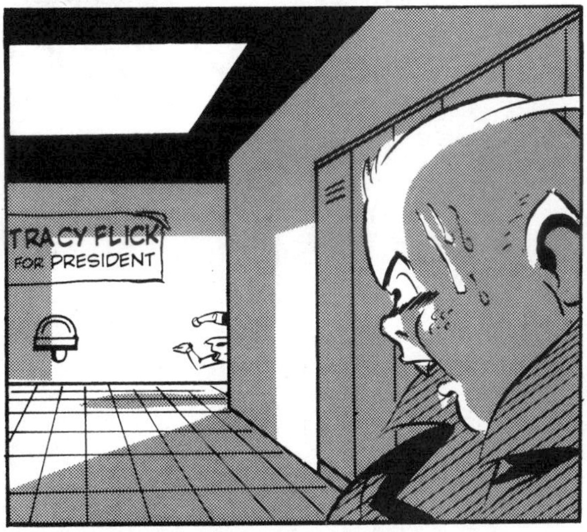
TRACY FLICK
FOR PRESIDENT

"ANYWAY, A WEEK LATER I WAS IN THE SCHOOL LIBRARY AFTER ***SUNSET.*** I NEEDED TO DO A BOOK REPORT AND I WAS CHECKING OUT THE CLASSICS. I THOUGHT I WAS ***ALONE,*** SINCE THE SCHOOL WAS CLOSED AT THAT HOUR. BUT I HEARD SOMEONE ***BELOW*** ME . . .

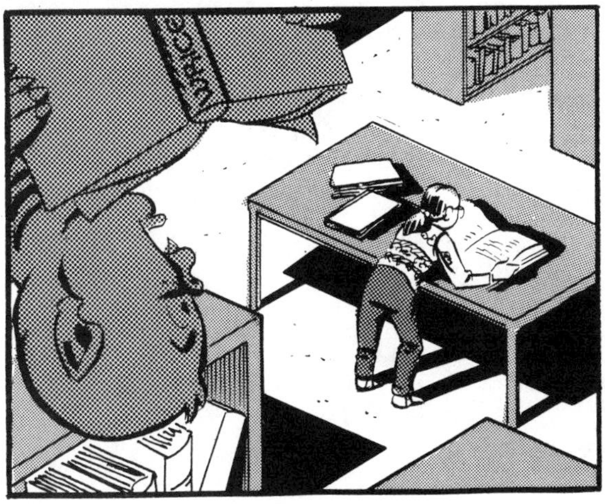

"IT WAS ***MYRTLE WINTERS.*** SURE, SHE WORKS IN THE LIBRARY, BUT IT WAS ***AFTER DARK*** . . . I WAS GONNA SWOOP DOWN INTO HER HAIR AND GIVE HER SUCH A ***FRIGHT***--BUT THEN I NOTICED WHAT ***BOOK*** SHE WAS LOOKIN' AT . . .

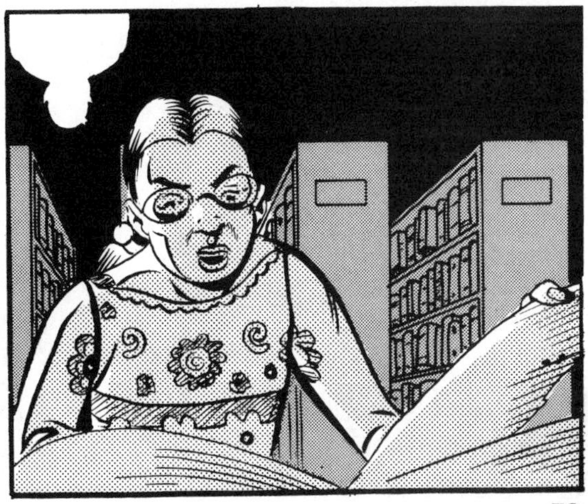

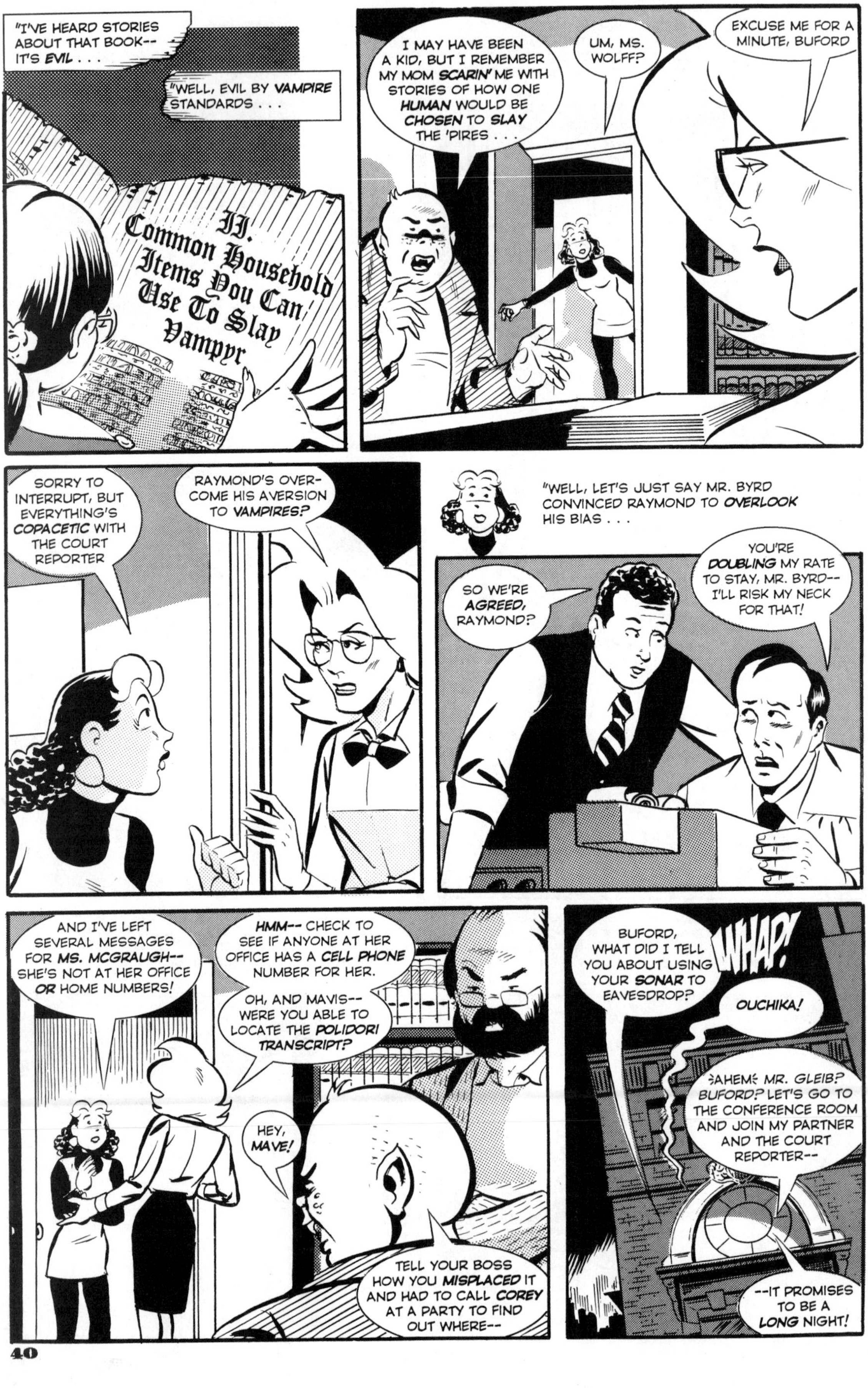
"I'VE HEARD STORIES ABOUT THAT BOOK-- IT'S EVIL . . .
"WELL, EVIL BY VAMPIRE STANDARDS . . .
II. Common Household Items You Can Use To Slay Vampyr
I MAY HAVE BEEN A KID, BUT I REMEMBER MY MOM SCARIN' ME WITH STORIES OF HOW ONE HUMAN WOULD BE CHOSEN TO SLAY THE 'PIRES . . .
UM, MS. WOLFF?
EXCUSE ME FOR A MINUTE, BUFORD
SORRY TO INTERRUPT, BUT EVERYTHING'S COPACETIC WITH THE COURT REPORTER
RAYMOND'S OVERCOME HIS AVERSION TO VAMPIRES?
"WELL, LET'S JUST SAY MR. BYRD CONVINCED RAYMOND TO OVERLOOK HIS BIAS . . .
SO WE'RE AGREED, RAYMOND?
YOU'RE DOUBLING MY RATE TO STAY, MR. BYRD-- I'LL RISK MY NECK FOR THAT!
AND I'VE LEFT SEVERAL MESSAGES FOR MS. MCGRAUGH-- SHE'S NOT AT HER OFFICE OR HOME NUMBERS!
HMM-- CHECK TO SEE IF ANYONE AT HER OFFICE HAS A CELL PHONE NUMBER FOR HER.
OH, AND MAVIS-- WERE YOU ABLE TO LOCATE THE POLIDORI TRANSCRIPT?
HEY, MAVE!
TELL YOUR BOSS HOW YOU MISPLACED IT AND HAD TO CALL COREY AT A PARTY TO FIND OUT WHERE--
BUFORD, WHAT DID I TELL YOU ABOUT USING YOUR SONAR TO EAVESDROP?
WHAP!
OUCHIKA!
AHEM MR. GLEIB? BUFORD? LET'S GO TO THE CONFERENCE ROOM AND JOIN MY PARTNER AND THE COURT REPORTER--
--IT PROMISES TO BE A LONG NIGHT!

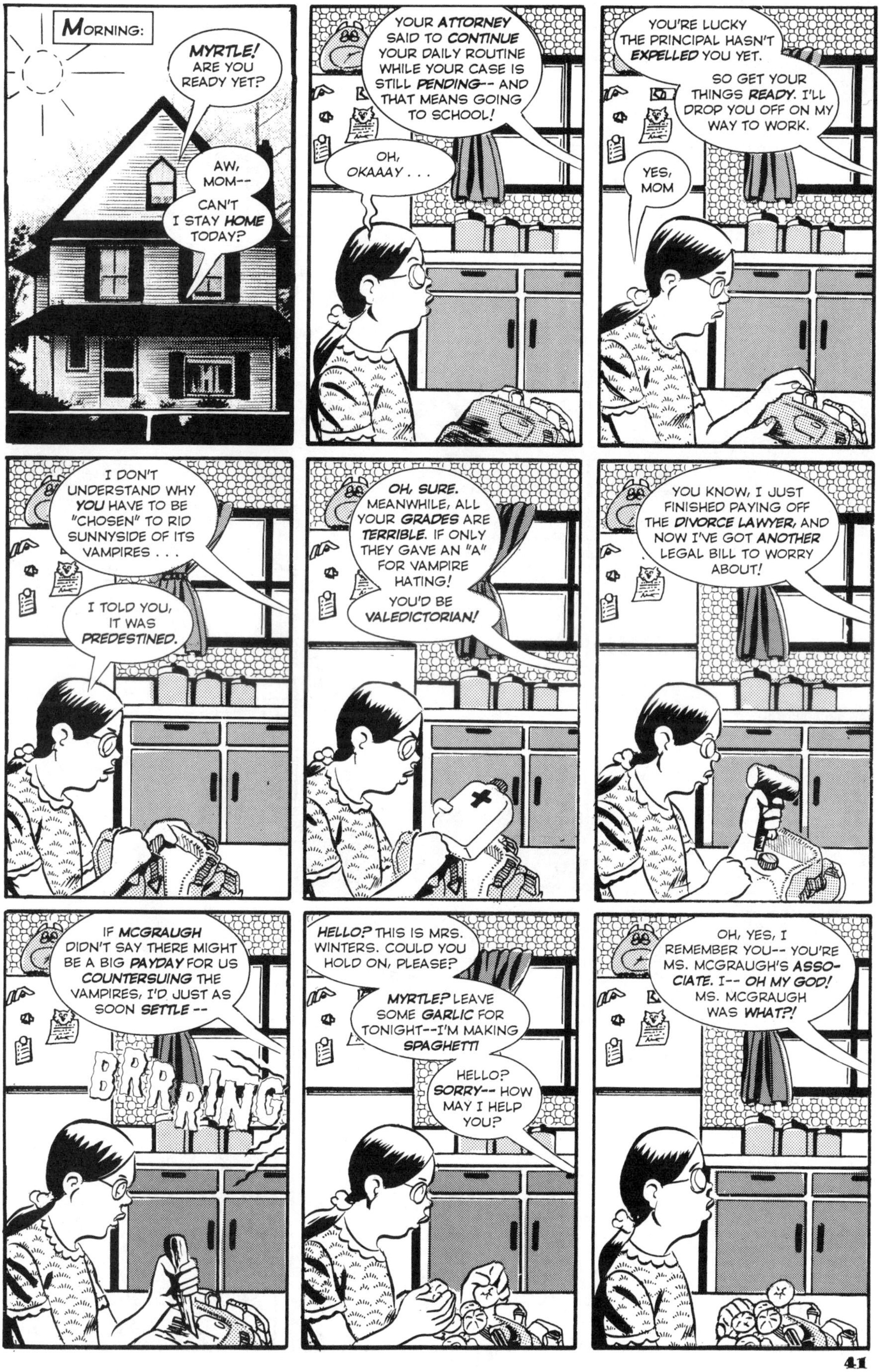
MORNING:
MYRTLE! ARE YOU READY YET?
AW, MOM-- CAN'T I STAY HOME TODAY?
YOUR ATTORNEY SAID TO CONTINUE YOUR DAILY ROUTINE WHILE YOUR CASE IS STILL PENDING-- AND THAT MEANS GOING TO SCHOOL!
OH, OKAAAY . . .
YOU'RE LUCKY THE PRINCIPAL HASN'T EXPELLED YOU YET.
SO GET YOUR THINGS READY. I'LL DROP YOU OFF ON MY WAY TO WORK.
YES, MOM
I DON'T UNDERSTAND WHY YOU HAVE TO BE "CHOSEN" TO RID SUNNYSIDE OF ITS VAMPIRES . . .
I TOLD YOU, IT WAS PREDESTINED.
OH, SURE. MEANWHILE, ALL YOUR GRADES ARE TERRIBLE. IF ONLY THEY GAVE AN "A" FOR VAMPIRE HATING!
YOU'D BE VALEDICTORIAN!
YOU KNOW, I JUST FINISHED PAYING OFF THE DIVORCE LAWYER, AND NOW I'VE GOT ANOTHER LEGAL BILL TO WORRY ABOUT!
IF MCGRAUGH DIDN'T SAY THERE MIGHT BE A BIG PAYDAY FOR US COUNTERSUING THE VAMPIRES, I'D JUST AS SOON SETTLE --
BRRRING
HELLO? THIS IS MRS. WINTERS. COULD YOU HOLD ON, PLEASE?
MYRTLE? LEAVE SOME GARLIC FOR TONIGHT--I'M MAKING SPAGHETTI
HELLO? SORRY-- HOW MAY I HELP YOU?
OH, YES, I REMEMBER YOU-- YOU'RE MS. MCGRAUGH'S ASSOCIATE. I-- OH MY GOD! MS. MCGRAUGH WAS WHAT?!

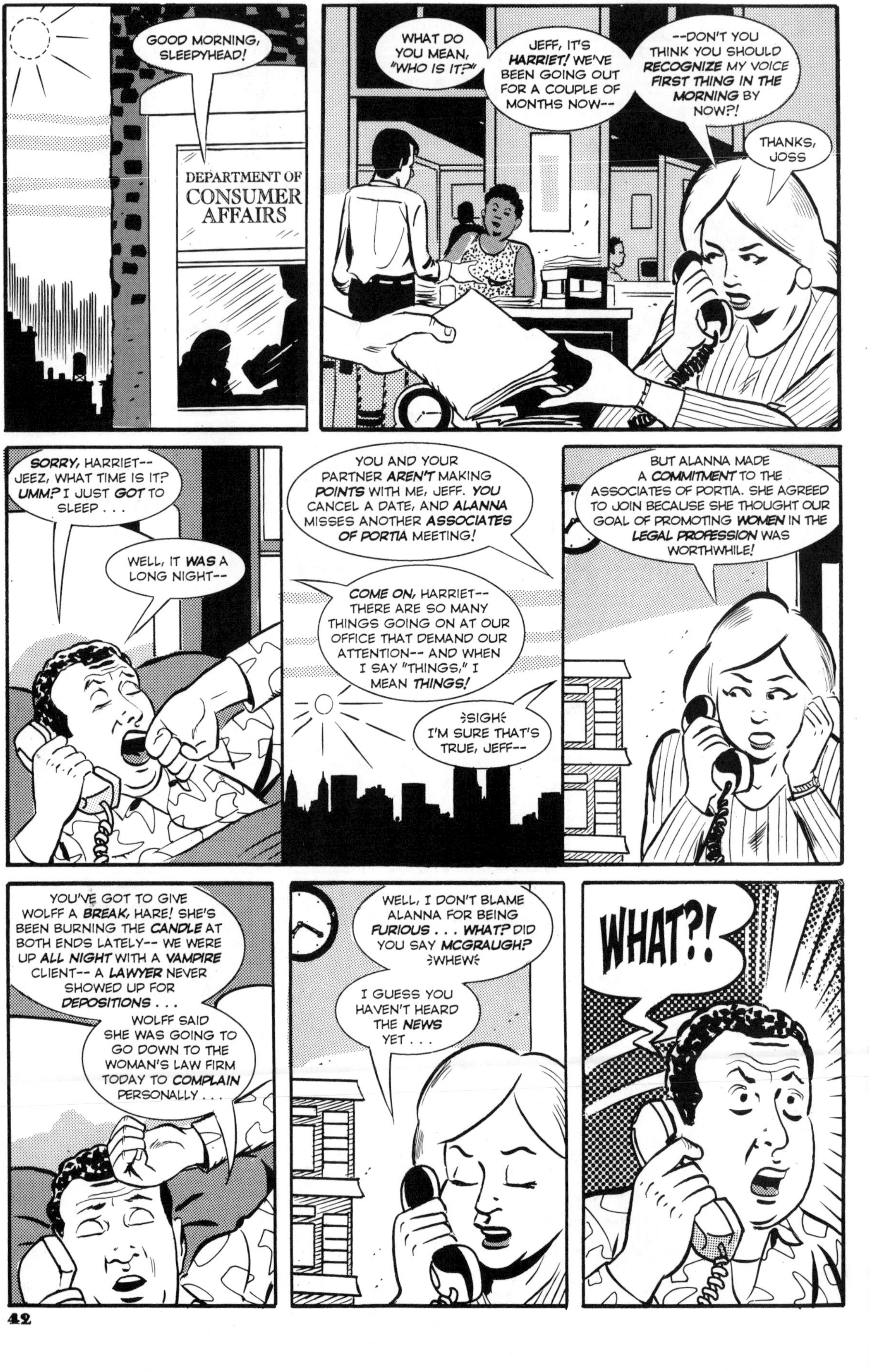

GOOD MORNING, SLEEPYHEAD!
DEPARTMENT OF CONSUMER AFFAIRS
WHAT DO YOU MEAN, "WHO IS IT?"
JEFF, IT'S HARRIET! WE'VE BEEN GOING OUT FOR A COUPLE OF MONTHS NOW--
--DON'T YOU THINK YOU SHOULD RECOGNIZE MY VOICE FIRST THING IN THE MORNING BY NOW?!
THANKS, JOSS
SORRY, HARRIET-- JEEZ, WHAT TIME IS IT? UMM? I JUST GOT TO SLEEP . . .
WELL, IT WAS A LONG NIGHT--
YOU AND YOUR PARTNER AREN'T MAKING POINTS WITH ME, JEFF. YOU CANCEL A DATE, AND ALANNA MISSES ANOTHER ASSOCIATES OF PORTIA MEETING!
COME ON, HARRIET-- THERE ARE SO MANY THINGS GOING ON AT OUR OFFICE THAT DEMAND OUR ATTENTION-- AND WHEN I SAY "THINGS," I MEAN THINGS!
SIGH I'M SURE THAT'S TRUE, JEFF--
BUT ALANNA MADE A COMMITMENT TO THE ASSOCIATES OF PORTIA. SHE AGREED TO JOIN BECAUSE SHE THOUGHT OUR GOAL OF PROMOTING WOMEN IN THE LEGAL PROFESSION WAS WORTHWHILE!
YOU'VE GOT TO GIVE WOLFF A BREAK, HARE! SHE'S BEEN BURNING THE CANDLE AT BOTH ENDS LATELY-- WE WERE UP ALL NIGHT WITH A VAMPIRE CLIENT-- A LAWYER NEVER SHOWED UP FOR DEPOSITIONS . . .
WOLFF SAID SHE WAS GOING TO GO DOWN TO THE WOMAN'S LAW FIRM TODAY TO COMPLAIN PERSONALLY . . .
WELL, I DON'T BLAME ALANNA FOR BEING FURIOUS . . . WHAT? DID YOU SAY MCGRAUGH? WHEW
I GUESS YOU HAVEN'T HEARD THE NEWS YET . . .
WHAT?!

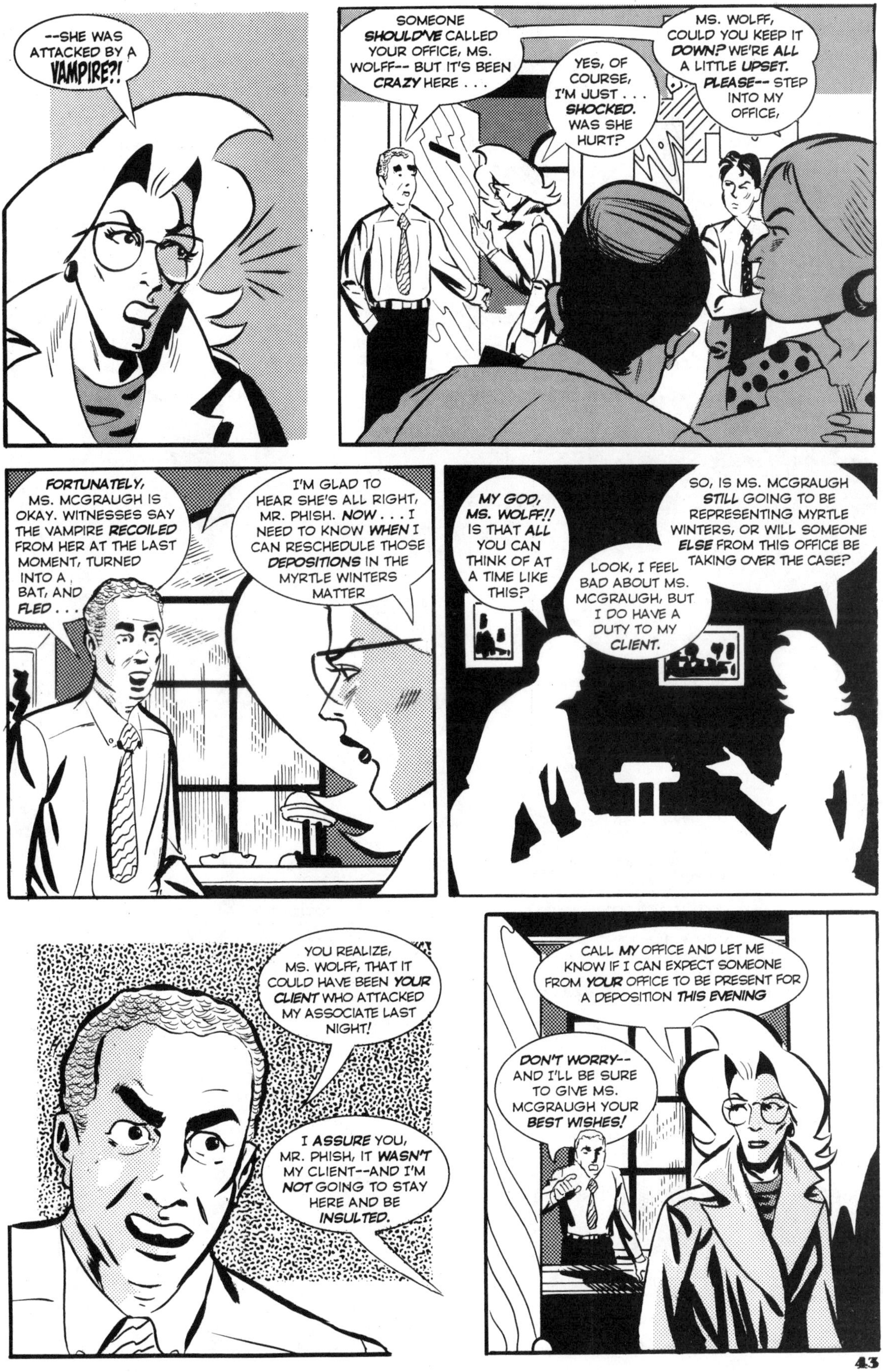
--SHE WAS ATTACKED BY A VAMPIRE?!
SOMEONE SHOULD'VE CALLED YOUR OFFICE, MS. WOLFF-- BUT IT'S BEEN CRAZY HERE . . .
YES, OF COURSE, I'M JUST . . . SHOCKED. WAS SHE HURT?
MS. WOLFF, COULD YOU KEEP IT DOWN? WE'RE ALL A LITTLE UPSET. PLEASE-- STEP INTO MY OFFICE,
FORTUNATELY, MS. MCGRAUGH IS OKAY. WITNESSES SAY THE VAMPIRE RECOILED FROM HER AT THE LAST MOMENT, TURNED INTO A BAT, AND FLED . . .
I'M GLAD TO HEAR SHE'S ALL RIGHT, MR. PHISH. NOW . . . I NEED TO KNOW WHEN I CAN RESCHEDULE THOSE DEPOSITIONS IN THE MYRTLE WINTERS MATTER
MY GOD, MS. WOLFF!! IS THAT ALL YOU CAN THINK OF AT A TIME LIKE THIS?
LOOK, I FEEL BAD ABOUT MS. MCGRAUGH, BUT I DO HAVE A DUTY TO MY CLIENT.
SO, IS MS. MCGRAUGH STILL GOING TO BE REPRESENTING MYRTLE WINTERS, OR WILL SOMEONE ELSE FROM THIS OFFICE BE TAKING OVER THE CASE?
YOU REALIZE, MS. WOLFF, THAT IT COULD HAVE BEEN YOUR CLIENT WHO ATTACKED MY ASSOCIATE LAST NIGHT!
I ASSURE YOU, MR. PHISH, IT WASN'T MY CLIENT--AND I'M NOT GOING TO STAY HERE AND BE INSULTED.
CALL MY OFFICE AND LET ME KNOW IF I CAN EXPECT SOMEONE FROM YOUR OFFICE TO BE PRESENT FOR A DEPOSITION THIS EVENING
DON'T WORRY-- AND I'LL BE SURE TO GIVE MS. MCGRAUGH YOUR BEST WISHES!

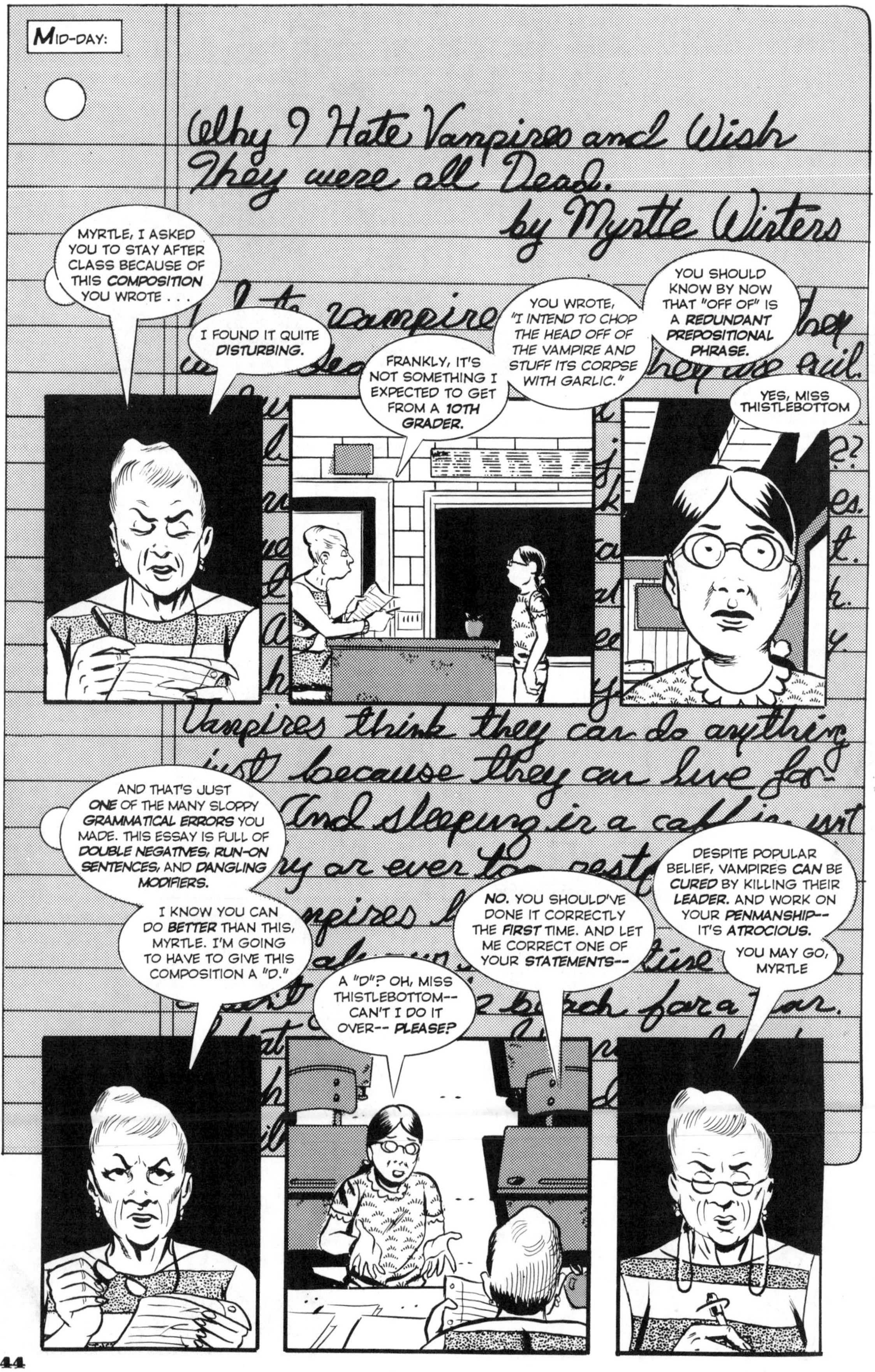
MID-DAY:
Why I Hate Vampires and Wish They were all Dead.
by Myrtle Winters
MYRTLE, I ASKED YOU TO STAY AFTER CLASS BECAUSE OF THIS COMPOSITION YOU WROTE . . .
I FOUND IT QUITE DISTURBING.
FRANKLY, IT'S NOT SOMETHING I EXPECTED TO GET FROM A 10TH GRADER.
YOU WROTE, "I INTEND TO CHOP THE HEAD OFF OF THE VAMPIRE AND STUFF ITS CORPSE WITH GARLIC."
YOU SHOULD KNOW BY NOW THAT "OFF OF" IS A REDUNDANT PREPOSITIONAL PHRASE.
YES, MISS THISTLEBOTTOM
Vampires think they can do anything
just because they can live for-
AND THAT'S JUST ONE OF THE MANY SLOPPY GRAMMATICAL ERRORS YOU MADE. THIS ESSAY IS FULL OF DOUBLE NEGATIVES, RUN-ON SENTENCES, AND DANGLING MODIFIERS.
I KNOW YOU CAN DO BETTER THAN THIS, MYRTLE. I'M GOING TO HAVE TO GIVE THIS COMPOSITION A "D."
A "D"? OH, MISS THISTLEBOTTOM-- CAN'T I DO IT OVER-- PLEASE?
NO. YOU SHOULD'VE DONE IT CORRECTLY THE FIRST TIME. AND LET ME CORRECT ONE OF YOUR STATEMENTS--
DESPITE POPULAR BELIEF, VAMPIRES CAN BE CURED BY KILLING THEIR LEADER. AND WORK ON YOUR PENMANSHIP-- IT'S ATROCIOUS.
YOU MAY GO, MYRTLE

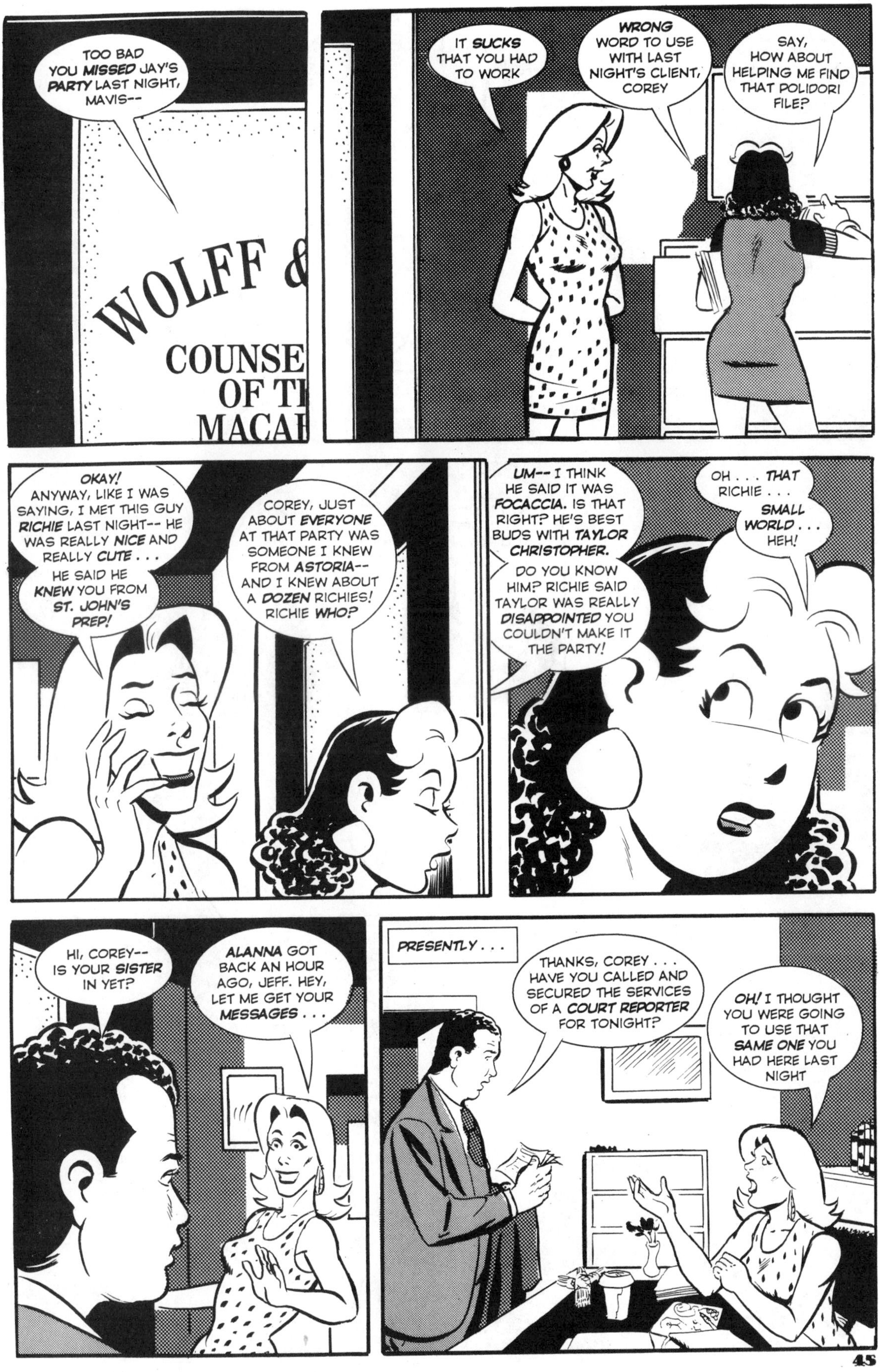
TOO BAD YOU MISSED JAY'S PARTY LAST NIGHT, MAVIS--
WOLFF &
COUNSE
OF TI
MACAI
IT SUCKS THAT YOU HAD TO WORK
WRONG WORD TO USE WITH LAST NIGHT'S CLIENT, COREY
SAY, HOW ABOUT HELPING ME FIND THAT POLIDORI FILE?
OKAY! ANYWAY, LIKE I WAS SAYING, I MET THIS GUY RICHIE LAST NIGHT-- HE WAS REALLY NICE AND REALLY CUTE . . .
HE SAID HE KNEW YOU FROM ST. JOHN'S PREP!
COREY, JUST ABOUT EVERYONE AT THAT PARTY WAS SOMEONE I KNEW FROM ASTORIA-- AND I KNEW ABOUT A DOZEN RICHIES! RICHIE WHO?
UM-- I THINK HE SAID IT WAS FOCACCIA. IS THAT RIGHT? HE'S BEST BUDS WITH TAYLOR CHRISTOPHER.
DO YOU KNOW HIM? RICHIE SAID TAYLOR WAS REALLY DISAPPOINTED YOU COULDN'T MAKE IT THE PARTY!
OH . . . THAT RICHIE . . .
SMALL WORLD . . . HEH!
HI, COREY-- IS YOUR SISTER IN YET?
ALANNA GOT BACK AN HOUR AGO, JEFF. HEY, LET ME GET YOUR MESSAGES . . .
PRESENTLY . . .
THANKS, COREY . . . HAVE YOU CALLED AND SECURED THE SERVICES OF A COURT REPORTER FOR TONIGHT?
OH! I THOUGHT YOU WERE GOING TO USE THAT SAME ONE YOU HAD HERE LAST NIGHT

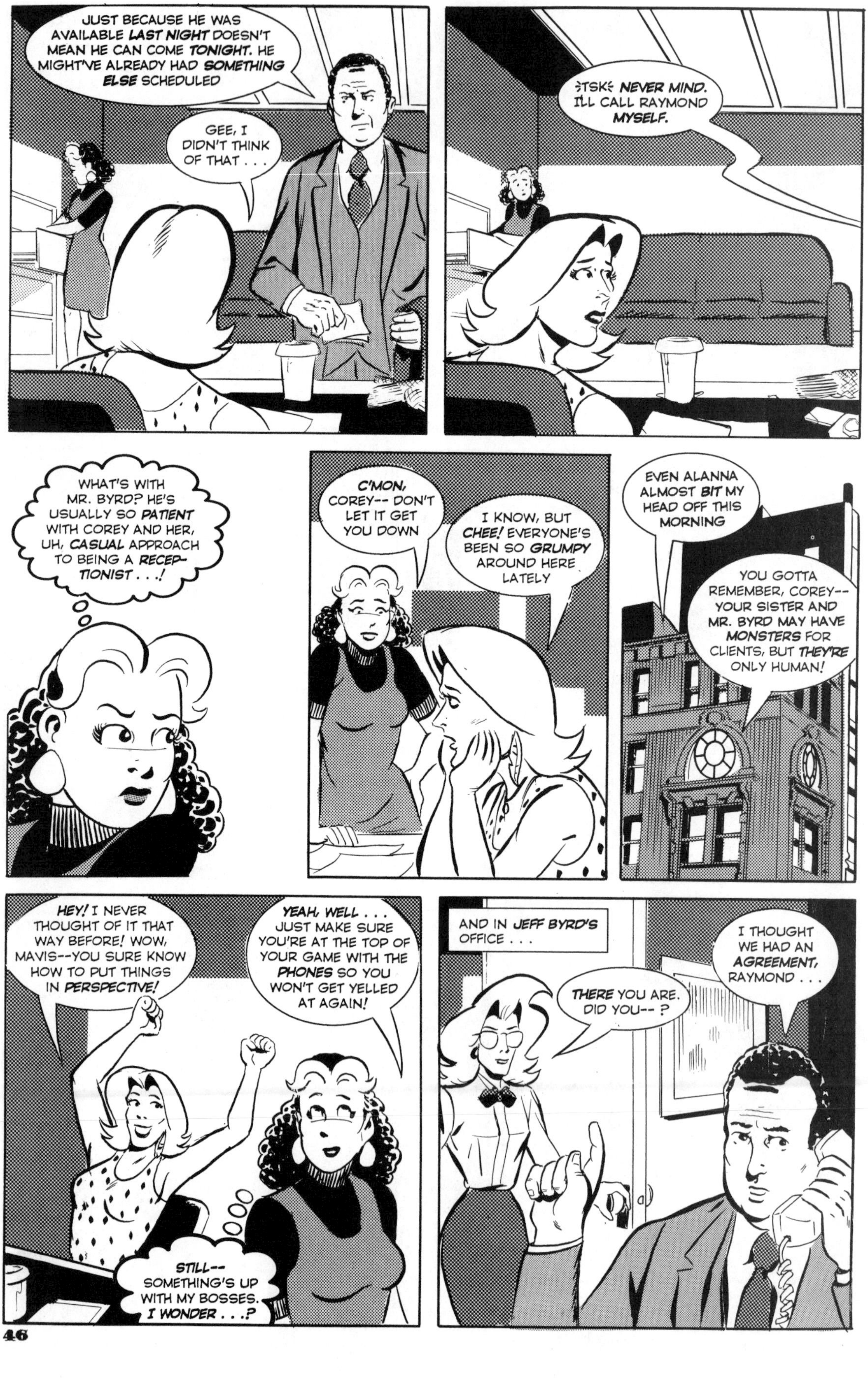
JUST BECAUSE HE WAS AVAILABLE LAST NIGHT DOESN'T MEAN HE CAN COME TONIGHT. HE MIGHT'VE ALREADY HAD SOMETHING ELSE SCHEDULED
GEE, I DIDN'T THINK OF THAT . . .
TSK NEVER MIND. I'LL CALL RAYMOND MYSELF.
WHAT'S WITH MR. BYRD? HE'S USUALLY SO PATIENT WITH COREY AND HER, UH, CASUAL APPROACH TO BEING A RECEP-TIONIST . . .!
C'MON, COREY-- DON'T LET IT GET YOU DOWN
I KNOW, BUT CHEE! EVERYONE'S BEEN SO GRUMPY AROUND HERE LATELY
EVEN ALANNA ALMOST BIT MY HEAD OFF THIS MORNING
YOU GOTTA REMEMBER, COREY-- YOUR SISTER AND MR. BYRD MAY HAVE MONSTERS FOR CLIENTS, BUT THEY'RE ONLY HUMAN!
HEY! I NEVER THOUGHT OF IT THAT WAY BEFORE! WOW, MAVIS--YOU SURE KNOW HOW TO PUT THINGS IN PERSPECTIVE!
YEAH, WELL . . . JUST MAKE SURE YOU'RE AT THE TOP OF YOUR GAME WITH THE PHONES SO YOU WON'T GET YELLED AT AGAIN!
STILL-- SOMETHING'S UP WITH MY BOSSES. I WONDER . . .?
AND IN JEFF BYRD'S OFFICE . . .
THERE YOU ARE. DID YOU-- ?
I THOUGHT WE HAD AN AGREEMENT, RAYMOND . . .

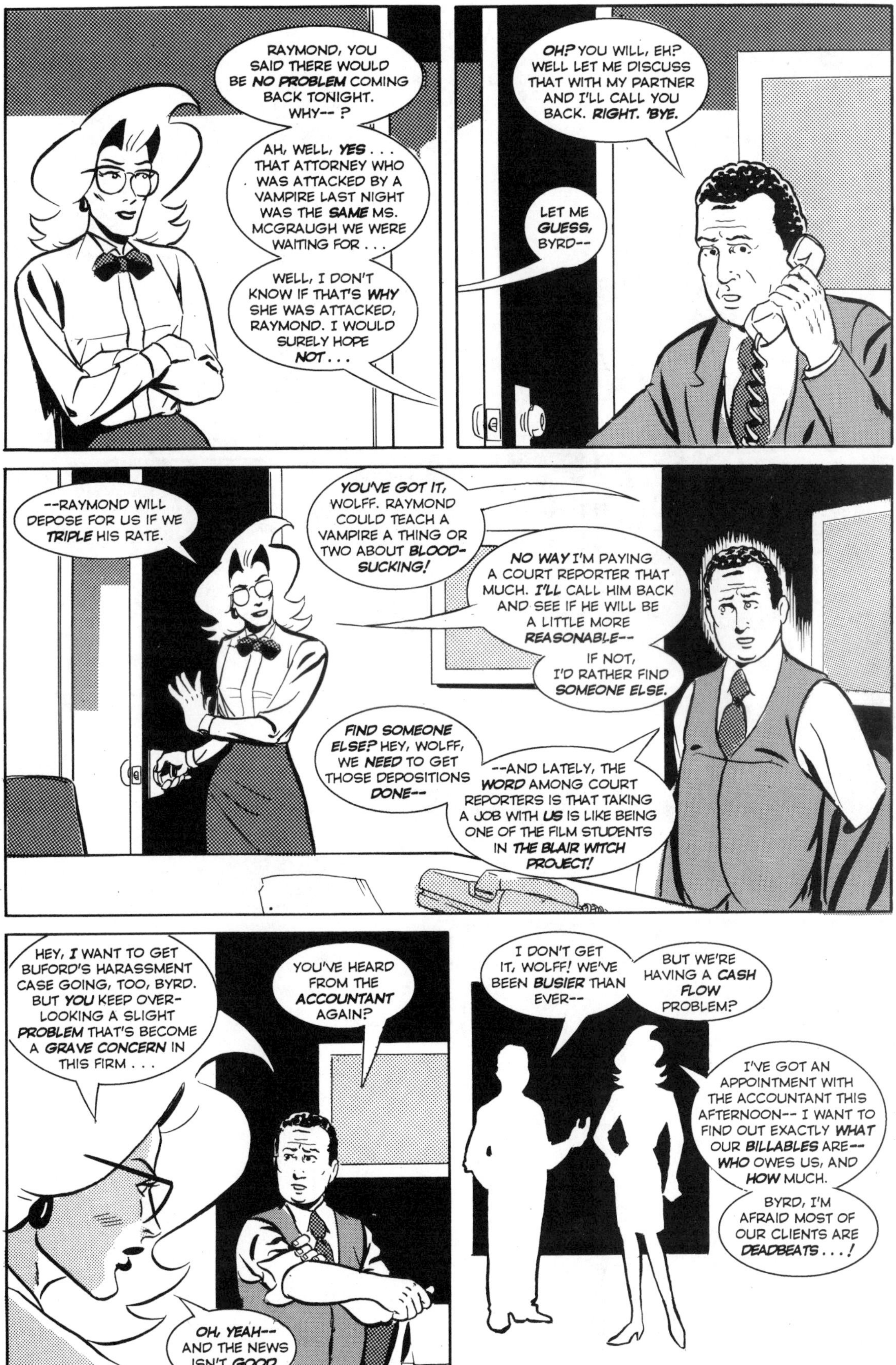
RAYMOND, YOU SAID THERE WOULD BE NO PROBLEM COMING BACK TONIGHT. WHY-- ?
AH, WELL, YES . . . THAT ATTORNEY WHO WAS ATTACKED BY A VAMPIRE LAST NIGHT WAS THE SAME MS. MCGRAUGH WE WERE WAITING FOR . . .
WELL, I DON'T KNOW IF THAT'S WHY SHE WAS ATTACKED, RAYMOND. I WOULD SURELY HOPE NOT . . .
OH? YOU WILL, EH? WELL LET ME DISCUSS THAT WITH MY PARTNER AND I'LL CALL YOU BACK. RIGHT. 'BYE.
LET ME GUESS, BYRD--
--RAYMOND WILL DEPOSE FOR US IF WE TRIPLE HIS RATE.
YOU'VE GOT IT, WOLFF. RAYMOND COULD TEACH A VAMPIRE A THING OR TWO ABOUT BLOOD-SUCKING!
NO WAY I'M PAYING A COURT REPORTER THAT MUCH. I'LL CALL HIM BACK AND SEE IF HE WILL BE A LITTLE MORE REASONABLE--
IF NOT, I'D RATHER FIND SOMEONE ELSE.
FIND SOMEONE ELSE? HEY, WOLFF, WE NEED TO GET THOSE DEPOSITIONS DONE--
--AND LATELY, THE WORD AMONG COURT REPORTERS IS THAT TAKING A JOB WITH US IS LIKE BEING ONE OF THE FILM STUDENTS IN THE BLAIR WITCH PROJECT!
HEY, I WANT TO GET BUFORD'S HARASSMENT CASE GOING, TOO, BYRD. BUT YOU KEEP OVER-LOOKING A SLIGHT PROBLEM THAT'S BECOME A GRAVE CONCERN IN THIS FIRM . . .
YOU'VE HEARD FROM THE ACCOUNTANT AGAIN?
OH, YEAH-- AND THE NEWS ISN'T GOOD.
I DON'T GET IT, WOLFF! WE'VE BEEN BUSIER THAN EVER--
BUT WE'RE HAVING A CASH FLOW PROBLEM?
I'VE GOT AN APPOINTMENT WITH THE ACCOUNTANT THIS AFTERNOON-- I WANT TO FIND OUT EXACTLY WHAT OUR BILLABLES ARE-- WHO OWES US, AND HOW MUCH.
BYRD, I'M AFRAID MOST OF OUR CLIENTS ARE DEADBEATS . . . !

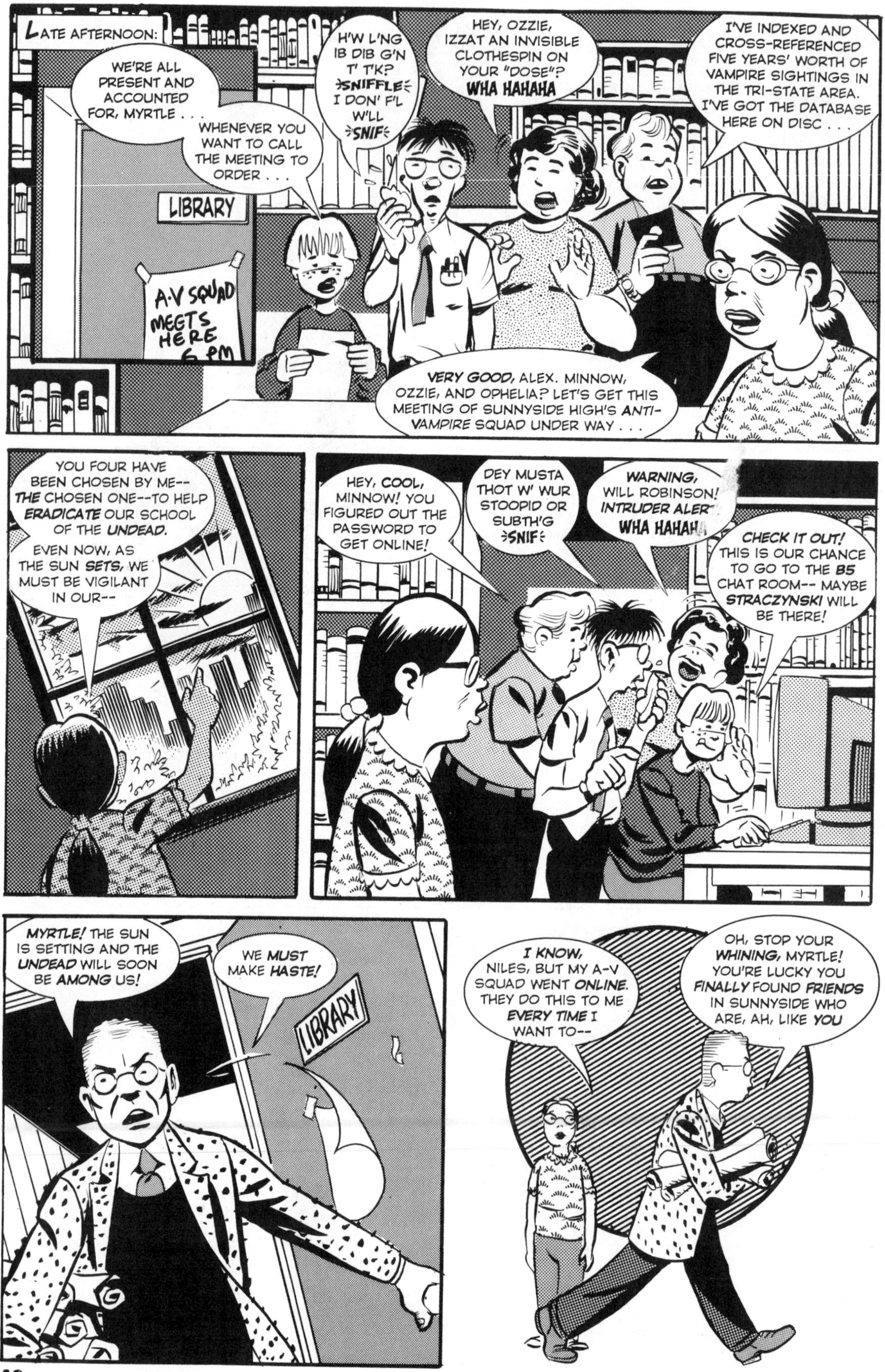
LATE AFTERNOON:
WE'RE ALL PRESENT AND ACCOUNTED FOR, MYRTLE . . .
WHENEVER YOU WANT TO CALL THE MEETING TO ORDER . . .
H'W L'NG IB DIB G'N T' T'K? *SNIFFLE* I DON' F'L W'LL *SNIF*
HEY, OZZIE, IZZAT AN INVISIBLE CLOTHESPIN ON YOUR "DOSE"? WHA HAHAHA
I'VE INDEXED AND CROSS-REFERENCED FIVE YEARS' WORTH OF VAMPIRE SIGHTINGS IN THE TRI-STATE AREA. I'VE GOT THE DATABASE HERE ON DISC . . .
LIBRARY
A-V SQUAD MEETS HERE 6 PM
VERY GOOD, ALEX. MINNOW, OZZIE, AND OPHELIA? LET'S GET THIS MEETING OF SUNNYSIDE HIGH'S ANTI-VAMPIRE SQUAD UNDER WAY . . .
YOU FOUR HAVE BEEN CHOSEN BY ME-- THE CHOSEN ONE--TO HELP ERADICATE OUR SCHOOL OF THE UNDEAD.
EVEN NOW, AS THE SUN SETS, WE MUST BE VIGILANT IN OUR--
HEY, COOL, MINNOW! YOU FIGURED OUT THE PASSWORD TO GET ONLINE!
DEY MUSTA THOT W' WUR STOOPID OR SUBTH'G *SNIF*
WARNING, WILL ROBINSON! INTRUDER ALERT! WHA HAHAHA
CHECK IT OUT! THIS IS OUR CHANCE TO GO TO THE B5 CHAT ROOM-- MAYBE STRACZYNSKI WILL BE THERE!
MYRTLE! THE SUN IS SETTING AND THE UNDEAD WILL SOON BE AMONG US!
WE MUST MAKE HASTE!
LIBRARY
I KNOW, NILES, BUT MY A-V SQUAD WENT ONLINE. THEY DO THIS TO ME EVERY TIME I WANT TO--
OH, STOP YOUR WHINING, MYRTLE! YOU'RE LUCKY YOU FINALLY FOUND FRIENDS IN SUNNYSIDE WHO ARE, AH, LIKE YOU

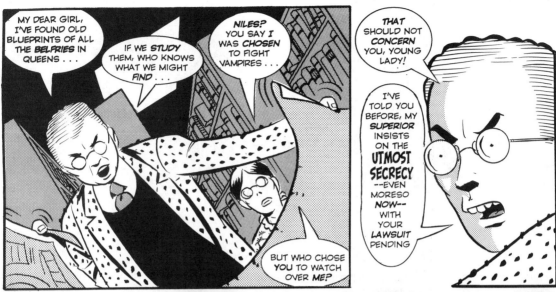

MY DEAR GIRL, I'VE FOUND OLD BLUEPRINTS OF ALL THE *BELFRIES* IN QUEENS . . .

IF WE *STUDY* THEM, WHO KNOWS WHAT WE MIGHT *FIND* . . .

NILES? YOU SAY *I* WAS *CHOSEN* TO FIGHT VAMPIRES . . .

THAT SHOULD NOT *CONCERN* YOU, YOUNG LADY!

I'VE TOLD YOU BEFORE, MY *SUPERIOR* INSISTS ON THE *UTMOST SECRECY* --EVEN MORESO *NOW*-- WITH YOUR *LAWSUIT* PENDING

BUT WHO CHOSE *YOU* TO WATCH OVER *ME?*

I'VE BEEN ADVISED TO BE VERY *CAREFUL* IN WHAT I SAY TO YOU, MYRTLE . . . WHY, IF A *LAWYER* GOT YOU UNDER *OATH* . . . I--I SHUDDER TO THINK WHAT YOU'D BE FORCED TO *REVEAL!*

I'D NEVER *BETRAY* YOU, NILES

I KNOW *YOU* WON'T, MYRTLE-- YOU AND THE A-V SQUAD HAVE BEEN MOST *DISCREET* . . .

AS *LIBRARIAN* I CAN GIVE THE FIVE OF YOU *ACCESS* TO THE FACILITIES AFTER SCHOOL HOURS TO *WORK, STUDY,* AND *DEVISE WAYS* FOR *DESTROYING* THE VAMPIRES AMONG US . . .

WELL, NILES, LATELY I FEEL LIKE *I'M THE ONE DOING ALL THE WORK*--

LOOK! IT'S ALMOST NIGHTTIME, AND ALL MY A-V SQUAD IS IN- TERESTED IN IS STUPID SCI-FI WEB SITES!

REALLY?

THAT WOULDN'T BE A SITE DEVOTED TO PATRICK STEWART, WOULD IT?

OH, YAS, C'P'N PICARD! ⇒SNIF⇐

NEXT GEN BEATS *VOYAGER* ANY DAY OF THE WEEK

BEAM ME UP, SNOTTY WHA HAHAHA

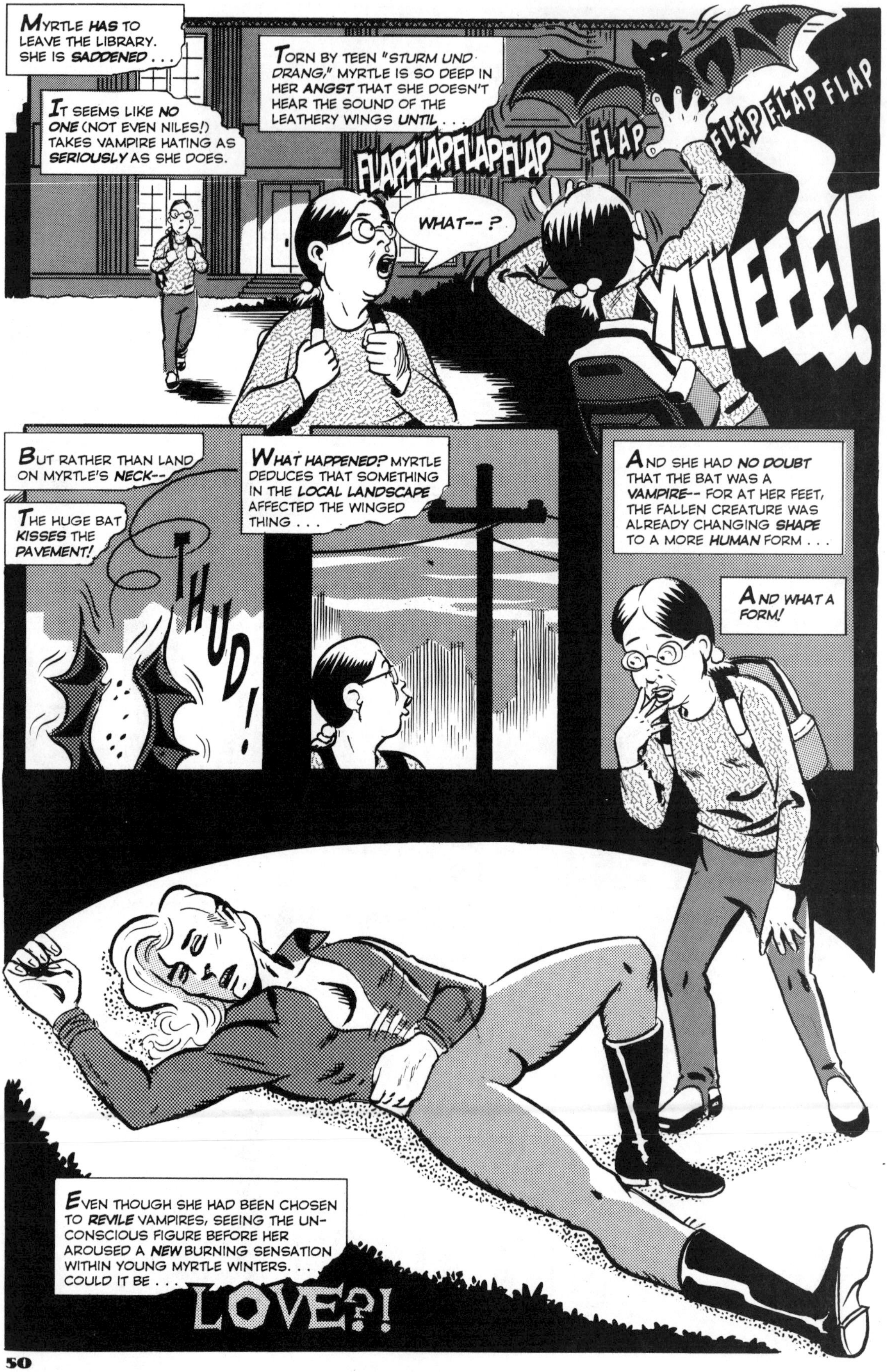
MYRTLE HAS TO LEAVE THE LIBRARY. SHE IS SADDENED . . .
IT SEEMS LIKE NO ONE (NOT EVEN NILES!) TAKES VAMPIRE HATING AS SERIOUSLY AS SHE DOES.
TORN BY TEEN "STURM UND DRANG," MYRTLE IS SO DEEP IN HER ANGST THAT SHE DOESN'T HEAR THE SOUND OF THE LEATHERY WINGS UNTIL . . .
FLAPFLAPFLAPFLAP
FLAP
FLAP FLAP FLAP FLAP
WHAT-- ?
YIIIEEE!
BUT RATHER THAN LAND ON MYRTLE'S NECK--
THE HUGE BAT KISSES THE PAVEMENT!
THUD!
WHAT HAPPENED? MYRTLE DEDUCES THAT SOMETHING IN THE LOCAL LANDSCAPE AFFECTED THE WINGED THING . . .
AND SHE HAD NO DOUBT THAT THE BAT WAS A VAMPIRE-- FOR AT HER FEET, THE FALLEN CREATURE WAS ALREADY CHANGING SHAPE TO A MORE HUMAN FORM . . .
AND WHAT A FORM!
EVEN THOUGH SHE HAD BEEN CHOSEN TO REVILE VAMPIRES, SEEING THE UNCONSCIOUS FIGURE BEFORE HER AROUSED A NEW BURNING SENSATION WITHIN YOUNG MYRTLE WINTERS. . . COULD IT BE . . .
LOVE?!

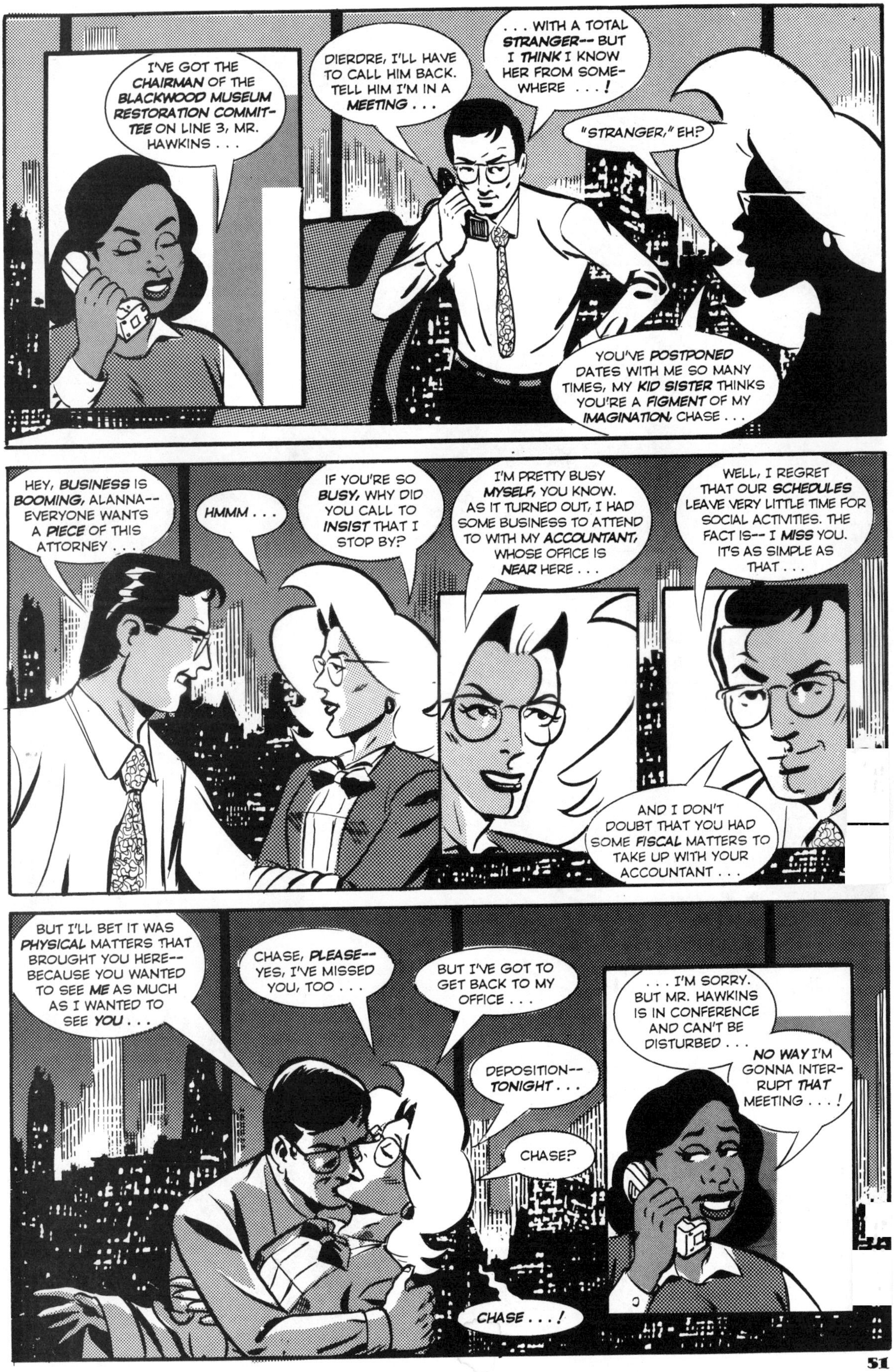
I'VE GOT THE CHAIRMAN OF THE BLACKWOOD MUSEUM RESTORATION COMMITTEE ON LINE 3, MR. HAWKINS . . .
DIERDRE, I'LL HAVE TO CALL HIM BACK. TELL HIM I'M IN A MEETING . . .
. . . WITH A TOTAL STRANGER-- BUT I THINK I KNOW HER FROM SOMEWHERE . . . !
"STRANGER," EH?
YOU'VE POSTPONED DATES WITH ME SO MANY TIMES, MY KID SISTER THINKS YOU'RE A FIGMENT OF MY IMAGINATION, CHASE . . .
HEY, BUSINESS IS BOOMING, ALANNA-- EVERYONE WANTS A PIECE OF THIS ATTORNEY . . .
HMMM . . .
IF YOU'RE SO BUSY, WHY DID YOU CALL TO INSIST THAT I STOP BY?
I'M PRETTY BUSY MYSELF, YOU KNOW. AS IT TURNED OUT, I HAD SOME BUSINESS TO ATTEND TO WITH MY ACCOUNTANT, WHOSE OFFICE IS NEAR HERE . . .
WELL, I REGRET THAT OUR SCHEDULES LEAVE VERY LITTLE TIME FOR SOCIAL ACTIVITIES. THE FACT IS-- I MISS YOU. IT'S AS SIMPLE AS THAT . . .
AND I DON'T DOUBT THAT YOU HAD SOME FISCAL MATTERS TO TAKE UP WITH YOUR ACCOUNTANT . . .
BUT I'LL BET IT WAS PHYSICAL MATTERS THAT BROUGHT YOU HERE-- BECAUSE YOU WANTED TO SEE ME AS MUCH AS I WANTED TO SEE YOU . . .
CHASE, PLEASE-- YES, I'VE MISSED YOU, TOO . . .
BUT I'VE GOT TO GET BACK TO MY OFFICE . . .
DEPOSITION-- TONIGHT . . .
CHASE?
CHASE . . . !
. . . I'M SORRY. BUT MR. HAWKINS IS IN CONFERENCE AND CAN'T BE DISTURBED . . .
NO WAY I'M GONNA INTERRUPT THAT MEETING . . . !

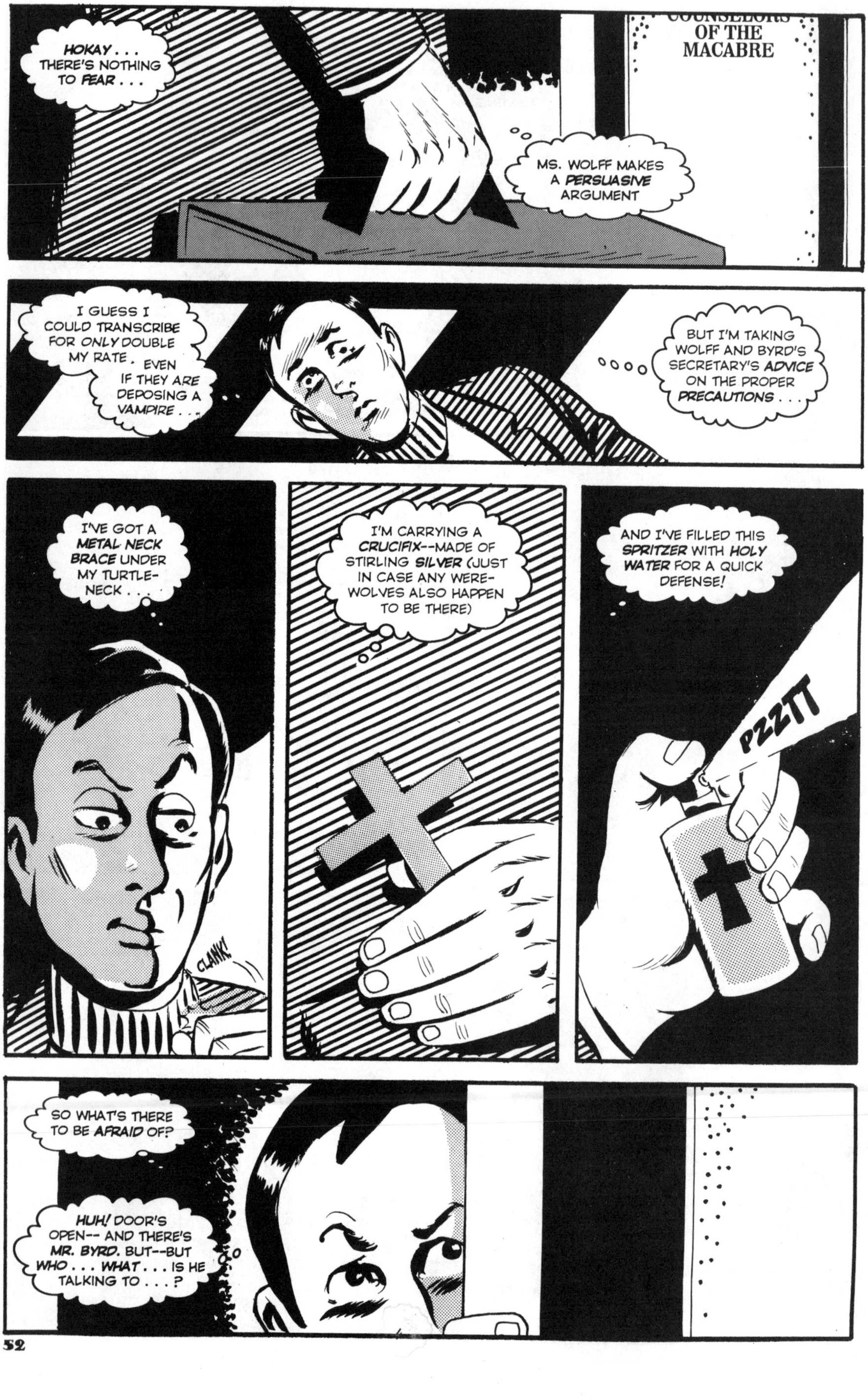
HOKAY . . . THERE'S NOTHING TO FEAR . . .
OF THE MACABRE
MS. WOLFF MAKES A PERSUASIVE ARGUMENT
I GUESS I COULD TRANSCRIBE FOR ONLY DOUBLE MY RATE. EVEN IF THEY ARE DEPOSING A VAMPIRE . . .
BUT I'M TAKING WOLFF AND BYRD'S SECRETARY'S ADVICE ON THE PROPER PRECAUTIONS . . .
I'VE GOT A METAL NECK BRACE UNDER MY TURTLE-NECK . . .
CLANK!
I'M CARRYING A CRUCIFIX--MADE OF STIRLING SILVER (JUST IN CASE ANY WERE-WOLVES ALSO HAPPEN TO BE THERE)
AND I'VE FILLED THIS SPRITZER WITH HOLY WATER FOR A QUICK DEFENSE!
PZZTT
SO WHAT'S THERE TO BE AFRAID OF?
HUH! DOOR'S OPEN-- AND THERE'S MR. BYRD. BUT--BUT WHO . . . WHAT . . . IS HE TALKING TO . . . ?

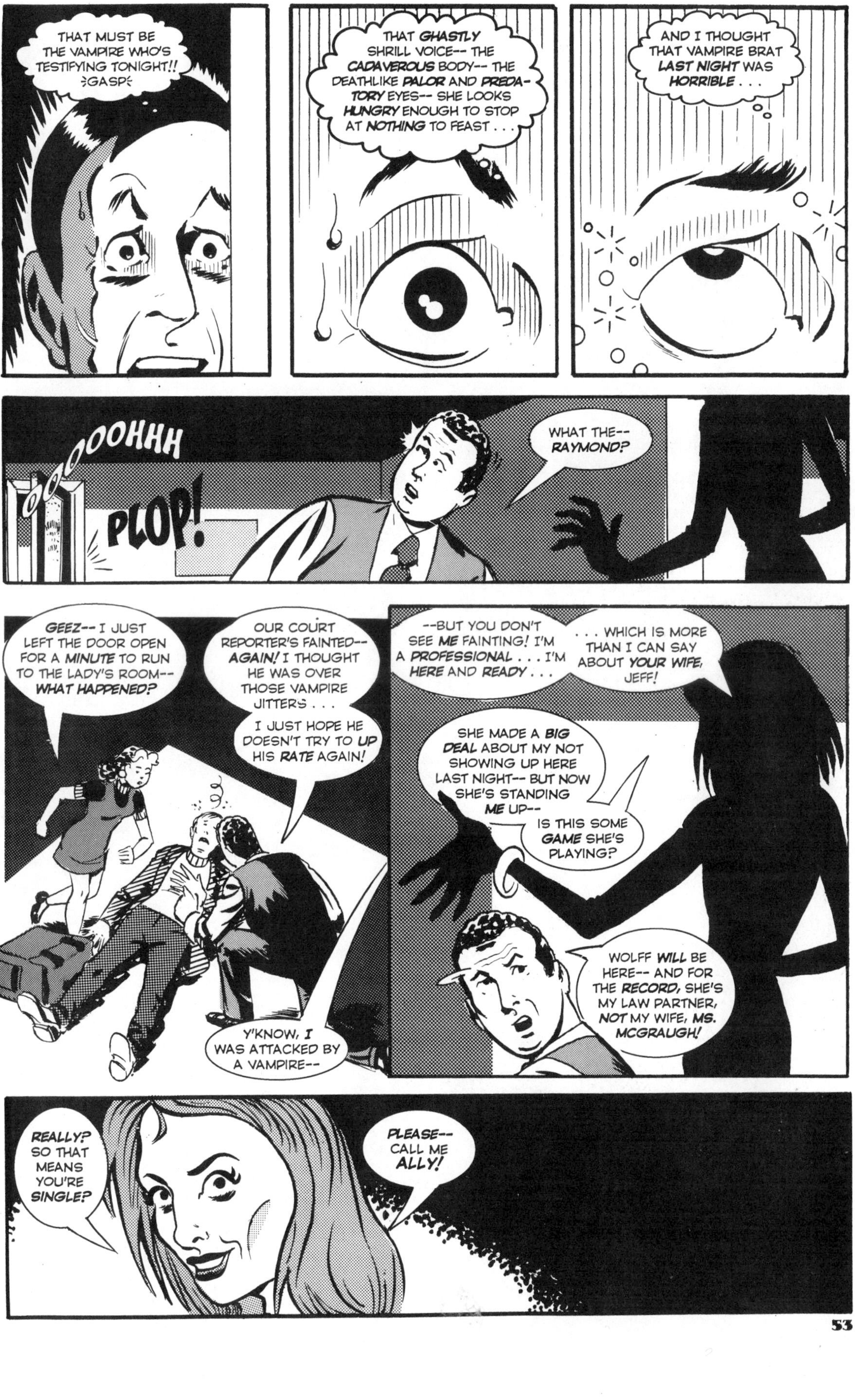
THAT MUST BE THE VAMPIRE WHO'S TESTIFYING TONIGHT!! GASP
THAT GHASTLY SHRILL VOICE-- THE CADAVEROUS BODY-- THE DEATHLIKE PALOR AND PREDA-TORY EYES-- SHE LOOKS HUNGRY ENOUGH TO STOP AT NOTHING TO FEAST . . .
AND I THOUGHT THAT VAMPIRE BRAT LAST NIGHT WAS HORRIBLE . . .
OOOOOOHHH
PLOP!
WHAT THE-- RAYMOND?
GEEZ-- I JUST LEFT THE DOOR OPEN FOR A MINUTE TO RUN TO THE LADY'S ROOM-- WHAT HAPPENED?
OUR COURT REPORTER'S FAINTED-- AGAIN! I THOUGHT HE WAS OVER THOSE VAMPIRE JITTERS . . .
I JUST HOPE HE DOESN'T TRY TO UP HIS RATE AGAIN!
Y'KNOW, I WAS ATTACKED BY A VAMPIRE--
--BUT YOU DON'T SEE ME FAINTING! I'M A PROFESSIONAL . . . I'M HERE AND READY . . .
. . . WHICH IS MORE THAN I CAN SAY ABOUT YOUR WIFE, JEFF!
SHE MADE A BIG DEAL ABOUT MY NOT SHOWING UP HERE LAST NIGHT-- BUT NOW SHE'S STANDING ME UP--
IS THIS SOME GAME SHE'S PLAYING?
WOLFF WILL BE HERE-- AND FOR THE RECORD, SHE'S MY LAW PARTNER, NOT MY WIFE, MS. MCGRAUGH!
REALLY? SO THAT MEANS YOU'RE SINGLE?
PLEASE-- CALL ME ALLY!

The Vampire Brat
Part 3

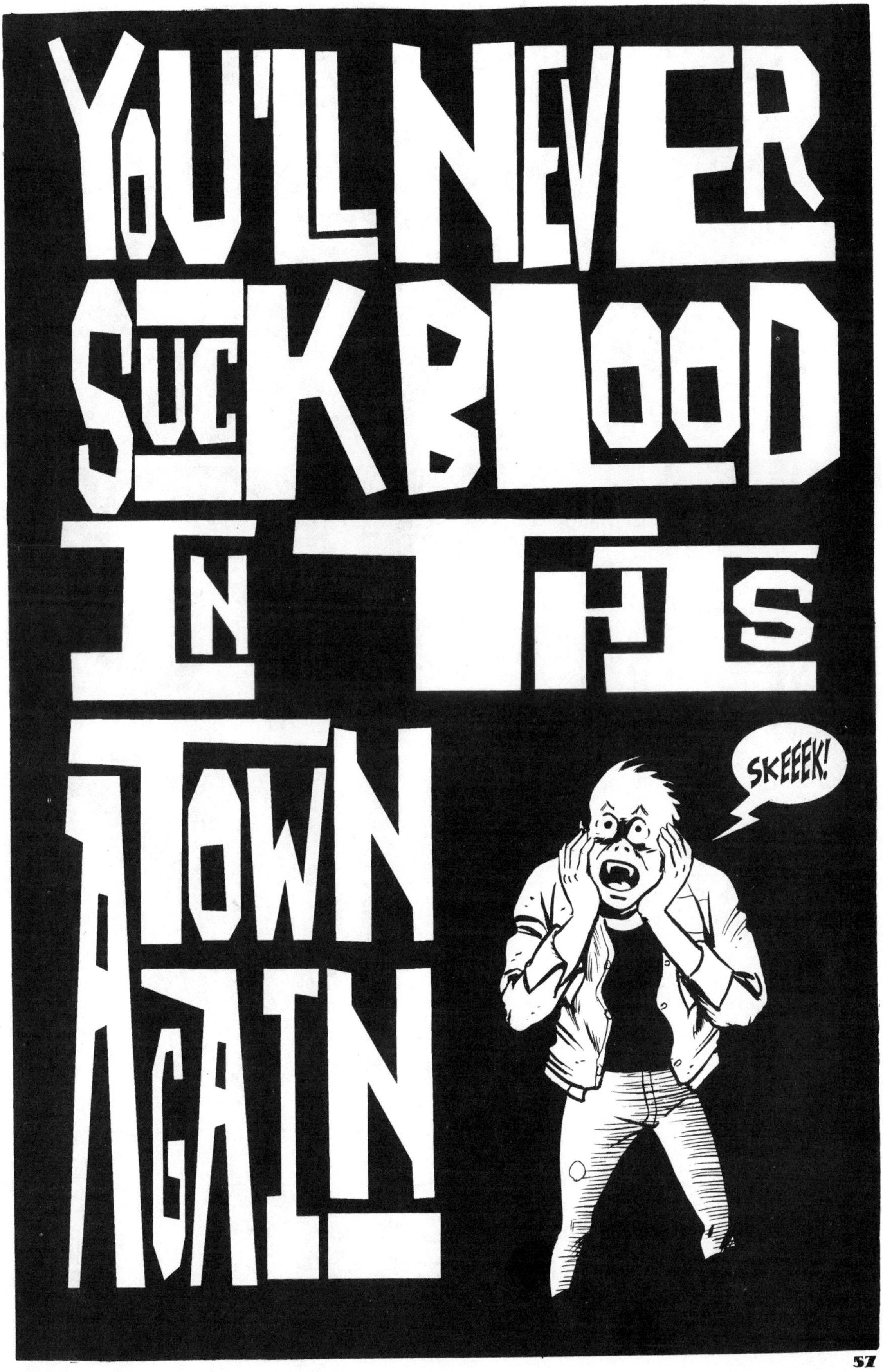
YOU'LL NEVER SUCK BLOOD IN THIS TOWN AGAIN
SKEEEK!

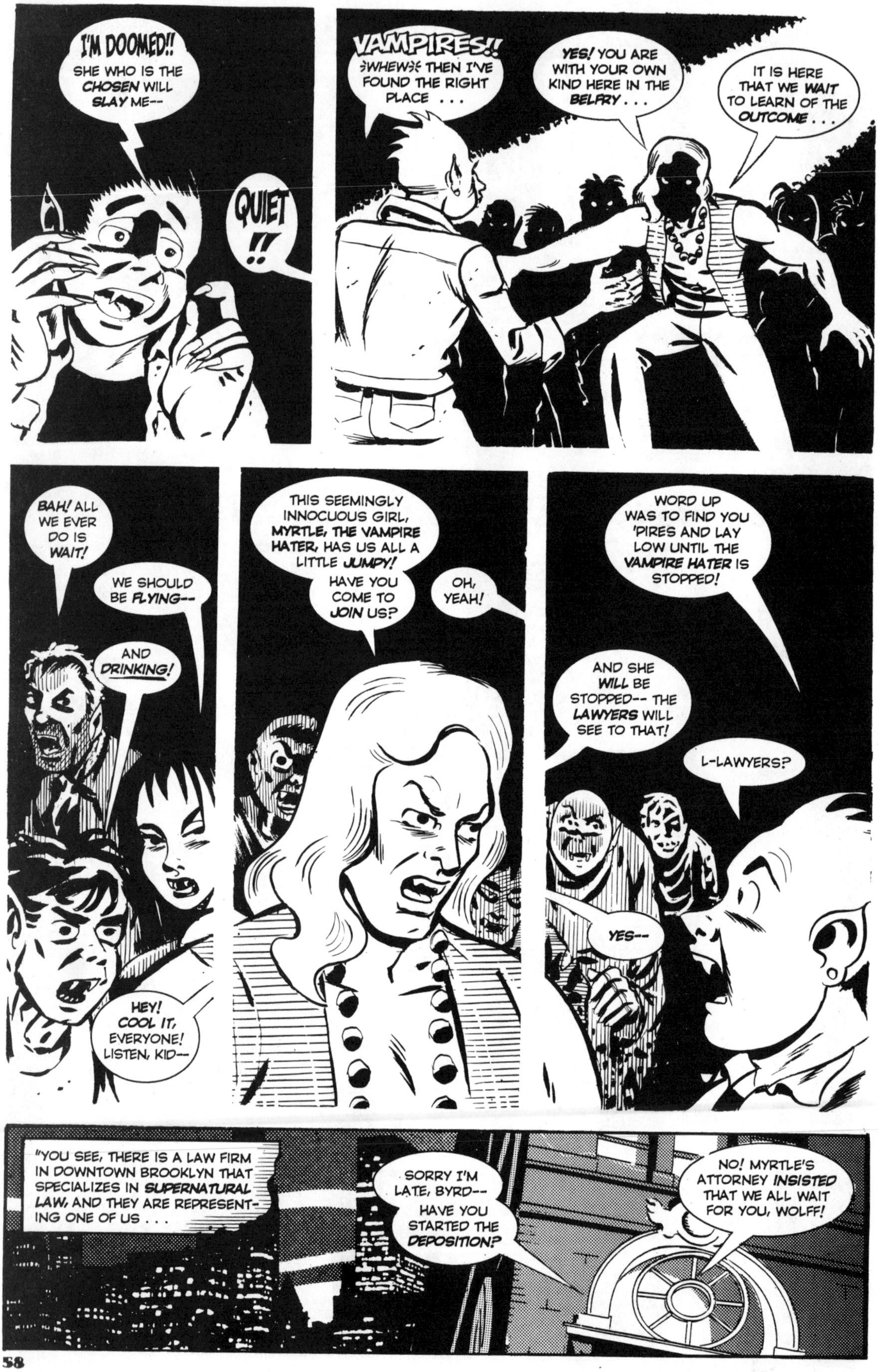
I'M DOOMED!!
SHE WHO IS THE CHOSEN WILL SLAY ME--
QUIET!!
VAMPIRES!!
WHEW THEN I'VE FOUND THE RIGHT PLACE . . .
YES! YOU ARE WITH YOUR OWN KIND HERE IN THE BELFRY . . .
IT IS HERE THAT WE WAIT TO LEARN OF THE OUTCOME . . .
BAH! ALL WE EVER DO IS WAIT!
WE SHOULD BE FLYING--
AND DRINKING!
HEY! COOL IT, EVERYONE! LISTEN, KID--
THIS SEEMINGLY INNOCUOUS GIRL, MYRTLE, THE VAMPIRE HATER, HAS US ALL A LITTLE JUMPY!
HAVE YOU COME TO JOIN US?
OH, YEAH!
WORD UP WAS TO FIND YOU 'PIRES AND LAY LOW UNTIL THE VAMPIRE HATER IS STOPPED!
AND SHE WILL BE STOPPED-- THE LAWYERS WILL SEE TO THAT!
L-LAWYERS?
YES--
"YOU SEE, THERE IS A LAW FIRM IN DOWNTOWN BROOKLYN THAT SPECIALIZES IN SUPERNATURAL LAW, AND THEY ARE REPRESENTING ONE OF US . . .
SORRY I'M LATE, BYRD--
HAVE YOU STARTED THE DEPOSITION?
NO! MYRTLE'S ATTORNEY INSISTED THAT WE ALL WAIT FOR YOU, WOLFF!

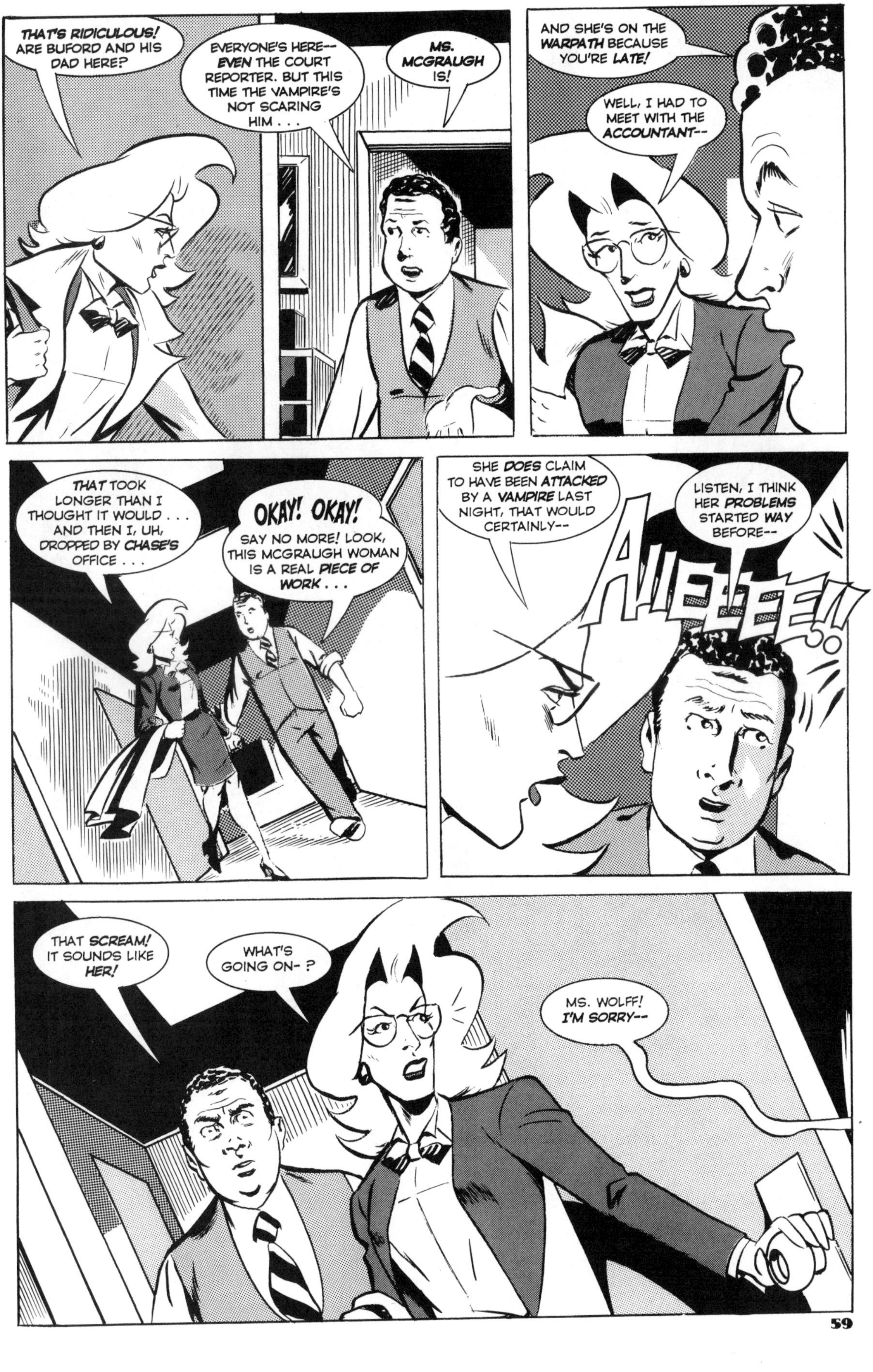
THAT'S RIDICULOUS! ARE BUFORD AND HIS DAD HERE?
EVERYONE'S HERE-- EVEN THE COURT REPORTER. BUT THIS TIME THE VAMPIRE'S NOT SCARING HIM . . .
MS. MCGRAUGH IS!
AND SHE'S ON THE WARPATH BECAUSE YOU'RE LATE!
WELL, I HAD TO MEET WITH THE ACCOUNTANT--
THAT TOOK LONGER THAN I THOUGHT IT WOULD . . . AND THEN I, UH, DROPPED BY CHASE'S OFFICE . . .
OKAY! OKAY!
SAY NO MORE! LOOK, THIS MCGRAUGH WOMAN IS A REAL PIECE OF WORK . . .
SHE DOES CLAIM TO HAVE BEEN ATTACKED BY A VAMPIRE LAST NIGHT, THAT WOULD CERTAINLY--
LISTEN, I THINK HER PROBLEMS STARTED WAY BEFORE--
AIEEEEE!!
THAT SCREAM! IT SOUNDS LIKE HER!
WHAT'S GOING ON- ?
MS. WOLFF! I'M SORRY--

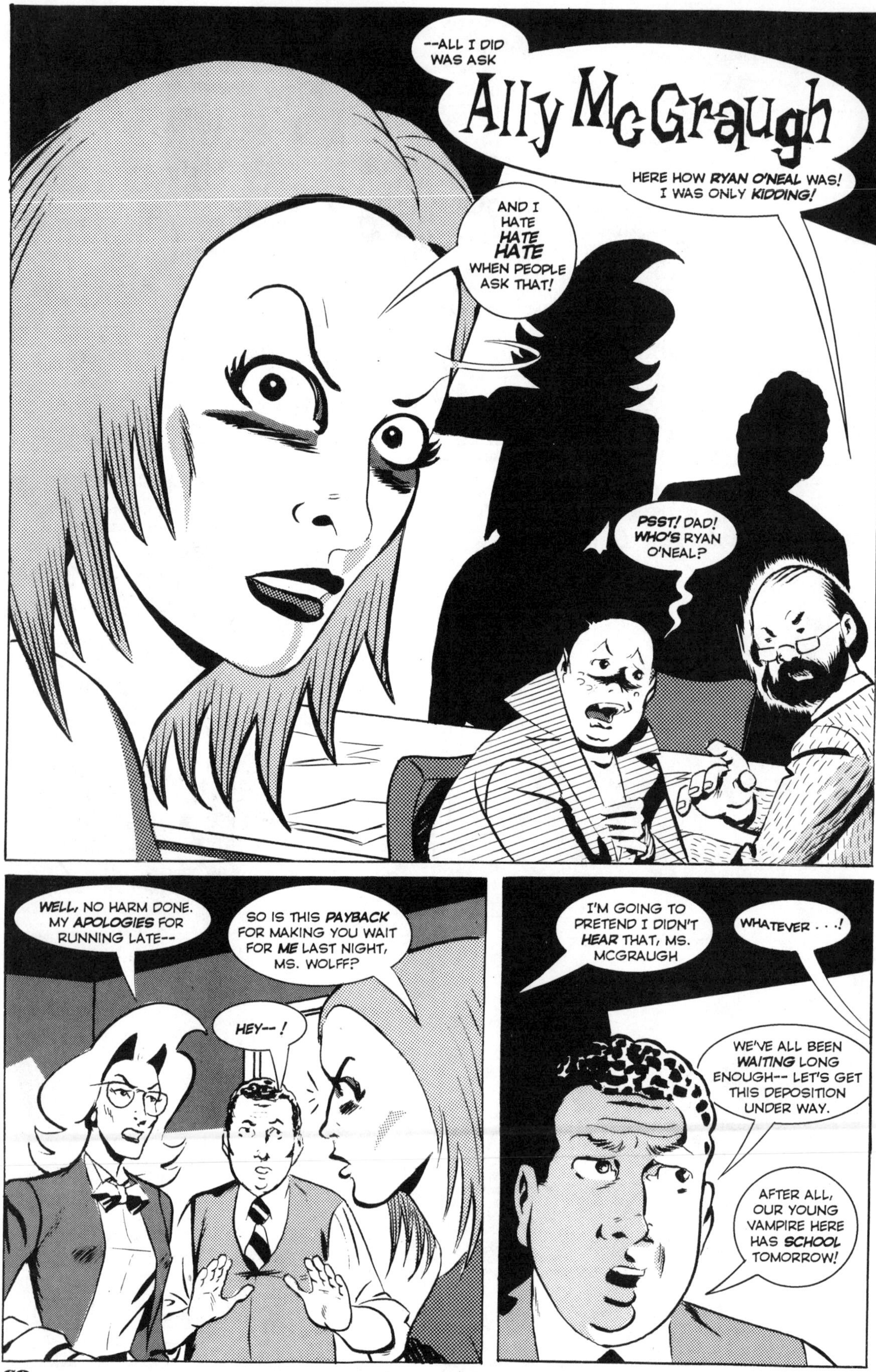
--ALL I DID WAS ASK
Ally McGraugh
HERE HOW RYAN O'NEAL WAS! I WAS ONLY KIDDING!
AND I HATE HATE HATE WHEN PEOPLE ASK THAT!
PSST! DAD! WHO'S RYAN O'NEAL?
WELL, NO HARM DONE. MY APOLOGIES FOR RUNNING LATE--
SO IS THIS PAYBACK FOR MAKING YOU WAIT FOR ME LAST NIGHT, MS. WOLFF?
HEY-- !
I'M GOING TO PRETEND I DIDN'T HEAR THAT, MS. MCGRAUGH
WHATEVER . . .!
WE'VE ALL BEEN WAITING LONG ENOUGH-- LET'S GET THIS DEPOSITION UNDER WAY.
AFTER ALL, OUR YOUNG VAMPIRE HERE HAS SCHOOL TOMORROW!

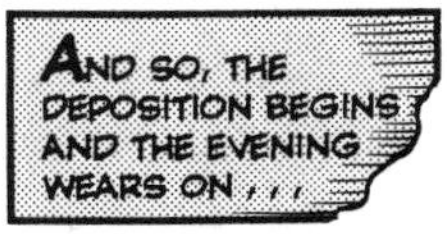
AND SO, THE DEPOSITION BEGINS AND THE EVENING WEARS ON . . .

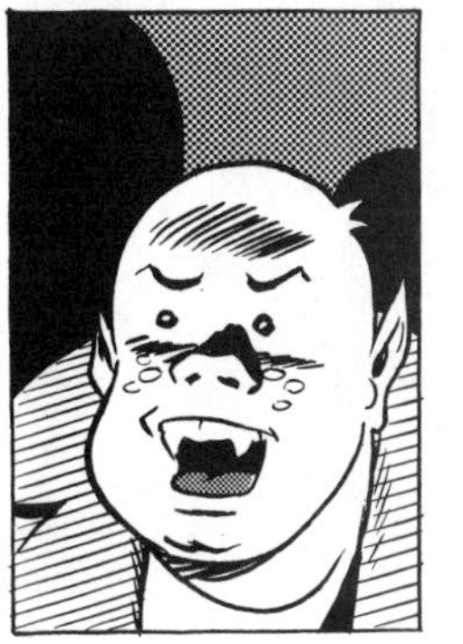

Buford Glieb: My dad says I'm a "hybrid"--my mom was a vampire and he's a human--I think!
Morty Glieb: I told you not to act stupid, you moron!
Alanna Wolff: Let your son continue, Mr. Glieb. You were saying about being a hybrid?
Buford Glieb: Well, I'm not the only one, see. There's a bunch of kids like me who go to Sunnyside High. We don't sleep in coffins, or things like that, but as we get older, our lay-- our lay--
Jeff Byrd: latent.
Buford Glieb: Yeah! Latent vampire powers start coming out. At least that's what my doctor says!
Alanna Wolff: And do the other kids at school know you're a vampire?
Buford Glieb: Well, they *didn't* until that vampire hater came along! We kept pretty much to ourselves. Going to school was tough enough, but then she comes along and starts busting my chops!

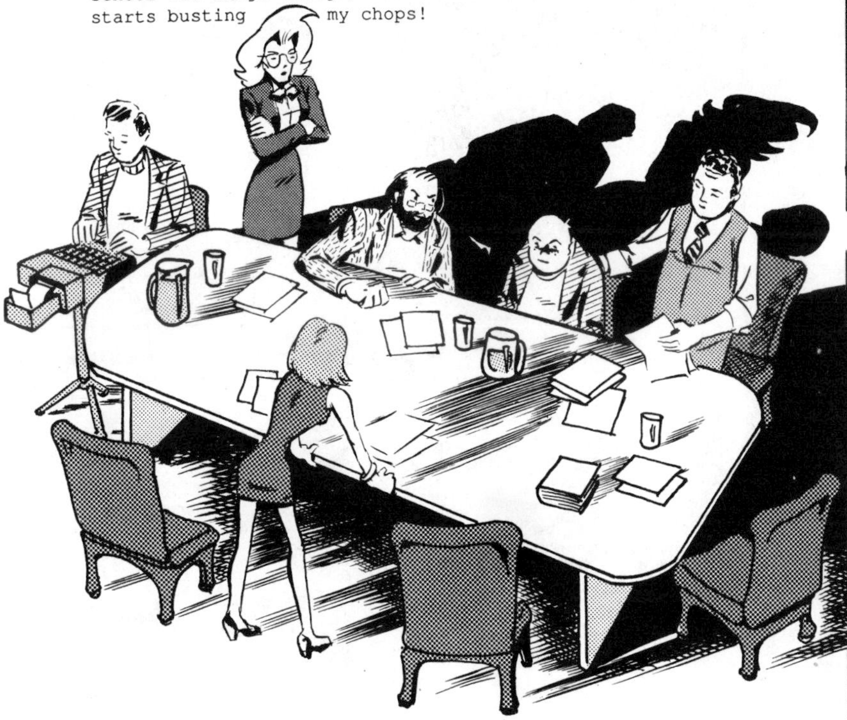

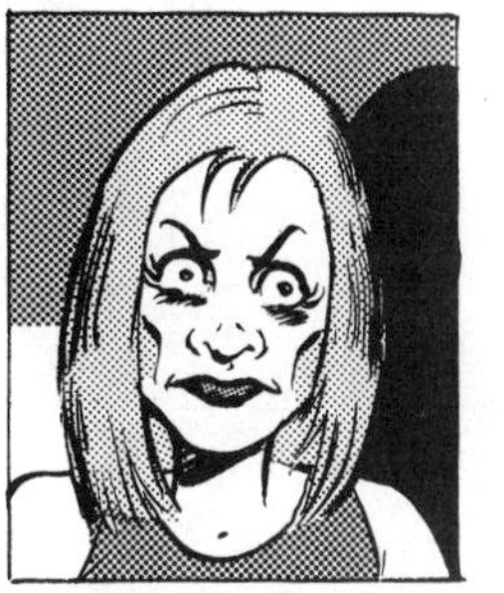

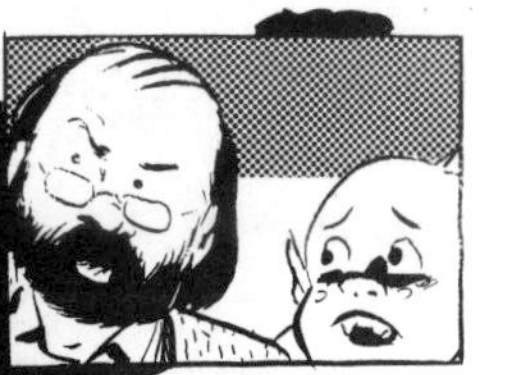

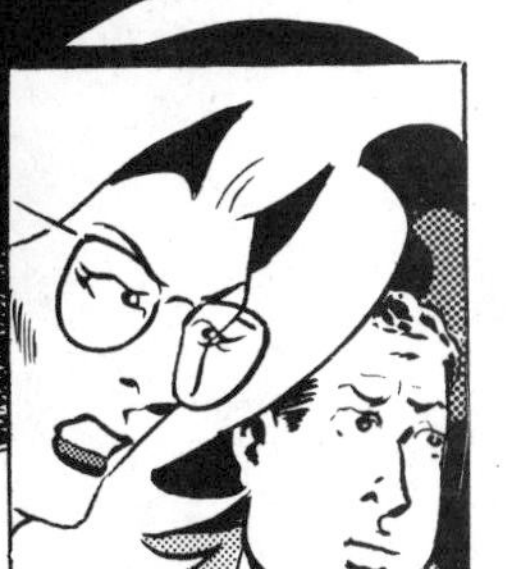

Alanna Wolff: Can you give an example, Buford?
Buford Glieb: I found a crucifix in my locker, and then my lunchbox was filled with garlic! It's embarrassing to go into convulsions in the middle of the lunchroom!
Morty Glieb: This Myrtle character sure seems to know a lot of ways to harass vampires.
Ally McGraugh: Would you please instruct Mr. Glieb that he is not the one being deposed?
Jeff Byrd: Mr. Glieb? Let Buford continue . . .
Ally McGraugh: Buford, can you tell me for the record when you first flashed your fangs at Myrtle Winters?
Alanna Wolff: Ms. McGraugh, I'd appreciate it if you wouldn't cross-examine when I have the witness.
Ally McGraugh: Hrumph! I wish I'd had a cross on me last night when that vampire attacked me . . .

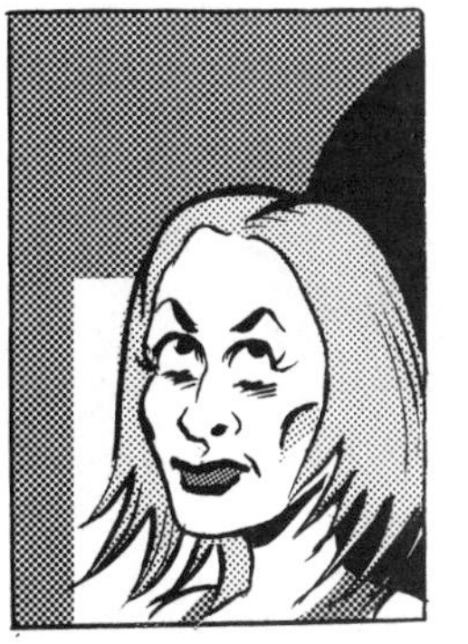

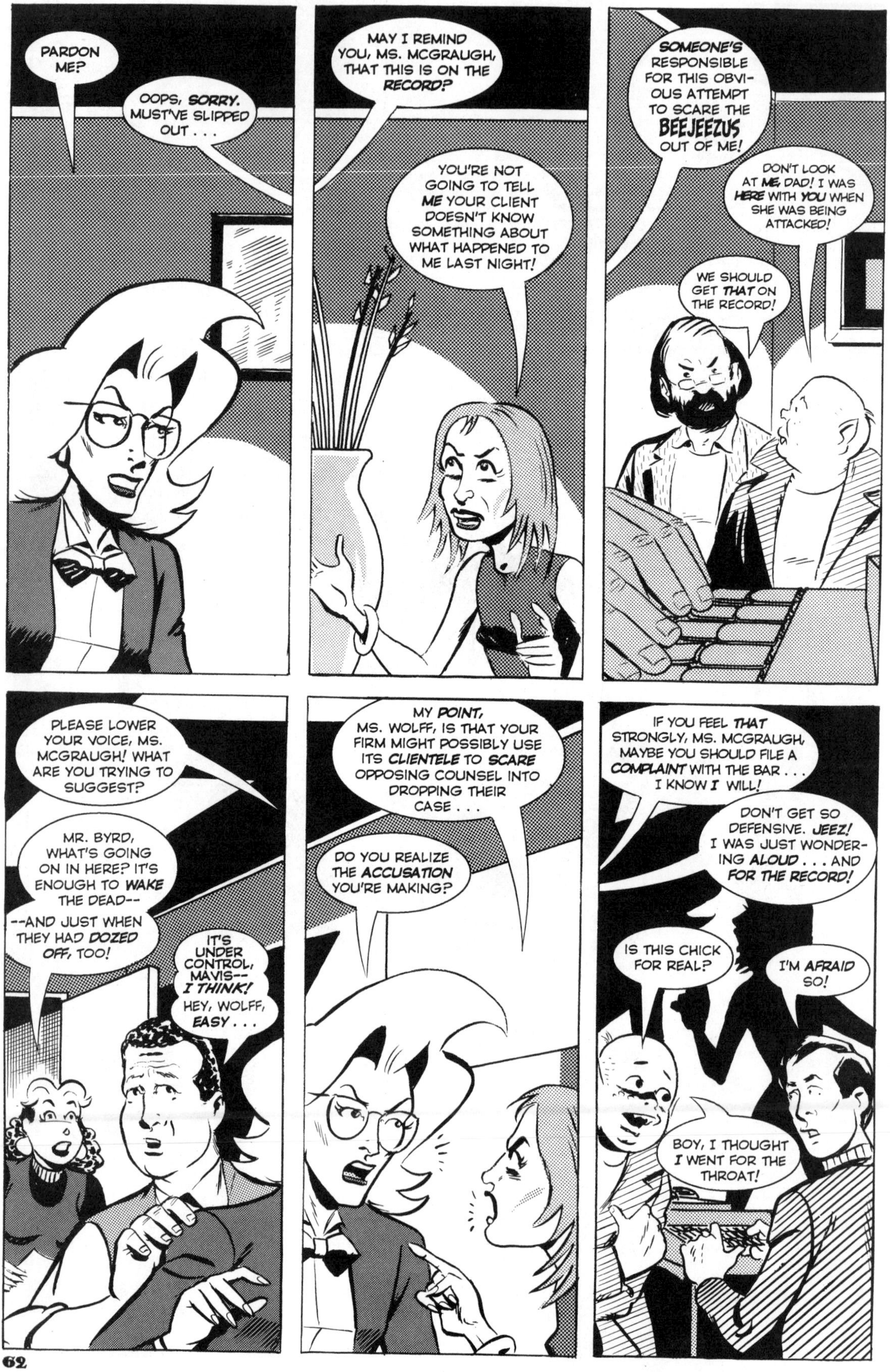
PARDON ME?
OOPS, SORRY. MUST'VE SLIPPED OUT . . .
MAY I REMIND YOU, MS. MCGRAUGH, THAT THIS IS ON THE RECORD?
YOU'RE NOT GOING TO TELL ME YOUR CLIENT DOESN'T KNOW SOMETHING ABOUT WHAT HAPPENED TO ME LAST NIGHT!
SOMEONE'S RESPONSIBLE FOR THIS OBVIOUS ATTEMPT TO SCARE THE BEEJEEZUS OUT OF ME!
DON'T LOOK AT ME, DAD! I WAS HERE WITH YOU WHEN SHE WAS BEING ATTACKED!
WE SHOULD GET THAT ON THE RECORD!
PLEASE LOWER YOUR VOICE, MS. MCGRAUGH! WHAT ARE YOU TRYING TO SUGGEST?
MR. BYRD, WHAT'S GOING ON IN HERE? IT'S ENOUGH TO WAKE THE DEAD--
--AND JUST WHEN THEY HAD DOZED OFF, TOO!
IT'S UNDER CONTROL, MAVIS-- I THINK! HEY, WOLFF, EASY . . .
MY POINT, MS. WOLFF, IS THAT YOUR FIRM MIGHT POSSIBLY USE ITS CLIENTELE TO SCARE OPPOSING COUNSEL INTO DROPPING THEIR CASE . . .
DO YOU REALIZE THE ACCUSATION YOU'RE MAKING?
IF YOU FEEL THAT STRONGLY, MS. MCGRAUGH, MAYBE YOU SHOULD FILE A COMPLAINT WITH THE BAR . . . I KNOW I WILL!
DON'T GET SO DEFENSIVE. JEEZ! I WAS JUST WONDERING ALOUD . . . AND FOR THE RECORD!
IS THIS CHICK FOR REAL?
I'M AFRAID SO!
BOY, I THOUGHT I WENT FOR THE THROAT!

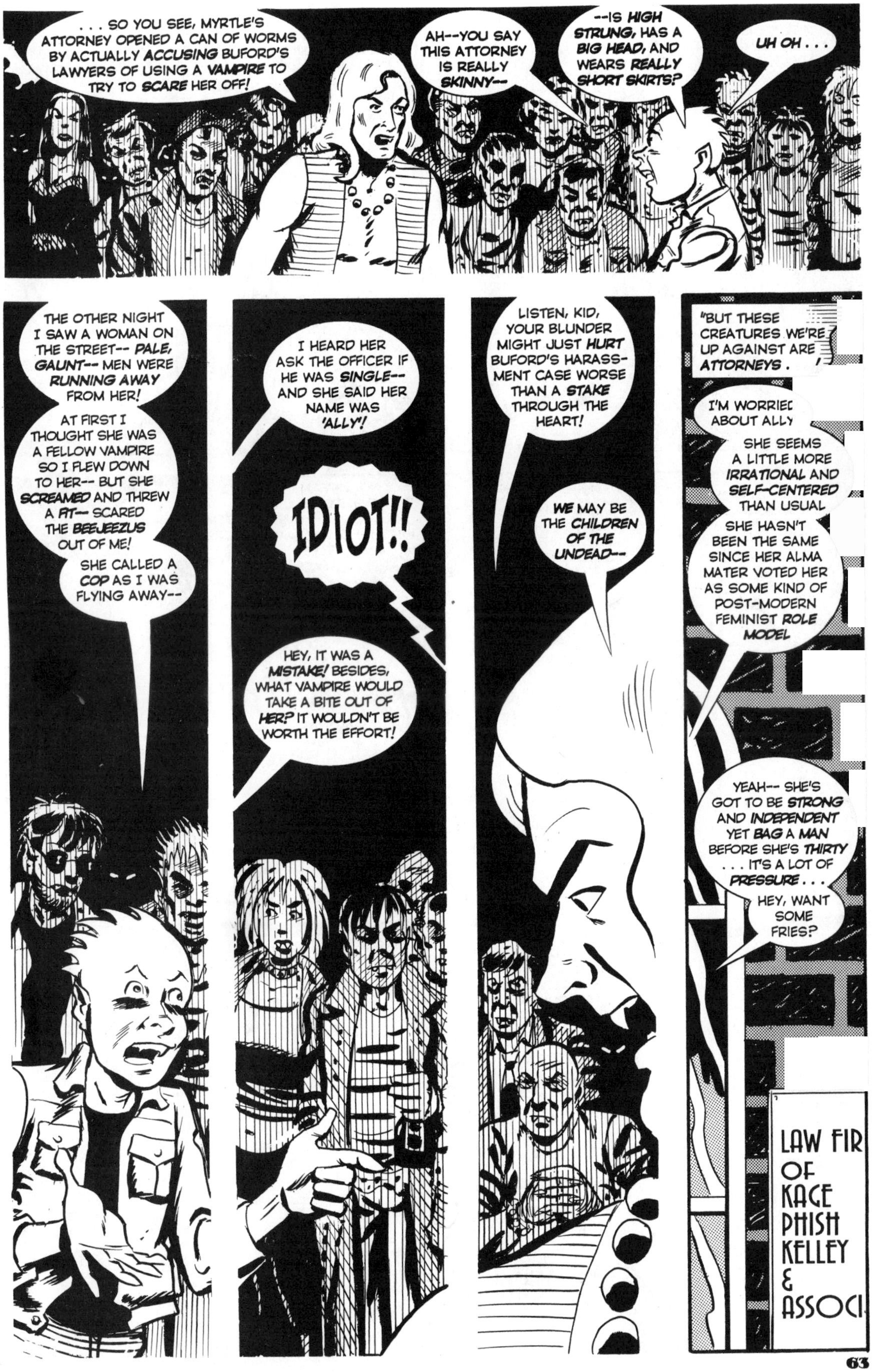

. . . SO YOU SEE, MYRTLE'S ATTORNEY OPENED A CAN OF WORMS BY ACTUALLY ACCUSING BUFORD'S LAWYERS OF USING A VAMPIRE TO TRY TO SCARE HER OFF!
AH--YOU SAY THIS ATTORNEY IS REALLY SKINNY--
--IS HIGH STRUNG, HAS A BIG HEAD, AND WEARS REALLY SHORT SKIRTS?
UH OH . . .
THE OTHER NIGHT I SAW A WOMAN ON THE STREET-- PALE, GAUNT-- MEN WERE RUNNING AWAY FROM HER!
AT FIRST I THOUGHT SHE WAS A FELLOW VAMPIRE SO I FLEW DOWN TO HER-- BUT SHE SCREAMED AND THREW A FIT-- SCARED THE BEEJEEZUS OUT OF ME!
SHE CALLED A COP AS I WAS FLYING AWAY--
I HEARD HER ASK THE OFFICER IF HE WAS SINGLE-- AND SHE SAID HER NAME WAS 'ALLY'!
IDIOT!!
HEY, IT WAS A MISTAKE! BESIDES, WHAT VAMPIRE WOULD TAKE A BITE OUT OF HER? IT WOULDN'T BE WORTH THE EFFORT!
LISTEN, KID, YOUR BLUNDER MIGHT JUST HURT BUFORD'S HARASS-MENT CASE WORSE THAN A STAKE THROUGH THE HEART!
WE MAY BE THE CHILDREN OF THE UNDEAD--
"BUT THESE CREATURES WE'RE UP AGAINST ARE ATTORNEYS .
I'M WORRIED ABOUT ALLY
SHE SEEMS A LITTLE MORE IRRATIONAL AND SELF-CENTERED THAN USUAL
SHE HASN'T BEEN THE SAME SINCE HER ALMA MATER VOTED HER AS SOME KIND OF POST-MODERN FEMINIST ROLE MODEL
YEAH-- SHE'S GOT TO BE STRONG AND INDEPENDENT YET BAG A MAN BEFORE SHE'S THIRTY . . . IT'S A LOT OF PRESSURE . . .
HEY, WANT SOME FRIES?
LAW FIR OF KAGE PHISH KELLEY & ASSOCI

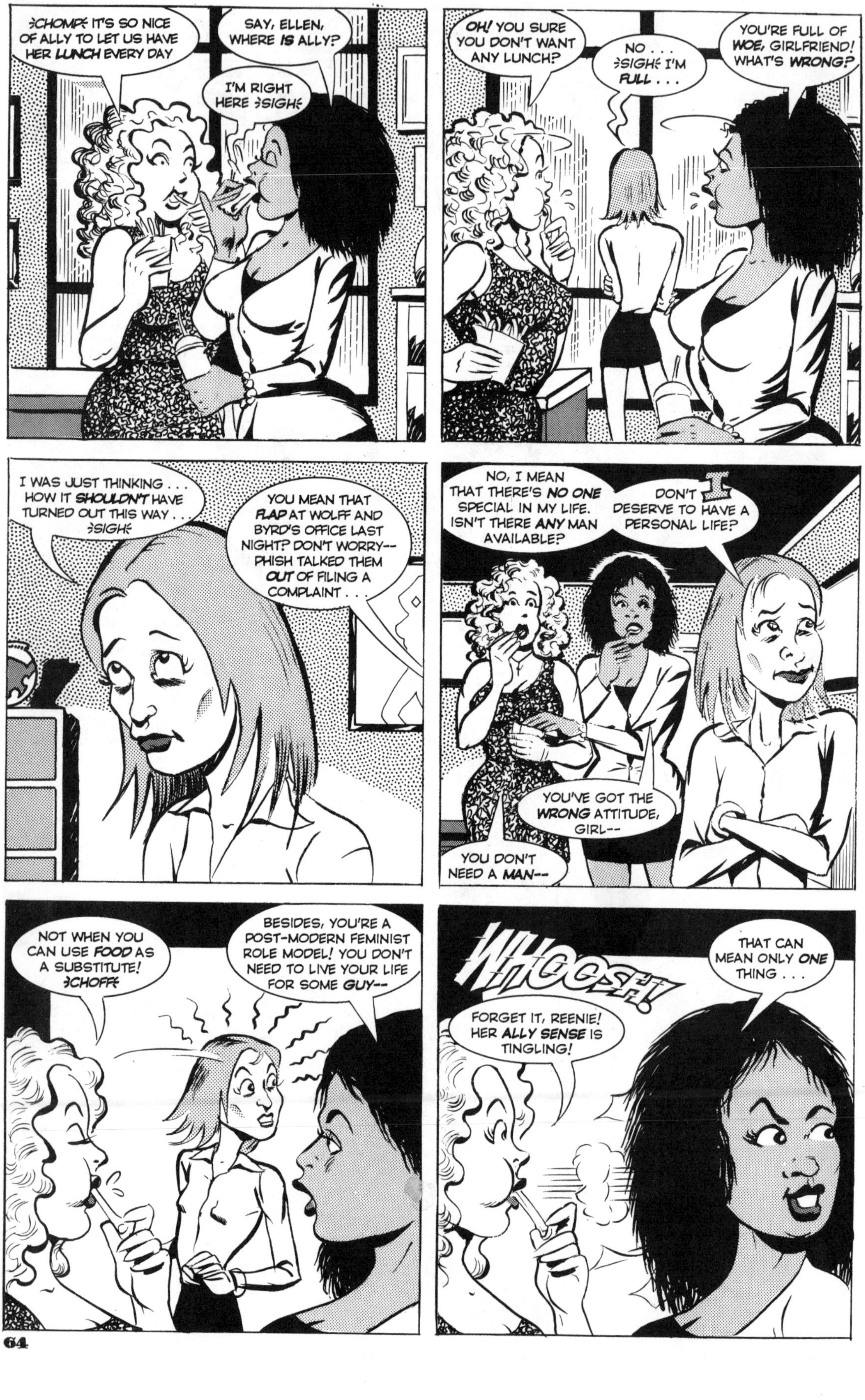

CHOMP IT'S SO NICE OF ALLY TO LET US HAVE HER LUNCH EVERY DAY
SAY, ELLEN, WHERE IS ALLY?
I'M RIGHT HERE *SIGH*
OH! YOU SURE YOU DON'T WANT ANY LUNCH?
NO . . . *SIGH* I'M FULL . . .
YOU'RE FULL OF WOE, GIRLFRIEND! WHAT'S WRONG?
I WAS JUST THINKING . . . HOW IT SHOULDN'T HAVE TURNED OUT THIS WAY . . . *SIGH*
YOU MEAN THAT FLAP AT WOLFF AND BYRD'S OFFICE LAST NIGHT? DON'T WORRY-- PHISH TALKED THEM OUT OF FILING A COMPLAINT . . .
NO, I MEAN THAT THERE'S NO ONE SPECIAL IN MY LIFE. ISN'T THERE ANY MAN AVAILABLE?
DON'T I DESERVE TO HAVE A PERSONAL LIFE?
YOU'VE GOT THE WRONG ATTITUDE, GIRL--
YOU DON'T NEED A MAN--
NOT WHEN YOU CAN USE FOOD AS A SUBSTITUTE! *CHOFF*
BESIDES, YOU'RE A POST-MODERN FEMINIST ROLE MODEL! YOU DON'T NEED TO LIVE YOUR LIFE FOR SOME GUY--
WHOOSH!
THAT CAN MEAN ONLY ONE THING . . .
FORGET IT, REENIE! HER ALLY SENSE IS TINGLING!

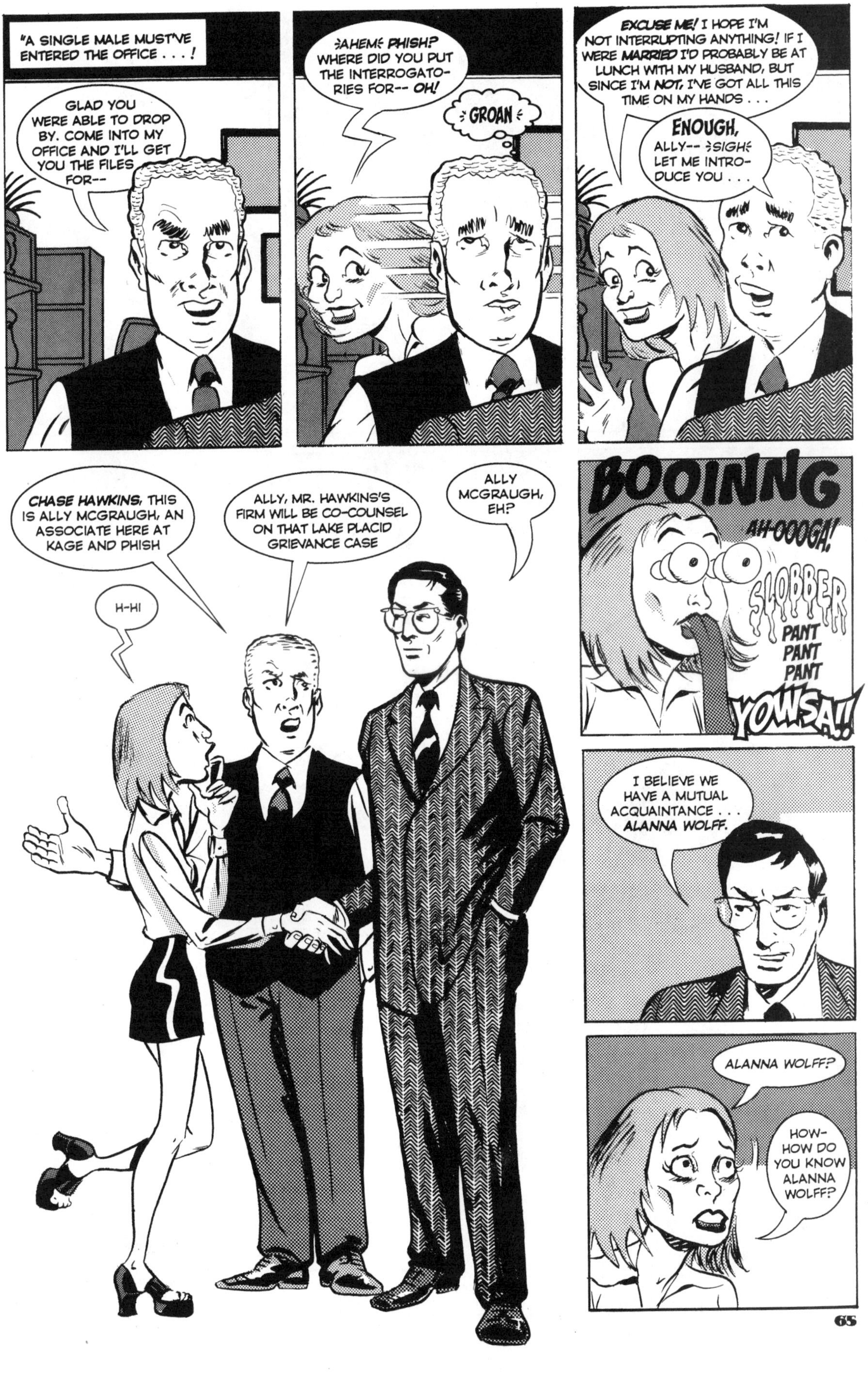
"A SINGLE MALE MUST'VE ENTERED THE OFFICE . . . !
GLAD YOU WERE ABLE TO DROP BY. COME INTO MY OFFICE AND I'LL GET YOU THE FILES FOR--
AHEM PHISH? WHERE DID YOU PUT THE INTERROGATORIES FOR-- OH!
GROAN
EXCUSE ME! I HOPE I'M NOT INTERRUPTING ANYTHING! IF I WERE MARRIED I'D PROBABLY BE AT LUNCH WITH MY HUSBAND, BUT SINCE I'M NOT, I'VE GOT ALL THIS TIME ON MY HANDS . . .
ENOUGH, ALLY-- SIGH LET ME INTRODUCE YOU . . .
CHASE HAWKINS, THIS IS ALLY MCGRAUGH, AN ASSOCIATE HERE AT KAGE AND PHISH
ALLY, MR. HAWKINS'S FIRM WILL BE CO-COUNSEL ON THAT LAKE PLACID GRIEVANCE CASE
ALLY MCGRAUGH, EH?
H-HI
BOOINNG
AH-OOOGA!
SLOBBER
PANT
PANT
PANT
YOWSA!!
I BELIEVE WE HAVE A MUTUAL ACQUAINTANCE . . . ALANNA WOLFF.
ALANNA WOLFF?
HOW-HOW DO YOU KNOW ALANNA WOLFF?

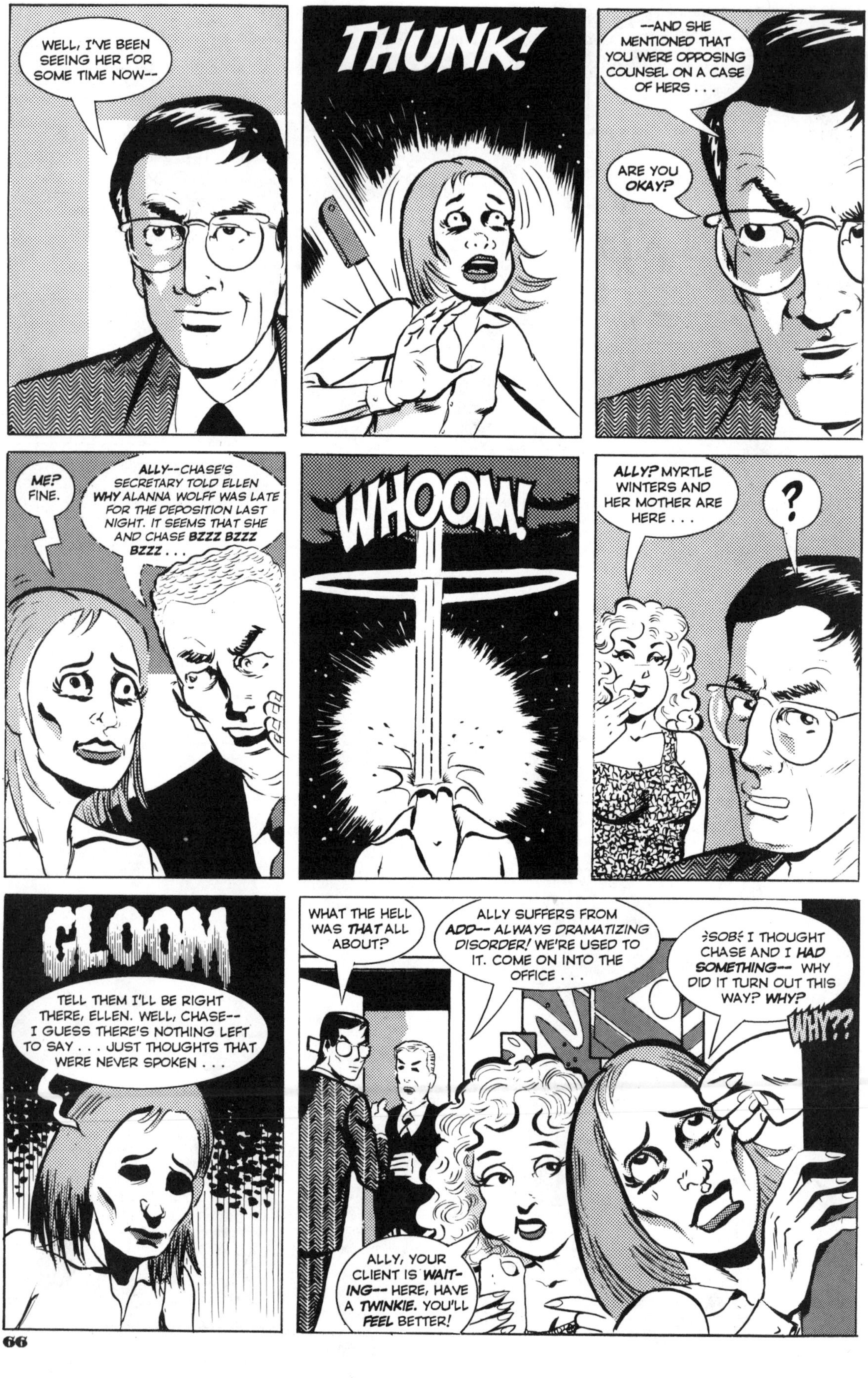
WELL, I'VE BEEN SEEING HER FOR SOME TIME NOW--
THUNK!
--AND SHE MENTIONED THAT YOU WERE OPPOSING COUNSEL ON A CASE OF HERS . . .
ARE YOU OKAY?
ME? FINE.
ALLY--CHASE'S SECRETARY TOLD ELLEN WHY ALANNA WOLFF WAS LATE FOR THE DEPOSITION LAST NIGHT. IT SEEMS THAT SHE AND CHASE BZZZ BZZZ BZZZ . . .
WHOOM!
ALLY? MYRTLE WINTERS AND HER MOTHER ARE HERE . . .
?
GLOOM
TELL THEM I'LL BE RIGHT THERE, ELLEN. WELL, CHASE-- I GUESS THERE'S NOTHING LEFT TO SAY . . . JUST THOUGHTS THAT WERE NEVER SPOKEN . . .
WHAT THE HELL WAS THAT ALL ABOUT?
ALLY SUFFERS FROM ADD-- ALWAYS DRAMATIZING DISORDER! WE'RE USED TO IT. COME ON INTO THE OFFICE . . .
SOB I THOUGHT CHASE AND I HAD SOMETHING-- WHY DID IT TURN OUT THIS WAY? WHY?
WHY??
ALLY, YOUR CLIENT IS WAIT-ING-- HERE, HAVE A TWINKIE. YOU'LL FEEL BETTER!

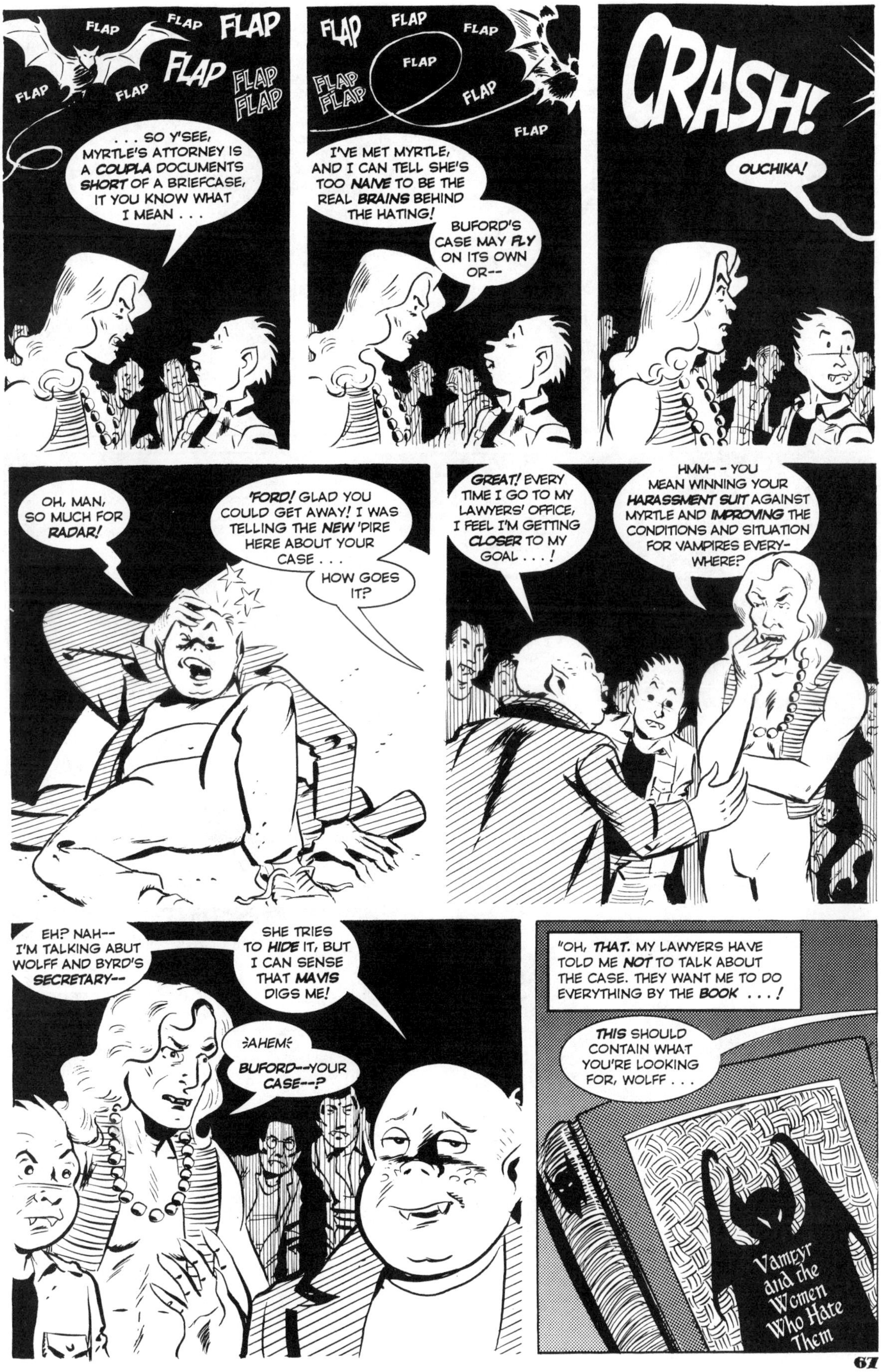
FLAP
FLAP
FLAP
FLAP
FLAP
FLAP
FLAP FLAP
. . . SO Y'SEE, MYRTLE'S ATTORNEY IS A COUPLA DOCUMENTS SHORT OF A BRIEFCASE, IT YOU KNOW WHAT I MEAN . . .
FLAP
FLAP
FLAP
FLAP FLAP
FLAP
FLAP
I'VE MET MYRTLE, AND I CAN TELL SHE'S TOO NAIVE TO BE THE REAL BRAINS BEHIND THE HATING!
BUFORD'S CASE MAY FLY ON ITS OWN OR--
CRASH!
OUCHIKA!
OH, MAN, SO MUCH FOR RADAR!
'FORD! GLAD YOU COULD GET AWAY! I WAS TELLING THE NEW 'PIRE HERE ABOUT YOUR CASE . . .
HOW GOES IT?
GREAT! EVERY TIME I GO TO MY LAWYERS' OFFICE, I FEEL I'M GETTING CLOSER TO MY GOAL . . . !
HMM-- - YOU MEAN WINNING YOUR HARASSMENT SUIT AGAINST MYRTLE AND IMPROVING THE CONDITIONS AND SITUATION FOR VAMPIRES EVERY-WHERE?
EH? NAH-- I'M TALKING ABUT WOLFF AND BYRD'S SECRETARY--
SHE TRIES TO HIDE IT, BUT I CAN SENSE THAT MAVIS DIGS ME!
AHEM
BUFORD--YOUR CASE--?
"OH, THAT. MY LAWYERS HAVE TOLD ME NOT TO TALK ABOUT THE CASE. THEY WANT ME TO DO EVERYTHING BY THE BOOK . . . !
THIS SHOULD CONTAIN WHAT YOU'RE LOOKING FOR, WOLFF . . .
Vampyr and the Women Who Hate Them

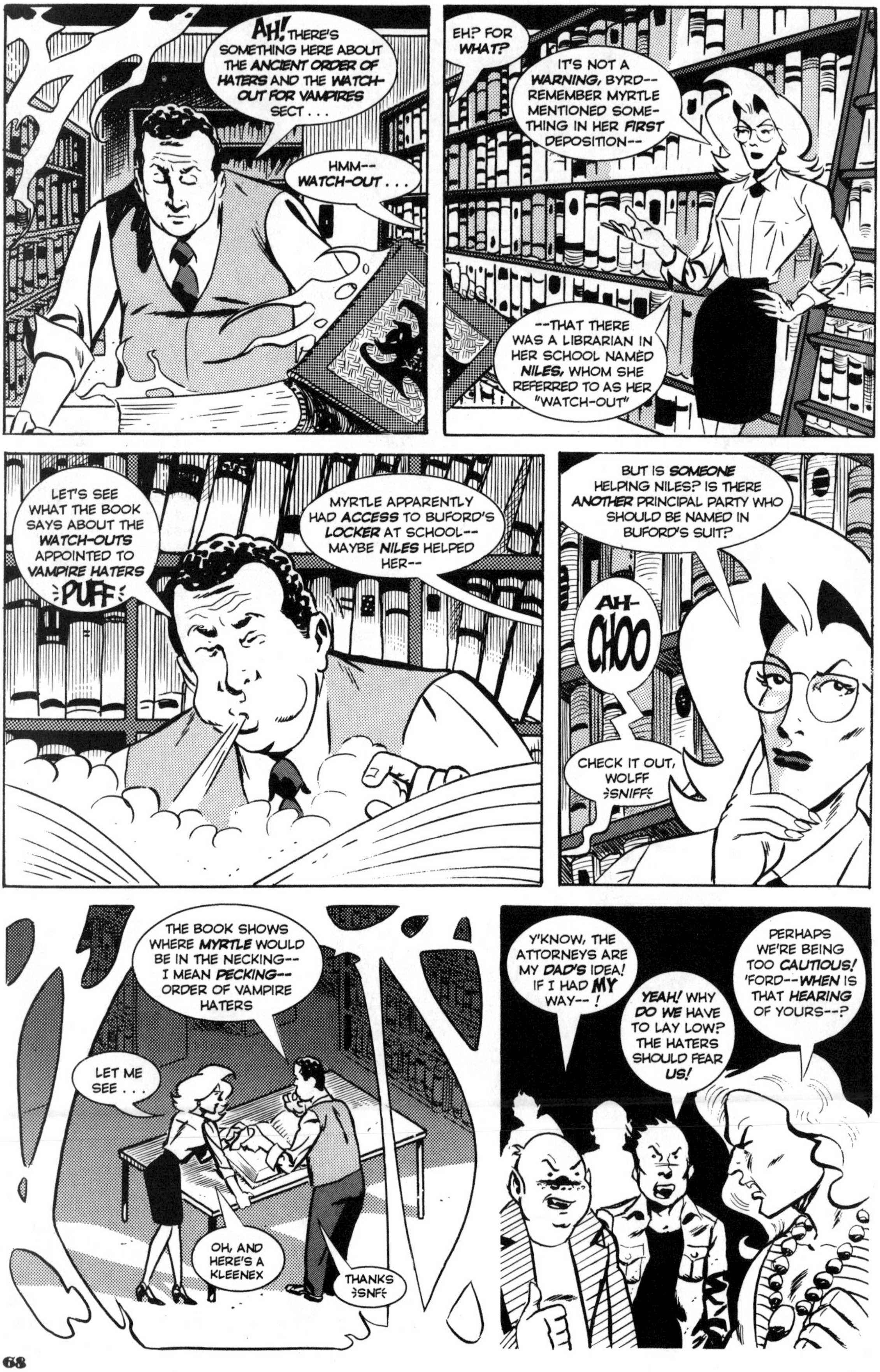
AH! THERE'S SOMETHING HERE ABOUT THE ANCIENT ORDER OF HATERS AND THE WATCH-OUT FOR VAMPIRES SECT . . .
HMM-- WATCH-OUT . . .
EH? FOR WHAT?
IT'S NOT A WARNING, BYRD-- REMEMBER MYRTLE MENTIONED SOMETHING IN HER FIRST DEPOSITION--
--THAT THERE WAS A LIBRARIAN IN HER SCHOOL NAMED NILES, WHOM SHE REFERRED TO AS HER "WATCH-OUT"
LET'S SEE WHAT THE BOOK SAYS ABOUT THE WATCH-OUTS APPOINTED TO VAMPIRE HATERS
PUFF
MYRTLE APPARENTLY HAD ACCESS TO BUFORD'S LOCKER AT SCHOOL-- MAYBE NILES HELPED HER--
BUT IS SOMEONE HELPING NILES? IS THERE ANOTHER PRINCIPAL PARTY WHO SHOULD BE NAMED IN BUFORD'S SUIT?
AH-CHOO
CHECK IT OUT, WOLFF SNIFF
THE BOOK SHOWS WHERE MYRTLE WOULD BE IN THE NECKING-- I MEAN PECKING-- ORDER OF VAMPIRE HATERS
LET ME SEE . . .
OH, AND HERE'S A KLEENEX
THANKS SNF
Y'KNOW, THE ATTORNEYS ARE MY DAD'S IDEA! IF I HAD MY WAY-- !
YEAH! WHY DO WE HAVE TO LAY LOW? THE HATERS SHOULD FEAR US!
PERHAPS WE'RE BEING TOO CAUTIOUS! 'FORD--WHEN IS THAT HEARING OF YOURS--?

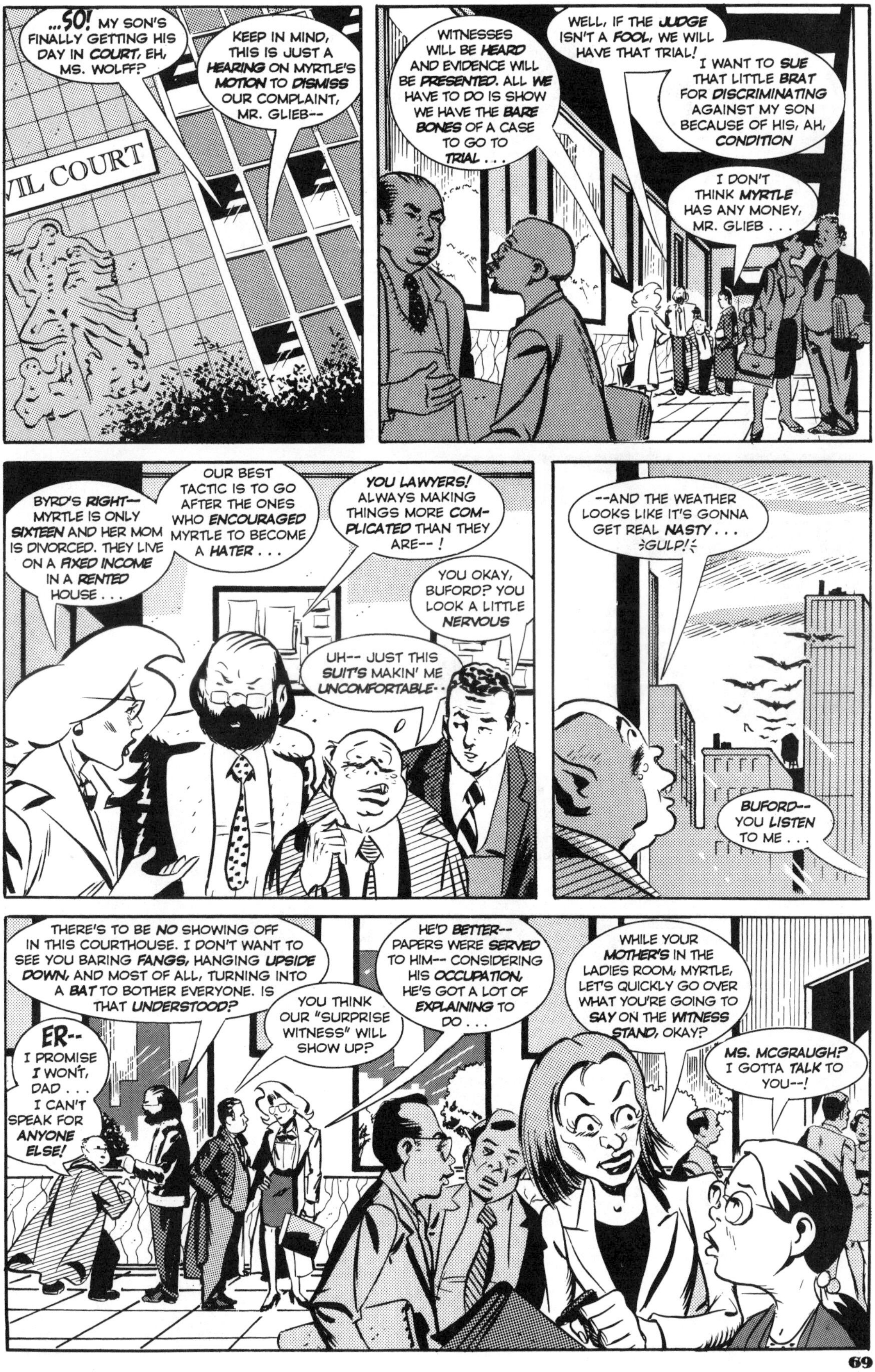
...SO! MY SON'S FINALLY GETTING HIS DAY IN COURT, EH, MS. WOLFF?
KEEP IN MIND, THIS IS JUST A HEARING ON MYRTLE'S MOTION TO DISMISS OUR COMPLAINT, MR. GLIEB--
VIL COURT
WITNESSES WILL BE HEARD AND EVIDENCE WILL BE PRESENTED. ALL WE HAVE TO DO IS SHOW WE HAVE THE BARE BONES OF A CASE TO GO TO TRIAL . . .
WELL, IF THE JUDGE ISN'T A FOOL, WE WILL HAVE THAT TRIAL!
I WANT TO SUE THAT LITTLE BRAT FOR DISCRIMINATING AGAINST MY SON BECAUSE OF HIS, AH, CONDITION
I DON'T THINK MYRTLE HAS ANY MONEY, MR. GLIEB . . .
BYRD'S RIGHT-- MYRTLE IS ONLY SIXTEEN AND HER MOM IS DIVORCED. THEY LIVE ON A FIXED INCOME IN A RENTED HOUSE . . .
OUR BEST TACTIC IS TO GO AFTER THE ONES WHO ENCOURAGED MYRTLE TO BECOME A HATER . . .
YOU LAWYERS! ALWAYS MAKING THINGS MORE COMPLICATED THAN THEY ARE-- !
YOU OKAY, BUFORD? YOU LOOK A LITTLE NERVOUS
UH-- JUST THIS SUIT'S MAKIN' ME UNCOMFORTABLE . . .
--AND THE WEATHER LOOKS LIKE IT'S GONNA GET REAL NASTY . . . GULP!
BUFORD-- YOU LISTEN TO ME . . .
THERE'S TO BE NO SHOWING OFF IN THIS COURTHOUSE. I DON'T WANT TO SEE YOU BARING FANGS, HANGING UPSIDE DOWN, AND MOST OF ALL, TURNING INTO A BAT TO BOTHER EVERYONE. IS THAT UNDERSTOOD?
ER-- I PROMISE I WON'T, DAD . . . I CAN'T SPEAK FOR ANYONE ELSE!
YOU THINK OUR "SURPRISE WITNESS" WILL SHOW UP?
HE'D BETTER-- PAPERS WERE SERVED TO HIM-- CONSIDERING HIS OCCUPATION, HE'S GOT A LOT OF EXPLAINING TO DO . . .
WHILE YOUR MOTHER'S IN THE LADIES ROOM, MYRTLE, LET'S QUICKLY GO OVER WHAT YOU'RE GOING TO SAY ON THE WITNESS STAND, OKAY?
MS. MCGRAUGH? I GOTTA TALK TO YOU--!

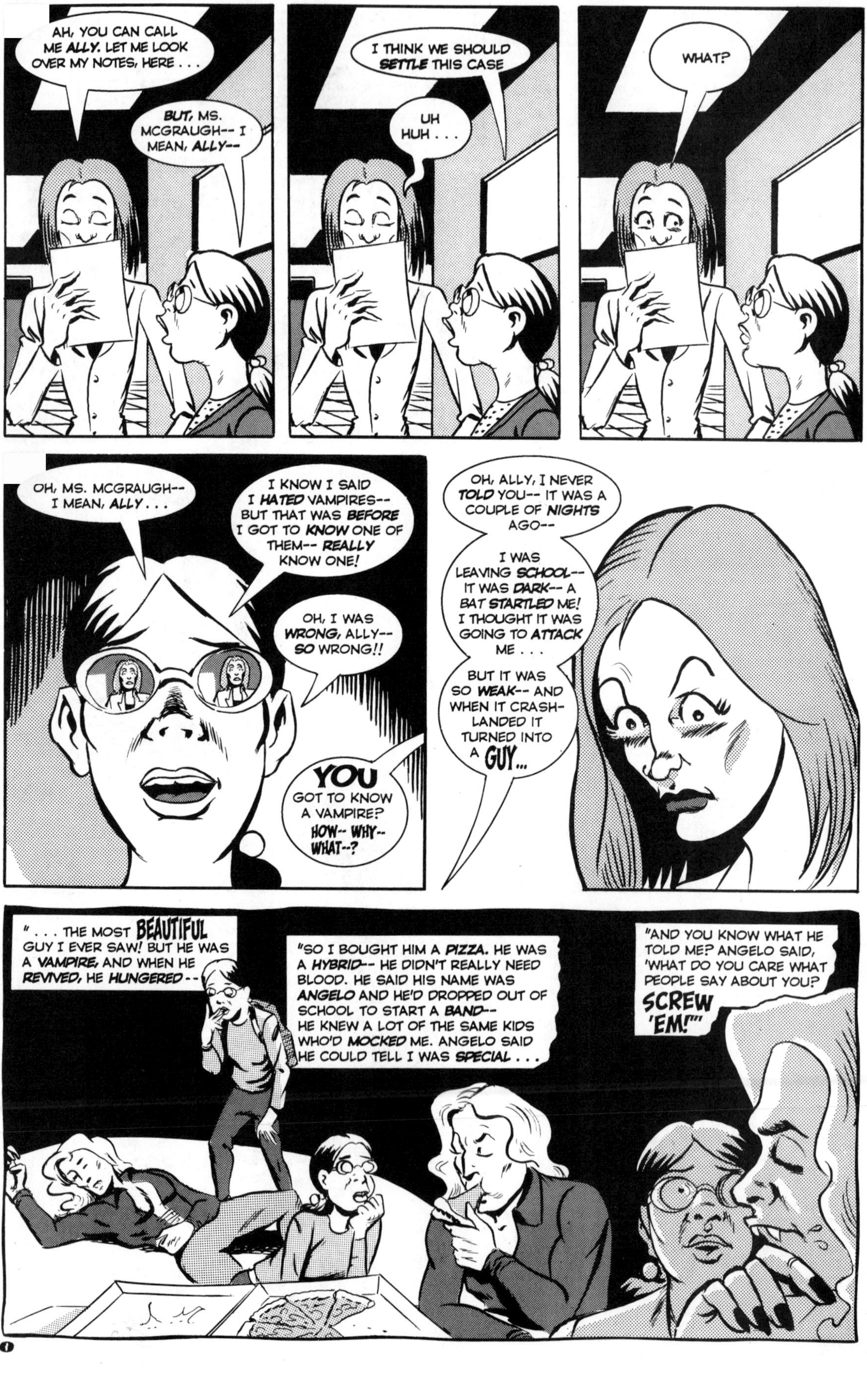

AH, YOU CAN CALL ME ALLY. LET ME LOOK OVER MY NOTES, HERE . . .
BUT, MS. MCGRAUGH-- I MEAN, ALLY--
I THINK WE SHOULD SETTLE THIS CASE
UH HUH . . .
WHAT?
OH, MS. MCGRAUGH-- I MEAN, ALLY . . .
I KNOW I SAID I HATED VAMPIRES-- BUT THAT WAS BEFORE I GOT TO KNOW ONE OF THEM-- REALLY KNOW ONE!
OH, I WAS WRONG, ALLY-- SO WRONG!!
YOU GOT TO KNOW A VAMPIRE? HOW-- WHY-- WHAT--?
OH, ALLY, I NEVER TOLD YOU-- IT WAS A COUPLE OF NIGHTS AGO--
I WAS LEAVING SCHOOL-- IT WAS DARK-- A BAT STARTLED ME! I THOUGHT IT WAS GOING TO ATTACK ME . . .
BUT IT WAS SO WEAK-- AND WHEN IT CRASH-LANDED IT TURNED INTO A GUY...
" . . . THE MOST BEAUTIFUL GUY I EVER SAW! BUT HE WAS A VAMPIRE, AND WHEN HE REVIVED, HE HUNGERED--
"SO I BOUGHT HIM A PIZZA. HE WAS A HYBRID-- HE DIDN'T REALLY NEED BLOOD. HE SAID HIS NAME WAS ANGELO AND HE'D DROPPED OUT OF SCHOOL TO START A BAND-- HE KNEW A LOT OF THE SAME KIDS WHO'D MOCKED ME. ANGELO SAID HE COULD TELL I WAS SPECIAL . . .
"AND YOU KNOW WHAT HE TOLD ME? ANGELO SAID, 'WHAT DO YOU CARE WHAT PEOPLE SAY ABOUT YOU? SCREW 'EM!'"

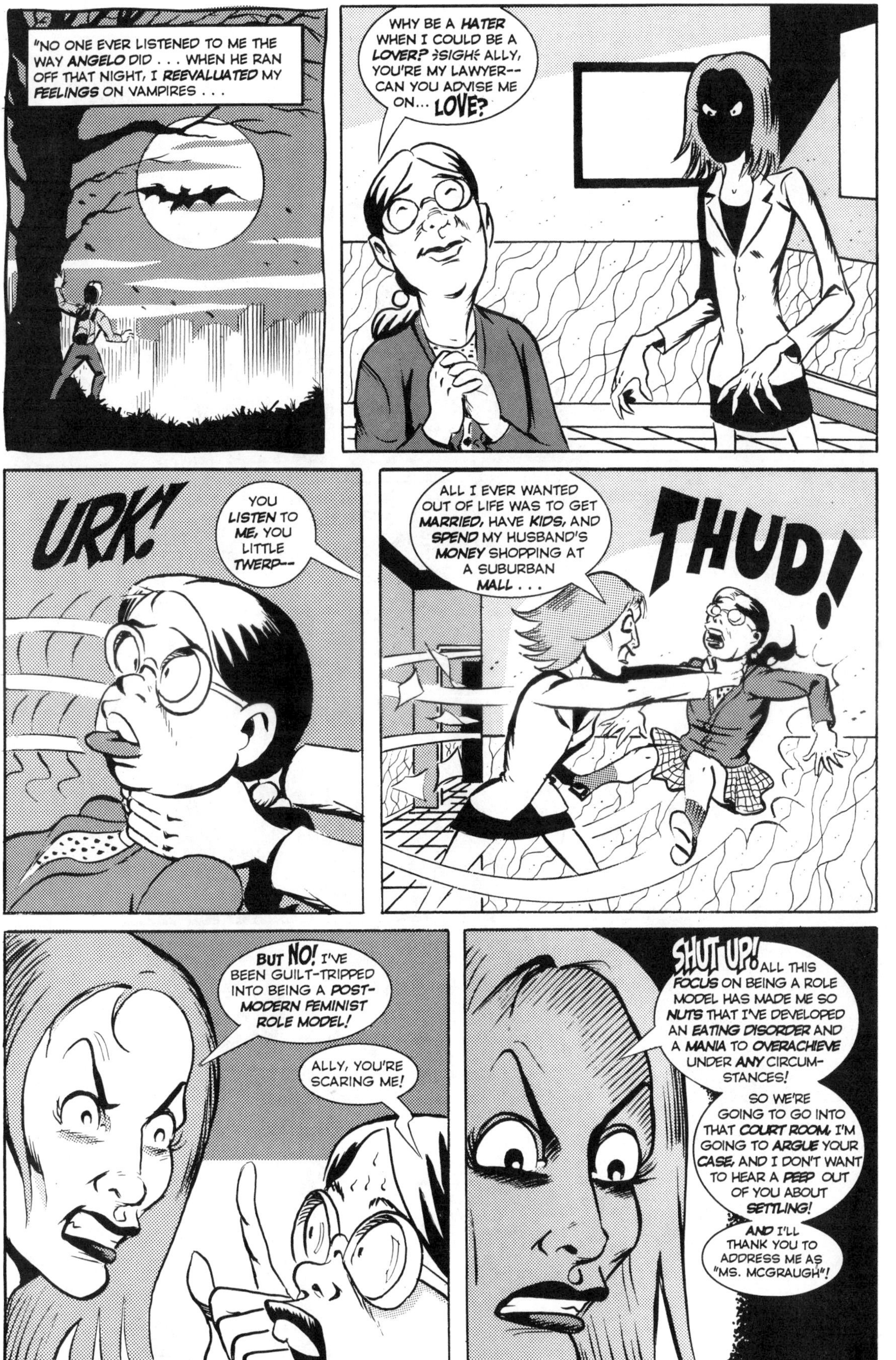

"NO ONE EVER LISTENED TO ME THE WAY ANGELO DID . . . WHEN HE RAN OFF THAT NIGHT, I REEVALUATED MY FEELINGS ON VAMPIRES . . .
WHY BE A HATER WHEN I COULD BE A LOVER? ;SIGH; ALLY, YOU'RE MY LAWYER-- CAN YOU ADVISE ME ON... LOVE?
URK!
YOU LISTEN TO ME, YOU LITTLE TWERP--
ALL I EVER WANTED OUT OF LIFE WAS TO GET MARRIED, HAVE KIDS, AND SPEND MY HUSBAND'S MONEY SHOPPING AT A SUBURBAN MALL . . .
THUD!
BUT NO! I'VE BEEN GUILT-TRIPPED INTO BEING A POST-MODERN FEMINIST ROLE MODEL!
ALLY, YOU'RE SCARING ME!
SHUT UP! ALL THIS FOCUS ON BEING A ROLE MODEL HAS MADE ME SO NUTS THAT I'VE DEVELOPED AN EATING DISORDER AND A MANIA TO OVERACHIEVE UNDER ANY CIRCUM-STANCES!
SO WE'RE GOING TO GO INTO THAT COURT ROOM, I'M GOING TO ARGUE YOUR CASE, AND I DON'T WANT TO HEAR A PEEP OUT OF YOU ABOUT SETTLING!
AND I'LL THANK YOU TO ADDRESS ME AS "MS. MCGRAUGH"!

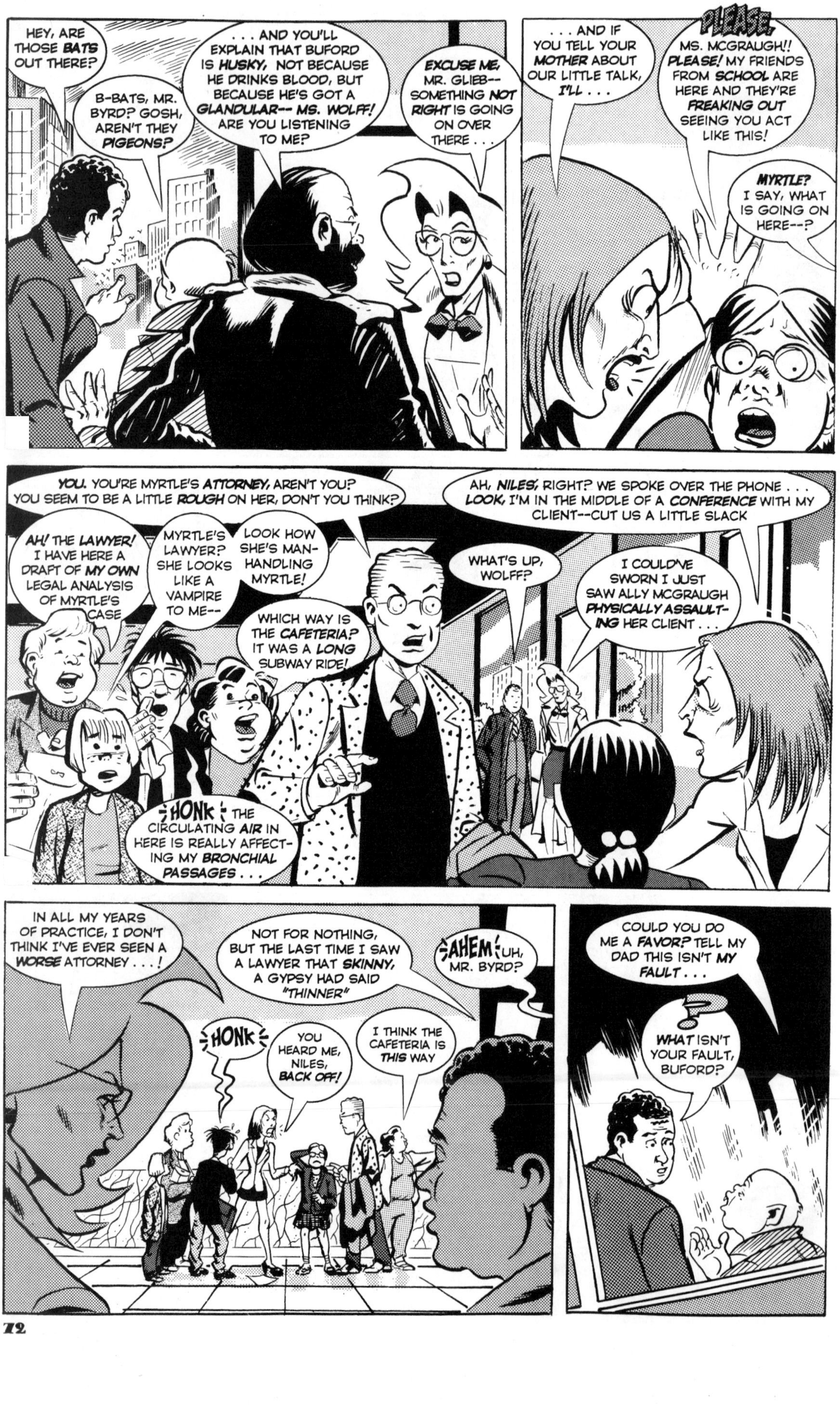

HEY, ARE THOSE BATS OUT THERE?
B-BATS, MR. BYRD? GOSH, AREN'T THEY PIGEONS?
. . . AND YOU'LL EXPLAIN THAT BUFORD IS HUSKY, NOT BECAUSE HE DRINKS BLOOD, BUT BECAUSE HE'S GOT A GLANDULAR-- MS. WOLFF! ARE YOU LISTENING TO ME?
EXCUSE ME, MR. GLIEB-- SOMETHING NOT RIGHT IS GOING ON OVER THERE . . .
. . . AND IF YOU TELL YOUR MOTHER ABOUT OUR LITTLE TALK, I'LL . . .
PLEASE,
MS. MCGRAUGH!! PLEASE! MY FRIENDS FROM SCHOOL ARE HERE AND THEY'RE FREAKING OUT SEEING YOU ACT LIKE THIS!
MYRTLE? I SAY, WHAT IS GOING ON HERE--?
YOU. YOU'RE MYRTLE'S ATTORNEY, AREN'T YOU? YOU SEEM TO BE A LITTLE ROUGH ON HER, DON'T YOU THINK?
AH, NILES, RIGHT? WE SPOKE OVER THE PHONE . . . LOOK, I'M IN THE MIDDLE OF A CONFERENCE WITH MY CLIENT--CUT US A LITTLE SLACK
AH! THE LAWYER! I HAVE HERE A DRAFT OF MY OWN LEGAL ANALYSIS OF MYRTLE'S CASE
MYRTLE'S LAWYER? SHE LOOKS LIKE A VAMPIRE TO ME--
LOOK HOW SHE'S MAN-HANDLING MYRTLE!
WHICH WAY IS THE CAFETERIA? IT WAS A LONG SUBWAY RIDE!
WHAT'S UP, WOLFF?
I COULD'VE SWORN I JUST SAW ALLY MCGRAUGH PHYSICALLY ASSAULTING HER CLIENT . . .
HONK THE CIRCULATING AIR IN HERE IS REALLY AFFECTING MY BRONCHIAL PASSAGES . . .
IN ALL MY YEARS OF PRACTICE, I DON'T THINK I'VE EVER SEEN A WORSE ATTORNEY . . . !
NOT FOR NOTHING, BUT THE LAST TIME I SAW A LAWYER THAT SKINNY, A GYPSY HAD SAID "THINNER"
AHEM UH, MR. BYRD?
HONK
YOU HEARD ME, NILES, BACK OFF!
I THINK THE CAFETERIA IS THIS WAY
COULD YOU DO ME A FAVOR? TELL MY DAD THIS ISN'T MY FAULT . . .
?
WHAT ISN'T YOUR FAULT, BUFORD?

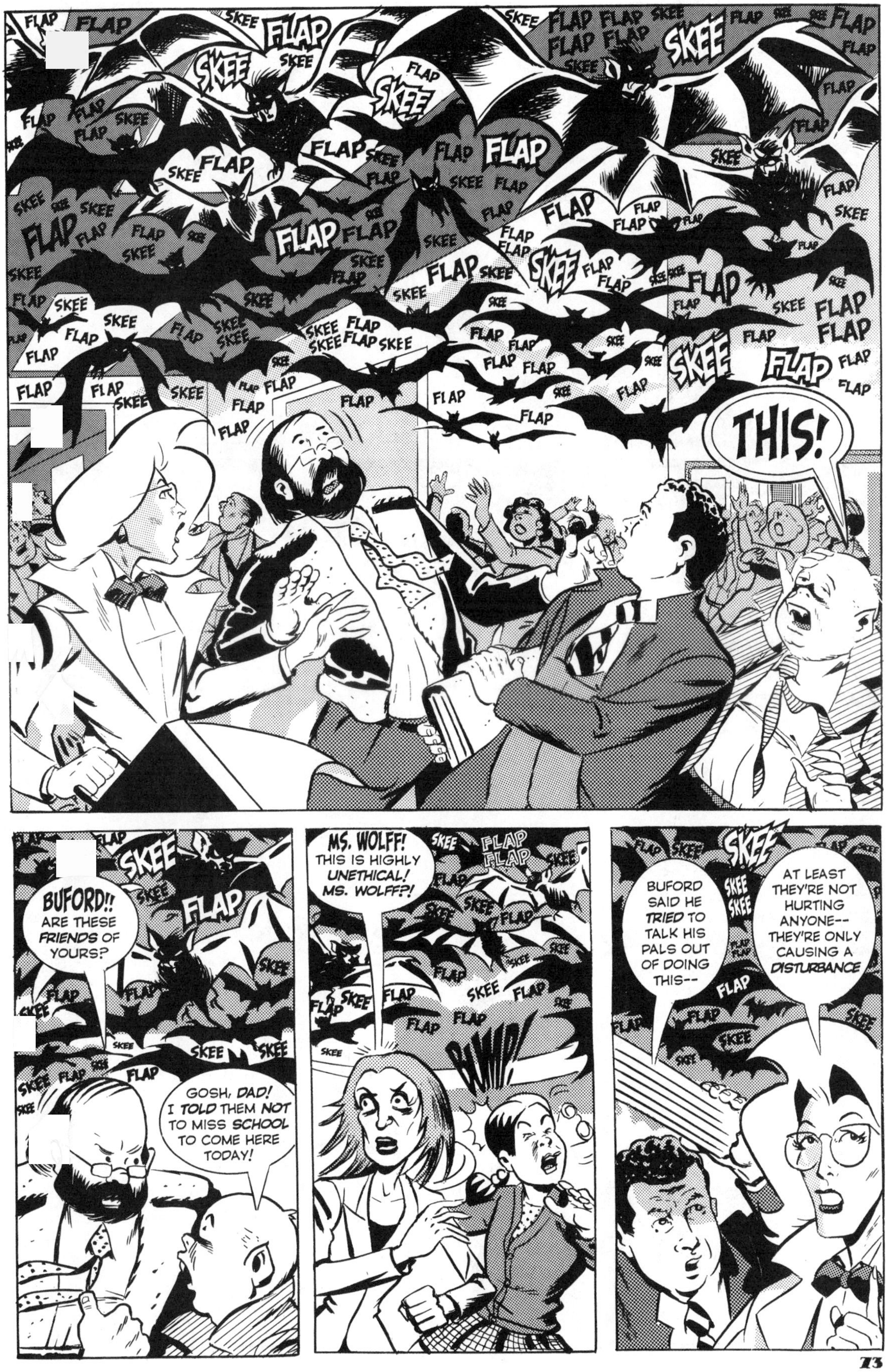
FLAP
SKEE
THIS!
BUFORD!! ARE THESE *FRIENDS* OF YOURS?
GOSH, *DAD!* I *TOLD* THEM *NOT* TO MISS *SCHOOL* TO COME HERE TODAY!
MS. WOLFF! THIS IS HIGHLY *UNETHICAL!* MS. WOLFF?!
BUMP!
BUFORD SAID HE *TRIED* TO TALK HIS PALS OUT OF DOING THIS--
AT LEAST THEY'RE NOT HURTING ANYONE-- THEY'RE ONLY CAUSING A *DISTURBANCE*

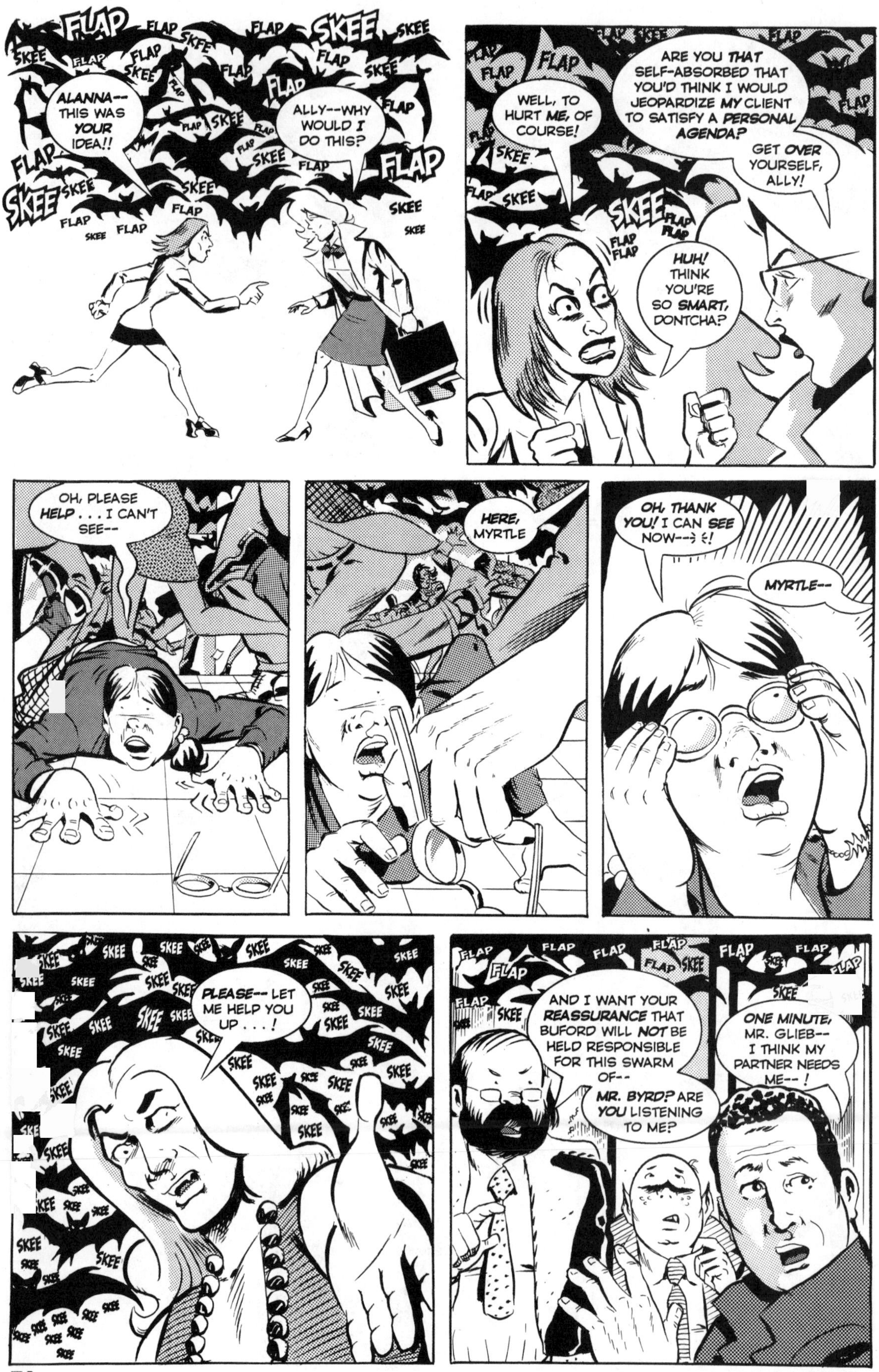
FLAP FLAP SKEE FLAP SKEE SKEE
ALANNA-- THIS WAS YOUR IDEA!!
ALLY--WHY WOULD I DO THIS?
WELL, TO HURT ME, OF COURSE!
ARE YOU THAT SELF-ABSORBED THAT YOU'D THINK I WOULD JEOPARDIZE MY CLIENT TO SATISFY A PERSONAL AGENDA?
GET OVER YOURSELF, ALLY!
HUH! THINK YOU'RE SO SMART, DONTCHA?
OH, PLEASE HELP . . . I CAN'T SEE--
HERE, MYRTLE
OH, THANK YOU! I CAN SEE NOW-- !
MYRTLE--
PLEASE-- LET ME HELP YOU UP . . . !
AND I WANT YOUR REASSURANCE THAT BUFORD WILL NOT BE HELD RESPONSIBLE FOR THIS SWARM OF--
MR. BYRD? ARE YOU LISTENING TO ME?
ONE MINUTE, MR. GLIEB-- I THINK MY PARTNER NEEDS ME-- !

FLAP SKEE SKEE SKEE SKEE FLAP FLAP FLAP FLAP SKEE FLAP SKEE SKEE FLAP

GOOD LORD! ¿CHOKE? WHAT IS THE *MEANING* OF THIS?

I'M *SORRY*, ALANNA, BUT I HAVEN'T STOPPED THINKING ABOUT *ALLY* SINCE I MET HER . . .

SURE, YOU'RE *LOGICAL*, *SENSIBLE*, *OBJECTIVE*, AND *INTELLIGENT*. BUT LET'S FACE IT-- OUR *CULTURE* IS *THREATENED* BY WOMEN LIKE *YOU*!

THAT'S WHY SOMEONE LIKE *ALLY* IS CELEBRATED--A "POST-MODERN FEMINIST ROLE MODEL" FOR THE *CON-FUSED* AND *MISGUIDED* TO FEEL *GOOD* ABOUT THEMSELVES!

DEEP DOWN, I GUESS I KNEW THE FEMINISM WAS ALL *LIP SERVICE*, BUT WHO CARES IF I FINALLY GET MY *MAN*?

I REALIZE THIS MAY NOT BE THE *BEST TIME* TO TELL YOU THIS, ALANNA, BUT I *LOVE* ALLY!

I KNOW IT *HURTS*, ALANNA, BUT MAYBE SOMEDAY WE CAN BE *FRIENDS*--?

SOB

ALLY?

OKAY, ALLY, YOU HAD YOUR *FUN*-- NOW I'M *OUT OF HERE*!

SO SOON? CAN'T I *INDULGE* IN MY *ADD* A LITTLE?

ALLY--

TWO WORDS, ALLY-- *GET REAL*!

NUTS! EVEN THE MEN IN MY *FANTASIES* WON'T STAY AROUND AND COMMIT . . . !

POP!

EARTH TO ALLY--

FLAP SKEE FLAP FLAP FLAP FLAP

WHA--?

IF YOU'D STOP *DAY-DREAMING* YOU'D SEE THAT YOU NEED TO TEND TO YOUR CLIENT BEFORE I SPEAK WITH THAT *VAMPIRE* AND HER . . .

SEE, MR. BYRD? ANGELO TOLD THE GUYS TO *SPLIT* AND THEY'RE LAMMING OUTTA HERE!

ANGELO? THAT'S ANGELO?!

"BOY, I'LL NEVER FORGET THE LOOK ON HER FACE . . .

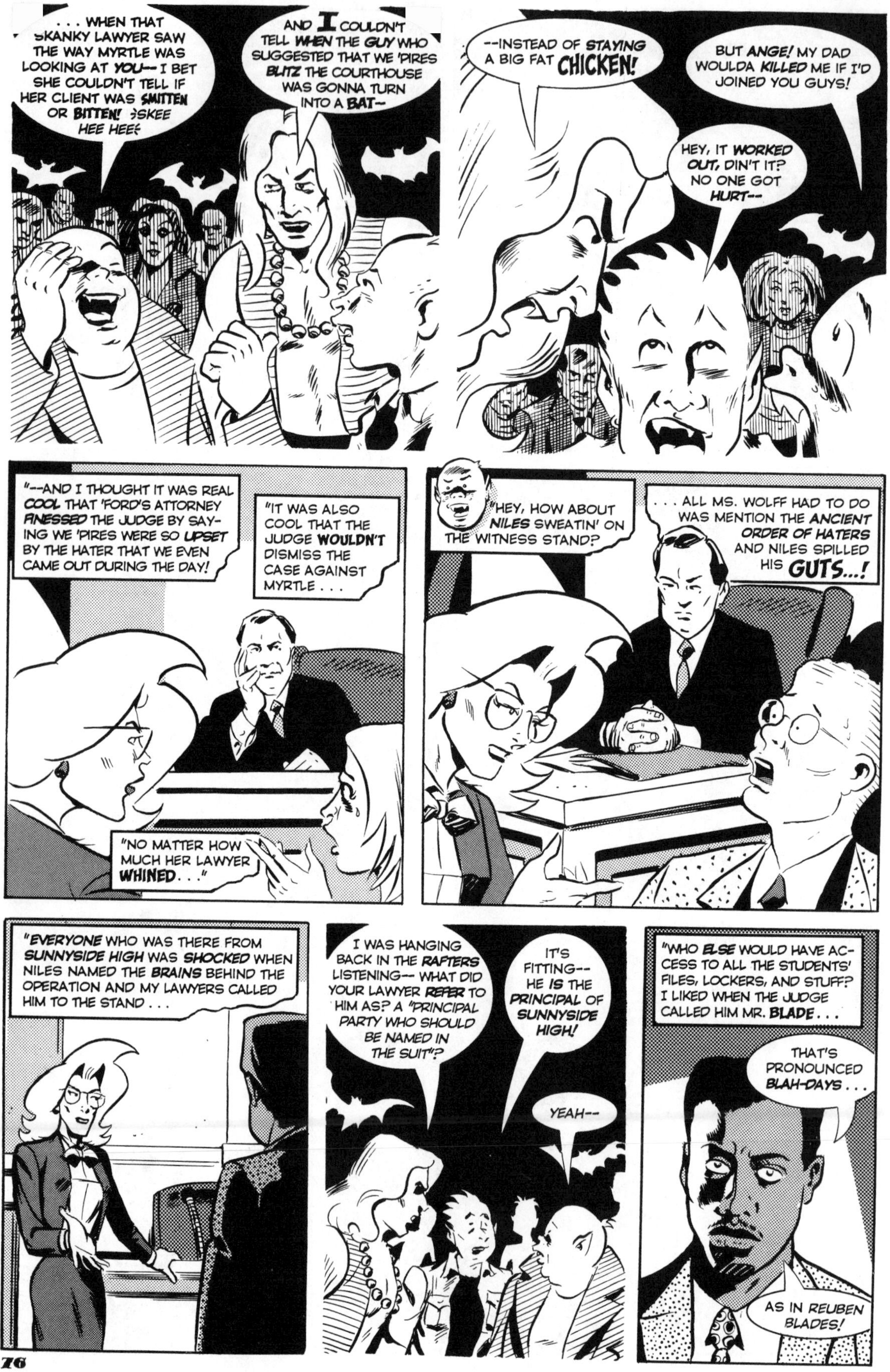

. . . WHEN THAT SKANKY LAWYER SAW THE WAY MYRTLE WAS LOOKING AT YOU-- I BET SHE COULDN'T TELL IF HER CLIENT WAS SMITTEN OR BITTEN! SKEE HEE HEE
AND I COULDN'T TELL WHEN THE GUY WHO SUGGESTED THAT WE 'PIRES BLITZ THE COURTHOUSE WAS GONNA TURN INTO A BAT--
--INSTEAD OF STAYING A BIG FAT CHICKEN!
BUT ANGE! MY DAD WOULDA KILLED ME IF I'D JOINED YOU GUYS!
HEY, IT WORKED OUT, DIN'T IT? NO ONE GOT HURT--
"--AND I THOUGHT IT WAS REAL COOL THAT 'FORD'S ATTORNEY FINESSED THE JUDGE BY SAYING WE 'PIRES WERE SO UPSET BY THE HATER THAT WE EVEN CAME OUT DURING THE DAY!
"IT WAS ALSO COOL THAT THE JUDGE WOULDN'T DISMISS THE CASE AGAINST MYRTLE . . .
"NO MATTER HOW MUCH HER LAWYER WHINED. . ."
"HEY, HOW ABOUT NILES SWEATIN' ON THE WITNESS STAND?
. . . ALL MS. WOLFF HAD TO DO WAS MENTION THE ANCIENT ORDER OF HATERS AND NILES SPILLED HIS GUTS...!
"EVERYONE WHO WAS THERE FROM SUNNYSIDE HIGH WAS SHOCKED WHEN NILES NAMED THE BRAINS BEHIND THE OPERATION AND MY LAWYERS CALLED HIM TO THE STAND . . .
I WAS HANGING BACK IN THE RAFTERS LISTENING-- WHAT DID YOUR LAWYER REFER TO HIM AS? A "PRINCIPAL PARTY WHO SHOULD BE NAMED IN THE SUIT"?
IT'S FITTING-- HE IS THE PRINCIPAL OF SUNNYSIDE HIGH!
YEAH--
"WHO ELSE WOULD HAVE ACCESS TO ALL THE STUDENTS' FILES, LOCKERS, AND STUFF? I LIKED WHEN THE JUDGE CALLED HIM MR. BLADE . . .
THAT'S PRONOUNCED BLAH-DAYS . . .
AS IN REUBEN BLADES!

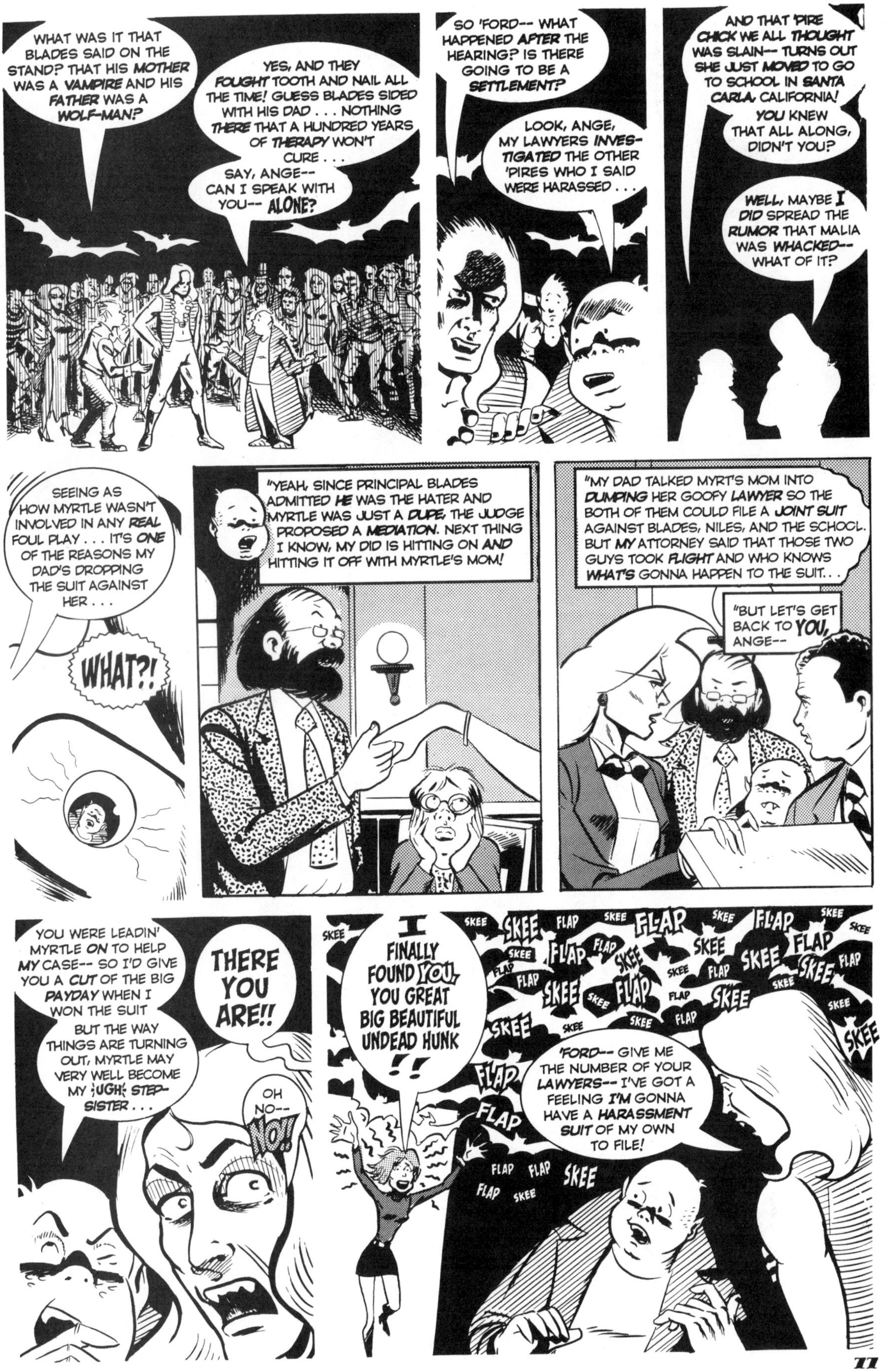

WHAT WAS IT THAT BLADES SAID ON THE STAND? THAT HIS MOTHER WAS A VAMPIRE AND HIS FATHER WAS A WOLF-MAN?
YES, AND THEY FOUGHT TOOTH AND NAIL ALL THE TIME! GUESS BLADES SIDED WITH HIS DAD . . . NOTHING THERE THAT A HUNDRED YEARS OF THERAPY WON'T CURE . . .
SAY, ANGE-- CAN I SPEAK WITH YOU-- ALONE?
SO 'FORD-- WHAT HAPPENED AFTER THE HEARING? IS THERE GOING TO BE A SETTLEMENT?
LOOK, ANGE, MY LAWYERS INVESTIGATED THE OTHER 'PIRES WHO I SAID WERE HARASSED . . .
AND THAT 'PIRE CHICK WE ALL THOUGHT WAS SLAIN-- TURNS OUT SHE JUST MOVED TO GO TO SCHOOL IN SANTA CARLA, CALIFORNIA!
YOU KNEW THAT ALL ALONG, DIDN'T YOU?
WELL, MAYBE I DID SPREAD THE RUMOR THAT MALIA WAS WHACKED-- WHAT OF IT?
SEEING AS HOW MYRTLE WASN'T INVOLVED IN ANY REAL FOUL PLAY . . . IT'S ONE OF THE REASONS MY DAD'S DROPPING THE SUIT AGAINST HER . . .
WHAT?!
"YEAH, SINCE PRINCIPAL BLADES ADMITTED HE WAS THE HATER AND MYRTLE WAS JUST A DUPE, THE JUDGE PROPOSED A MEDIATION. NEXT THING I KNOW, MY DID IS HITTING ON AND HITTING IT OFF WITH MYRTLE'S MOM!
"MY DAD TALKED MYRT'S MOM INTO DUMPING HER GOOFY LAWYER SO THE BOTH OF THEM COULD FILE A JOINT SUIT AGAINST BLADES, NILES, AND THE SCHOOL. BUT MY ATTORNEY SAID THAT THOSE TWO GUYS TOOK FLIGHT AND WHO KNOWS WHAT'S GONNA HAPPEN TO THE SUIT . . .
"BUT LET'S GET BACK TO YOU, ANGE--
YOU WERE LEADIN' MYRTLE ON TO HELP MY CASE-- SO I'D GIVE YOU A CUT OF THE BIG PAYDAY WHEN I WON THE SUIT
BUT THE WAY THINGS ARE TURNING OUT, MYRTLE MAY VERY WELL BECOME MY ¡UGH! STEP-SISTER . . .
THERE YOU ARE!!
OH NO-- NO!!
I FINALLY FOUND YOU, YOU GREAT BIG BEAUTIFUL UNDEAD HUNK !!
SKEE SKEE FLAP SKEE FLAP SKEE FLAP SKEE SKEE FLAP FLAP SKEE FLAP SKEE FLAP SKEE FLAP
'FORD-- GIVE ME THE NUMBER OF YOUR LAWYERS-- I'VE GOT A FEELING I'M GONNA HAVE A HARASSMENT SUIT OF MY OWN TO FILE!
FLAP FLAP FLAP SKEE FLAP SKEE

Fashionably Late

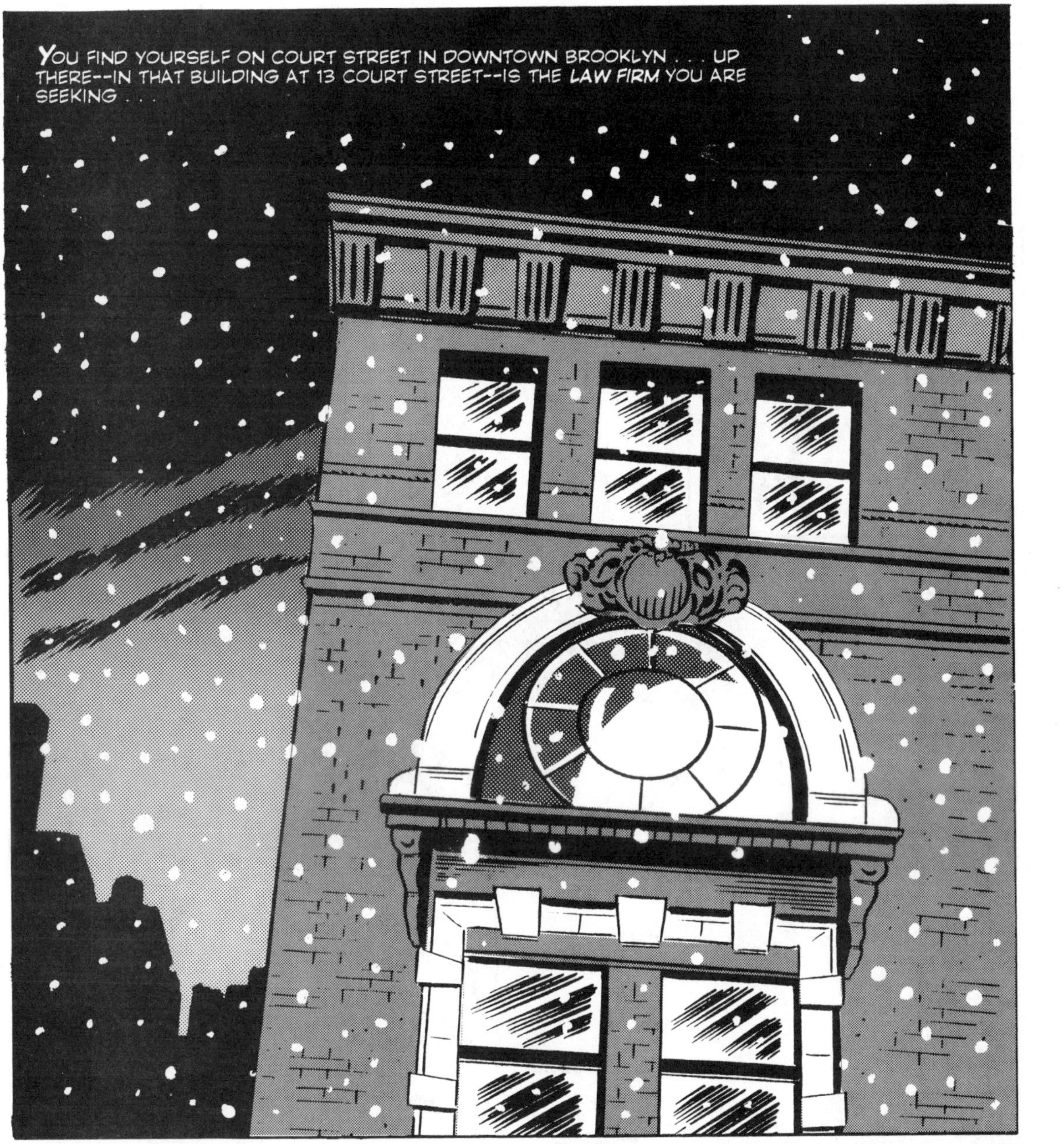
YOU FIND YOURSELF ON COURT STREET IN DOWNTOWN BROOKLYN . . . UP THERE--IN THAT BUILDING AT 13 COURT STREET--IS THE LAW FIRM YOU ARE SEEKING . . .

THE POLICY OF THIS FIRM IS THAT NO ONE CAN SEE THE ATTORNEYS WITHOUT AN APPOINTMENT . . .

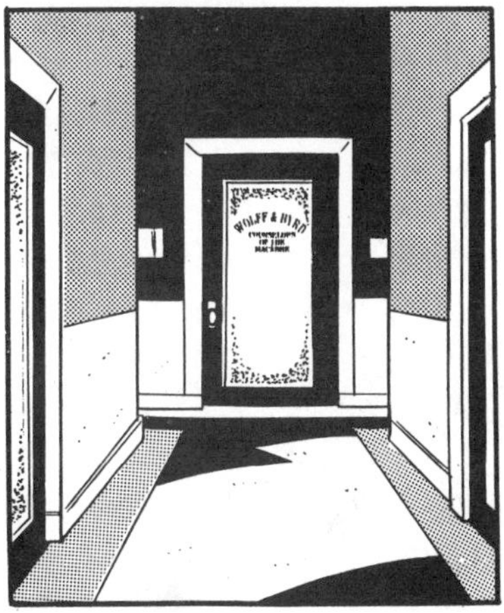

TONIGHT, HOWEVER, WHAT YOU WOULD NEED TO GAIN ENTRANCE IS AN INVITATION!

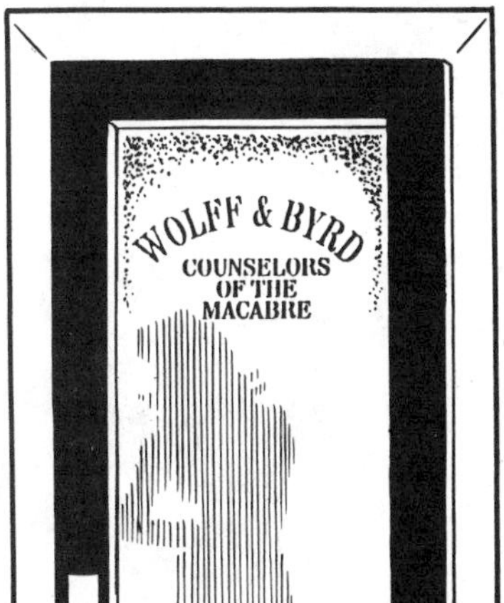
WOLFF & BYRD
COUNSELORS OF THE MACABRE

FOR TONIGHT THE MAIN SPIRITS ARE THE KIND ONE DRINKS . . . AND THE WORD PARTY DOESN'T MEAN 'DEFENDANT' OR 'PLAINTIFF'!

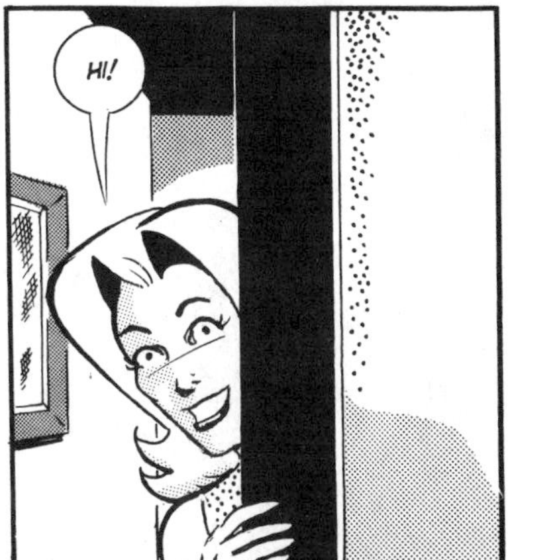
HI!

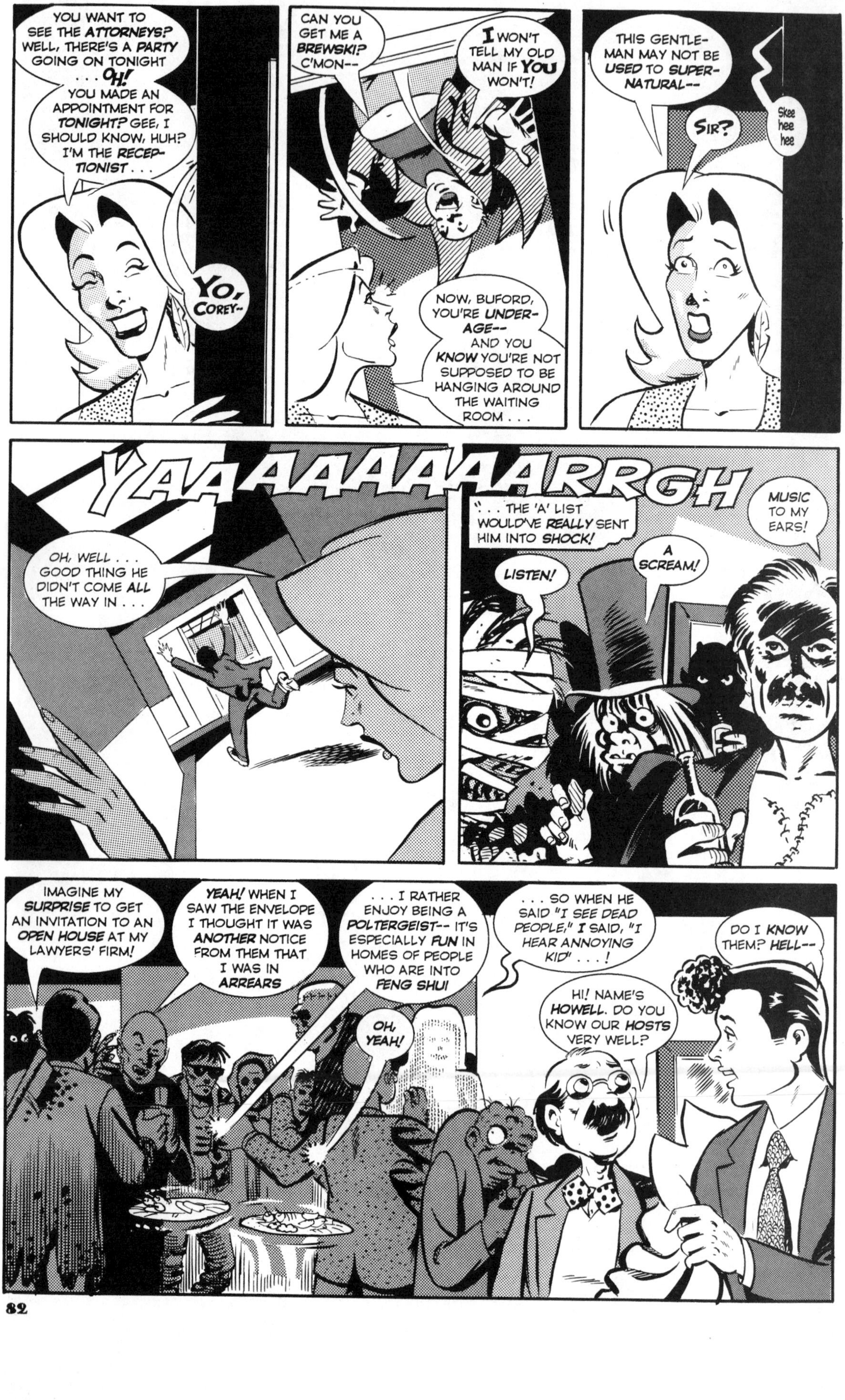

YOU WANT TO SEE THE ATTORNEYS? WELL, THERE'S A PARTY GOING ON TONIGHT . . . OH!
YOU MADE AN APPOINTMENT FOR TONIGHT? GEE, I SHOULD KNOW, HUH? I'M THE RECEPTIONIST . . .
YO, COREY--
CAN YOU GET ME A BREWSKI? C'MON--
I WON'T TELL MY OLD MAN IF YOU WON'T!
NOW, BUFORD, YOU'RE UNDERAGE-- AND YOU KNOW YOU'RE NOT SUPPOSED TO BE HANGING AROUND THE WAITING ROOM . . .
THIS GENTLEMAN MAY NOT BE USED TO SUPERNATURAL--
SIR?
Skee hee hee
YAAAAAAAAARRGH
OH, WELL . . . GOOD THING HE DIDN'T COME ALL THE WAY IN . . .
". . . THE 'A' LIST WOULD'VE REALLY SENT HIM INTO SHOCK!
LISTEN!
A SCREAM!
MUSIC TO MY EARS!
IMAGINE MY SURPRISE TO GET AN INVITATION TO AN OPEN HOUSE AT MY LAWYERS' FIRM!
YEAH! WHEN I SAW THE ENVELOPE I THOUGHT IT WAS ANOTHER NOTICE FROM THEM THAT I WAS IN ARREARS
. . . I RATHER ENJOY BEING A POLTERGEIST-- IT'S ESPECIALLY FUN IN HOMES OF PEOPLE WHO ARE INTO FENG SHUI
OH, YEAH!
. . . SO WHEN HE SAID "I SEE DEAD PEOPLE," I SAID, "I HEAR ANNOYING KID" . . . !
DO I KNOW THEM? HELL--
HI! NAME'S HOWELL. DO YOU KNOW OUR HOSTS VERY WELL?

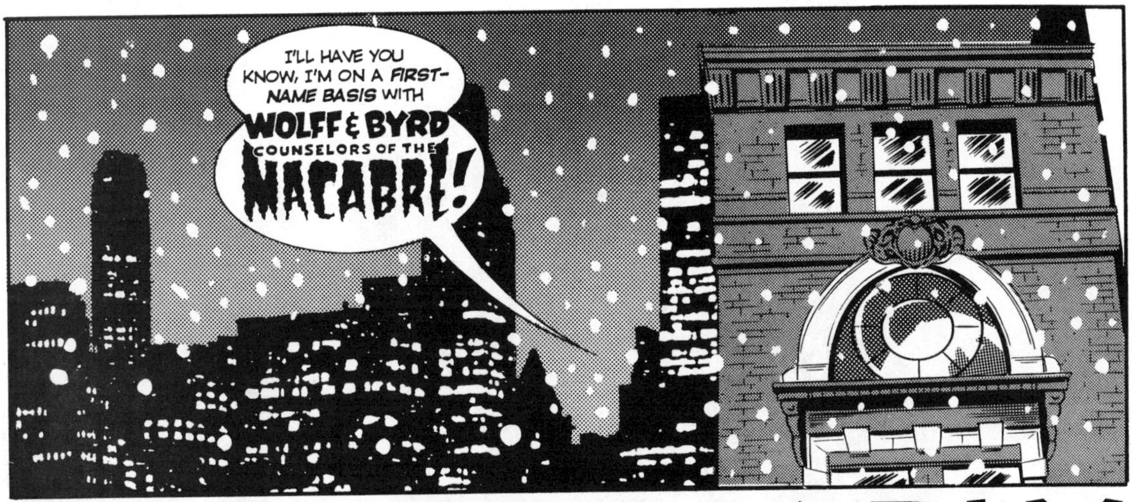
I'LL HAVE YOU KNOW, I'M ON A FIRST-NAME BASIS WITH
WOLFF & BYRD COUNSELORS OF THE MACABRE!

FASHIONABLY LATE

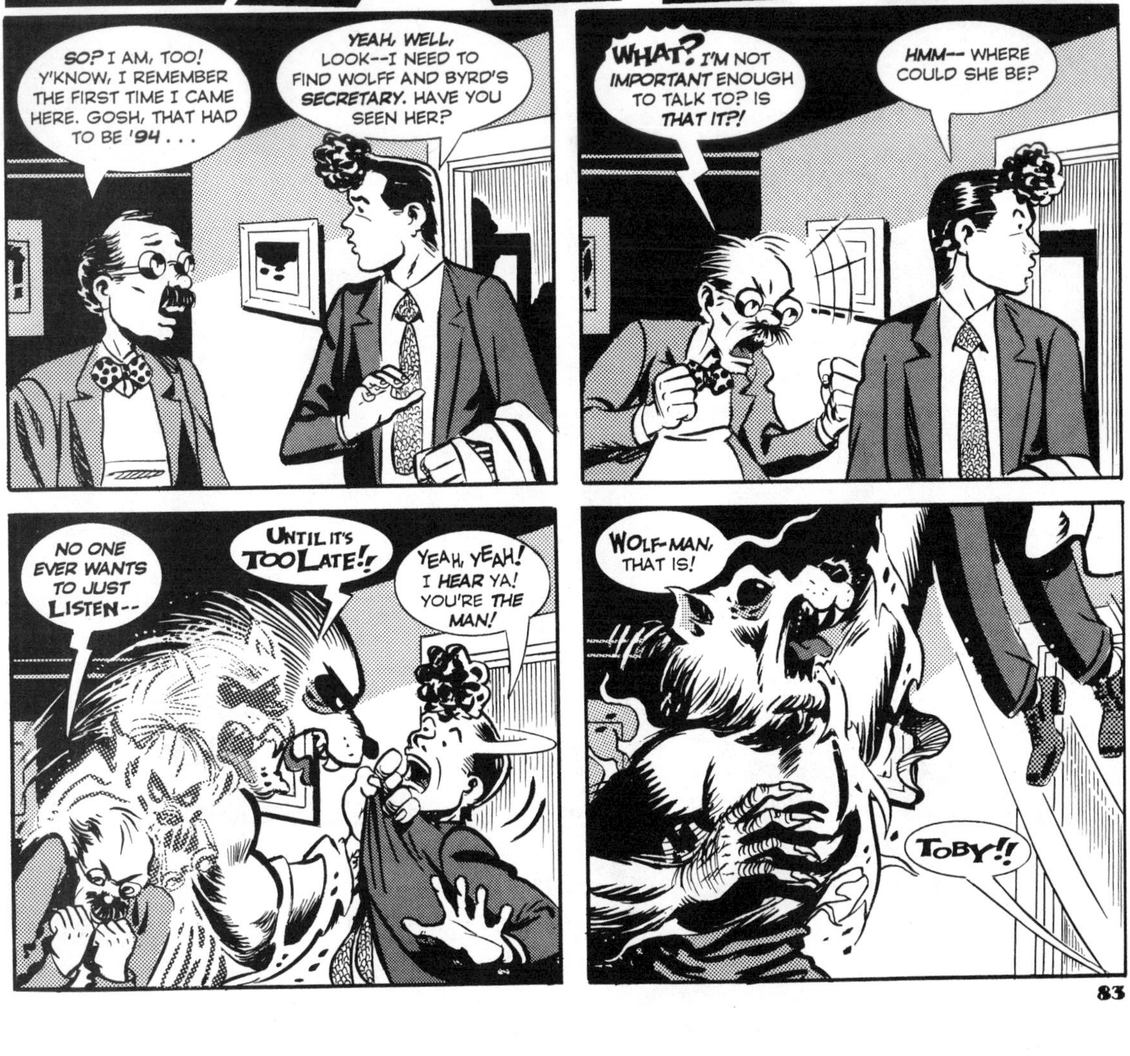
SO? I AM, TOO! Y'KNOW, I REMEMBER THE FIRST TIME I CAME HERE. GOSH, THAT HAD TO BE '94 . . .
YEAH, WELL, LOOK--I NEED TO FIND WOLFF AND BYRD'S SECRETARY. HAVE YOU SEEN HER?
WHAT? I'M NOT IMPORTANT ENOUGH TO TALK TO? IS THAT IT?!
HMM-- WHERE COULD SHE BE?
NO ONE EVER WANTS TO JUST LISTEN--
UNTIL IT'S TOO LATE!!
YEAH, YEAH! I HEAR YA! YOU'RE THE MAN!
WOLF-MAN, THAT IS!
TOBY!!

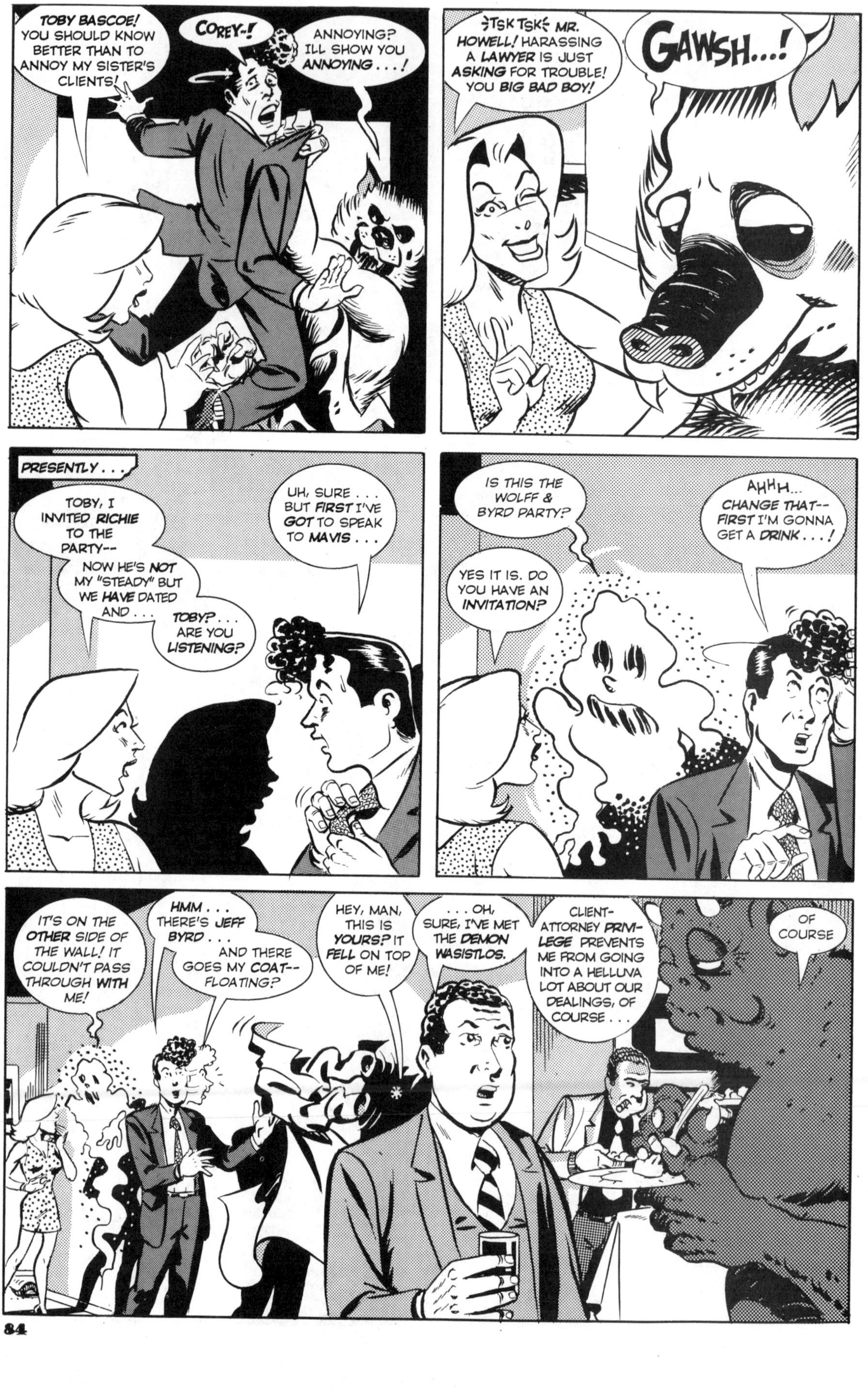
TOBY BASCOE! YOU SHOULD KNOW BETTER THAN TO ANNOY MY SISTER'S CLIENTS!
COREY--!
ANNOYING? I'LL SHOW YOU ANNOYING . . . !
TSK TSK MR. HOWELL! HARASSING A LAWYER IS JUST ASKING FOR TROUBLE! YOU BIG BAD BOY!
GAWSH...!
PRESENTLY . . .
TOBY, I INVITED RICHIE TO THE PARTY--
NOW HE'S NOT MY "STEADY" BUT WE HAVE DATED AND . . .
TOBY? . . . ARE YOU LISTENING?
UH, SURE . . . BUT FIRST I'VE GOT TO SPEAK TO MAVIS . . .
IS THIS THE WOLFF & BYRD PARTY?
YES IT IS. DO YOU HAVE AN INVITATION?
AHHH... CHANGE THAT-- FIRST I'M GONNA GET A DRINK . . . !
IT'S ON THE OTHER SIDE OF THE WALL! IT COULDN'T PASS THROUGH WITH ME!
HMM . . . THERE'S JEFF BYRD . . .
AND THERE GOES MY COAT-- FLOATING?
HEY, MAN, THIS IS YOURS? IT FELL ON TOP OF ME!
. . . OH, SURE, I'VE MET THE DEMON WASISTLOS.
CLIENT-ATTORNEY PRIVI-LEGE PREVENTS ME FROM GOING INTO A HELLUVA LOT ABOUT OUR DEALINGS, OF COURSE . . .
OF COURSE

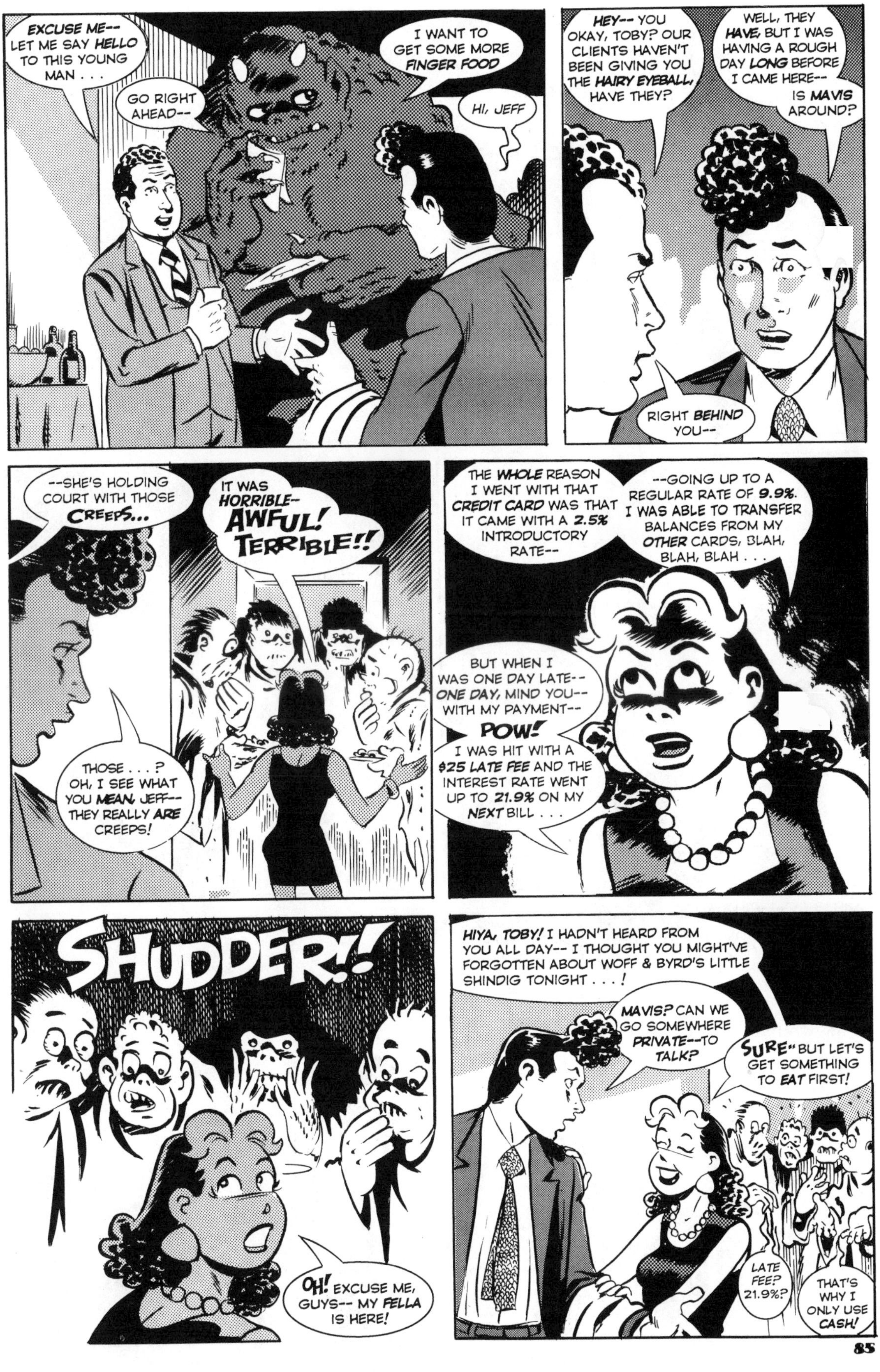
EXCUSE ME-- LET ME SAY HELLO TO THIS YOUNG MAN . . .
GO RIGHT AHEAD--
I WANT TO GET SOME MORE FINGER FOOD
HI, JEFF
HEY-- YOU OKAY, TOBY? OUR CLIENTS HAVEN'T BEEN GIVING YOU THE HAIRY EYEBALL, HAVE THEY?
WELL, THEY HAVE, BUT I WAS HAVING A ROUGH DAY LONG BEFORE I CAME HERE--
IS MAVIS AROUND?
RIGHT BEHIND YOU--
--SHE'S HOLDING COURT WITH THOSE CREEPS...
IT WAS HORRIBLE-- AWFUL! TERRIBLE!!
THOSE . . .? OH, I SEE WHAT YOU MEAN, JEFF-- THEY REALLY ARE CREEPS!
THE WHOLE REASON I WENT WITH THAT CREDIT CARD WAS THAT IT CAME WITH A 2.5% INTRODUCTORY RATE--
--GOING UP TO A REGULAR RATE OF 9.9%. I WAS ABLE TO TRANSFER BALANCES FROM MY OTHER CARDS, BLAH, BLAH, BLAH . . .
BUT WHEN I WAS ONE DAY LATE-- ONE DAY, MIND YOU-- WITH MY PAYMENT--
POW!
I WAS HIT WITH A $25 LATE FEE AND THE INTEREST RATE WENT UP TO 21.9% ON MY NEXT BILL . . .
SHUDDER!!
OH! EXCUSE ME, GUYS-- MY FELLA IS HERE!
HIYA, TOBY! I HADN'T HEARD FROM YOU ALL DAY-- I THOUGHT YOU MIGHT'VE FORGOTTEN ABOUT WOFF & BYRD'S LITTLE SHINDIG TONIGHT . . . !
MAVIS? CAN WE GO SOMEWHERE PRIVATE--TO TALK?
SURE" BUT LET'S GET SOMETHING TO EAT FIRST!
LATE FEE? 21.9%?
THAT'S WHY I ONLY USE CASH!

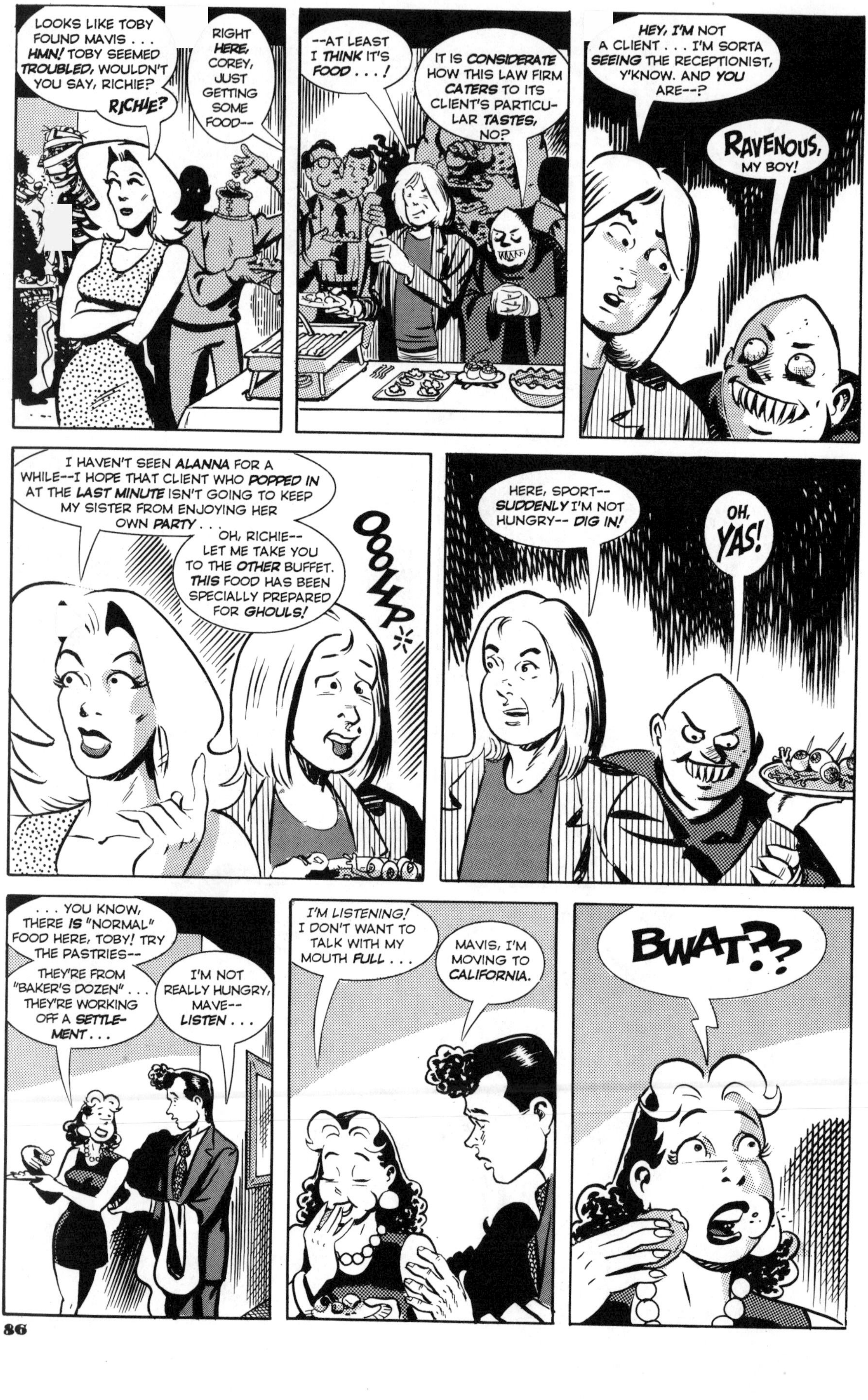

LOOKS LIKE TOBY FOUND MAVIS . . . HMN! TOBY SEEMED TROUBLED, WOULDN'T YOU SAY, RICHIE? RICHIE?
RIGHT HERE, COREY, JUST GETTING SOME FOOD--
--AT LEAST I THINK IT'S FOOD . . . !
IT IS CONSIDERATE HOW THIS LAW FIRM CATERS TO ITS CLIENT'S PARTICULAR TASTES, NO?
HEY, I'M NOT A CLIENT . . . I'M SORTA SEEING THE RECEPTIONIST, Y'KNOW. AND YOU ARE--?
RAVENOUS, MY BOY!
I HAVEN'T SEEN ALANNA FOR A WHILE--I HOPE THAT CLIENT WHO POPPED IN AT THE LAST MINUTE ISN'T GOING TO KEEP MY SISTER FROM ENJOYING HER OWN PARTY . . .
OH, RICHIE-- LET ME TAKE YOU TO THE OTHER BUFFET. THIS FOOD HAS BEEN SPECIALLY PREPARED FOR GHOULS!
OOOLLP
HERE, SPORT-- SUDDENLY I'M NOT HUNGRY-- DIG IN!
OH, YAS!
. . . YOU KNOW, THERE IS "NORMAL" FOOD HERE, TOBY! TRY THE PASTRIES--
THEY'RE FROM "BAKER'S DOZEN" . . . THEY'RE WORKING OFF A SETTLEMENT . . .
I'M NOT REALLY HUNGRY, MAVE-- LISTEN . . .
I'M LISTENING! I DON'T WANT TO TALK WITH MY MOUTH FULL . . .
MAVIS, I'M MOVING TO CALIFORNIA.
BWAT?!?

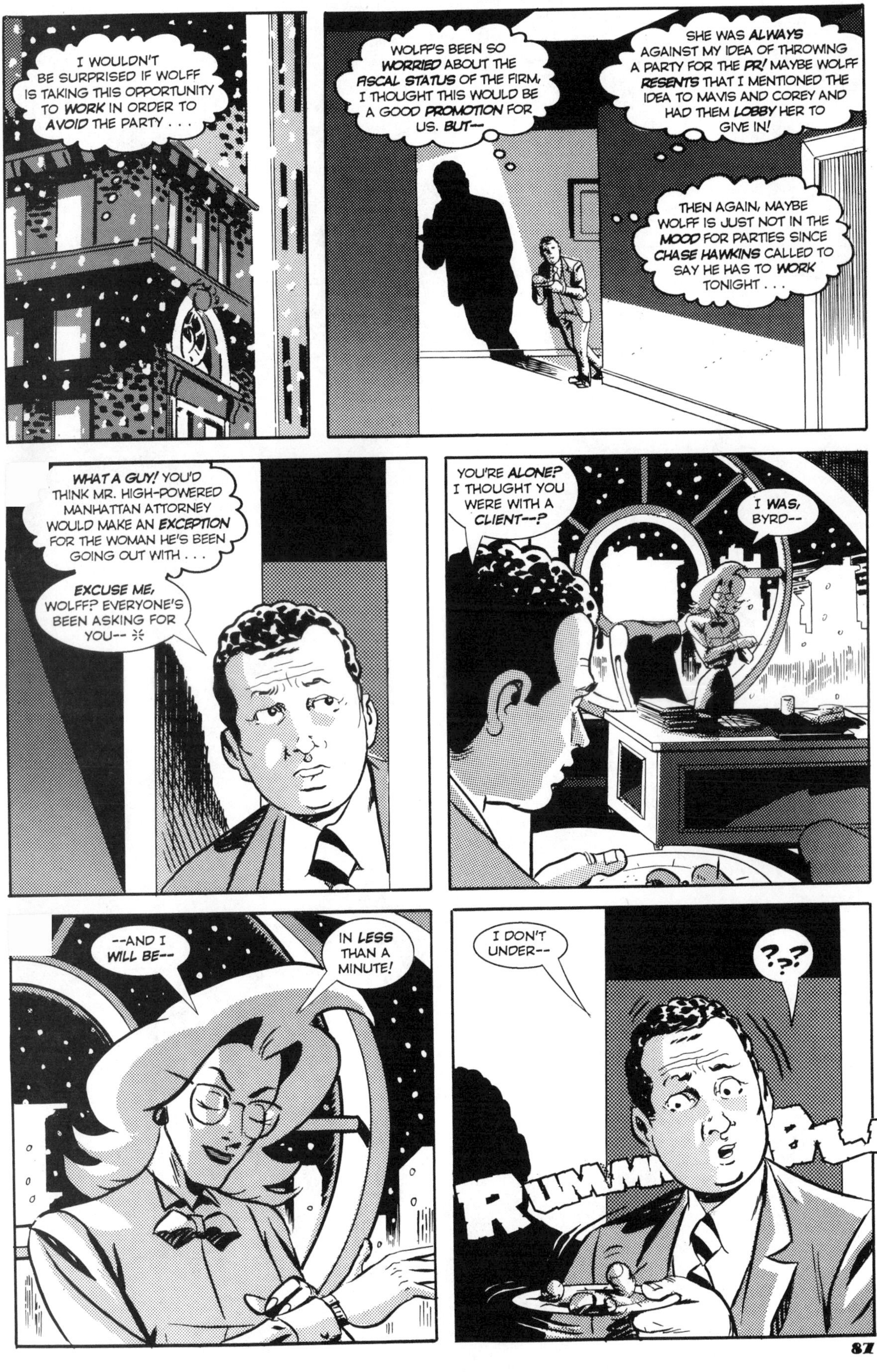
I WOULDN'T BE SURPRISED IF WOLFF IS TAKING THIS OPPORTUNITY TO WORK IN ORDER TO AVOID THE PARTY . . .
WOLFF'S BEEN SO WORRIED ABOUT THE FISCAL STATUS OF THE FIRM, I THOUGHT THIS WOULD BE A GOOD PROMOTION FOR US. BUT--
SHE WAS ALWAYS AGAINST MY IDEA OF THROWING A PARTY FOR THE PR! MAYBE WOLFF RESENTS THAT I MENTIONED THE IDEA TO MAVIS AND COREY AND HAD THEM LOBBY HER TO GIVE IN!
THEN AGAIN, MAYBE WOLFF IS JUST NOT IN THE MOOD FOR PARTIES SINCE CHASE HAWKINS CALLED TO SAY HE HAS TO WORK TONIGHT . . .
WHAT A GUY! YOU'D THINK MR. HIGH-POWERED MANHATTAN ATTORNEY WOULD MAKE AN EXCEPTION FOR THE WOMAN HE'S BEEN GOING OUT WITH . . .
EXCUSE ME, WOLFF? EVERYONE'S BEEN ASKING FOR YOU--
YOU'RE ALONE? I THOUGHT YOU WERE WITH A CLIENT--?
I WAS, BYRD--
--AND I WILL BE--
IN LESS THAN A MINUTE!
I DON'T UNDER--
???
RUMMBLE

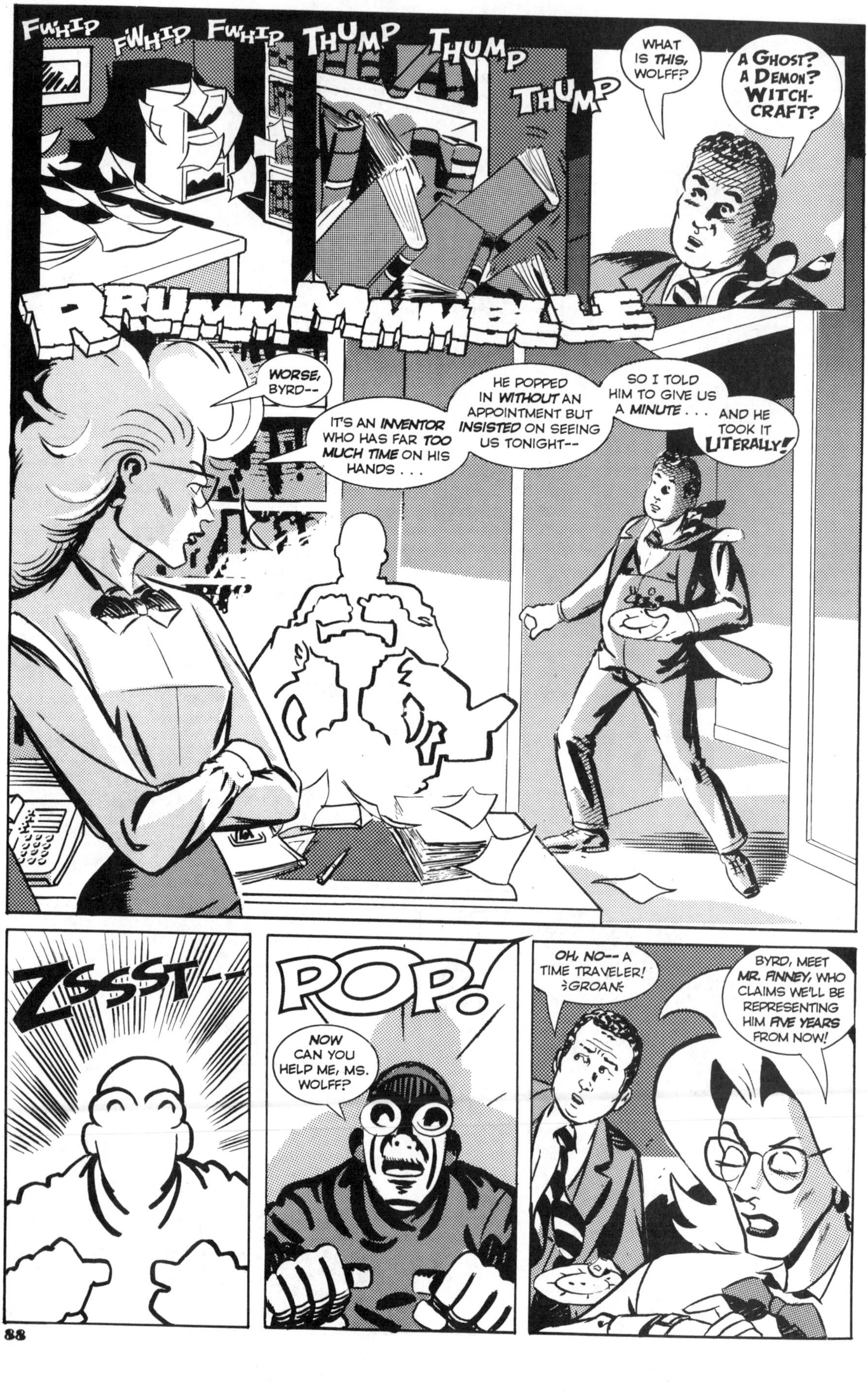
FWHIP FWHIP FWHIP THUMP THUMP THUMP
WHAT IS THIS, WOLFF?
A GHOST? A DEMON? WITCH-CRAFT?
RRUMMMMMMBLLE
WORSE, BYRD--
IT'S AN INVENTOR WHO HAS FAR TOO MUCH TIME ON HIS HANDS . . .
HE POPPED IN WITHOUT AN APPOINTMENT BUT INSISTED ON SEEING US TONIGHT--
SO I TOLD HIM TO GIVE US A MINUTE . . .
AND HE TOOK IT LITERALLY!
ZSSST--
POP!
NOW CAN YOU HELP ME, MS. WOLFF?
OH, NO-- A TIME TRAVELER! GROAN
BYRD, MEET MR. FINNEY, WHO CLAIMS WE'LL BE REPRESENTING HIM FIVE YEARS FROM NOW!

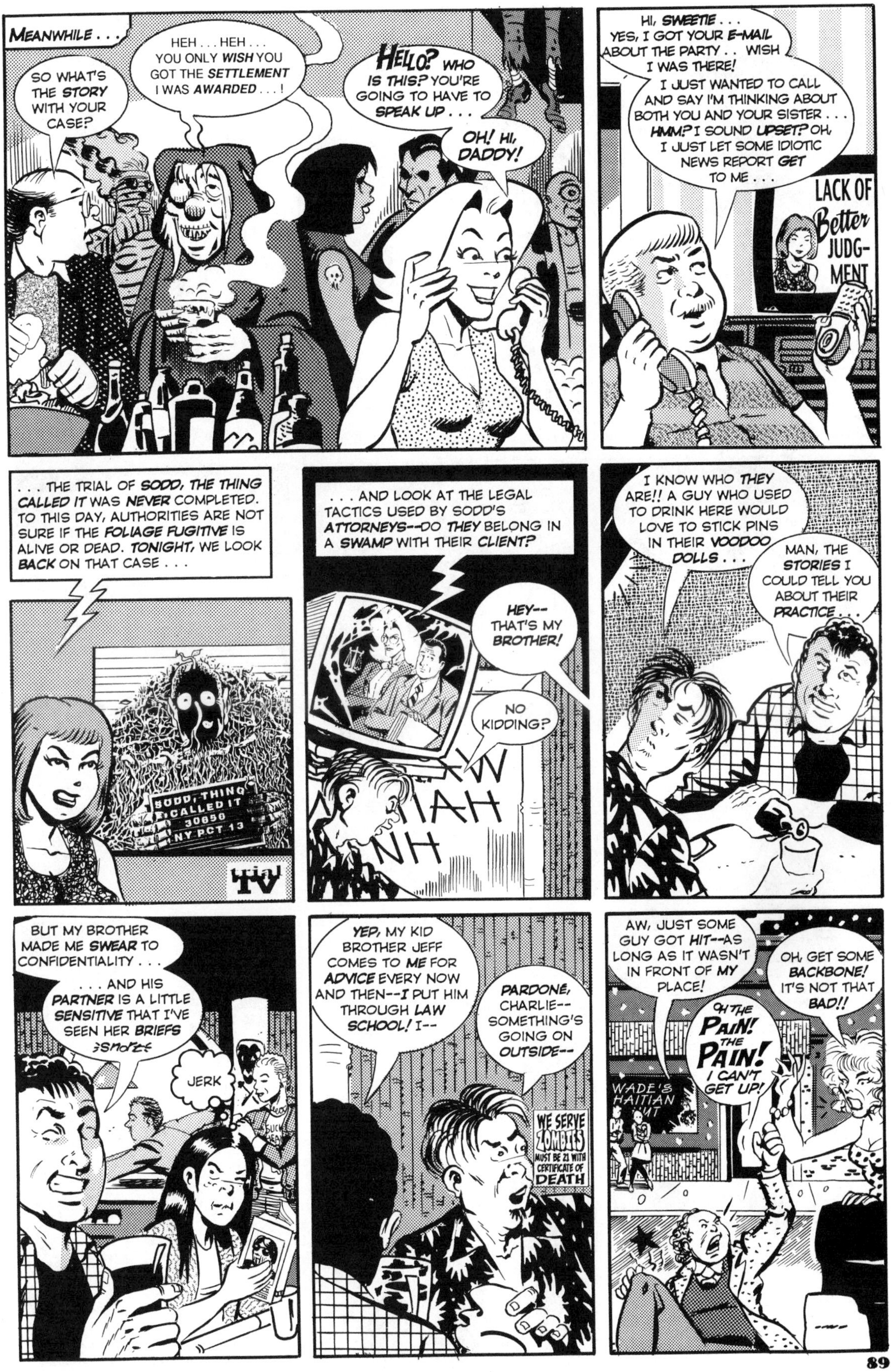

MEANWHILE . . .
SO WHAT'S THE STORY WITH YOUR CASE?
HEH . . . HEH . . . YOU ONLY WISH YOU GOT THE SETTLEMENT I WAS AWARDED . . . !
HELLO? WHO IS THIS? YOU'RE GOING TO HAVE TO SPEAK UP . . .
OH! HI, DADDY!
HI, SWEETIE . . . YES, I GOT YOUR E-MAIL ABOUT THE PARTY . . WISH I WAS THERE!
I JUST WANTED TO CALL AND SAY I'M THINKING ABOUT BOTH YOU AND YOUR SISTER . . . HMM? I SOUND UPSET? OH, I JUST LET SOME IDIOTIC NEWS REPORT GET TO ME . . .
LACK OF Better JUDG-MENT
. . . THE TRIAL OF SODD, THE THING CALLED IT WAS NEVER COMPLETED. TO THIS DAY, AUTHORITIES ARE NOT SURE IF THE FOLIAGE FUGITIVE IS ALIVE OR DEAD. TONIGHT, WE LOOK BACK ON THAT CASE . . .
SODD, THING CALLED IT 30850 NY PCT 13
trial TV
. . . AND LOOK AT THE LEGAL TACTICS USED BY SODD'S ATTORNEYS--DO THEY BELONG IN A SWAMP WITH THEIR CLIENT?
HEY-- THAT'S MY BROTHER!
NO KIDDING?
I KNOW WHO THEY ARE!! A GUY WHO USED TO DRINK HERE WOULD LOVE TO STICK PINS IN THEIR VOODOO DOLLS . . .
MAN, THE STORIES I COULD TELL YOU ABOUT THEIR PRACTICE . . .
BUT MY BROTHER MADE ME SWEAR TO CONFIDENTIALITY . . .
. . . AND HIS PARTNER IS A LITTLE SENSITIVE THAT I'VE SEEN HER BRIEFS
JERK
YEP, MY KID BROTHER JEFF COMES TO ME FOR ADVICE EVERY NOW AND THEN--I PUT HIM THROUGH LAW SCHOOL! I--
PARDONE, CHARLIE-- SOMETHING'S GOING ON OUTSIDE--
WE SERVE ZOMBIES MUST BE 21 WITH CERTIFICATE OF DEATH
AW, JUST SOME GUY GOT HIT--AS LONG AS IT WASN'T IN FRONT OF MY PLACE!
OH THE PAIN! THE PAIN! I CAN'T GET UP!
OH, GET SOME BACKBONE! IT'S NOT THAT BAD!!
WADE'S HAITIAN

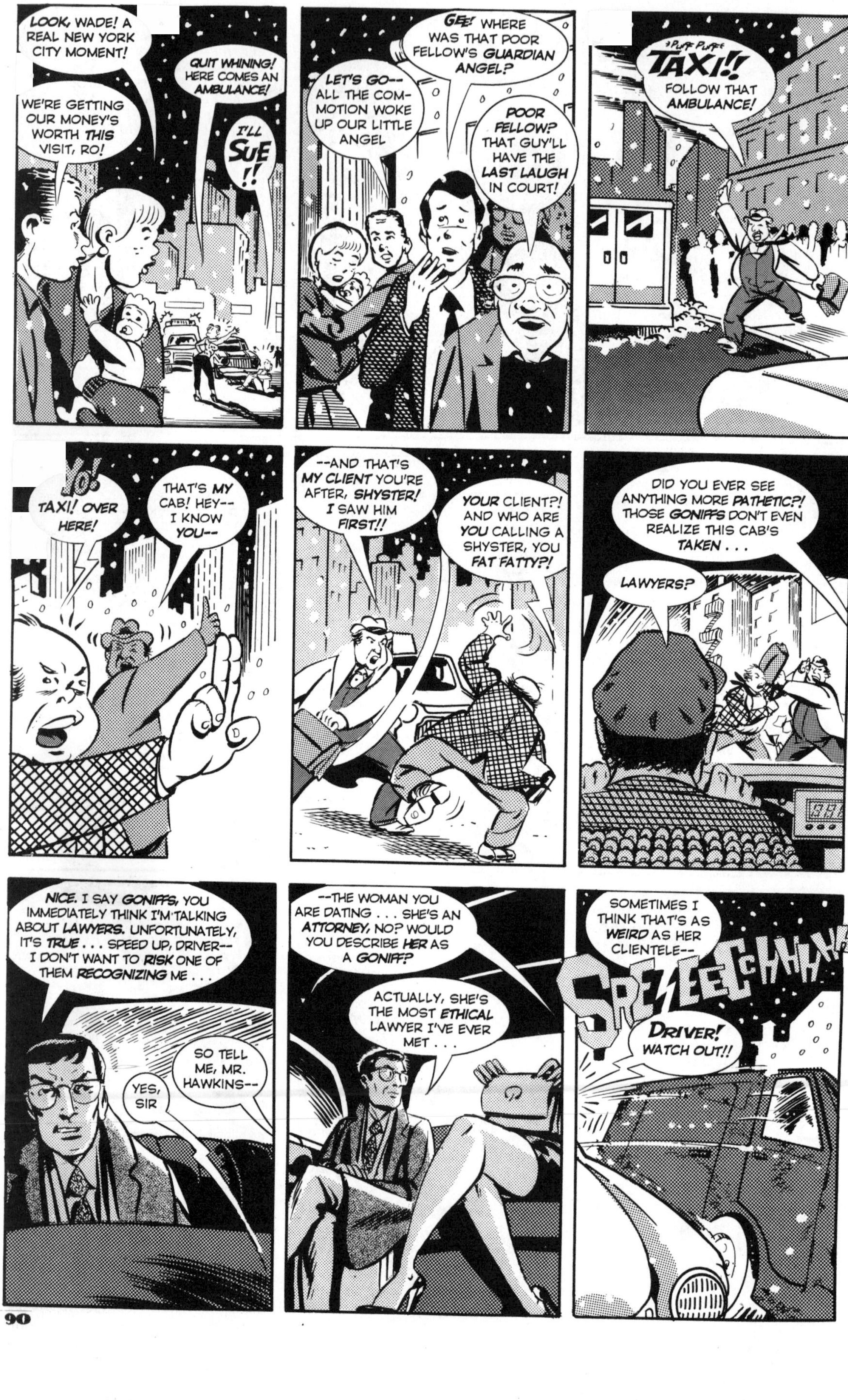
LOOK, WADE! A REAL NEW YORK CITY MOMENT!
WE'RE GETTING OUR MONEY'S WORTH THIS VISIT, RO!
QUIT WHINING! HERE COMES AN AMBULANCE!
I'LL SUE!!
GEE! WHERE WAS THAT POOR FELLOW'S GUARDIAN ANGEL?
LET'S GO-- ALL THE COMMOTION WOKE UP OUR LITTLE ANGEL
POOR FELLOW? THAT GUY'LL HAVE THE LAST LAUGH IN COURT!
PUFF PUFF
TAXI!! FOLLOW THAT AMBULANCE!
YO! TAXI! OVER HERE!
THAT'S MY CAB! HEY-- I KNOW YOU--
--AND THAT'S MY CLIENT YOU'RE AFTER, SHYSTER! I SAW HIM FIRST!!
YOUR CLIENT?! AND WHO ARE YOU CALLING A SHYSTER, YOU FAT FATTY?!
DID YOU EVER SEE ANYTHING MORE PATHETIC?! THOSE GONIFFS DON'T EVEN REALIZE THIS CAB'S TAKEN . . .
LAWYERS?
NICE. I SAY GONIFFS, YOU IMMEDIATELY THINK I'M TALKING ABOUT LAWYERS. UNFORTUNATELY, IT'S TRUE . . . SPEED UP, DRIVER-- I DON'T WANT TO RISK ONE OF THEM RECOGNIZING ME . . .
YES, SIR
SO TELL ME, MR. HAWKINS--
--THE WOMAN YOU ARE DATING . . . SHE'S AN ATTORNEY, NO? WOULD YOU DESCRIBE HER AS A GONIFF?
ACTUALLY, SHE'S THE MOST ETHICAL LAWYER I'VE EVER MET . . .
SOMETIMES I THINK THAT'S AS WEIRD AS HER CLIENTELE--
SREEECHHHHHH
DRIVER! WATCH OUT!!

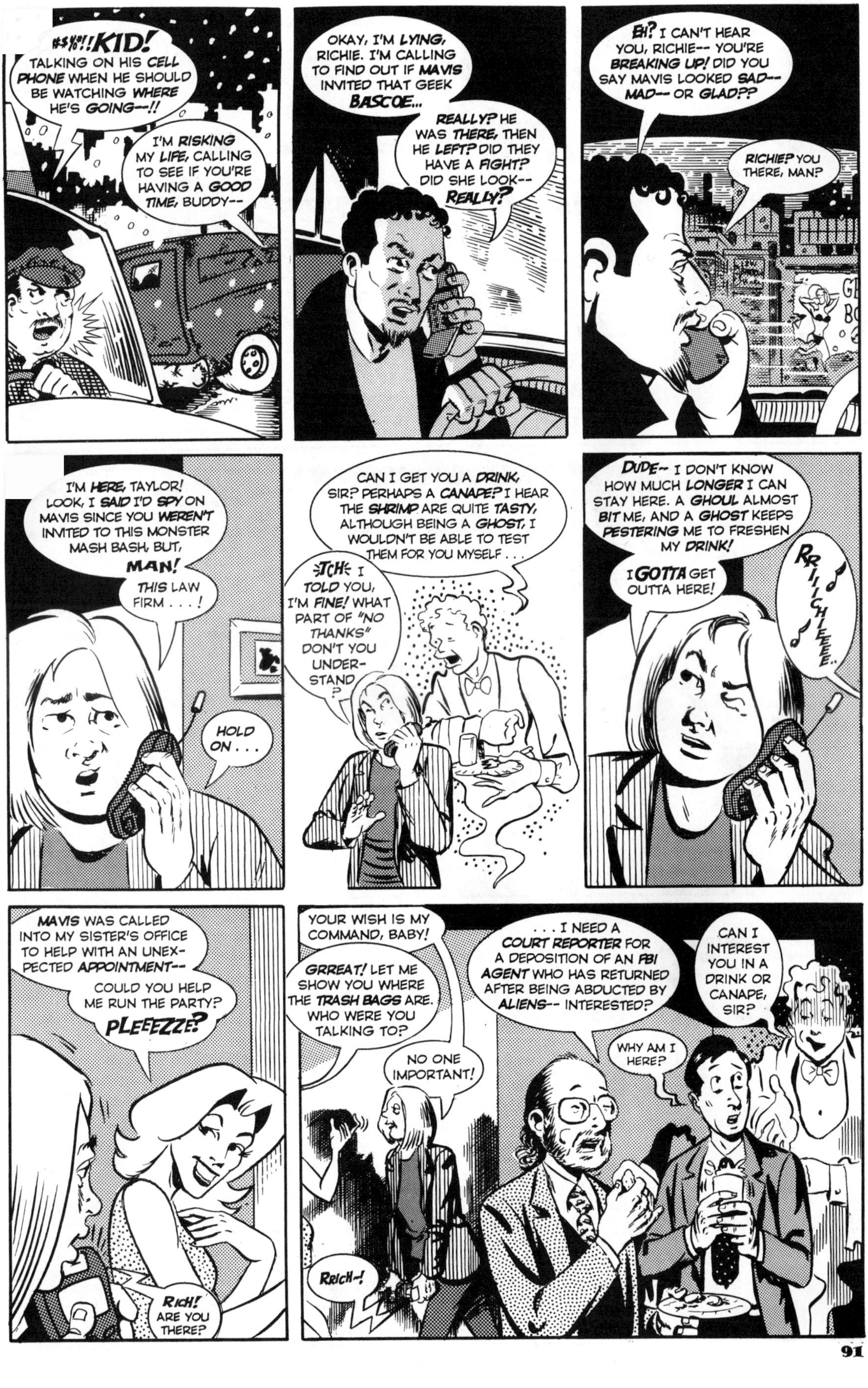
#$%*!! KID! TALKING ON HIS CELL PHONE WHEN HE SHOULD BE WATCHING WHERE HE'S GOING--!!
I'M RISKING MY LIFE, CALLING TO SEE IF YOU'RE HAVING A GOOD TIME, BUDDY--
OKAY, I'M LYING, RICHIE. I'M CALLING TO FIND OUT IF MAVIS INVITED THAT GEEK BASCOE...
REALLY? HE WAS THERE, THEN HE LEFT? DID THEY HAVE A FIGHT? DID SHE LOOK-- REALLY?
EH? I CAN'T HEAR YOU, RICHIE-- YOU'RE BREAKING UP! DID YOU SAY MAVIS LOOKED SAD-- MAD-- OR GLAD??
RICHIE? YOU THERE, MAN?
I'M HERE, TAYLOR! LOOK, I SAID I'D SPY ON MAVIS SINCE YOU WEREN'T INVITED TO THIS MONSTER MASH BASH, BUT, MAN!
THIS LAW FIRM . . . !
HOLD ON . . .
CAN I GET YOU A DRINK, SIR? PERHAPS A CANAPE? I HEAR THE SHRIMP ARE QUITE TASTY, ALTHOUGH BEING A GHOST, I WOULDN'T BE ABLE TO TEST THEM FOR YOU MYSELF . . .
TCH I TOLD YOU, I'M FINE! WHAT PART OF "NO THANKS" DON'T YOU UNDER-STAND?
DUDE-- I DON'T KNOW HOW MUCH LONGER I CAN STAY HERE. A GHOUL ALMOST BIT ME, AND A GHOST KEEPS PESTERING ME TO FRESHEN MY DRINK!
I GOTTA GET OUTTA HERE!
RRIIICHIEEEE..
MAVIS WAS CALLED INTO MY SISTER'S OFFICE TO HELP WITH AN UNEX-PECTED APPOINTMENT--
COULD YOU HELP ME RUN THE PARTY? PLEEEZZE?
RICH! ARE YOU THERE?
YOUR WISH IS MY COMMAND, BABY!
GRREAT! LET ME SHOW YOU WHERE THE TRASH BAGS ARE. WHO WERE YOU TALKING TO?
NO ONE IMPORTANT!
RRICH-!
. . . I NEED A COURT REPORTER FOR A DEPOSITION OF AN FBI AGENT WHO HAS RETURNED AFTER BEING ABDUCTED BY ALIENS-- INTERESTED?
WHY AM I HERE?
CAN I INTEREST YOU IN A DRINK OR CANAPE, SIR?

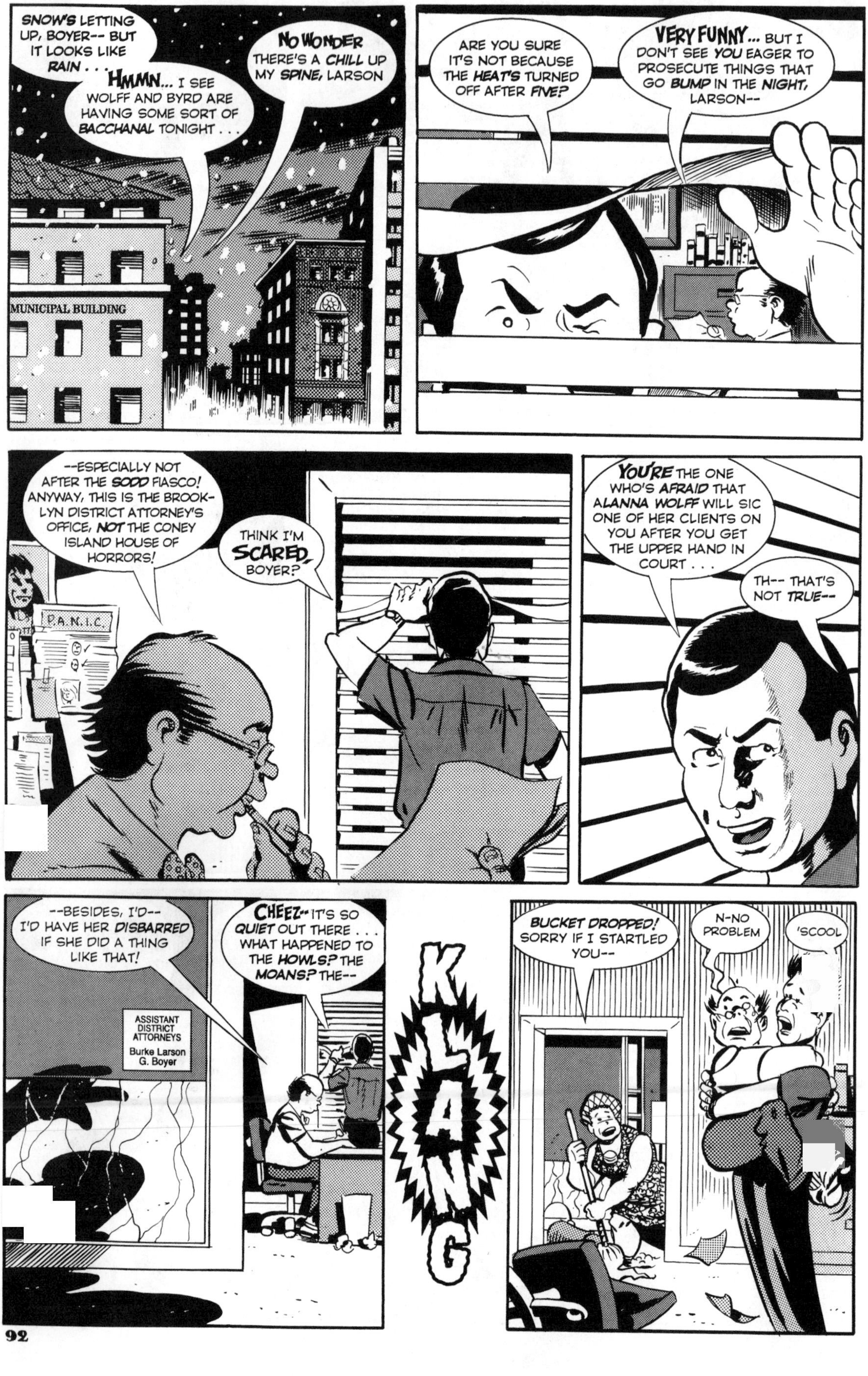

SNOW'S LETTING UP, BOYER-- BUT IT LOOKS LIKE RAIN . . .
HMMN... I SEE WOLFF AND BYRD ARE HAVING SOME SORT OF BACCHANAL TONIGHT . . .
NO WONDER THERE'S A CHILL UP MY SPINE, LARSON
MUNICIPAL BUILDING
ARE YOU SURE IT'S NOT BECAUSE THE HEAT'S TURNED OFF AFTER FIVE?
VERY FUNNY... BUT I DON'T SEE YOU EAGER TO PROSECUTE THINGS THAT GO BUMP IN THE NIGHT, LARSON--
--ESPECIALLY NOT AFTER THE SODD FIASCO! ANYWAY, THIS IS THE BROOKLYN DISTRICT ATTORNEY'S OFFICE, NOT THE CONEY ISLAND HOUSE OF HORRORS!
THINK I'M SCARED, BOYER?
P.A.N.I.C.
YOU'RE THE ONE WHO'S AFRAID THAT ALANNA WOLFF WILL SIC ONE OF HER CLIENTS ON YOU AFTER YOU GET THE UPPER HAND IN COURT . . .
TH-- THAT'S NOT TRUE--
--BESIDES, I'D-- I'D HAVE HER DISBARRED IF SHE DID A THING LIKE THAT!
ASSISTANT DISTRICT ATTORNEYS
Burke Larson
G. Boyer
CHEEZ-- IT'S SO QUIET OUT THERE . . . WHAT HAPPENED TO THE HOWLS? THE MOANS? THE--
KLANG
BUCKET DROPPED! SORRY IF I STARTLED YOU--
N-NO PROBLEM
'SCOOL

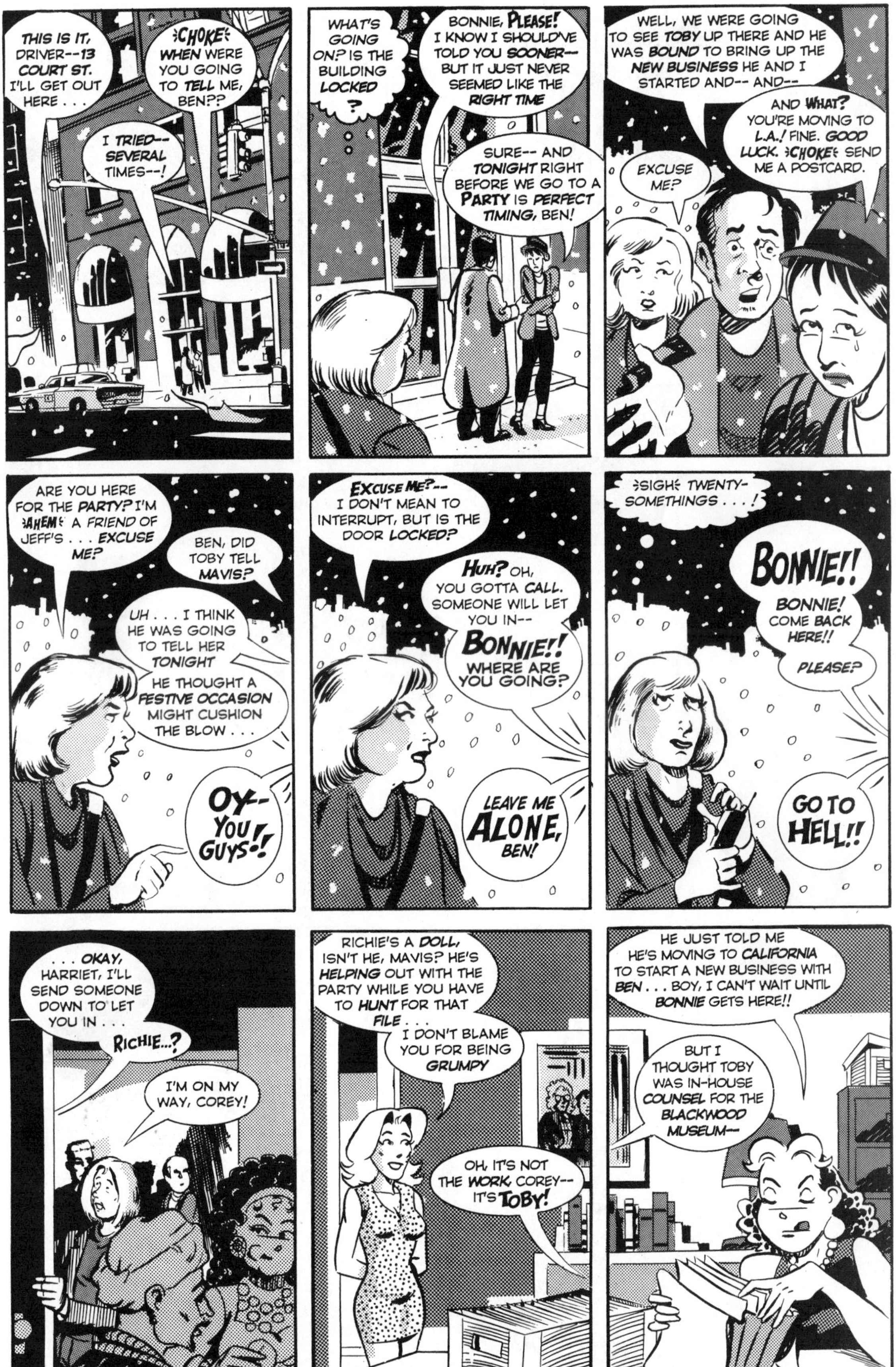
THIS IS IT, DRIVER--13 COURT ST. I'LL GET OUT HERE . . .
CHOKE WHEN WERE YOU GOING TO TELL ME, BEN??
I TRIED-- SEVERAL TIMES--!
WHAT'S GOING ON? IS THE BUILDING LOCKED?
BONNIE, PLEASE! I KNOW I SHOULD'VE TOLD YOU SOONER-- BUT IT JUST NEVER SEEMED LIKE THE RIGHT TIME
SURE-- AND TONIGHT RIGHT BEFORE WE GO TO A PARTY IS PERFECT TIMING, BEN!
WELL, WE WERE GOING TO SEE TOBY UP THERE AND HE WAS BOUND TO BRING UP THE NEW BUSINESS HE AND I STARTED AND-- AND--
AND WHAT? YOU'RE MOVING TO L.A.! FINE. GOOD LUCK. *CHOKE* SEND ME A POSTCARD.
EXCUSE ME?
ARE YOU HERE FOR THE PARTY? I'M *AHEM* A FRIEND OF JEFF'S . . . EXCUSE ME?
BEN, DID TOBY TELL MAVIS?
UH . . . I THINK HE WAS GOING TO TELL HER TONIGHT
HE THOUGHT A FESTIVE OCCASION MIGHT CUSHION THE BLOW . . .
OY-YOU GUYS-!!
EXCUSE ME?-- I DON'T MEAN TO INTERRUPT, BUT IS THE DOOR LOCKED?
HUH? OH, YOU GOTTA CALL. SOMEONE WILL LET YOU IN--
BONNIE!! WHERE ARE YOU GOING?
LEAVE ME ALONE, BEN!
SIGH TWENTY-SOMETHINGS . . . !
BONNIE!!
BONNIE! COME BACK HERE!!
PLEASE?
GO TO HELL!!
. . . OKAY, HARRIET, I'LL SEND SOMEONE DOWN TO LET YOU IN . . .
RICHIE...?
I'M ON MY WAY, COREY!
RICHIE'S A DOLL, ISN'T HE, MAVIS? HE'S HELPING OUT WITH THE PARTY WHILE YOU HAVE TO HUNT FOR THAT FILE . . .
I DON'T BLAME YOU FOR BEING GRUMPY
OH, IT'S NOT THE WORK, COREY-- IT'S TOBY!
HE JUST TOLD ME HE'S MOVING TO CALIFORNIA TO START A NEW BUSINESS WITH BEN . . . BOY, I CAN'T WAIT UNTIL BONNIE GETS HERE!!
BUT I THOUGHT TOBY WAS IN-HOUSE COUNSEL FOR THE BLACKWOOD MUSEUM--

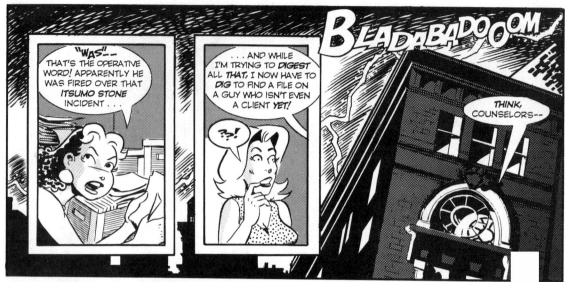

"WAS"-- THAT'S THE OPERATIVE WORD! APPARENTLY HE WAS FIRED OVER THAT ITSUMO STONE INCIDENT . . .

. . . AND WHILE I'M TRYING TO DIGEST ALL THAT, I NOW HAVE TO DIG TO FIND A FILE ON A GUY WHO ISN'T EVEN A CLIENT YET!

??!

BLADABADOOOM!

THINK, COUNSELORS--

ALTHOUGH I COME FROM YOUR FUTURE . . .

WE'VE MET SEVERAL TIMES IN THE PAST . . .

AND NOW I NEED TO KNOW WHAT IS HAPPENING WITH MY CASE IN THE PRESENT!

ARE YOU SURE MY NAME DOESN'T RING A BELL?

WELL?

I'M WITH YOU, WOLFF--

I'VE NEVER MET HIM BEFORE IN MY LIFE!

VLADABADOOMM!

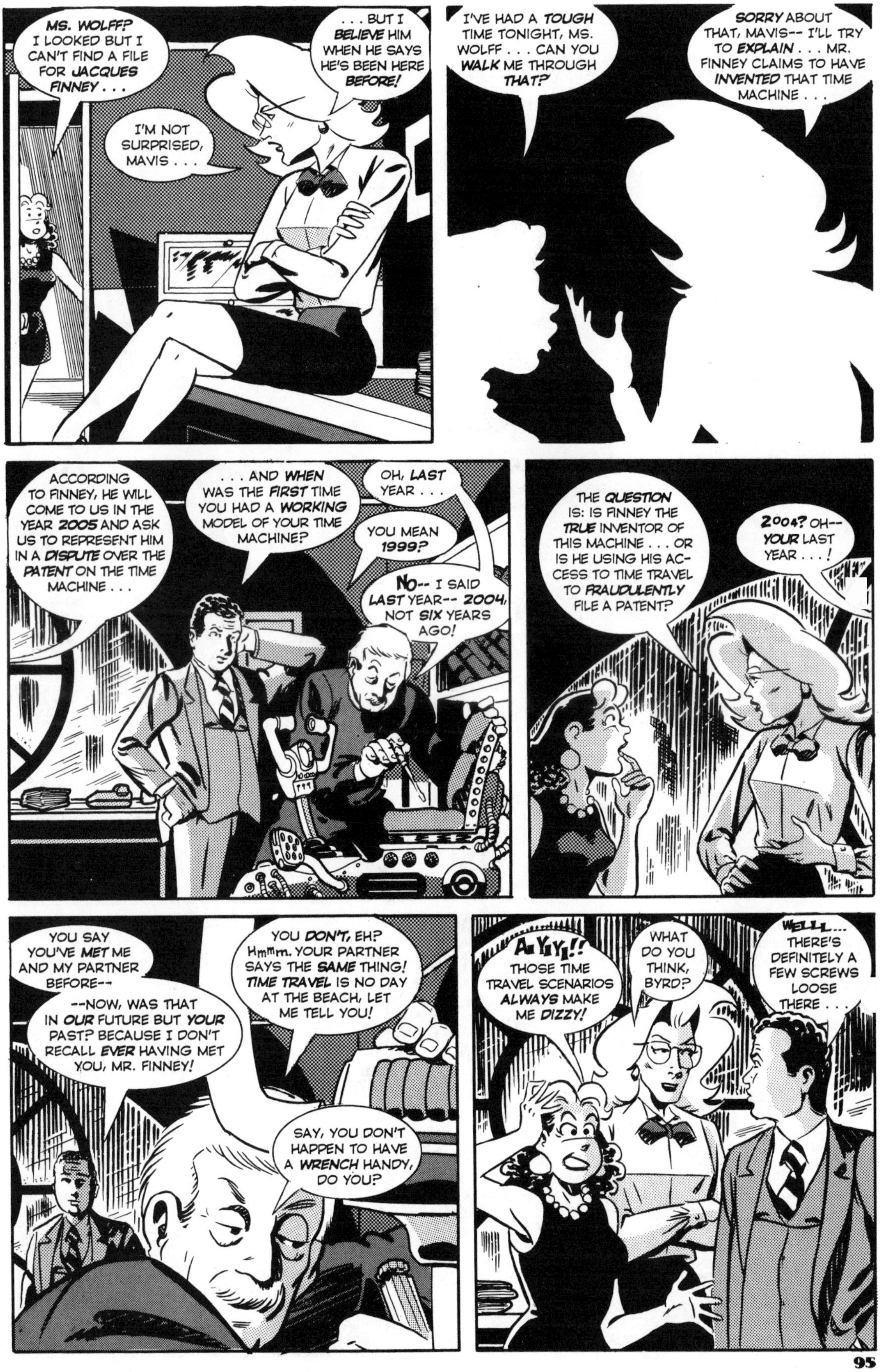
MS. WOLFF? I LOOKED BUT I CAN'T FIND A FILE FOR JACQUES FINNEY . . .
I'M NOT SURPRISED, MAVIS . . .
. . . BUT I BELIEVE HIM WHEN HE SAYS HE'S BEEN HERE BEFORE!
I'VE HAD A TOUGH TIME TONIGHT, MS. WOLFF . . . CAN YOU WALK ME THROUGH THAT?
SORRY ABOUT THAT, MAVIS-- I'LL TRY TO EXPLAIN . . . MR. FINNEY CLAIMS TO HAVE INVENTED THAT TIME MACHINE . . .
ACCORDING TO FINNEY, HE WILL COME TO US IN THE YEAR 2005 AND ASK US TO REPRESENT HIM IN A DISPUTE OVER THE PATENT ON THE TIME MACHINE . . .
. . . AND WHEN WAS THE FIRST TIME YOU HAD A WORKING MODEL OF YOUR TIME MACHINE?
OH, LAST YEAR . . .
YOU MEAN 1999?
NO-- I SAID LAST YEAR-- 2004, NOT SIX YEARS AGO!
THE QUESTION IS: IS FINNEY THE TRUE INVENTOR OF THIS MACHINE . . . OR IS HE USING HIS ACCESS TO TIME TRAVEL TO FRAUDULENTLY FILE A PATENT?
2004? OH-- YOUR LAST YEAR . . . !
YOU SAY YOU'VE MET ME AND MY PARTNER BEFORE--
--NOW, WAS THAT IN OUR FUTURE BUT YOUR PAST? BECAUSE I DON'T RECALL EVER HAVING MET YOU, MR. FINNEY!
YOU DON'T, EH? Hmmm. YOUR PARTNER SAYS THE SAME THING! TIME TRAVEL IS NO DAY AT THE BEACH, LET ME TELL YOU!
SAY, YOU DON'T HAPPEN TO HAVE A WRENCH HANDY, DO YOU?
AYIYI!! THOSE TIME TRAVEL SCENARIOS ALWAYS MAKE ME DIZZY!
WHAT DO YOU THINK, BYRD?
WELL... THERE'S DEFINITELY A FEW SCREWS LOOSE THERE . . .

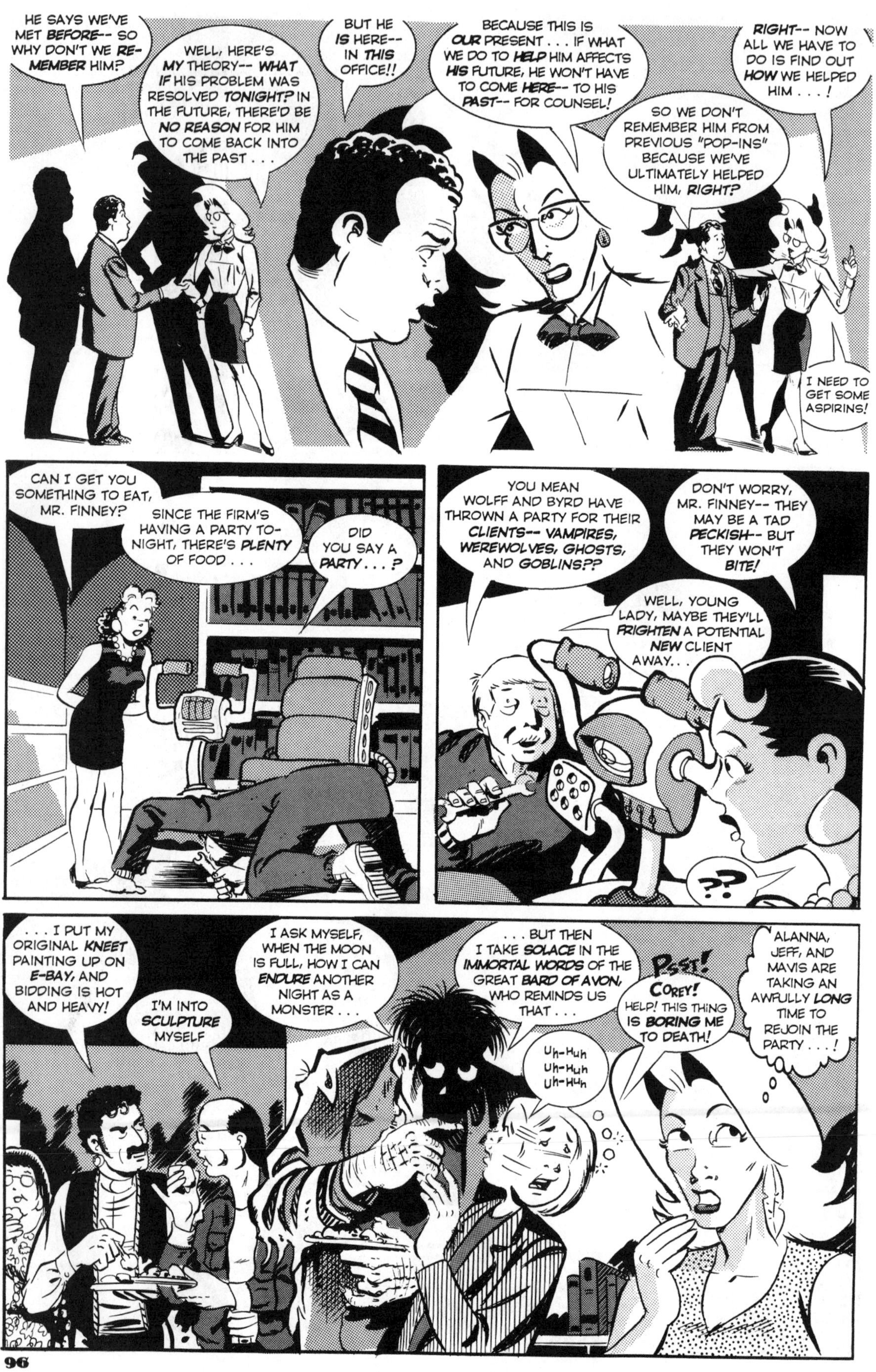
HE SAYS WE'VE MET BEFORE-- SO WHY DON'T WE REMEMBER HIM?
WELL, HERE'S MY THEORY-- WHAT IF HIS PROBLEM WAS RESOLVED TONIGHT? IN THE FUTURE, THERE'D BE NO REASON FOR HIM TO COME BACK INTO THE PAST . . .
BUT HE IS HERE-- IN THIS OFFICE!!
BECAUSE THIS IS OUR PRESENT . . . IF WHAT WE DO TO HELP HIM AFFECTS HIS FUTURE, HE WON'T HAVE TO COME HERE-- TO HIS PAST-- FOR COUNSEL!
SO WE DON'T REMEMBER HIM FROM PREVIOUS "POP-INS" BECAUSE WE'VE ULTIMATELY HELPED HIM, RIGHT?
RIGHT-- NOW ALL WE HAVE TO DO IS FIND OUT HOW WE HELPED HIM . . . !
I NEED TO GET SOME ASPIRINS!
CAN I GET YOU SOMETHING TO EAT, MR. FINNEY?
SINCE THE FIRM'S HAVING A PARTY TONIGHT, THERE'S PLENTY OF FOOD . . .
DID YOU SAY A PARTY . . . ?
YOU MEAN WOLFF AND BYRD HAVE THROWN A PARTY FOR THEIR CLIENTS-- VAMPIRES, WEREWOLVES, GHOSTS, AND GOBLINS??
DON'T WORRY, MR. FINNEY-- THEY MAY BE A TAD PECKISH-- BUT THEY WON'T BITE!
WELL, YOUNG LADY, MAYBE THEY'LL FRIGHTEN A POTENTIAL NEW CLIENT AWAY. . .
??
. . . I PUT MY ORIGINAL KNEET PAINTING UP ON E-BAY, AND BIDDING IS HOT AND HEAVY!
I'M INTO SCULPTURE MYSELF
I ASK MYSELF, WHEN THE MOON IS FULL, HOW I CAN ENDURE ANOTHER NIGHT AS A MONSTER . . .
. . . BUT THEN I TAKE SOLACE IN THE IMMORTAL WORDS OF THE GREAT BARD OF AVON, WHO REMINDS US THAT . . .
Uh-Huh Uh-Huh Uh-Huh
PSST! COREY! HELP! THIS THING IS BORING ME TO DEATH!
ALANNA, JEFF, AND MAVIS ARE TAKING AN AWFULLY LONG TIME TO REJOIN THE PARTY . . . !

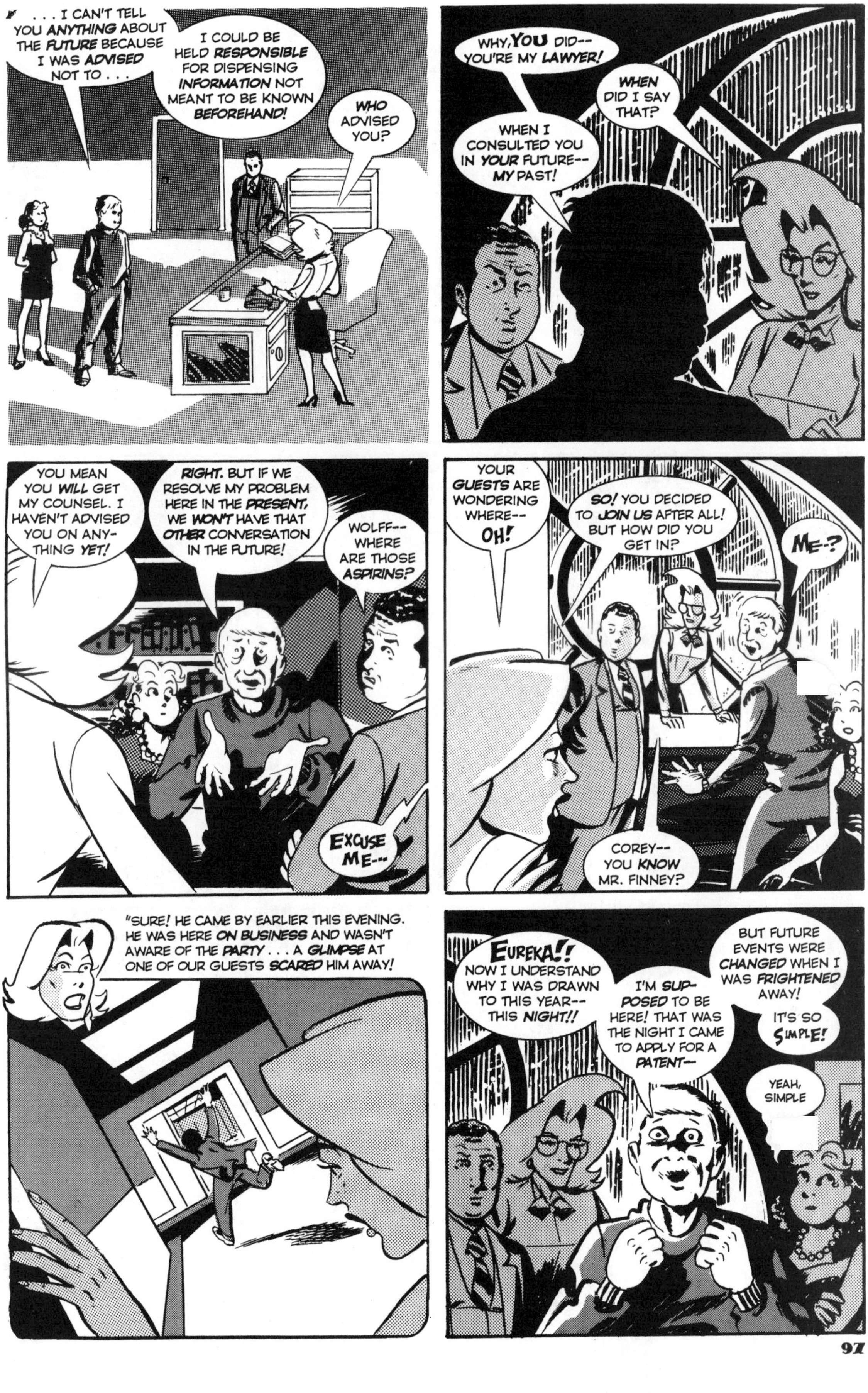
. . . I CAN'T TELL YOU ANYTHING ABOUT THE FUTURE BECAUSE I WAS ADVISED NOT TO . . .
I COULD BE HELD RESPONSIBLE FOR DISPENSING INFORMATION NOT MEANT TO BE KNOWN BEFOREHAND!
WHO ADVISED YOU?
WHY, YOU DID-- YOU'RE MY LAWYER!
WHEN DID I SAY THAT?
WHEN I CONSULTED YOU IN YOUR FUTURE-- MY PAST!
YOU MEAN YOU WILL GET MY COUNSEL. I HAVEN'T ADVISED YOU ON ANY-THING YET!
RIGHT. BUT IF WE RESOLVE MY PROBLEM HERE IN THE PRESENT, WE WON'T HAVE THAT OTHER CONVERSATION IN THE FUTURE!
WOLFF-- WHERE ARE THOSE ASPIRINS?
EXCUSE ME--
YOUR GUESTS ARE WONDERING WHERE-- OH!
SO! YOU DECIDED TO JOIN US AFTER ALL! BUT HOW DID YOU GET IN?
ME-?
COREY-- YOU KNOW MR. FINNEY?
"SURE! HE CAME BY EARLIER THIS EVENING. HE WAS HERE ON BUSINESS AND WASN'T AWARE OF THE PARTY . . . A GLIMPSE AT ONE OF OUR GUESTS SCARED HIM AWAY!
EUREKA!! NOW I UNDERSTAND WHY I WAS DRAWN TO THIS YEAR-- THIS NIGHT!!
I'M SUP-POSED TO BE HERE! THAT WAS THE NIGHT I CAME TO APPLY FOR A PATENT--
BUT FUTURE EVENTS WERE CHANGED WHEN I WAS FRIGHTENED AWAY!
IT'S SO SIMPLE!
YEAH, SIMPLE

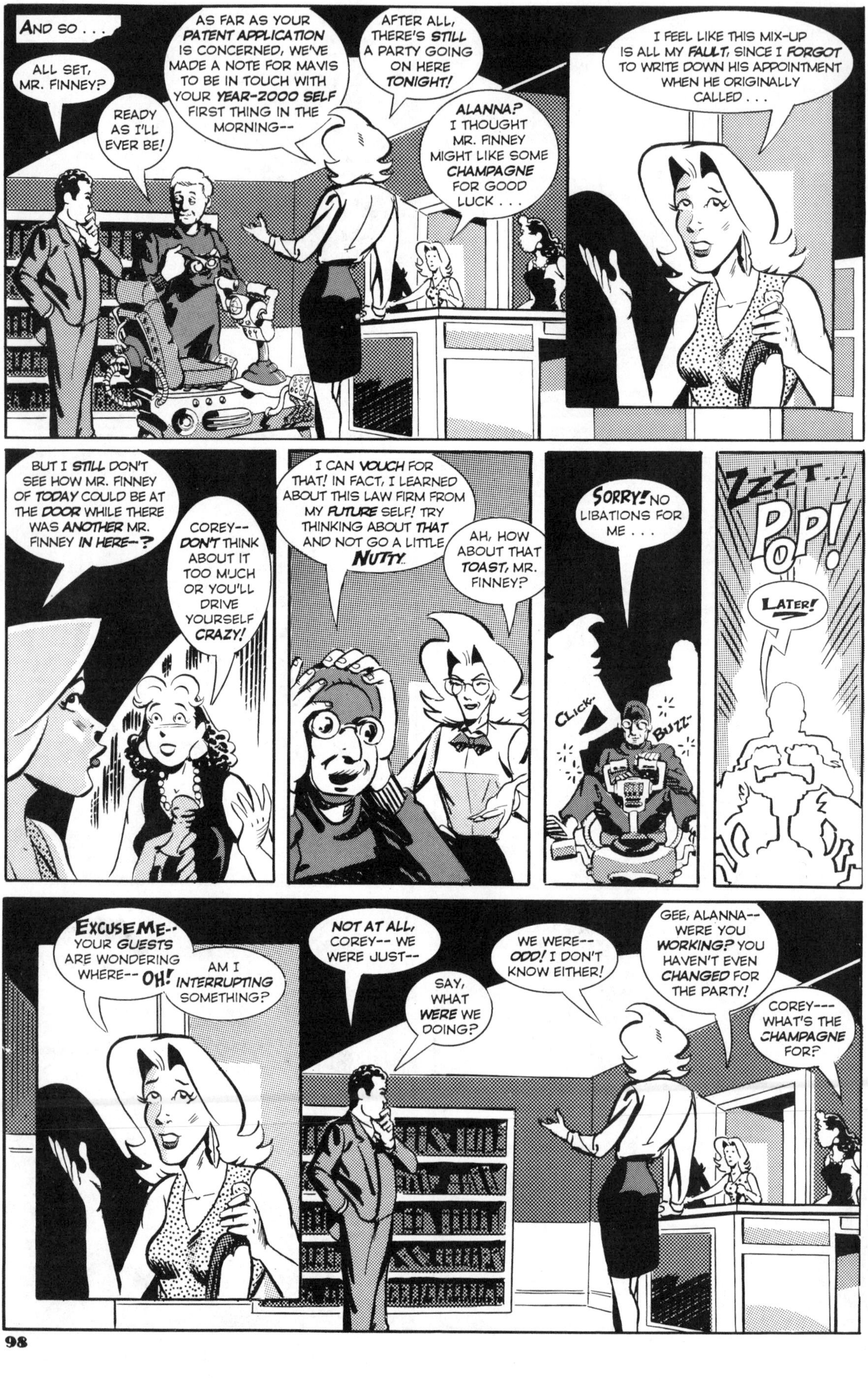
AND SO . . .
ALL SET, MR. FINNEY?
READY AS I'LL EVER BE!
AS FAR AS YOUR PATENT APPLICATION IS CONCERNED, WE'VE MADE A NOTE FOR MAVIS TO BE IN TOUCH WITH YOUR YEAR-2000 SELF FIRST THING IN THE MORNING--
AFTER ALL, THERE'S STILL A PARTY GOING ON HERE TONIGHT!
ALANNA? I THOUGHT MR. FINNEY MIGHT LIKE SOME CHAMPAGNE FOR GOOD LUCK . . .
I FEEL LIKE THIS MIX-UP IS ALL MY FAULT, SINCE I FORGOT TO WRITE DOWN HIS APPOINTMENT WHEN HE ORIGINALLY CALLED . . .
BUT I STILL DON'T SEE HOW MR. FINNEY OF TODAY COULD BE AT THE DOOR WHILE THERE WAS ANOTHER MR. FINNEY IN HERE--?
COREY-- DON'T THINK ABOUT IT TOO MUCH OR YOU'LL DRIVE YOURSELF CRAZY!
I CAN VOUCH FOR THAT! IN FACT, I LEARNED ABOUT THIS LAW FIRM FROM MY FUTURE SELF! TRY THINKING ABOUT THAT AND NOT GO A LITTLE NUTTY...
AH, HOW ABOUT THAT TOAST, MR. FINNEY?
SORRY! NO LIBATIONS FOR ME . . .
CLICK..
BUZZ..
ZZZT...
POP!
LATER!
EXCUSE ME-- YOUR GUESTS ARE WONDERING WHERE-- OH!
AM I INTERRUPTING SOMETHING?
NOT AT ALL, COREY-- WE WERE JUST--
SAY, WHAT WERE WE DOING?
WE WERE-- ODD! I DON'T KNOW EITHER!
GEE, ALANNA-- WERE YOU WORKING? YOU HAVEN'T EVEN CHANGED FOR THE PARTY!
COREY--- WHAT'S THE CHAMPAGNE FOR?

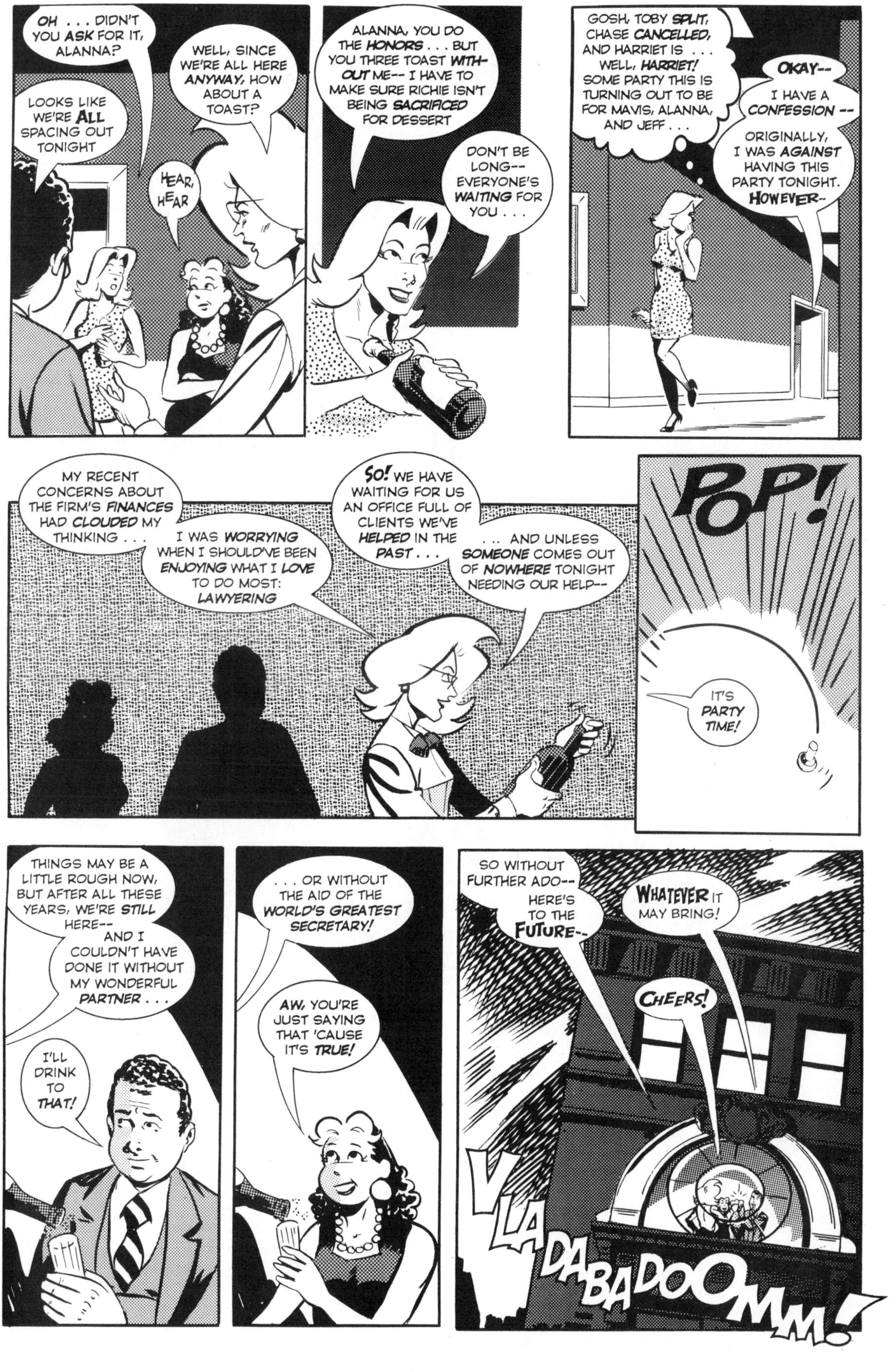
OH . . . DIDN'T YOU ASK FOR IT, ALANNA?
LOOKS LIKE WE'RE ALL SPACING OUT TONIGHT
WELL, SINCE WE'RE ALL HERE ANYWAY, HOW ABOUT A TOAST?
HEAR, HEAR
ALANNA, YOU DO THE HONORS . . . BUT YOU THREE TOAST WITH-OUT ME-- I HAVE TO MAKE SURE RICHIE ISN'T BEING SACRIFICED FOR DESSERT
DON'T BE LONG-- EVERYONE'S WAITING FOR YOU . . .
GOSH, TOBY SPLIT, CHASE CANCELLED, AND HARRIET IS . . . WELL, HARRIET! SOME PARTY THIS IS TURNING OUT TO BE FOR MAVIS, ALANNA, AND JEFF . . .
OKAY--
I HAVE A CONFESSION --
ORIGINALLY, I WAS AGAINST HAVING THIS PARTY TONIGHT. HOWEVER--
MY RECENT CONCERNS ABOUT THE FIRM'S FINANCES HAD CLOUDED MY THINKING . . .
I WAS WORRYING WHEN I SHOULD'VE BEEN ENJOYING WHAT I LOVE TO DO MOST: LAWYERING
SO! WE HAVE WAITING FOR US AN OFFICE FULL OF CLIENTS WE'VE HELPED IN THE PAST . . .
. . . AND UNLESS SOMEONE COMES OUT OF NOWHERE TONIGHT NEEDING OUR HELP--
POP!
IT'S PARTY TIME!
THINGS MAY BE A LITTLE ROUGH NOW, BUT AFTER ALL THESE YEARS, WE'RE STILL HERE--
AND I COULDN'T HAVE DONE IT WITHOUT MY WONDERFUL PARTNER . . .
I'LL DRINK TO THAT!
. . . OR WITHOUT THE AID OF THE WORLD'S GREATEST SECRETARY!
AW, YOU'RE JUST SAYING THAT 'CAUSE IT'S TRUE!
SO WITHOUT FURTHER ADO--
HERE'S TO THE FUTURE--
WHATEVER IT MAY BRING!
CHEERS!
VLADABADOOMM!

Black Market Souls

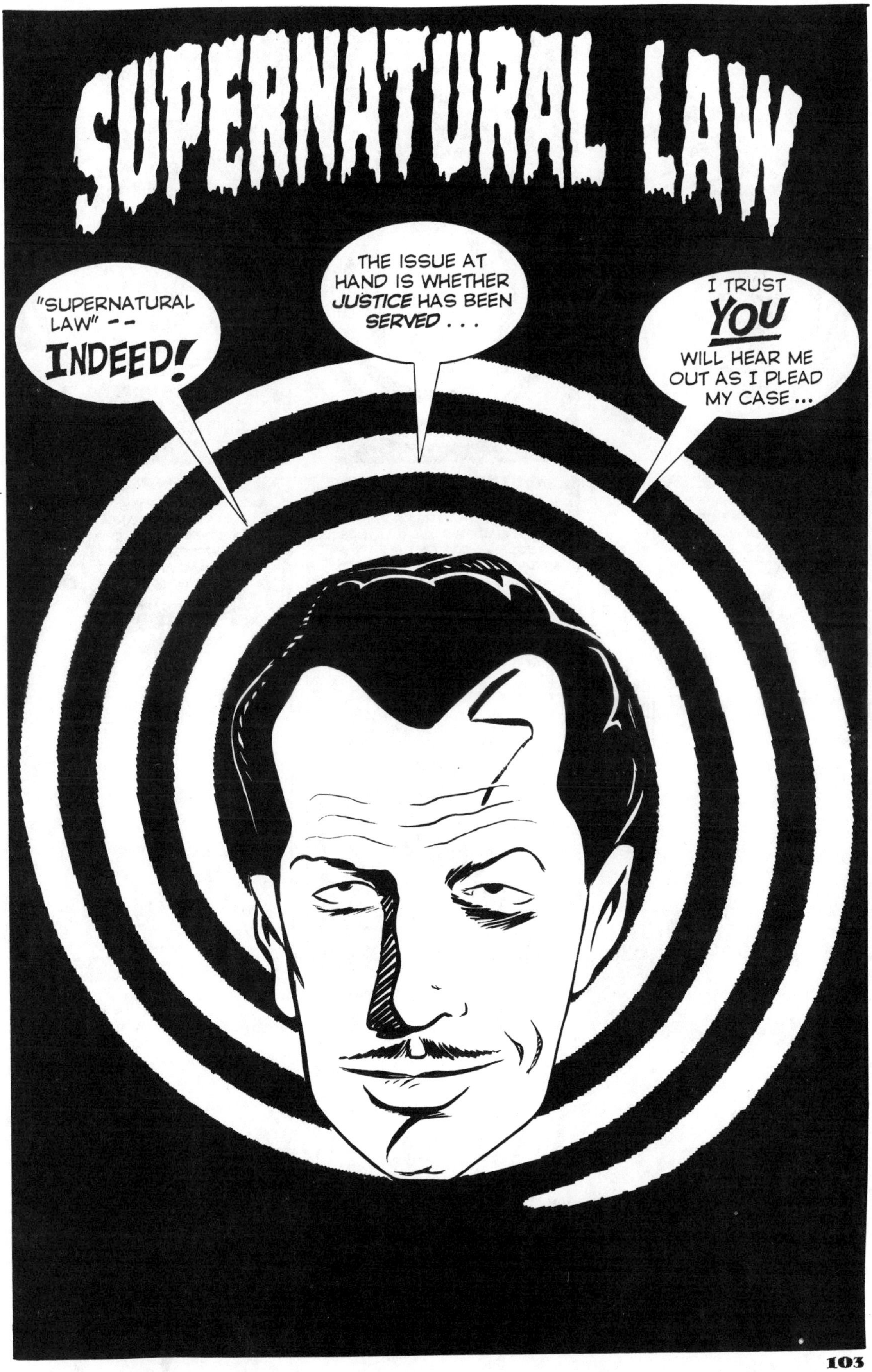
SUPERNATURAL LAW
"SUPERNATURAL LAW" -- INDEED!
THE ISSUE AT HAND IS WHETHER JUSTICE HAS BEEN SERVED . . .
I TRUST YOU WILL HEAR ME OUT AS I PLEAD MY CASE ...

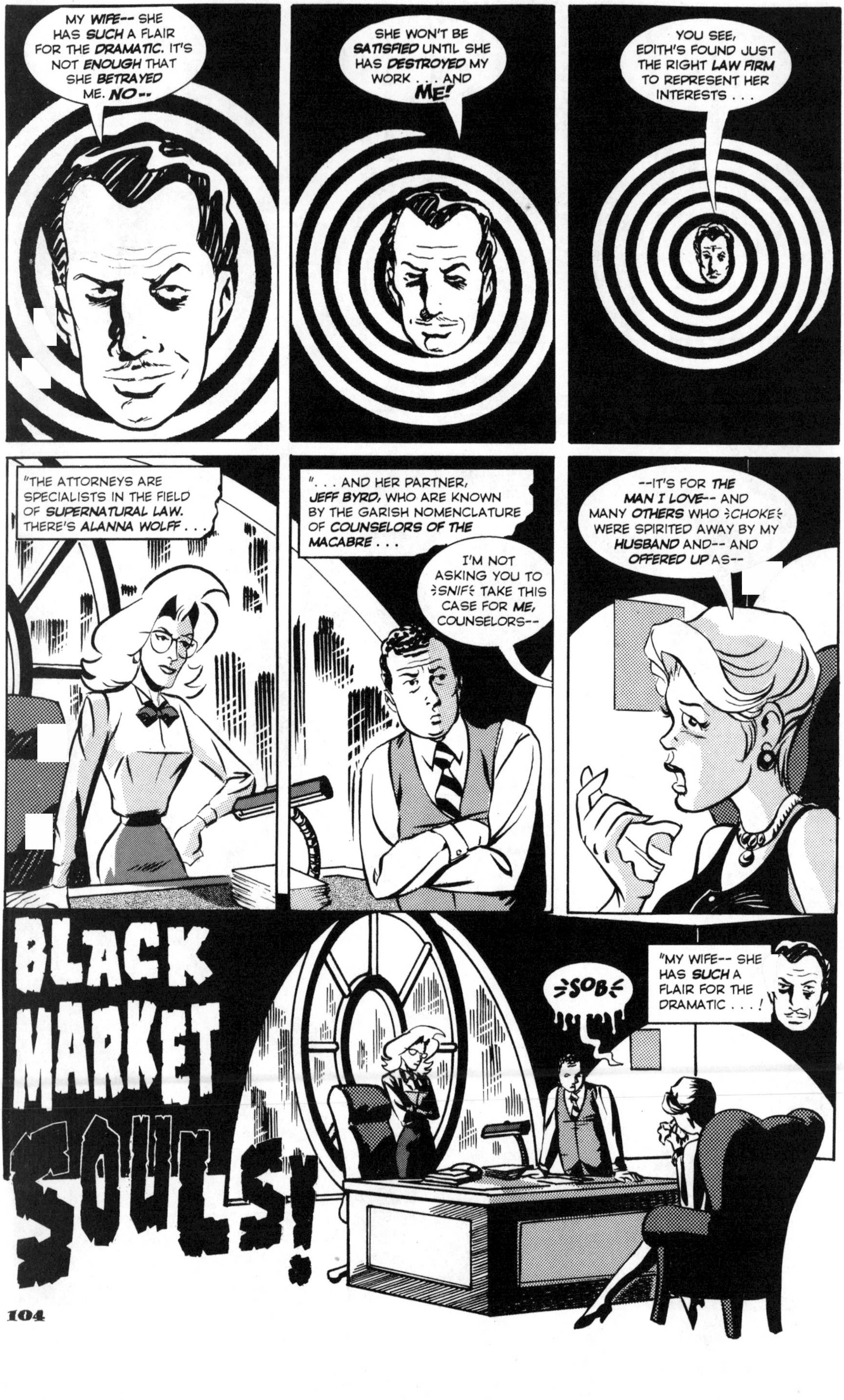
MY WIFE-- SHE HAS SUCH A FLAIR FOR THE DRAMATIC. IT'S NOT ENOUGH THAT SHE BETRAYED ME. NO--
SHE WON'T BE SATISFIED UNTIL SHE HAS DESTROYED MY WORK . . . AND ME!
YOU SEE, EDITH'S FOUND JUST THE RIGHT LAW FIRM TO REPRESENT HER INTERESTS . . .
"THE ATTORNEYS ARE SPECIALISTS IN THE FIELD OF SUPERNATURAL LAW. THERE'S ALANNA WOLFF . . .
". . . AND HER PARTNER, JEFF BYRD, WHO ARE KNOWN BY THE GARISH NOMENCLATURE OF COUNSELORS OF THE MACABRE . . .
I'M NOT ASKING YOU TO SNIF TAKE THIS CASE FOR ME, COUNSELORS--
--IT'S FOR THE MAN I LOVE-- AND MANY OTHERS WHO CHOKE WERE SPIRITED AWAY BY MY HUSBAND AND-- AND OFFERED UP AS--
BLACK MARKET SOULS!
SOB
"MY WIFE-- SHE HAS SUCH A FLAIR FOR THE DRAMATIC . . . !

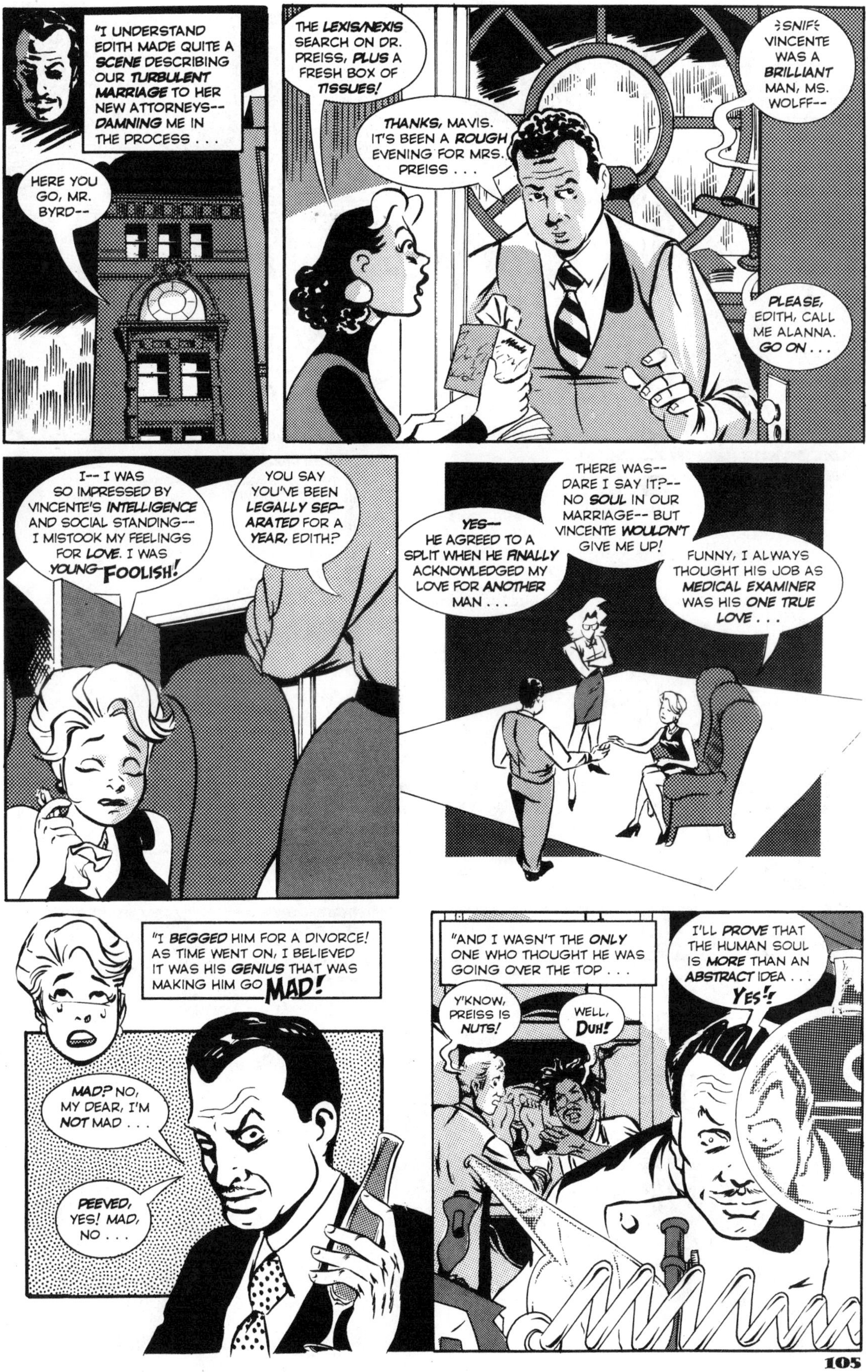
"I UNDERSTAND EDITH MADE QUITE A SCENE DESCRIBING OUR TURBULENT MARRIAGE TO HER NEW ATTORNEYS-- DAMNING ME IN THE PROCESS . . .
HERE YOU GO, MR. BYRD--
THE LEXIS/NEXIS SEARCH ON DR. PREISS, PLUS A FRESH BOX OF TISSUES!
THANKS, MAVIS. IT'S BEEN A ROUGH EVENING FOR MRS. PREISS . . .
SNIF VINCENTE WAS A BRILLIANT MAN, MS. WOLFF--
PLEASE, EDITH, CALL ME ALANNA. GO ON . . .
I-- I WAS SO IMPRESSED BY VINCENTE'S INTELLIGENCE AND SOCIAL STANDING-- I MISTOOK MY FEELINGS FOR LOVE. I WAS YOUNG-FOOLISH!
YOU SAY YOU'VE BEEN LEGALLY SEPARATED FOR A YEAR, EDITH?
YES-- HE AGREED TO A SPLIT WHEN HE FINALLY ACKNOWLEDGED MY LOVE FOR ANOTHER MAN . . .
THERE WAS-- DARE I SAY IT?-- NO SOUL IN OUR MARRIAGE-- BUT VINCENTE WOULDN'T GIVE ME UP!
FUNNY, I ALWAYS THOUGHT HIS JOB AS MEDICAL EXAMINER WAS HIS ONE TRUE LOVE . . .
"I BEGGED HIM FOR A DIVORCE! AS TIME WENT ON, I BELIEVED IT WAS HIS GENIUS THAT WAS MAKING HIM GO MAD!
MAD? NO, MY DEAR, I'M NOT MAD . . .
PEEVED, YES! MAD, NO . . .
"AND I WASN'T THE ONLY ONE WHO THOUGHT HE WAS GOING OVER THE TOP . . .
Y'KNOW, PREISS IS NUTS!
WELL, DUH!
I'LL PROVE THAT THE HUMAN SOUL IS MORE THAN AN ABSTRACT IDEA . . . YES!!

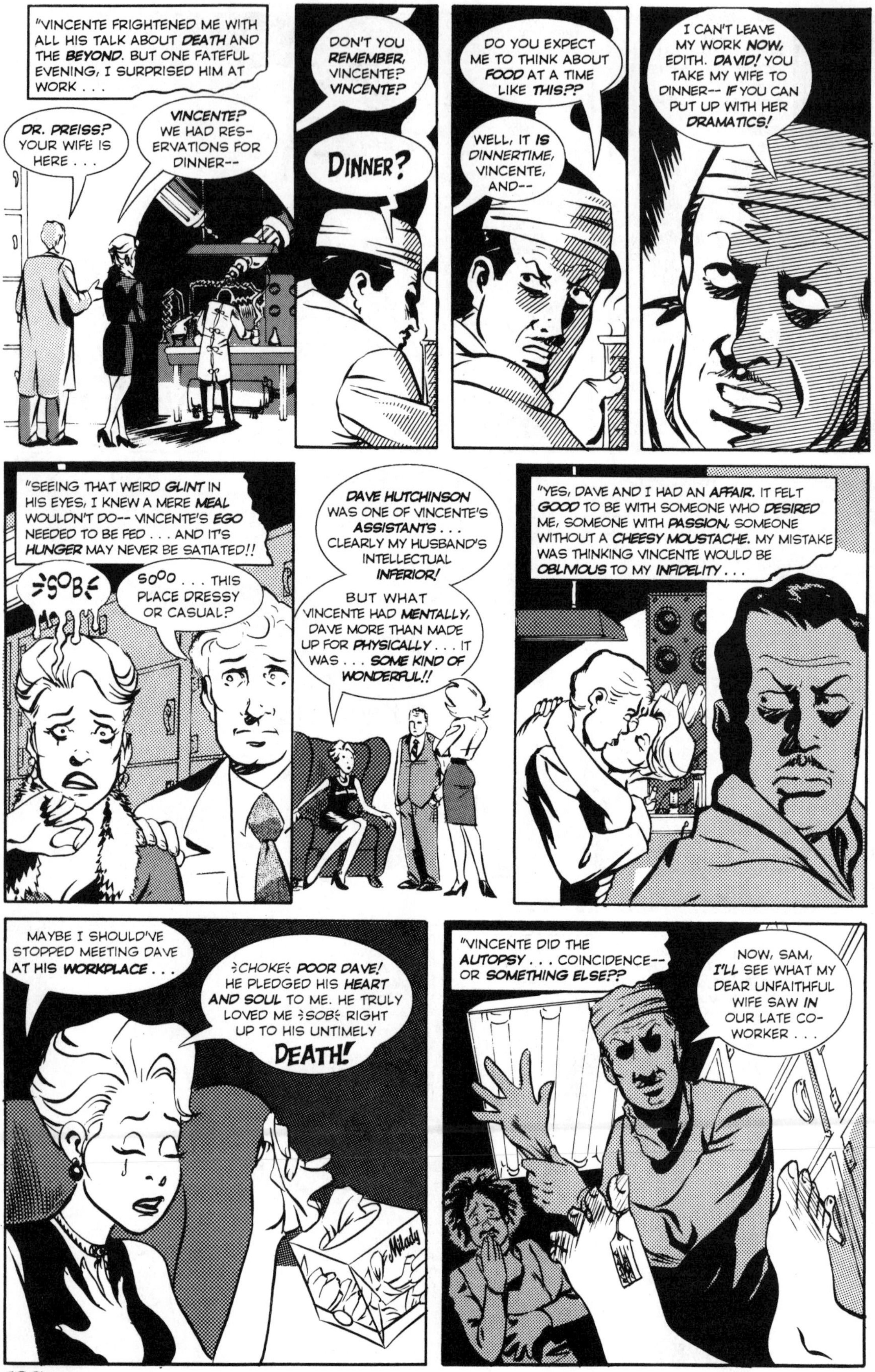
"VINCENTE FRIGHTENED ME WITH ALL HIS TALK ABOUT DEATH AND THE BEYOND. BUT ONE FATEFUL EVENING, I SURPRISED HIM AT WORK . . .
DR. PREISS? YOUR WIFE IS HERE . . .
VINCENTE? WE HAD RESERVATIONS FOR DINNER--
DON'T YOU REMEMBER, VINCENTE? VINCENTE?
DINNER?
DO YOU EXPECT ME TO THINK ABOUT FOOD AT A TIME LIKE THIS??
WELL, IT IS DINNERTIME, VINCENTE, AND--
I CAN'T LEAVE MY WORK NOW, EDITH. DAVID! YOU TAKE MY WIFE TO DINNER-- IF YOU CAN PUT UP WITH HER DRAMATICS!
"SEEING THAT WEIRD GLINT IN HIS EYES, I KNEW A MERE MEAL WOULDN'T DO-- VINCENTE'S EGO NEEDED TO BE FED . . . AND IT'S HUNGER MAY NEVER BE SATIATED!!
SOB
SOOO . . . THIS PLACE DRESSY OR CASUAL?
DAVE HUTCHINSON WAS ONE OF VINCENTE'S ASSISTANTS . . . CLEARLY MY HUSBAND'S INTELLECTUAL INFERIOR!
BUT WHAT VINCENTE HAD MENTALLY, DAVE MORE THAN MADE UP FOR PHYSICALLY . . . IT WAS . . . SOME KIND OF WONDERFUL!!
"YES, DAVE AND I HAD AN AFFAIR. IT FELT GOOD TO BE WITH SOMEONE WHO DESIRED ME, SOMEONE WITH PASSION, SOMEONE WITHOUT A CHEESY MOUSTACHE. MY MISTAKE WAS THINKING VINCENTE WOULD BE OBLIVIOUS TO MY INFIDELITY . . .
MAYBE I SHOULD'VE STOPPED MEETING DAVE AT HIS WORKPLACE . . .
CHOKE POOR DAVE! HE PLEDGED HIS HEART AND SOUL TO ME. HE TRULY LOVED ME SOB RIGHT UP TO HIS UNTIMELY DEATH!
Milady
"VINCENTE DID THE AUTOPSY . . . COINCIDENCE-- OR SOMETHING ELSE??
NOW, SAM, I'LL SEE WHAT MY DEAR UNFAITHFUL WIFE SAW IN OUR LATE CO-WORKER . . .

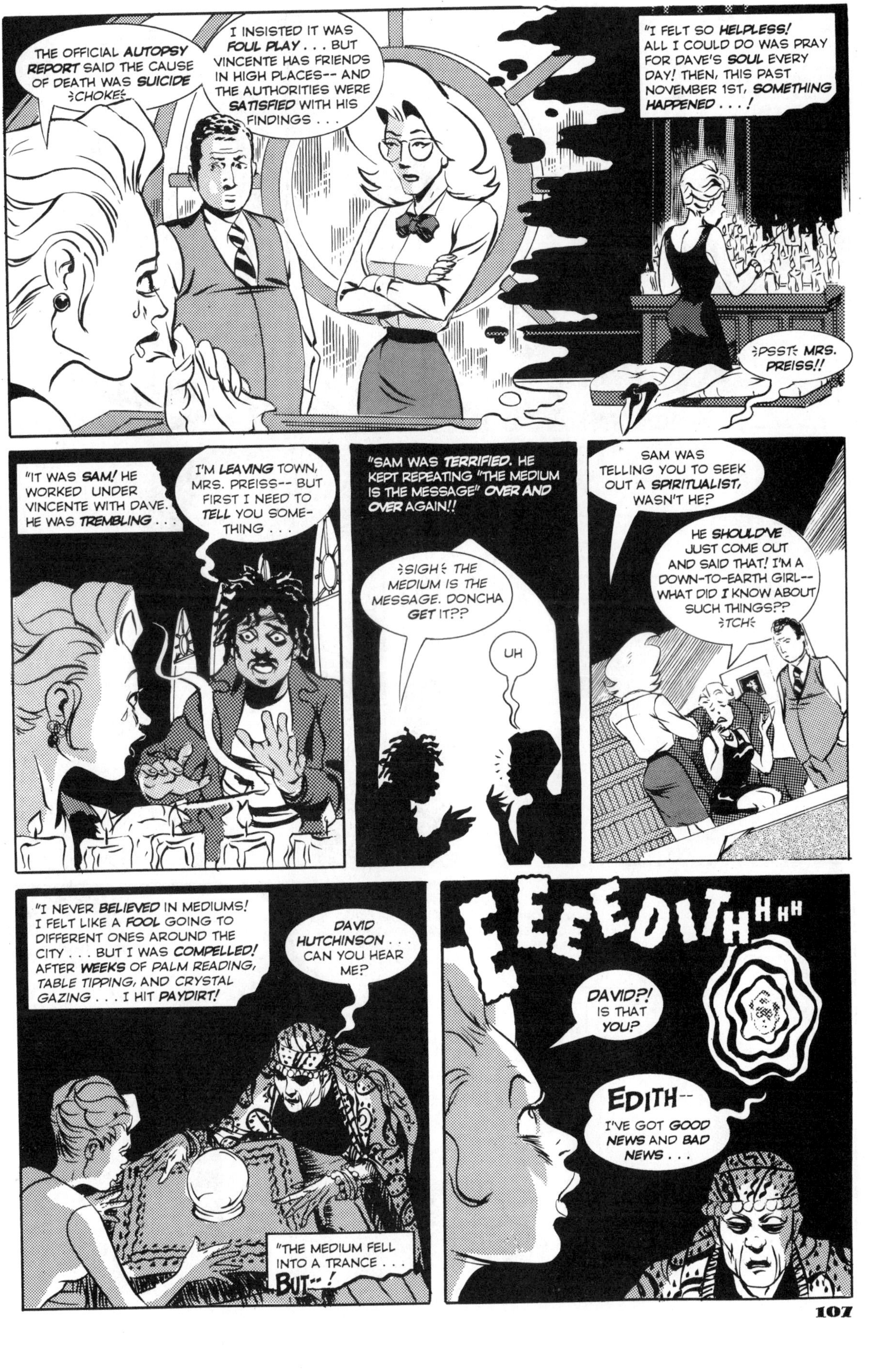
THE OFFICIAL AUTOPSY REPORT SAID THE CAUSE OF DEATH WAS SUICIDE
CHOKE
I INSISTED IT WAS FOUL PLAY . . . BUT VINCENTE HAS FRIENDS IN HIGH PLACES-- AND THE AUTHORITIES WERE SATISFIED WITH HIS FINDINGS . . .
"I FELT SO HELPLESS! ALL I COULD DO WAS PRAY FOR DAVE'S SOUL EVERY DAY! THEN, THIS PAST NOVEMBER 1ST, SOMETHING HAPPENED . . . !
PSST MRS. PREISS!!
"IT WAS SAM! HE WORKED UNDER VINCENTE WITH DAVE. HE WAS TREMBLING . . .
I'M LEAVING TOWN, MRS. PREISS-- BUT FIRST I NEED TO TELL YOU SOMETHING . . .
"SAM WAS TERRIFIED. HE KEPT REPEATING "THE MEDIUM IS THE MESSAGE" OVER AND OVER AGAIN!!
SIGH THE MEDIUM IS THE MESSAGE. DONCHA GET IT??
UH
SAM WAS TELLING YOU TO SEEK OUT A SPIRITUALIST, WASN'T HE?
HE SHOULD'VE JUST COME OUT AND SAID THAT! I'M A DOWN-TO-EARTH GIRL-- WHAT DID I KNOW ABOUT SUCH THINGS??
TCH
"I NEVER BELIEVED IN MEDIUMS! I FELT LIKE A FOOL GOING TO DIFFERENT ONES AROUND THE CITY . . . BUT I WAS COMPELLED! AFTER WEEKS OF PALM READING, TABLE TIPPING, AND CRYSTAL GAZING . . . I HIT PAYDIRT!
DAVID HUTCHINSON . . . CAN YOU HEAR ME?
"THE MEDIUM FELL INTO A TRANCE . . . BUT--!
EEEEDITHHHH
DAVID?! IS THAT YOU?
EDITH-- I'VE GOT GOOD NEWS AND BAD NEWS . . .

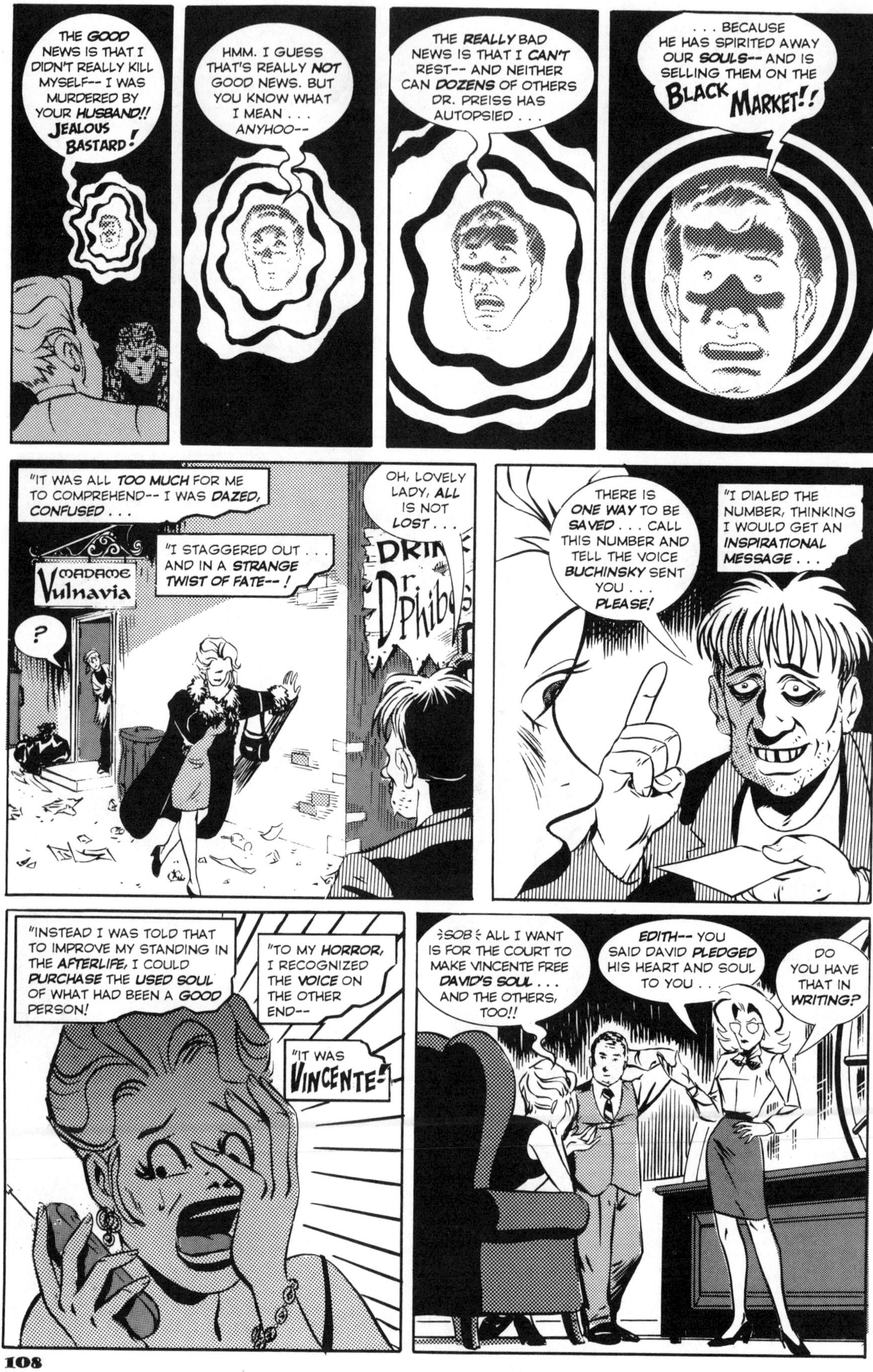
THE GOOD NEWS IS THAT I DIDN'T REALLY KILL MYSELF-- I WAS MURDERED BY YOUR HUSBAND!! JEALOUS BASTARD!
HMM. I GUESS THAT'S REALLY NOT GOOD NEWS. BUT YOU KNOW WHAT I MEAN . . . ANYHOO--
THE REALLY BAD NEWS IS THAT I CAN'T REST-- AND NEITHER CAN DOZENS OF OTHERS DR. PREISS HAS AUTOPSIED . . .
. . . BECAUSE HE HAS SPIRITED AWAY OUR SOULS-- AND IS SELLING THEM ON THE BLACK MARKET!!
"IT WAS ALL TOO MUCH FOR ME TO COMPREHEND-- I WAS DAZED, CONFUSED . . .
MADAME Vulnavia
"I STAGGERED OUT . . . AND IN A STRANGE TWIST OF FATE-- !
?
OH, LOVELY LADY, ALL IS NOT LOST . . .
DRIN
Dr. Phib
THERE IS ONE WAY TO BE SAVED . . . CALL THIS NUMBER AND TELL THE VOICE BUCHINSKY SENT YOU . . . PLEASE!
"I DIALED THE NUMBER, THINKING I WOULD GET AN INSPIRATIONAL MESSAGE . . .
"INSTEAD I WAS TOLD THAT TO IMPROVE MY STANDING IN THE AFTERLIFE, I COULD PURCHASE THE USED SOUL OF WHAT HAD BEEN A GOOD PERSON!
"TO MY HORROR, I RECOGNIZED THE VOICE ON THE OTHER END--
"IT WAS VINCENTE!
≥SOB≤ ALL I WANT IS FOR THE COURT TO MAKE VINCENTE FREE DAVID'S SOUL . . . AND THE OTHERS, TOO!!
EDITH-- YOU SAID DAVID PLEDGED HIS HEART AND SOUL TO YOU . . .
DO YOU HAVE THAT IN WRITING?

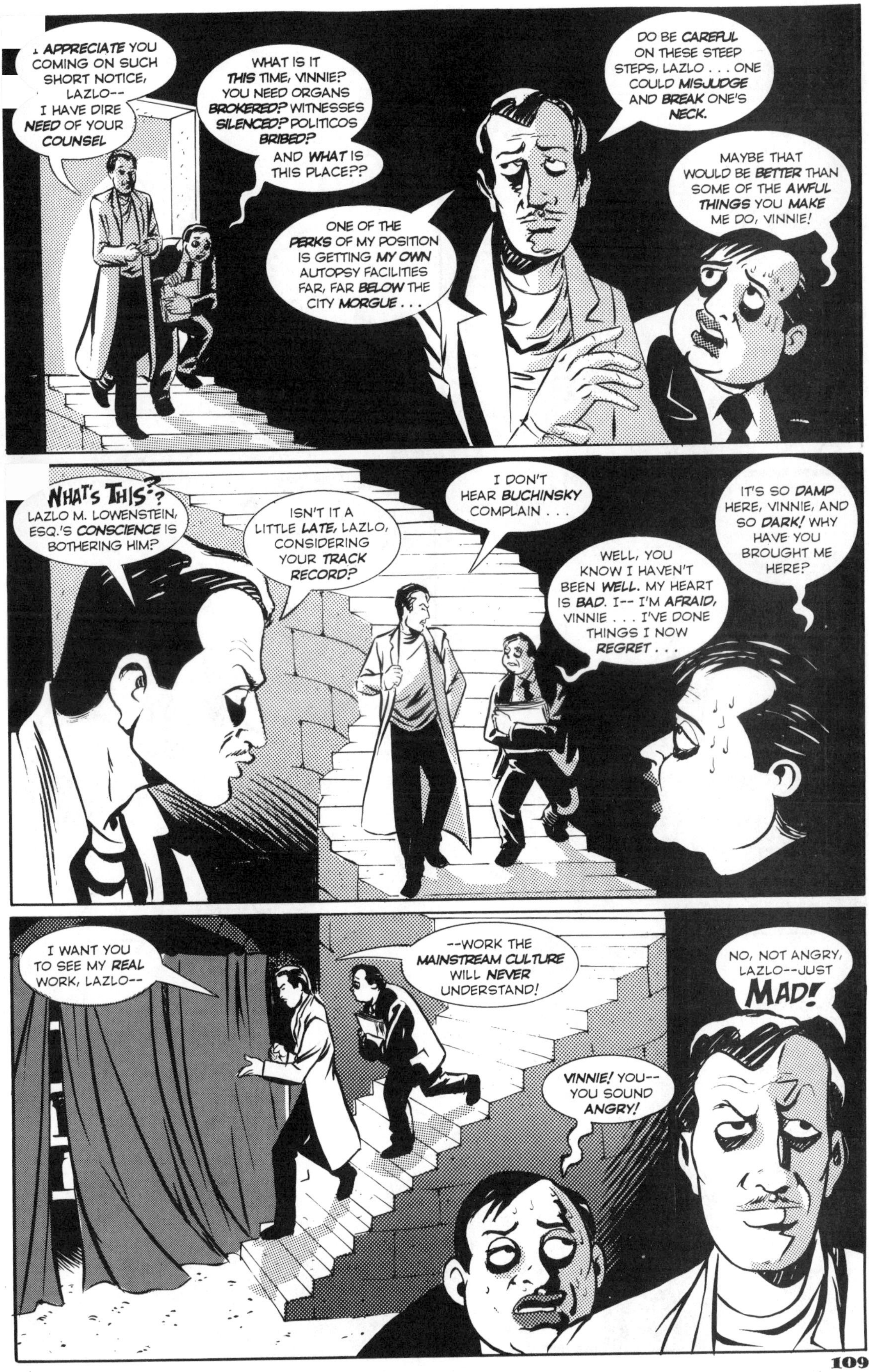
I APPRECIATE YOU COMING ON SUCH SHORT NOTICE, LAZLO-- I HAVE DIRE NEED OF YOUR COUNSEL
WHAT IS IT THIS TIME, VINNIE? YOU NEED ORGANS BROKERED? WITNESSES SILENCED? POLITICOS BRIBED?
AND WHAT IS THIS PLACE??
ONE OF THE PERKS OF MY POSITION IS GETTING MY OWN AUTOPSY FACILITIES FAR, FAR BELOW THE CITY MORGUE . . .
DO BE CAREFUL ON THESE STEEP STEPS, LAZLO . . . ONE COULD MISJUDGE AND BREAK ONE'S NECK.
MAYBE THAT WOULD BE BETTER THAN SOME OF THE AWFUL THINGS YOU MAKE ME DO, VINNIE!
WHAT'S THIS?? LAZLO M. LOWENSTEIN, ESQ.'S CONSCIENCE IS BOTHERING HIM?
ISN'T IT A LITTLE LATE, LAZLO, CONSIDERING YOUR TRACK RECORD?
I DON'T HEAR BUCHINSKY COMPLAIN . . .
IT'S SO DAMP HERE, VINNIE, AND SO DARK! WHY HAVE YOU BROUGHT ME HERE?
WELL, YOU KNOW I HAVEN'T BEEN WELL. MY HEART IS BAD. I-- I'M AFRAID, VINNIE . . . I'VE DONE THINGS I NOW REGRET . . .
I WANT YOU TO SEE MY REAL WORK, LAZLO--
--WORK THE MAINSTREAM CULTURE WILL NEVER UNDERSTAND!
VINNIE! YOU-- YOU SOUND ANGRY!
NO, NOT ANGRY, LAZLO--JUST MAD!

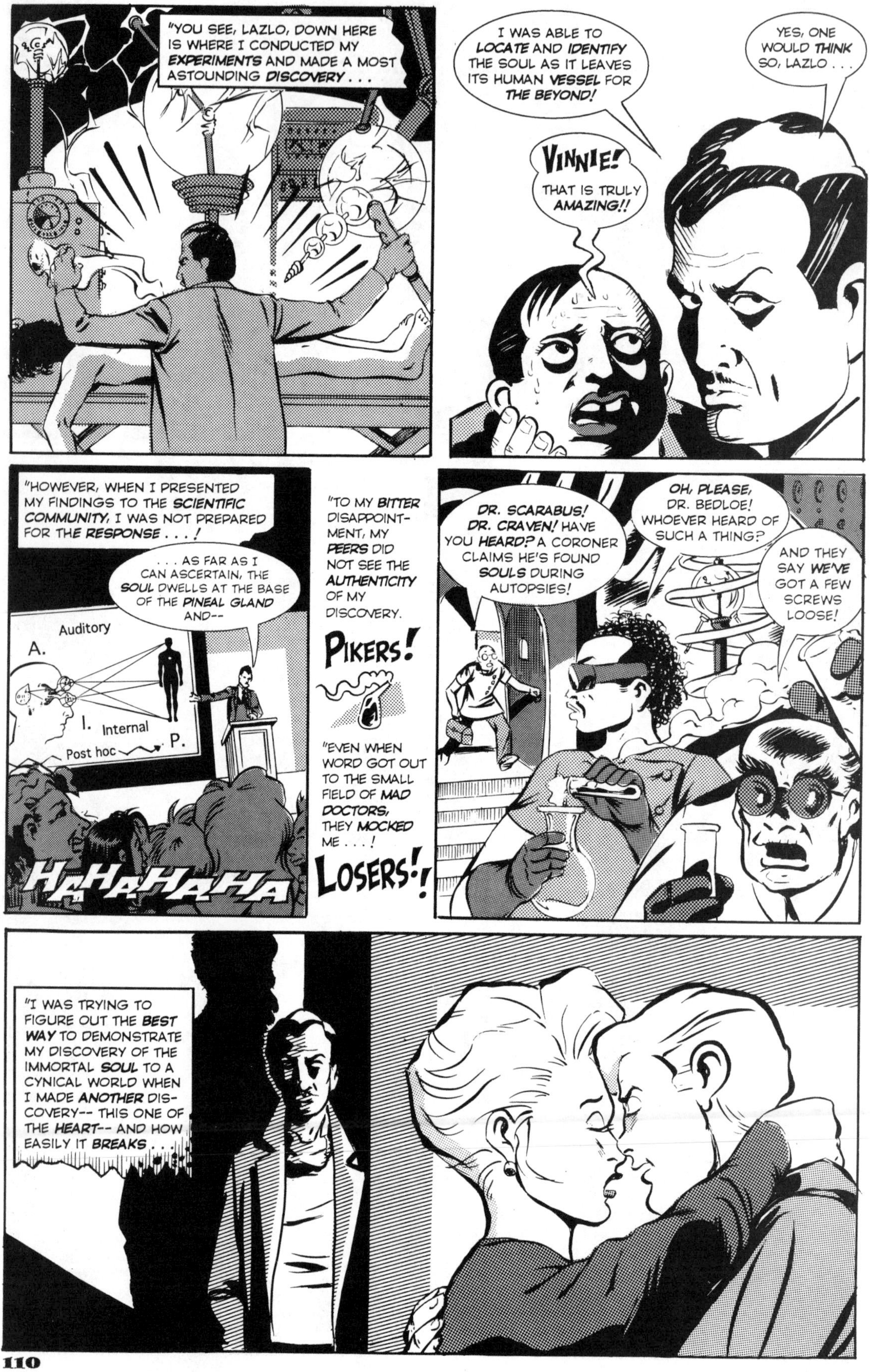
"YOU SEE, LAZLO, DOWN HERE IS WHERE I CONDUCTED MY EXPERIMENTS AND MADE A MOST ASTOUNDING DISCOVERY . . .
I WAS ABLE TO LOCATE AND IDENTIFY THE SOUL AS IT LEAVES ITS HUMAN VESSEL FOR THE BEYOND!
VINNIE! THAT IS TRULY AMAZING!!
YES, ONE WOULD THINK SO, LAZLO . . .
"HOWEVER, WHEN I PRESENTED MY FINDINGS TO THE SCIENTIFIC COMMUNITY, I WAS NOT PREPARED FOR THE RESPONSE . . . !
. . . AS FAR AS I CAN ASCERTAIN, THE SOUL DWELLS AT THE BASE OF THE PINEAL GLAND AND--
Auditory
A.
I.
Internal
P.
Post hoc
HAHAHAHAHA
"TO MY BITTER DISAPPOINT-MENT, MY PEERS DID NOT SEE THE AUTHENTICITY OF MY DISCOVERY.
PIKERS!
"EVEN WHEN WORD GOT OUT TO THE SMALL FIELD OF MAD DOCTORS, THEY MOCKED ME . . . !
LOSERS!!
DR. SCARABUS! DR. CRAVEN! HAVE YOU HEARD? A CORONER CLAIMS HE'S FOUND SOULS DURING AUTOPSIES!
OH, PLEASE, DR. BEDLOE! WHOEVER HEARD OF SUCH A THING?
AND THEY SAY WE'VE GOT A FEW SCREWS LOOSE!
"I WAS TRYING TO FIGURE OUT THE BEST WAY TO DEMONSTRATE MY DISCOVERY OF THE IMMORTAL SOUL TO A CYNICAL WORLD WHEN I MADE ANOTHER DIS-COVERY-- THIS ONE OF THE HEART-- AND HOW EASILY IT BREAKS . . .

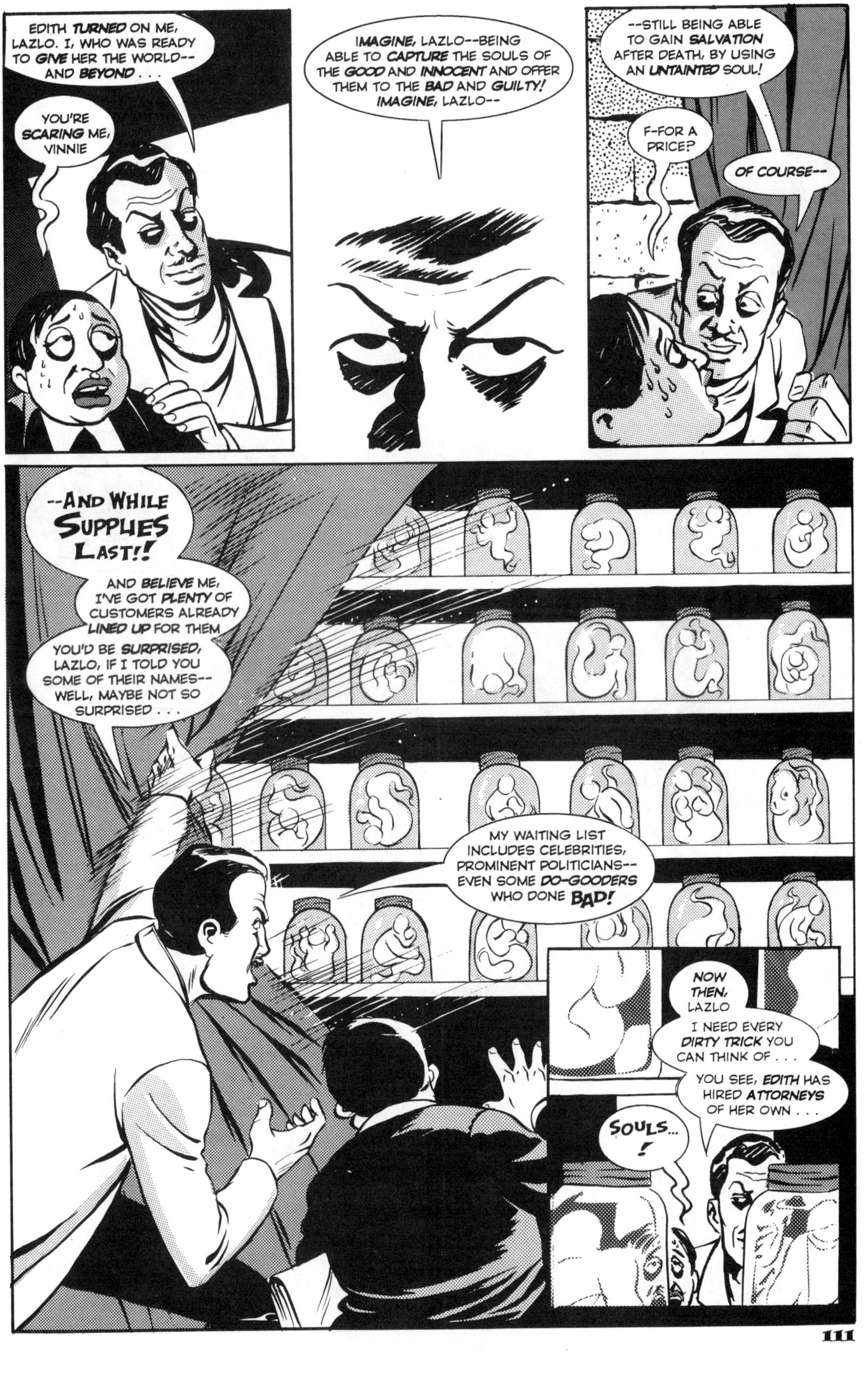
EDITH TURNED ON ME, LAZLO. I, WHO WAS READY TO GIVE HER THE WORLD-- AND BEYOND . . .
YOU'RE SCARING ME, VINNIE
IMAGINE, LAZLO--BEING ABLE TO CAPTURE THE SOULS OF THE GOOD AND INNOCENT AND OFFER THEM TO THE BAD AND GUILTY! IMAGINE, LAZLO--
--STILL BEING ABLE TO GAIN SALVATION AFTER DEATH, BY USING AN UNTAINTED SOUL!
F-FOR A PRICE?
OF COURSE--
--AND WHILE SUPPLIES LAST!!
AND BELIEVE ME, I'VE GOT PLENTY OF CUSTOMERS ALREADY LINED UP FOR THEM
YOU'D BE SURPRISED, LAZLO, IF I TOLD YOU SOME OF THEIR NAMES-- WELL, MAYBE NOT SO SURPRISED . . .
MY WAITING LIST INCLUDES CELEBRITIES, PROMINENT POLITICIANS-- EVEN SOME DO-GOODERS WHO DONE BAD!
NOW THEN, LAZLO
I NEED EVERY DIRTY TRICK YOU CAN THINK OF . . .
YOU SEE, EDITH HAS HIRED ATTORNEYS OF HER OWN . . .
SOULS... !

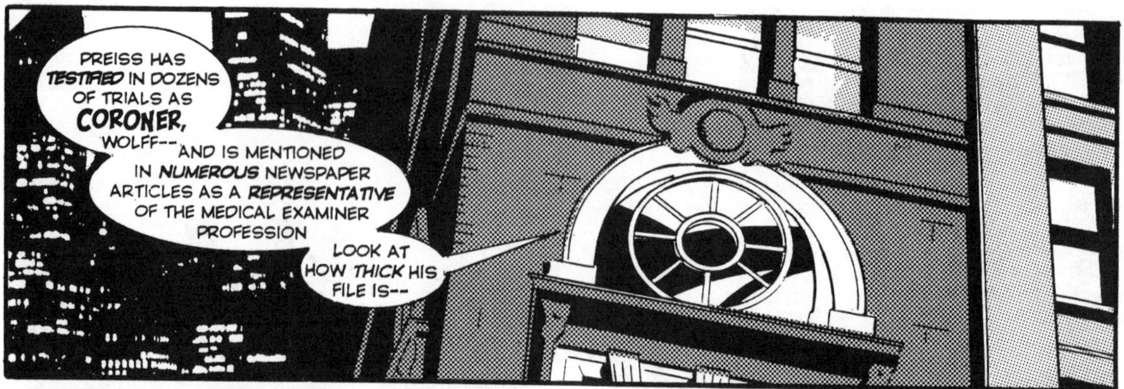
PREISS HAS TESTIFIED IN DOZENS OF TRIALS AS CORONER, WOLFF--
AND IS MENTIONED IN NUMEROUS NEWSPAPER ARTICLES AS A REPRESENTATIVE OF THE MEDICAL EXAMINER PROFESSION
LOOK AT HOW THICK HIS FILE IS--

PART TWO SOLE MATES

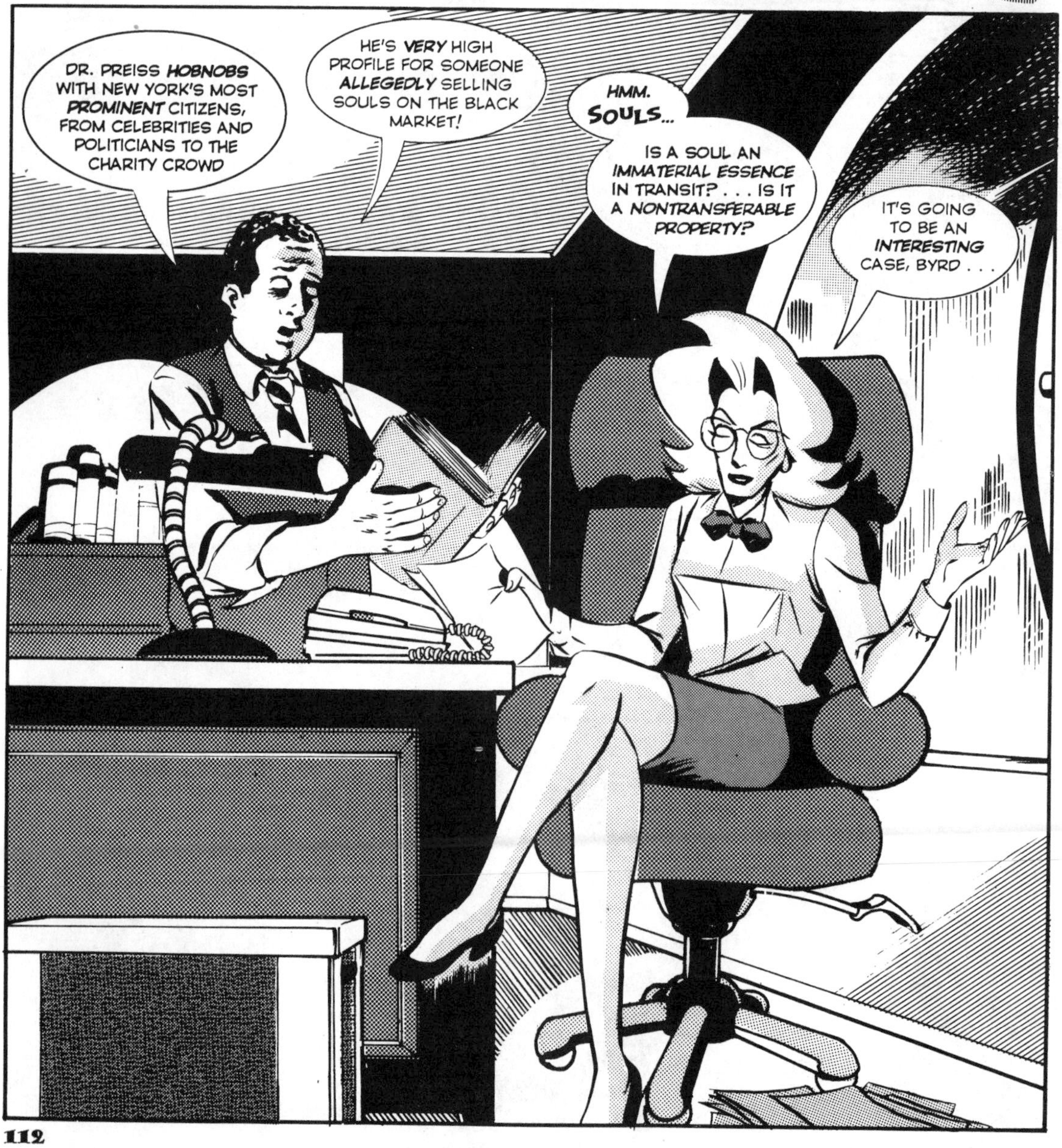
DR. PREISS HOBNOBS WITH NEW YORK'S MOST PROMINENT CITIZENS, FROM CELEBRITIES AND POLITICIANS TO THE CHARITY CROWD
HE'S VERY HIGH PROFILE FOR SOMEONE ALLEGEDLY SELLING SOULS ON THE BLACK MARKET!
HMM. SOULS...
IS A SOUL AN IMMATERIAL ESSENCE IN TRANSIT? . . . IS IT A NONTRANSFERABLE PROPERTY?
IT'S GOING TO BE AN INTERESTING CASE, BYRD . . .

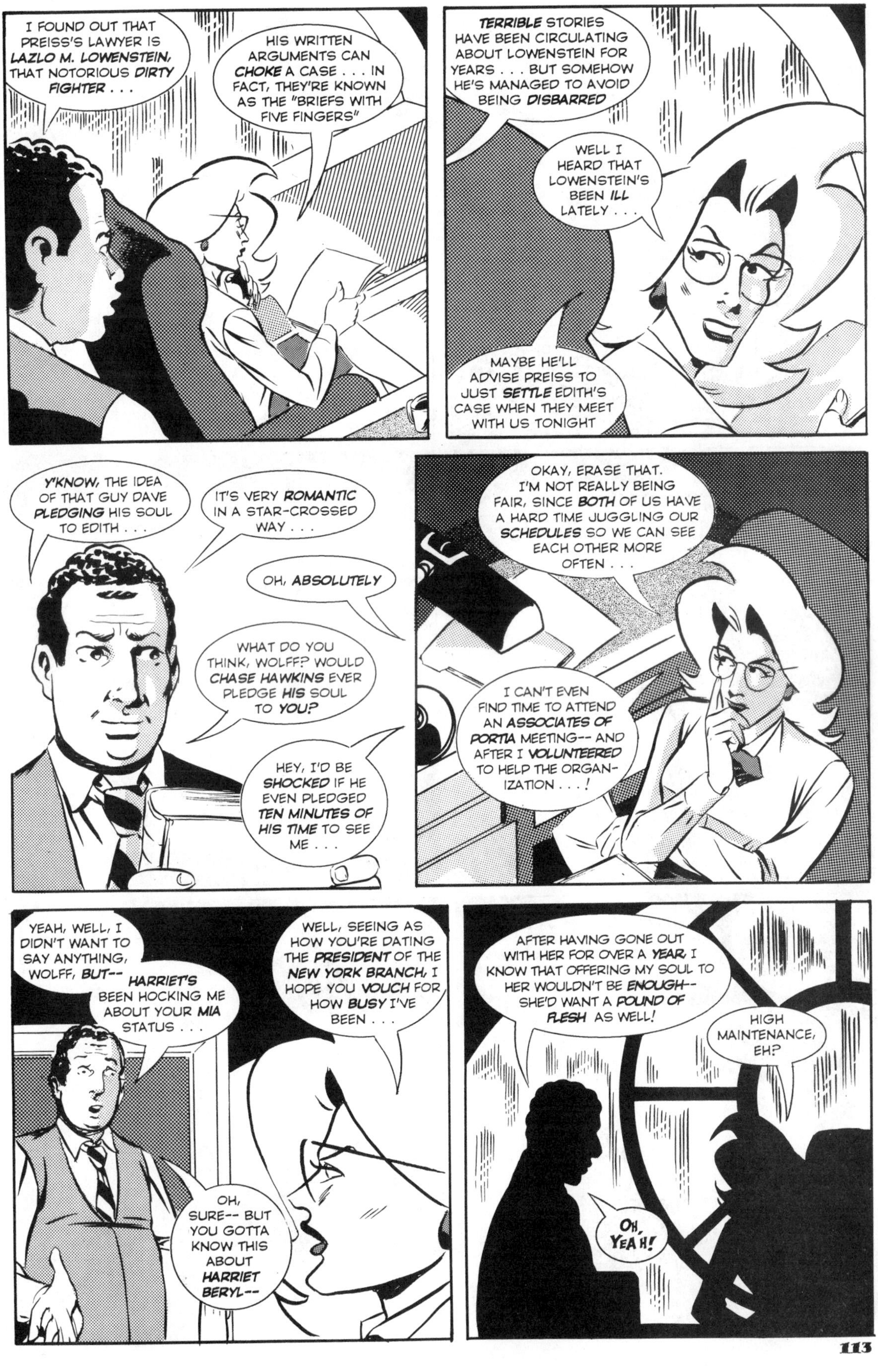

I FOUND OUT THAT PREISS'S LAWYER IS LAZLO M. LOWENSTEIN, THAT NOTORIOUS DIRTY FIGHTER . . .
HIS WRITTEN ARGUMENTS CAN CHOKE A CASE . . . IN FACT, THEY'RE KNOWN AS THE "BRIEFS WITH FIVE FINGERS"
TERRIBLE STORIES HAVE BEEN CIRCULATING ABOUT LOWENSTEIN FOR YEARS . . . BUT SOMEHOW HE'S MANAGED TO AVOID BEING DISBARRED
WELL I HEARD THAT LOWENSTEIN'S BEEN ILL LATELY . . .
MAYBE HE'LL ADVISE PREISS TO JUST SETTLE EDITH'S CASE WHEN THEY MEET WITH US TONIGHT
Y'KNOW, THE IDEA OF THAT GUY DAVE PLEDGING HIS SOUL TO EDITH . . .
IT'S VERY ROMANTIC IN A STAR-CROSSED WAY . . .
OH, ABSOLUTELY
WHAT DO YOU THINK, WOLFF? WOULD CHASE HAWKINS EVER PLEDGE HIS SOUL TO YOU?
HEY, I'D BE SHOCKED IF HE EVEN PLEDGED TEN MINUTES OF HIS TIME TO SEE ME . . .
OKAY, ERASE THAT. I'M NOT REALLY BEING FAIR, SINCE BOTH OF US HAVE A HARD TIME JUGGLING OUR SCHEDULES SO WE CAN SEE EACH OTHER MORE OFTEN . . .
I CAN'T EVEN FIND TIME TO ATTEND AN ASSOCIATES OF PORTIA MEETING-- AND AFTER I VOLUNTEERED TO HELP THE ORGAN-IZATION . . . !
YEAH, WELL, I DIDN'T WANT TO SAY ANYTHING, WOLFF, BUT-- HARRIET'S BEEN HOCKING ME ABOUT YOUR MIA STATUS . . .
WELL, SEEING AS HOW YOU'RE DATING THE PRESIDENT OF THE NEW YORK BRANCH, I HOPE YOU VOUCH FOR HOW BUSY I'VE BEEN . . .
OH, SURE-- BUT YOU GOTTA KNOW THIS ABOUT HARRIET BERYL--
AFTER HAVING GONE OUT WITH HER FOR OVER A YEAR, I KNOW THAT OFFERING MY SOUL TO HER WOULDN'T BE ENOUGH-- SHE'D WANT A POUND OF FLESH AS WELL!
HIGH MAINTENANCE, EH?
OH, YEAH!

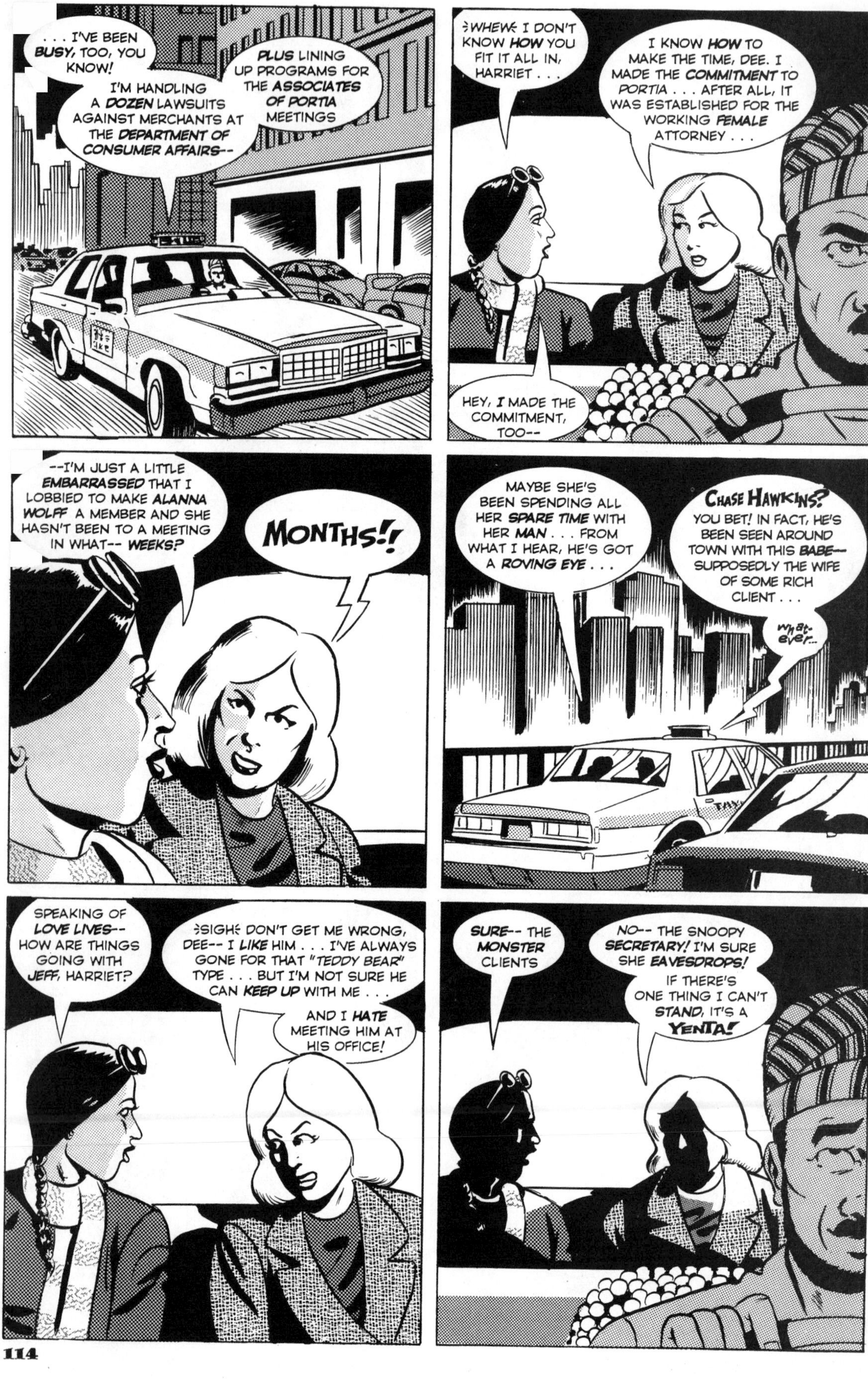

. . . I'VE BEEN BUSY, TOO, YOU KNOW!
I'M HANDLING A DOZEN LAWSUITS AGAINST MERCHANTS AT THE DEPARTMENT OF CONSUMER AFFAIRS--
PLUS LINING UP PROGRAMS FOR THE ASSOCIATES OF PORTIA MEETINGS
WHEW I DON'T KNOW HOW YOU FIT IT ALL IN, HARRIET . . .
I KNOW HOW TO MAKE THE TIME, DEE. I MADE THE COMMITMENT TO PORTIA . . . AFTER ALL, IT WAS ESTABLISHED FOR THE WORKING FEMALE ATTORNEY . . .
HEY, I MADE THE COMMITMENT, TOO--
--I'M JUST A LITTLE EMBARRASSED THAT I LOBBIED TO MAKE ALANNA WOLFF A MEMBER AND SHE HASN'T BEEN TO A MEETING IN WHAT-- WEEKS?
MONTHS!!
MAYBE SHE'S BEEN SPENDING ALL HER SPARE TIME WITH HER MAN . . . FROM WHAT I HEAR, HE'S GOT A ROVING EYE . . .
CHASE HAWKINS? YOU BET! IN FACT, HE'S BEEN SEEN AROUND TOWN WITH THIS BABE-- SUPPOSEDLY THE WIFE OF SOME RICH CLIENT . . .
what-ever...
SPEAKING OF LOVE LIVES-- HOW ARE THINGS GOING WITH JEFF, HARRIET?
SIGH DON'T GET ME WRONG, DEE-- I LIKE HIM . . . I'VE ALWAYS GONE FOR THAT "TEDDY BEAR" TYPE . . . BUT I'M NOT SURE HE CAN KEEP UP WITH ME . . .
AND I HATE MEETING HIM AT HIS OFFICE!
SURE-- THE MONSTER CLIENTS
NO-- THE SNOOPY SECRETARY! I'M SURE SHE EAVESDROPS!
IF THERE'S ONE THING I CAN'T STAND, IT'S A YENTA!

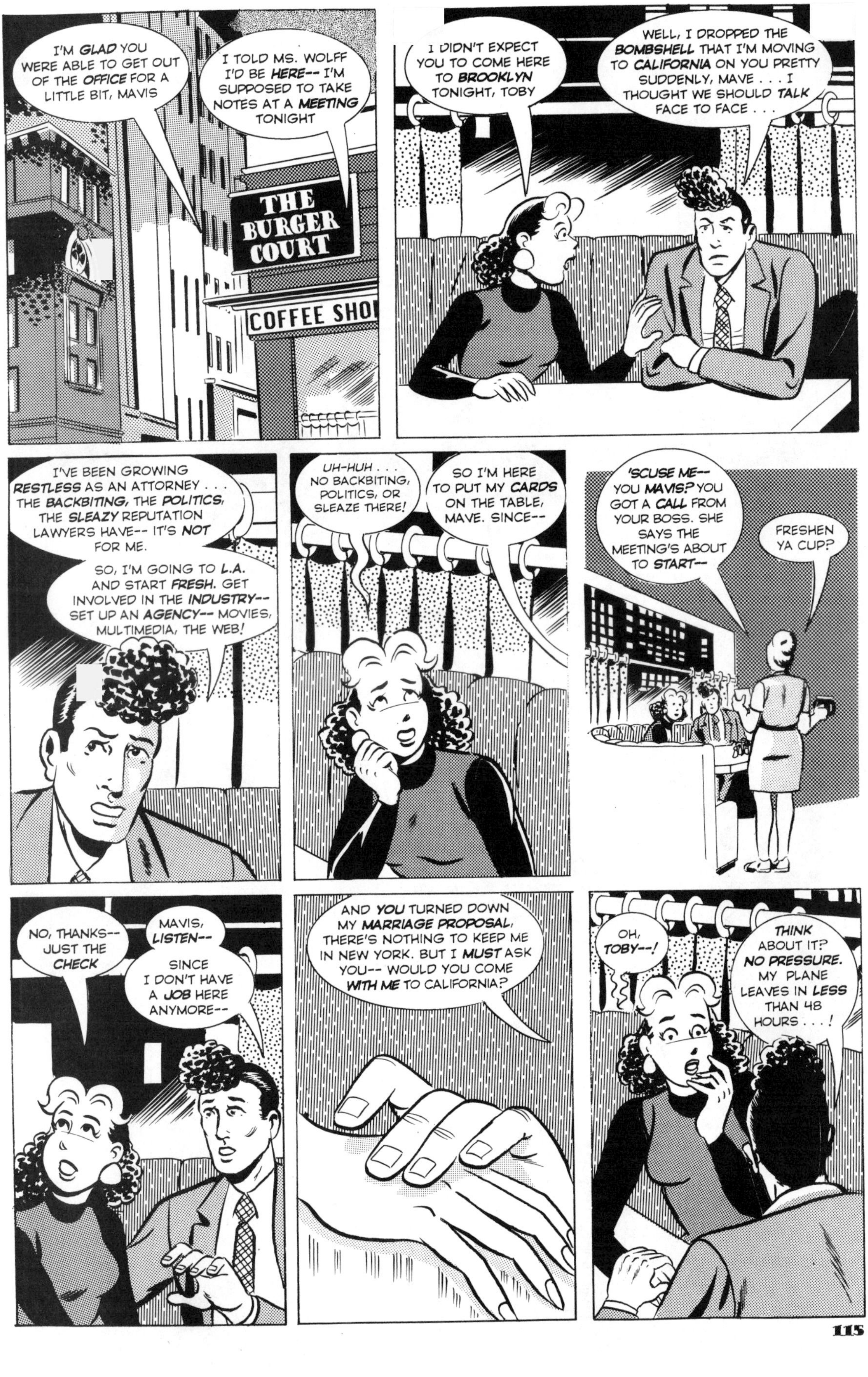
I'M GLAD YOU WERE ABLE TO GET OUT OF THE OFFICE FOR A LITTLE BIT, MAVIS
I TOLD MS. WOLFF I'D BE HERE-- I'M SUPPOSED TO TAKE NOTES AT A MEETING TONIGHT
THE BURGER COURT
COFFEE SHO
I DIDN'T EXPECT YOU TO COME HERE TO BROOKLYN TONIGHT, TOBY
WELL, I DROPPED THE BOMBSHELL THAT I'M MOVING TO CALIFORNIA ON YOU PRETTY SUDDENLY, MAVE . . . I THOUGHT WE SHOULD TALK FACE TO FACE . . .
I'VE BEEN GROWING RESTLESS AS AN ATTORNEY . . . THE BACKBITING, THE POLITICS, THE SLEAZY REPUTATION LAWYERS HAVE-- IT'S NOT FOR ME.
SO, I'M GOING TO L.A. AND START FRESH. GET INVOLVED IN THE INDUSTRY-- SET UP AN AGENCY-- MOVIES, MULTIMEDIA, THE WEB!
UH-HUH . . . NO BACKBITING, POLITICS, OR SLEAZE THERE!
SO I'M HERE TO PUT MY CARDS ON THE TABLE, MAVE. SINCE--
'SCUSE ME-- YOU MAVIS? YOU GOT A CALL FROM YOUR BOSS. SHE SAYS THE MEETING'S ABOUT TO START--
FRESHEN YA CUP?
NO, THANKS-- JUST THE CHECK
MAVIS, LISTEN--
SINCE I DON'T HAVE A JOB HERE ANYMORE--
AND YOU TURNED DOWN MY MARRIAGE PROPOSAL, THERE'S NOTHING TO KEEP ME IN NEW YORK. BUT I MUST ASK YOU-- WOULD YOU COME WITH ME TO CALIFORNIA?
OH, TOBY--!
THINK ABOUT IT? NO PRESSURE. MY PLANE LEAVES IN LESS THAN 48 HOURS . . . !

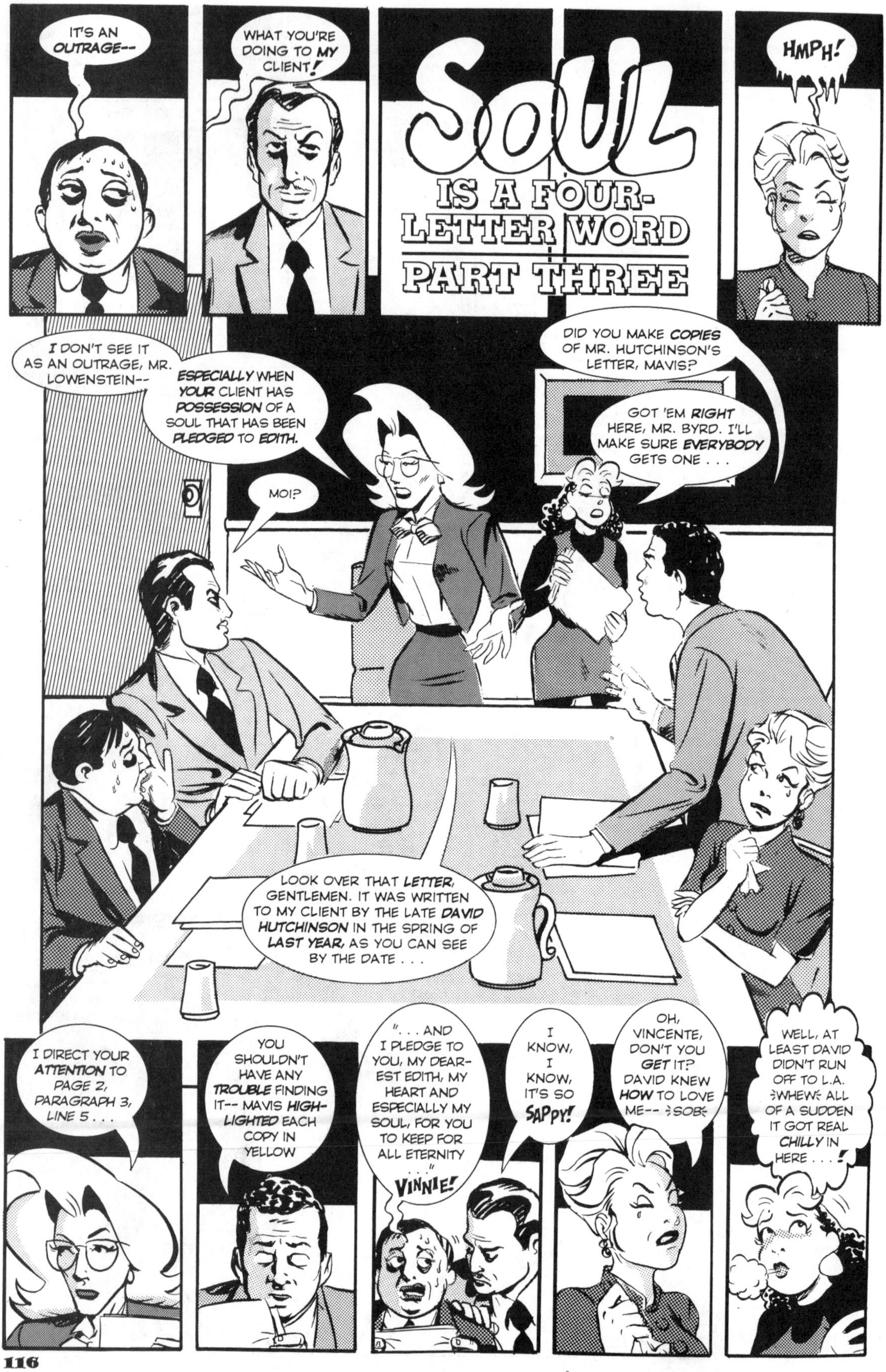
IT'S AN OUTRAGE--
WHAT YOU'RE DOING TO MY CLIENT!
SOUL IS A FOUR-LETTER WORD
PART THREE
HMPH!
I DON'T SEE IT AS AN OUTRAGE, MR. LOWENSTEIN--
ESPECIALLY WHEN YOUR CLIENT HAS POSSESSION OF A SOUL THAT HAS BEEN PLEDGED TO EDITH.
DID YOU MAKE COPIES OF MR. HUTCHINSON'S LETTER, MAVIS?
GOT 'EM RIGHT HERE, MR. BYRD. I'LL MAKE SURE EVERYBODY GETS ONE . . .
MOI!?
LOOK OVER THAT LETTER, GENTLEMEN. IT WAS WRITTEN TO MY CLIENT BY THE LATE DAVID HUTCHINSON IN THE SPRING OF LAST YEAR, AS YOU CAN SEE BY THE DATE . . .
I DIRECT YOUR ATTENTION TO PAGE 2, PARAGRAPH 3, LINE 5 . . .
YOU SHOULDN'T HAVE ANY TROUBLE FINDING IT-- MAVIS HIGHLIGHTED EACH COPY IN YELLOW
". . . AND I PLEDGE TO YOU, MY DEAREST EDITH, MY HEART AND ESPECIALLY MY SOUL, FOR YOU TO KEEP FOR ALL ETERNITY . . ."
VINNIE!
I KNOW, I KNOW, IT'S SO SAPPY!
OH, VINCENTE, DON'T YOU GET IT? DAVID KNEW HOW TO LOVE ME-- ≯SOB≮
WELL, AT LEAST DAVID DIDN'T RUN OFF TO L.A. ≯WHEW≮ ALL OF A SUDDEN IT GOT REAL CHILLY IN HERE . . . !

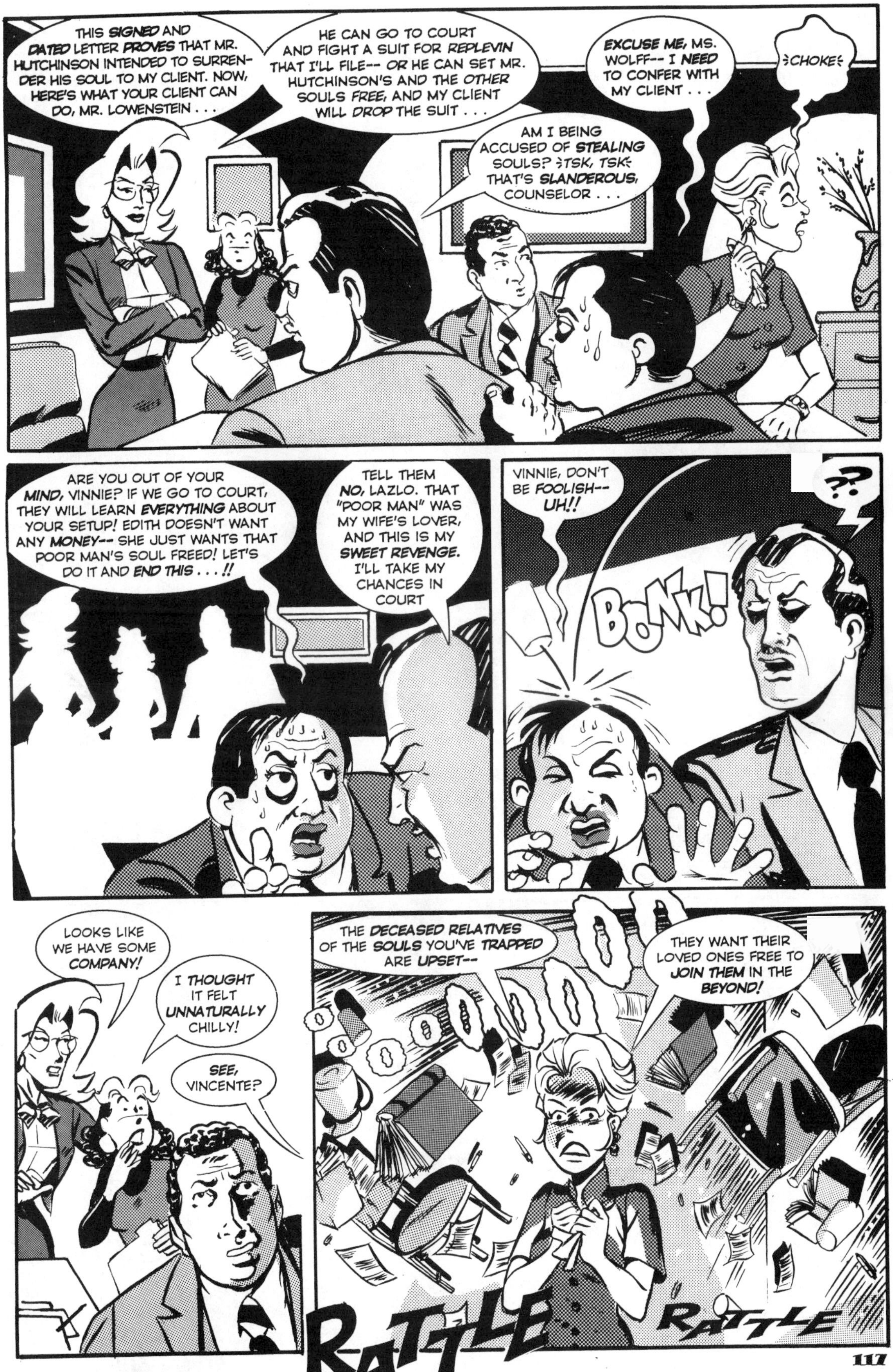

THIS SIGNED AND DATED LETTER PROVES THAT MR. HUTCHINSON INTENDED TO SURRENDER HIS SOUL TO MY CLIENT. NOW, HERE'S WHAT YOUR CLIENT CAN DO, MR. LOWENSTEIN . . .
HE CAN GO TO COURT AND FIGHT A SUIT FOR REPLEVIN THAT I'LL FILE-- OR HE CAN SET MR. HUTCHINSON'S AND THE OTHER SOULS FREE, AND MY CLIENT WILL DROP THE SUIT . . .
AM I BEING ACCUSED OF STEALING SOULS? TSK, TSK THAT'S SLANDEROUS, COUNSELOR . . .
EXCUSE ME, MS. WOLFF-- I NEED TO CONFER WITH MY CLIENT . . .
CHOKE
ARE YOU OUT OF YOUR MIND, VINNIE? IF WE GO TO COURT, THEY WILL LEARN EVERYTHING ABOUT YOUR SETUP! EDITH DOESN'T WANT ANY MONEY-- SHE JUST WANTS THAT POOR MAN'S SOUL FREED! LET'S DO IT AND END THIS . . . !!
TELL THEM NO, LAZLO. THAT "POOR MAN" WAS MY WIFE'S LOVER, AND THIS IS MY SWEET REVENGE. I'LL TAKE MY CHANCES IN COURT
VINNIE, DON'T BE FOOLISH-- UH!!
?!
BONK!
LOOKS LIKE WE HAVE SOME COMPANY!
I THOUGHT IT FELT UNNATURALLY CHILLY!
SEE, VINCENTE?
THE DECEASED RELATIVES OF THE SOULS YOU'VE TRAPPED ARE UPSET--
THEY WANT THEIR LOVED ONES FREE TO JOIN THEM IN THE BEYOND!
RATTLE
RATTLE

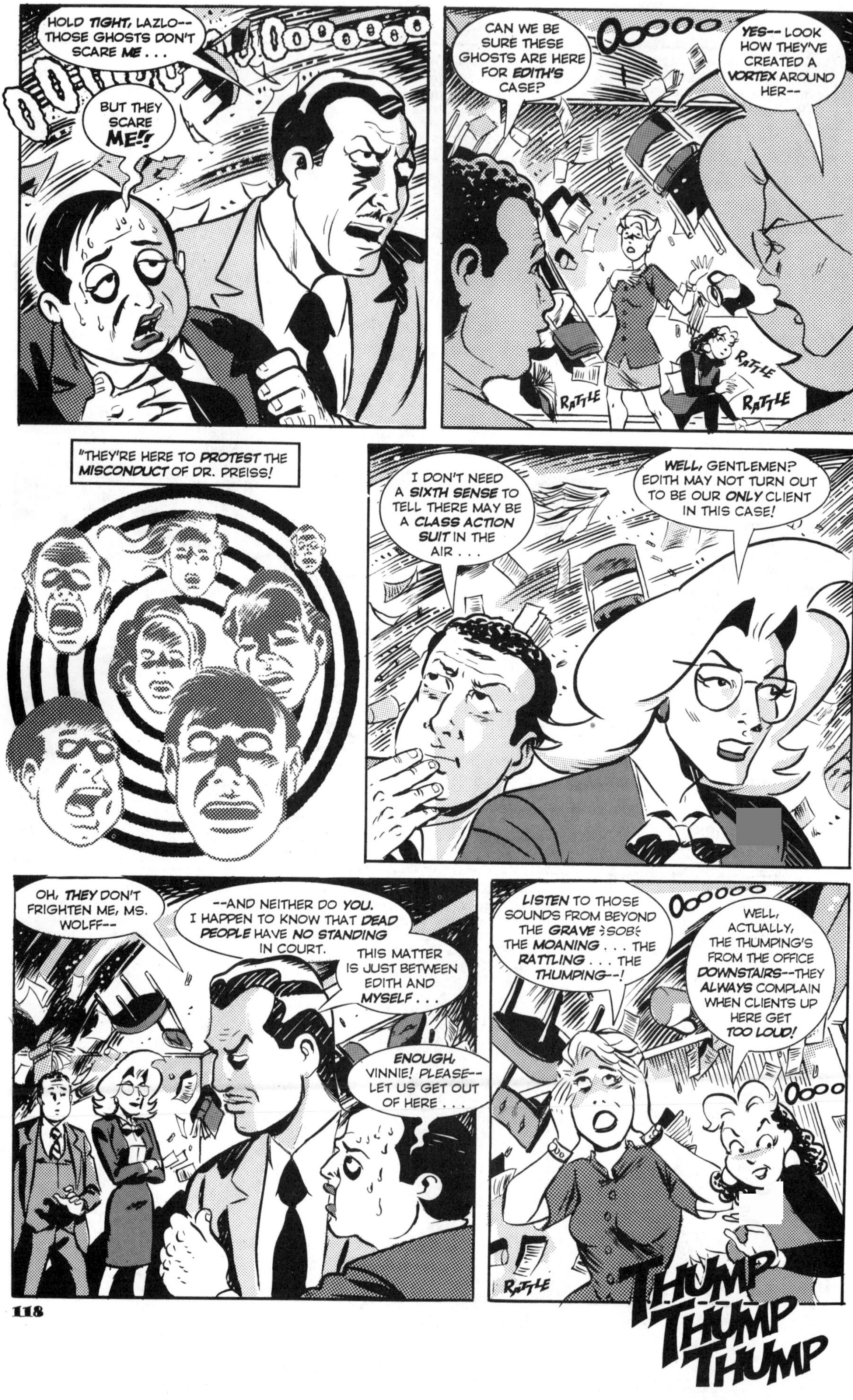
HOLD TIGHT, LAZLO-- THOSE GHOSTS DON'T SCARE ME . . .
BUT THEY SCARE ME!!
CAN WE BE SURE THESE GHOSTS ARE HERE FOR EDITH'S CASE?
OOOOO
YES-- LOOK HOW THEY'VE CREATED A VORTEX AROUND HER--
RATTLE
RATTLE
RATTLE
"THEY'RE HERE TO PROTEST THE MISCONDUCT OF DR. PREISS!
I DON'T NEED A SIXTH SENSE TO TELL THERE MAY BE A CLASS ACTION SUIT IN THE AIR . . .
WELL, GENTLEMEN? EDITH MAY NOT TURN OUT TO BE OUR ONLY CLIENT IN THIS CASE!
OH, THEY DON'T FRIGHTEN ME, MS. WOLFF--
--AND NEITHER DO YOU. I HAPPEN TO KNOW THAT DEAD PEOPLE HAVE NO STANDING IN COURT.
THIS MATTER IS JUST BETWEEN EDITH AND MYSELF . . .
ENOUGH, VINNIE! PLEASE-- LET US GET OUT OF HERE . . .
LISTEN TO THOSE SOUNDS FROM BEYOND THE GRAVE ⁓SOB⁓ THE MOANING . . . THE RATTLING . . . THE THUMPING--!
OOOOOO
WELL, ACTUALLY, THE THUMPING'S FROM THE OFFICE DOWNSTAIRS--THEY ALWAYS COMPLAIN WHEN CLIENTS UP HERE GET TOO LOUD!
OOOO
RATTLE
THUMP THUMP THUMP

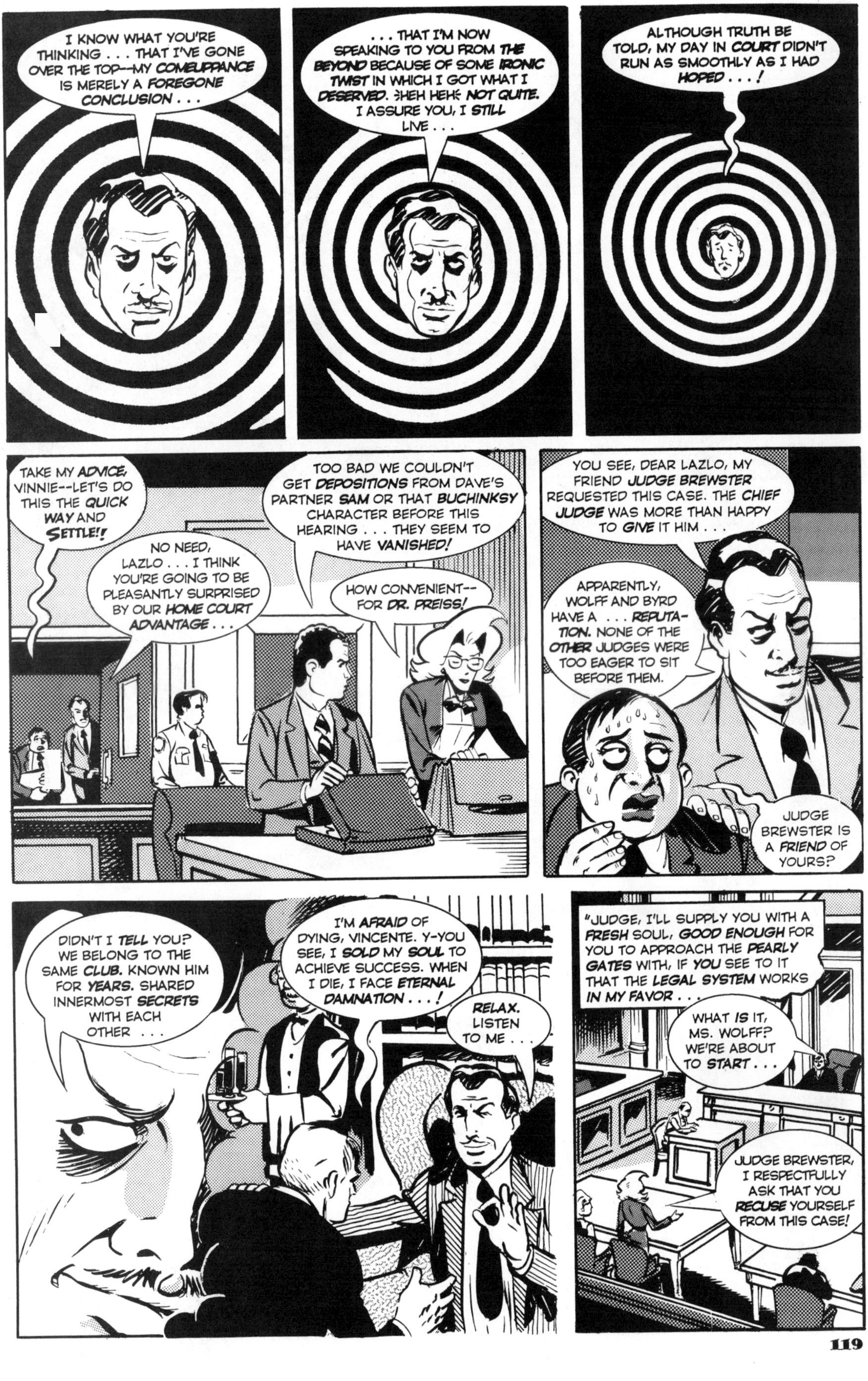
I KNOW WHAT YOU'RE THINKING . . . THAT I'VE GONE OVER THE TOP--MY COMEUPPANCE IS MERELY A FOREGONE CONCLUSION . . .
. . . THAT I'M NOW SPEAKING TO YOU FROM THE BEYOND BECAUSE OF SOME IRONIC TWIST IN WHICH I GOT WHAT I DESERVED. HEH HEH NOT QUITE. I ASSURE YOU, I STILL LIVE . . .
ALTHOUGH TRUTH BE TOLD, MY DAY IN COURT DIDN'T RUN AS SMOOTHLY AS I HAD HOPED . . . !
TAKE MY ADVICE, VINNIE--LET'S DO THIS THE QUICK WAY AND SETTLE!!
NO NEED, LAZLO . . . I THINK YOU'RE GOING TO BE PLEASANTLY SURPRISED BY OUR HOME COURT ADVANTAGE . . .
TOO BAD WE COULDN'T GET DEPOSITIONS FROM DAVE'S PARTNER SAM OR THAT BUCHINKSY CHARACTER BEFORE THIS HEARING . . . THEY SEEM TO HAVE VANISHED!
HOW CONVENIENT-- FOR DR. PREISS!
YOU SEE, DEAR LAZLO, MY FRIEND JUDGE BREWSTER REQUESTED THIS CASE. THE CHIEF JUDGE WAS MORE THAN HAPPY TO GIVE IT HIM . . .
APPARENTLY, WOLFF AND BYRD HAVE A . . . REPUTATION. NONE OF THE OTHER JUDGES WERE TOO EAGER TO SIT BEFORE THEM.
JUDGE BREWSTER IS A FRIEND OF YOURS?
DIDN'T I TELL YOU? WE BELONG TO THE SAME CLUB. KNOWN HIM FOR YEARS. SHARED INNERMOST SECRETS WITH EACH OTHER . . .
I'M AFRAID OF DYING, VINCENTE. Y-YOU SEE, I SOLD MY SOUL TO ACHIEVE SUCCESS. WHEN I DIE, I FACE ETERNAL DAMNATION . . . !
RELAX. LISTEN TO ME . . .
"JUDGE, I'LL SUPPLY YOU WITH A FRESH SOUL, GOOD ENOUGH FOR YOU TO APPROACH THE PEARLY GATES WITH, IF YOU SEE TO IT THAT THE LEGAL SYSTEM WORKS IN MY FAVOR . . .
WHAT IS IT, MS. WOLFF? WE'RE ABOUT TO START . . .
JUDGE BREWSTER, I RESPECTFULLY ASK THAT YOU RECUSE YOURSELF FROM THIS CASE!

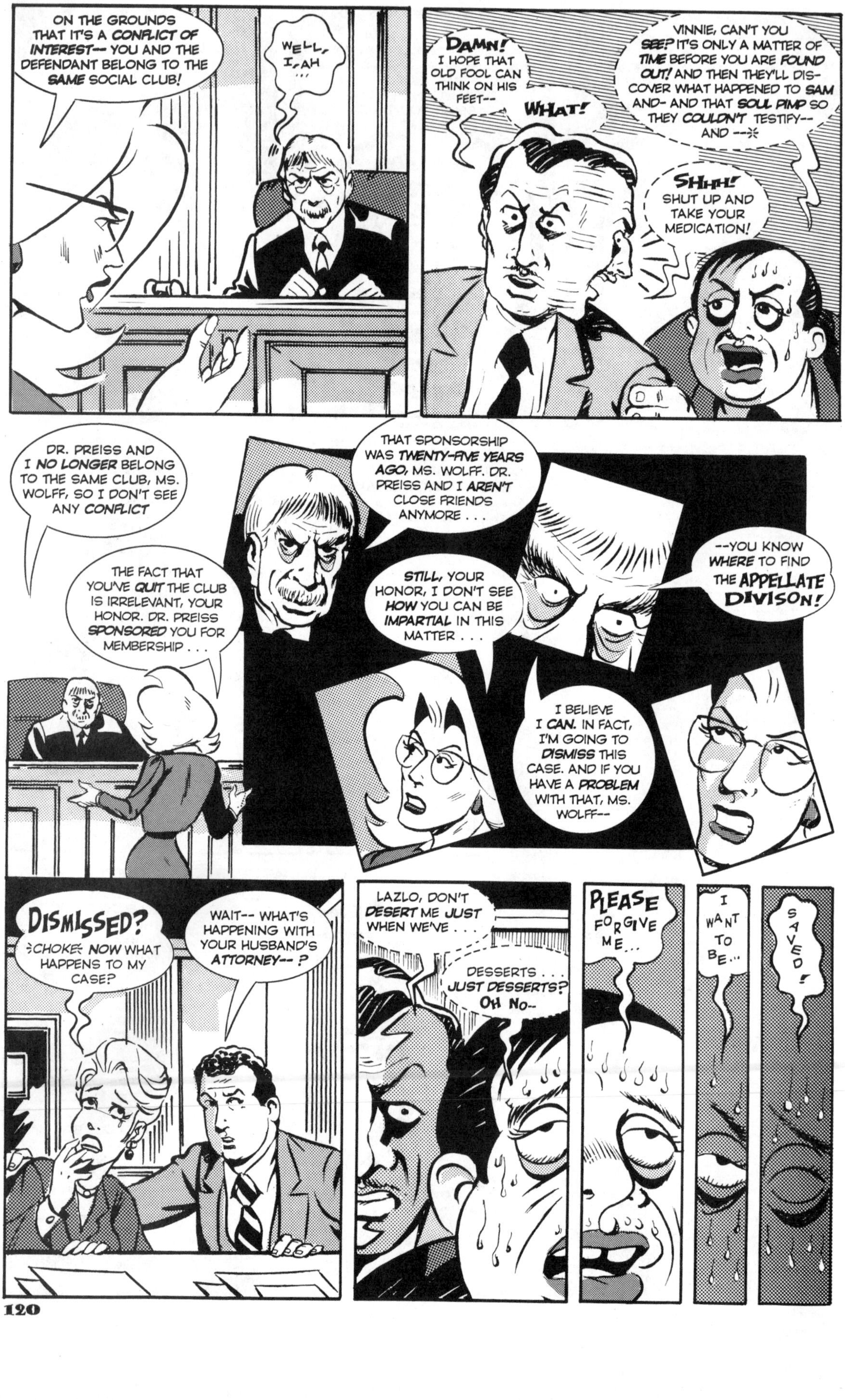
ON THE GROUNDS THAT IT'S A CONFLICT OF INTEREST-- YOU AND THE DEFENDANT BELONG TO THE SAME SOCIAL CLUB!
WELL, I, AH ...
DAMN! I HOPE THAT OLD FOOL CAN THINK ON HIS FEET--
WHAT!
VINNIE, CAN'T YOU SEE? IT'S ONLY A MATTER OF TIME BEFORE YOU ARE FOUND OUT! AND THEN THEY'LL DISCOVER WHAT HAPPENED TO SAM AND- AND THAT SOUL PIMP SO THEY COULDN'T TESTIFY-- AND --
SHHH! SHUT UP AND TAKE YOUR MEDICATION!
DR. PREISS AND I NO LONGER BELONG TO THE SAME CLUB, MS. WOLFF, SO I DON'T SEE ANY CONFLICT
THE FACT THAT YOU'VE QUIT THE CLUB IS IRRELEVANT, YOUR HONOR. DR. PREISS SPONSORED YOU FOR MEMBERSHIP . . .
THAT SPONSORSHIP WAS TWENTY-FIVE YEARS AGO, MS. WOLFF. DR. PREISS AND I AREN'T CLOSE FRIENDS ANYMORE . . .
STILL, YOUR HONOR, I DON'T SEE HOW YOU CAN BE IMPARTIAL IN THIS MATTER . . .
I BELIEVE I CAN. IN FACT, I'M GOING TO DISMISS THIS CASE. AND IF YOU HAVE A PROBLEM WITH THAT, MS. WOLFF--
--YOU KNOW WHERE TO FIND THE APPELLATE DIVISON!
DISMISSED? CHOKE NOW WHAT HAPPENS TO MY CASE?
WAIT-- WHAT'S HAPPENING WITH YOUR HUSBAND'S ATTORNEY-- ?
LAZLO, DON'T DESERT ME JUST WHEN WE'VE . . .
DESSERTS . . . JUST DESSERTS? OH NO--
PLEASE FORGIVE ME...
I WANT TO BE...
SAVED!

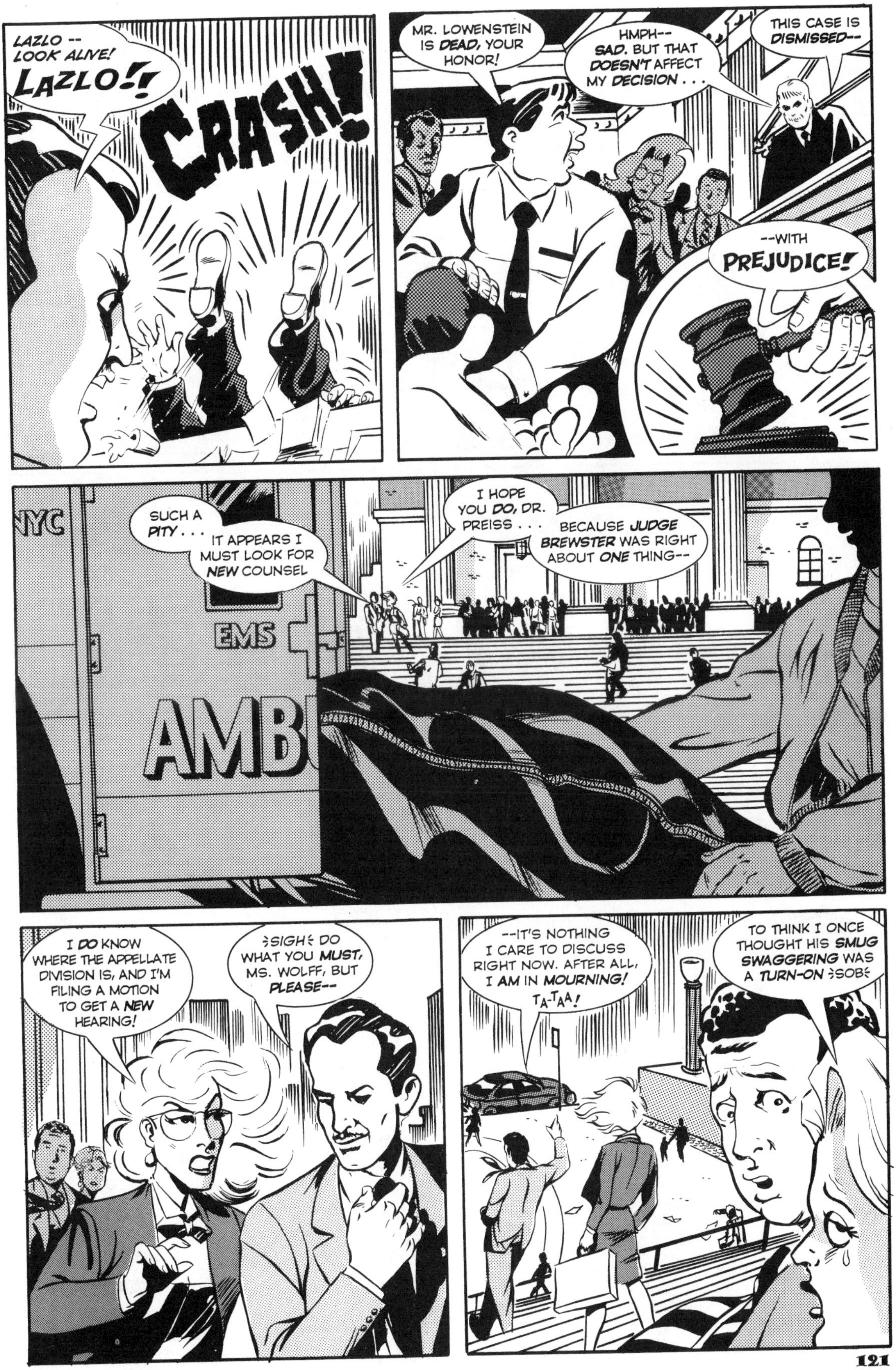
LAZLO -- LOOK ALIVE! LAZLO!!
CRASH!
MR. LOWENSTEIN IS DEAD, YOUR HONOR!
HMPH-- SAD. BUT THAT DOESN'T AFFECT MY DECISION . . .
THIS CASE IS DISMISSED--
--WITH PREJUDICE!
NYC
EMS
AMB
SUCH A PITY . . .
IT APPEARS I MUST LOOK FOR NEW COUNSEL
I HOPE YOU DO, DR. PREISS . . .
BECAUSE JUDGE BREWSTER WAS RIGHT ABOUT ONE THING--
I DO KNOW WHERE THE APPELLATE DIVISION IS, AND I'M FILING A MOTION TO GET A NEW HEARING!
SIGH DO WHAT YOU MUST, MS. WOLFF, BUT PLEASE--
--IT'S NOTHING I CARE TO DISCUSS RIGHT NOW. AFTER ALL, I AM IN MOURNING!
TA-TAA!
TO THINK I ONCE THOUGHT HIS SMUG SWAGGERING WAS A TURN-ON SOB

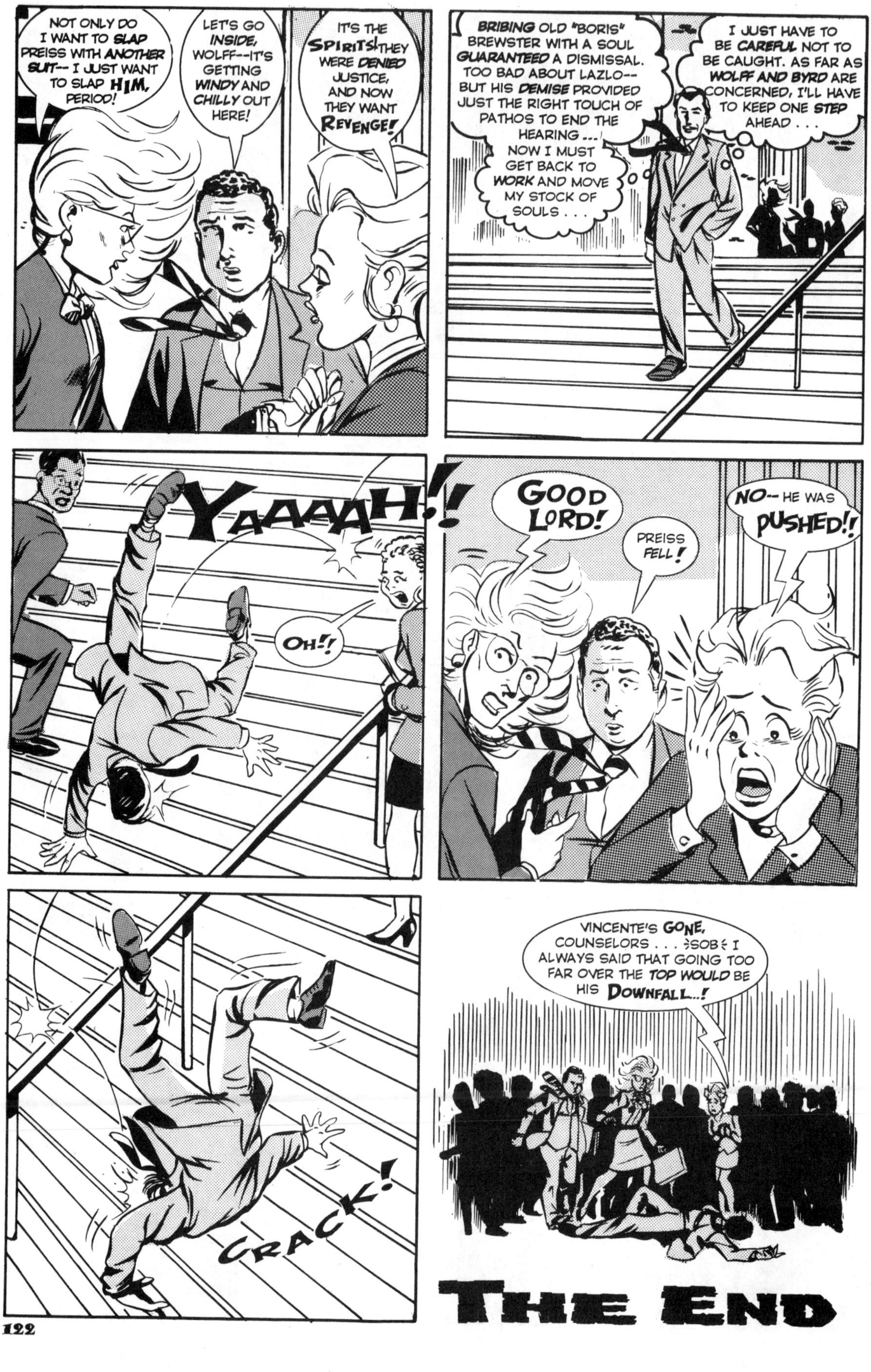
NOT ONLY DO I WANT TO SLAP PREISS WITH ANOTHER SUIT-- I JUST WANT TO SLAP HIM, PERIOD!
LET'S GO INSIDE, WOLFF--IT'S GETTING WINDY AND CHILLY OUT HERE!
IT'S THE SPIRITS! THEY WERE DENIED JUSTICE, AND NOW THEY WANT REVENGE!
BRIBING OLD "BORIS" BREWSTER WITH A SOUL GUARANTEED A DISMISSAL. TOO BAD ABOUT LAZLO-- BUT HIS DEMISE PROVIDED JUST THE RIGHT TOUCH OF PATHOS TO END THE HEARING ...
NOW I MUST GET BACK TO WORK AND MOVE MY STOCK OF SOULS . . .
I JUST HAVE TO BE CAREFUL NOT TO BE CAUGHT. AS FAR AS WOLFF AND BYRD ARE CONCERNED, I'LL HAVE TO KEEP ONE STEP AHEAD . . .
YAAAAH!!
OH!?
GOOD LORD!
PREISS FELL!
NO-- HE WAS PUSHED!!
CRACK!
VINCENTE'S GONE, COUNSELORS . . . SOB I ALWAYS SAID THAT GOING TOO FAR OVER THE TOP WOULD BE HIS DOWNFALL..!
THE END

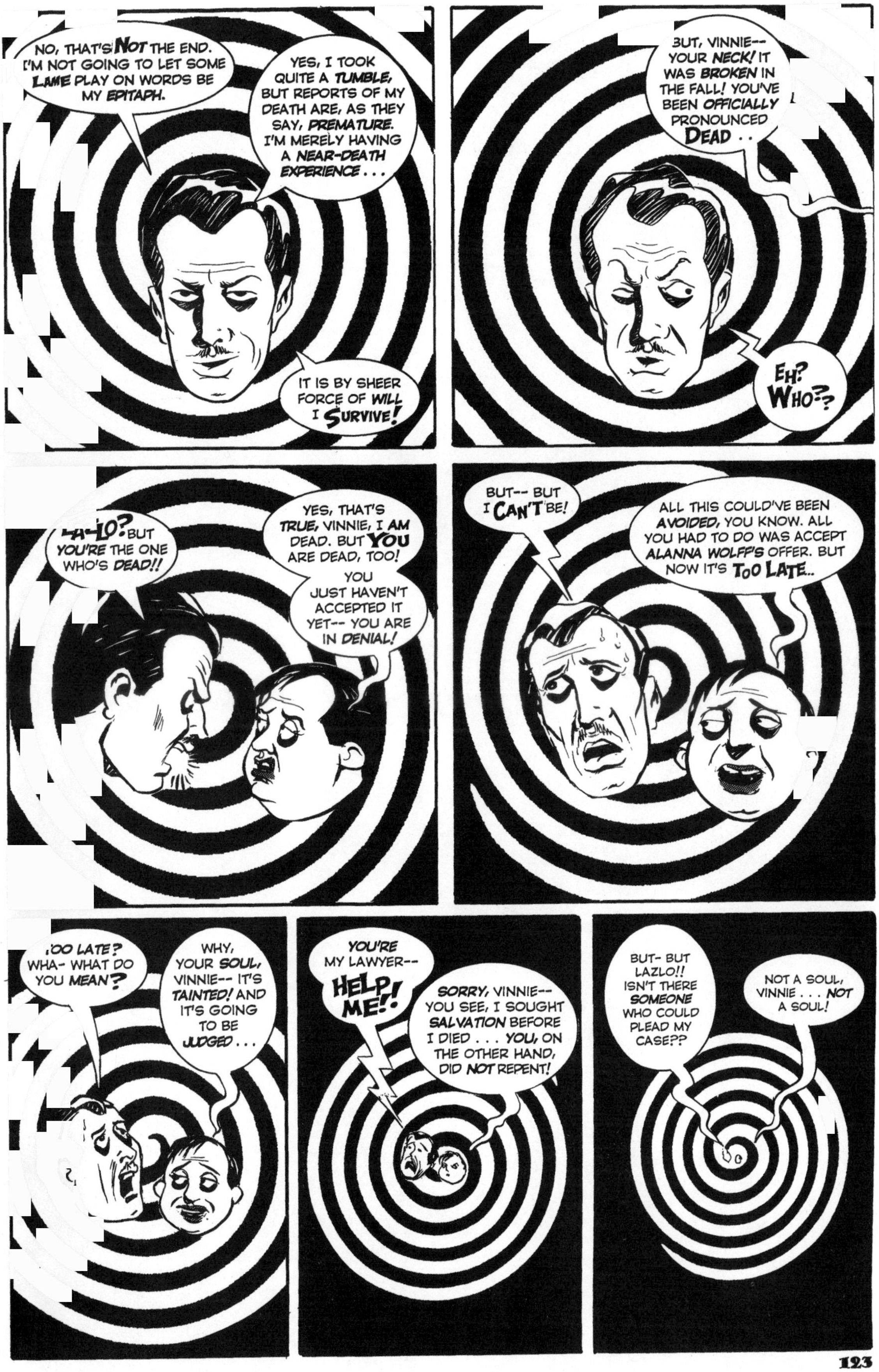

NO, THAT'S NOT THE END. I'M NOT GOING TO LET SOME LAME PLAY ON WORDS BE MY EPITAPH.
YES, I TOOK QUITE A TUMBLE, BUT REPORTS OF MY DEATH ARE, AS THEY SAY, PREMATURE. I'M MERELY HAVING A NEAR-DEATH EXPERIENCE . . .
IT IS BY SHEER FORCE OF WILL I SURVIVE!
BUT, VINNIE-- YOUR NECK! IT WAS BROKEN IN THE FALL! YOU'VE BEEN OFFICIALLY PRONOUNCED DEAD . .
EH? WHO??
BUT YOU'RE THE ONE WHO'S DEAD!!
YES, THAT'S TRUE, VINNIE, I AM DEAD. BUT YOU ARE DEAD, TOO!
YOU JUST HAVEN'T ACCEPTED IT YET-- YOU ARE IN DENIAL!
BUT-- BUT I CAN'T BE!
ALL THIS COULD'VE BEEN AVOIDED, YOU KNOW. ALL YOU HAD TO DO WAS ACCEPT ALANNA WOLFF'S OFFER. BUT NOW IT'S TOO LATE..
OO LATE? WHA- WHAT DO YOU MEAN?
WHY, YOUR SOUL, VINNIE-- IT'S TAINTED! AND IT'S GOING TO BE JUDGED . . .
YOU'RE MY LAWYER-- HELP ME!!
SORRY, VINNIE-- YOU SEE, I SOUGHT SALVATION BEFORE I DIED . . . YOU, ON THE OTHER HAND, DID NOT REPENT!
BUT- BUT LAZLO!! ISN'T THERE SOMEONE WHO COULD PLEAD MY CASE??
NOT A SOUL, VINNIE . . . NOT A SOUL!

Courting Disaster

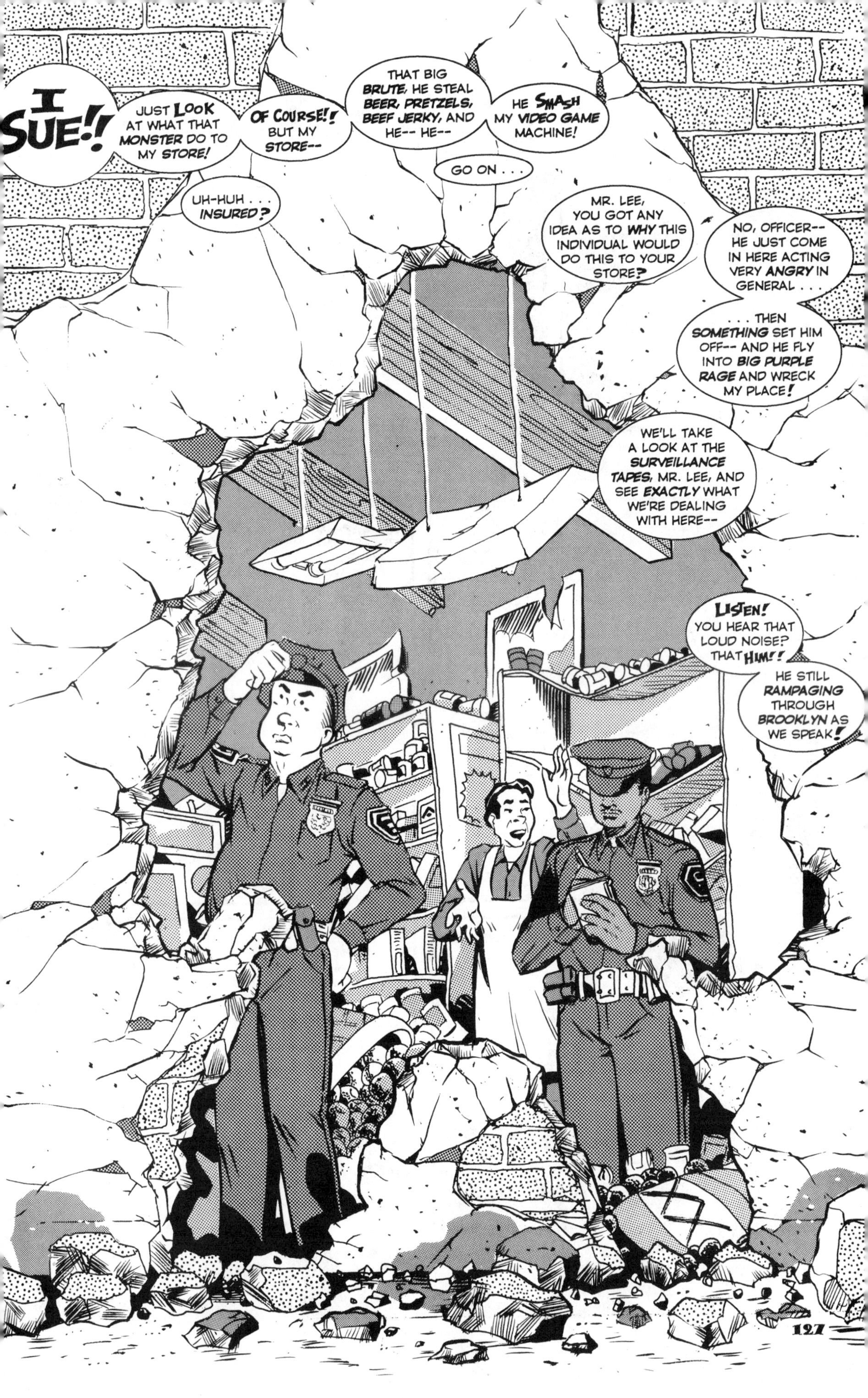

I SUE!!
JUST LOOK AT WHAT THAT MONSTER DO TO MY STORE!
UH-HUH . . . INSURED?
OF COURSE!! BUT MY STORE--
THAT BIG BRUTE, HE STEAL BEER, PRETZELS, BEEF JERKY, AND HE-- HE--
GO ON . . .
HE SMASH MY VIDEO GAME MACHINE!
MR. LEE, YOU GOT ANY IDEA AS TO WHY THIS INDIVIDUAL WOULD DO THIS TO YOUR STORE?
NO, OFFICER-- HE JUST COME IN HERE ACTING VERY ANGRY IN GENERAL . . .
. . . THEN SOMETHING SET HIM OFF-- AND HE FLY INTO BIG PURPLE RAGE AND WRECK MY PLACE!
WE'LL TAKE A LOOK AT THE SURVEILLANCE TAPES, MR. LEE, AND SEE EXACTLY WHAT WE'RE DEALING WITH HERE--
LISTEN! YOU HEAR THAT LOUD NOISE? THAT HIM!!
HE STILL RAMPAGING THROUGH BROOKLYN AS WE SPEAK!

WHOOM! ...'RE GOING TO SPEAK UP-- SPEAK UP--

WHOOM! I CAN'T HEAR YOU

WOLFF & B
COUNSELO
OF THE
MACABRE

WHOOM! ...FINALLY SUBSIDING! MUST BE ALL THE *STREET CONSTRUCTION!* HOLD PLEASE...

THIS IS THE LAW OFFICES OF WOLFF AND BYRD, COUNSELORS OF THE MACABRE. *COREY* SPEAKING. HOW MAY I HELP YOU?

WHY, HELLO, *DOCTOR!* YES, MY SISTER--I MEAN *MS.* WOLFF--SAYS THE PAPERWORK'S DONE-- YOU CAN PICK UP, UH, YOUR *EXPERIMENT.*

YOU'LL SEND SOMEONE? *GOOD!* BYE BYE!

HELLO? *RICHIE?* SORRY TO KEEP YOU ON *HOLD,* BUT I *AM* AT *WORK,* Y'KNOW-- ONE SEC...

¿AHEM¿ EXCUSE ME...?

GRUNT.

YOUR *MASTER* SAID *FRITZ* WILL COME BY FOR YOU.

SO JUST TAKE A SEAT OR HANG BACK AND RELAX, OKAY?

GRUNT.

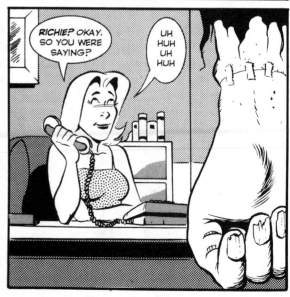

RICHIE? OKAY. SO YOU WERE SAYING?

UH HUH UH HUH

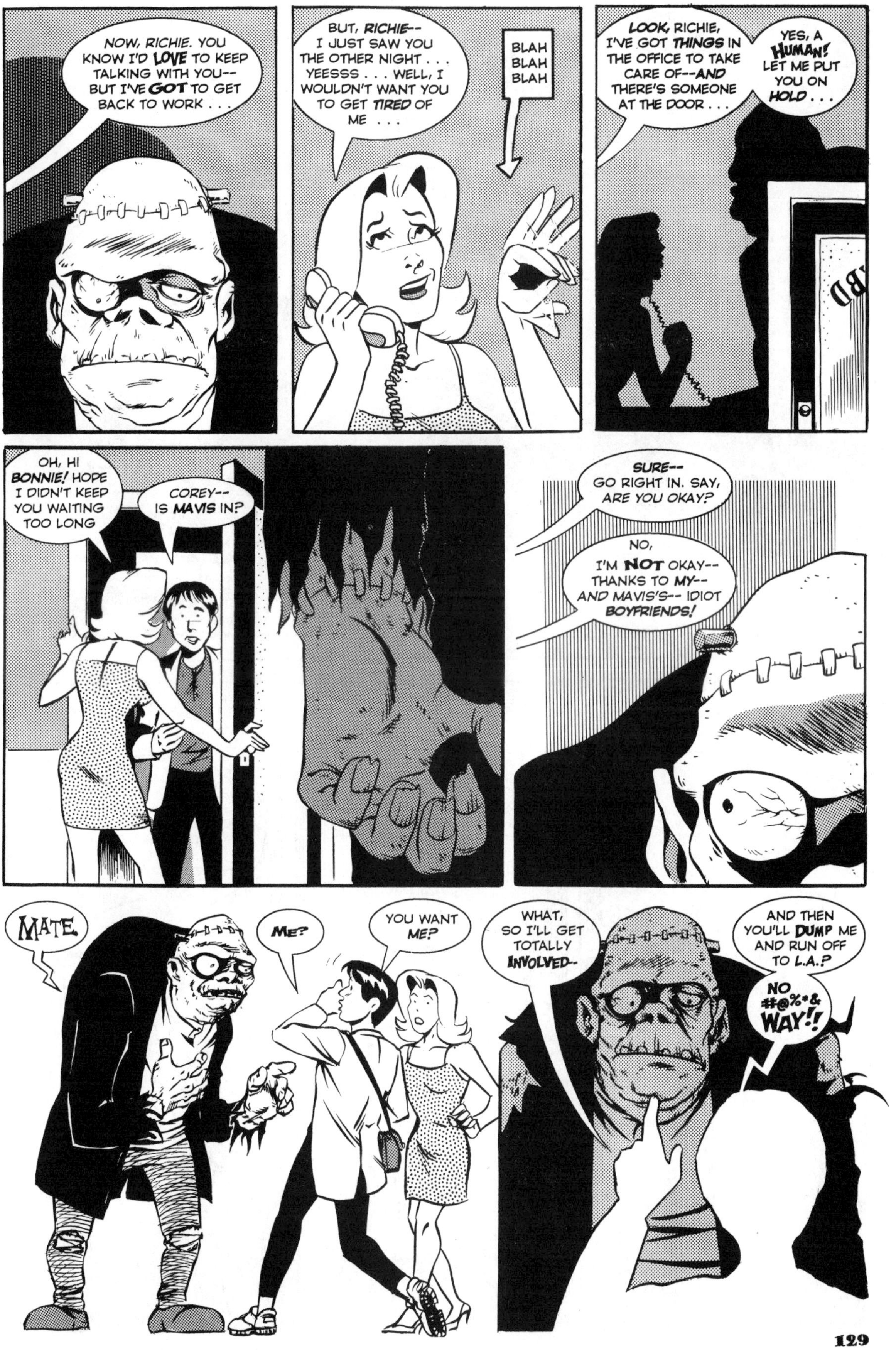
NOW, RICHIE. YOU KNOW I'D LOVE TO KEEP TALKING WITH YOU-- BUT I'VE GOT TO GET BACK TO WORK . . .
BUT, RICHIE-- I JUST SAW YOU THE OTHER NIGHT . . . YEESSS . . . WELL, I WOULDN'T WANT YOU TO GET TIRED OF ME . . .
BLAH BLAH BLAH
LOOK, RICHIE, I'VE GOT THINGS IN THE OFFICE TO TAKE CARE OF--AND THERE'S SOMEONE AT THE DOOR . . .
YES, A HUMAN! LET ME PUT YOU ON HOLD . . .
OH, HI BONNIE! HOPE I DIDN'T KEEP YOU WAITING TOO LONG
COREY-- IS MAVIS IN?
SURE-- GO RIGHT IN. SAY, ARE YOU OKAY?
NO, I'M NOT OKAY-- THANKS TO MY-- AND MAVIS'S-- IDIOT BOYFRIENDS!
MATE.
ME?
YOU WANT ME?
WHAT, SO I'LL GET TOTALLY INVOLVED..
AND THEN YOU'LL DUMP ME AND RUN OFF TO L.A.?
NO #@%*& WAY!!

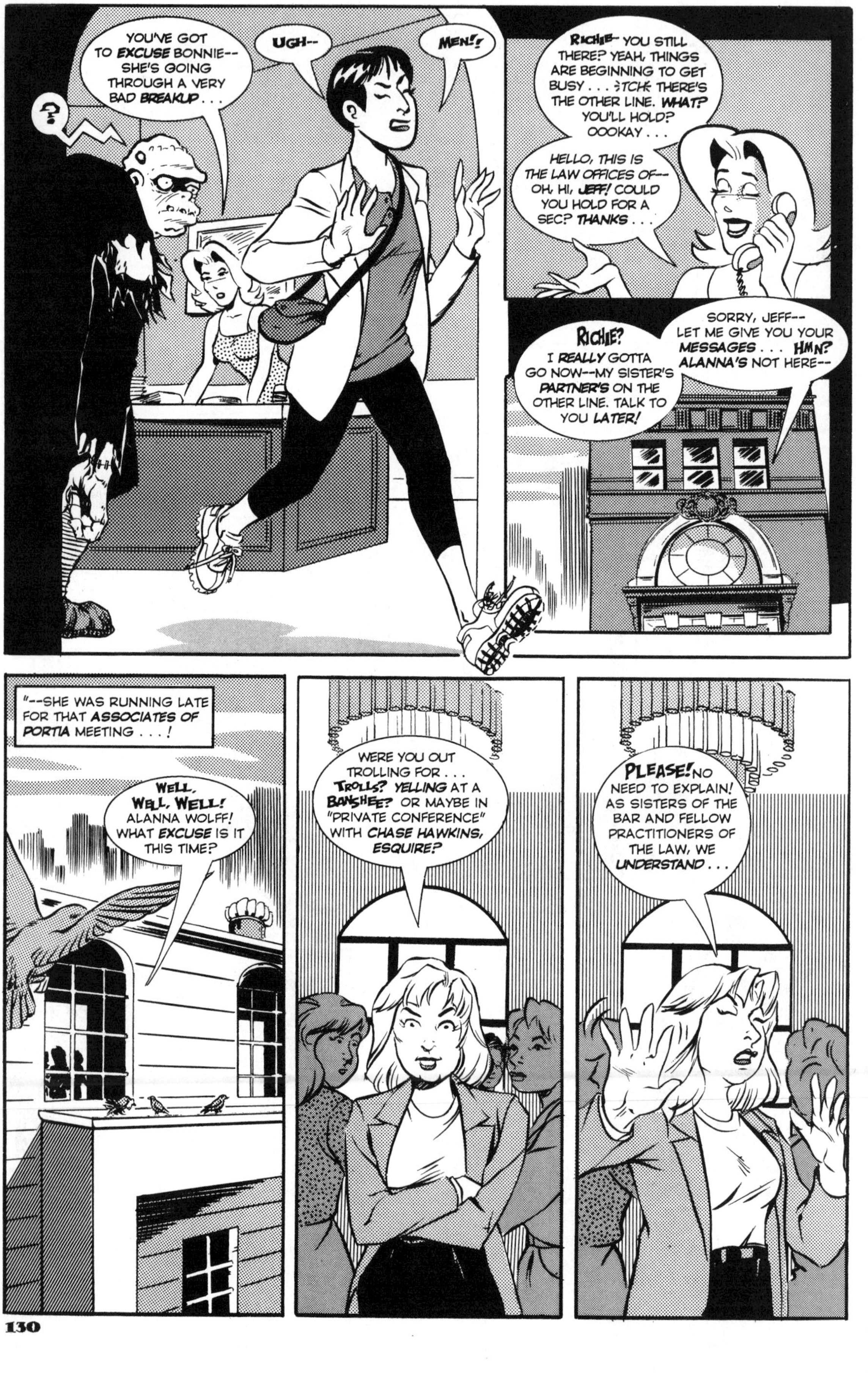

YOU'VE GOT TO EXCUSE BONNIE-- SHE'S GOING THROUGH A VERY BAD BREAKUP . . .
UGH--
MEN!?
?
RICHIE-- YOU STILL THERE? YEAH, THINGS ARE BEGINNING TO GET BUSY . . . TCH! THERE'S THE OTHER LINE. WHAT? YOU'LL HOLD? OOOKAY . . .
HELLO, THIS IS THE LAW OFFICES OF-- OH, HI, JEFF! COULD YOU HOLD FOR A SEC? THANKS . . .
RICHIE? I REALLY GOTTA GO NOW--MY SISTER'S PARTNER'S ON THE OTHER LINE. TALK TO YOU LATER!
SORRY, JEFF-- LET ME GIVE YOU YOUR MESSAGES . . . HMN? ALANNA'S NOT HERE--
"--SHE WAS RUNNING LATE FOR THAT ASSOCIATES OF PORTIA MEETING . . . !
WELL, WELL, WELL! ALANNA WOLFF! WHAT EXCUSE IS IT THIS TIME?
WERE YOU OUT TROLLING FOR . . . TROLLS? YELLING AT A BANSHEE? OR MAYBE IN "PRIVATE CONFERENCE" WITH CHASE HAWKINS, ESQUIRE?
PLEASE! NO NEED TO EXPLAIN! AS SISTERS OF THE BAR AND FELLOW PRACTITIONERS OF THE LAW, WE UNDERSTAND . . .

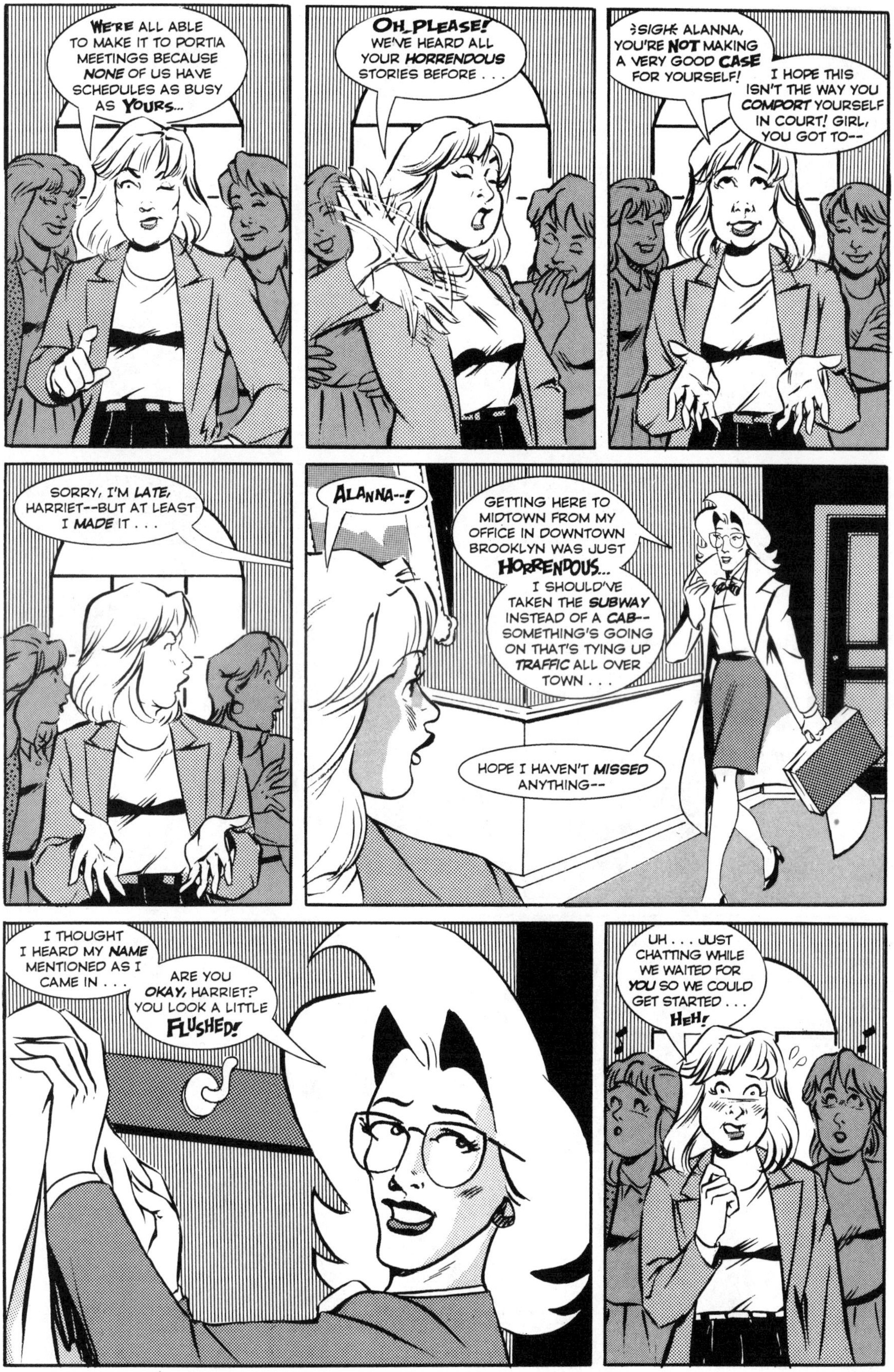
WE'RE ALL ABLE TO MAKE IT TO PORTIA MEETINGS BECAUSE NONE OF US HAVE SCHEDULES AS BUSY AS YOURS...
OH, PLEASE! WE'VE HEARD ALL YOUR HORRENDOUS STORIES BEFORE . . .
SIGH ALANNA, YOU'RE NOT MAKING A VERY GOOD CASE FOR YOURSELF!
I HOPE THIS ISN'T THE WAY YOU COMPORT YOURSELF IN COURT! GIRL, YOU GOT TO--
SORRY, I'M LATE, HARRIET--BUT AT LEAST I MADE IT . . .
ALANNA--!
GETTING HERE TO MIDTOWN FROM MY OFFICE IN DOWNTOWN BROOKLYN WAS JUST HORRENDOUS...
I SHOULD'VE TAKEN THE SUBWAY INSTEAD OF A CAB-- SOMETHING'S GOING ON THAT'S TYING UP TRAFFIC ALL OVER TOWN . . .
HOPE I HAVEN'T MISSED ANYTHING--
I THOUGHT I HEARD MY NAME MENTIONED AS I CAME IN . . .
ARE YOU OKAY, HARRIET? YOU LOOK A LITTLE FLUSHED!
UH . . . JUST CHATTING WHILE WE WAITED FOR YOU SO WE COULD GET STARTED . . .
HEH!

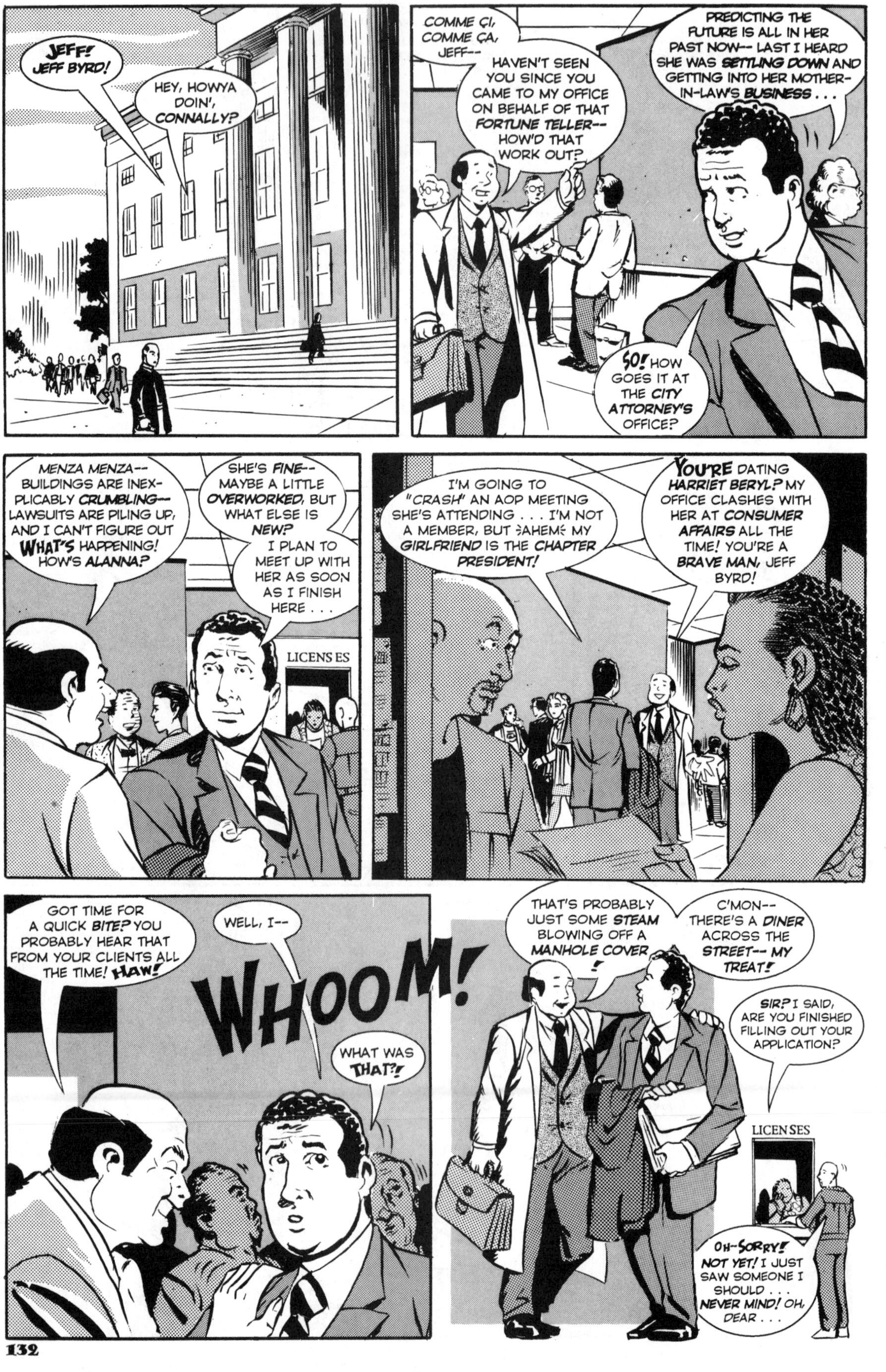
JEFF! JEFF BYRD!
HEY, HOWYA DOIN', CONNALLY?
COMME ÇI, COMME ÇA, JEFF--
HAVEN'T SEEN YOU SINCE YOU CAME TO MY OFFICE ON BEHALF OF THAT FORTUNE TELLER-- HOW'D THAT WORK OUT?
PREDICTING THE FUTURE IS ALL IN HER PAST NOW-- LAST I HEARD SHE WAS SETTLING DOWN AND GETTING INTO HER MOTHER-IN-LAW'S BUSINESS . . .
SO! HOW GOES IT AT THE CITY ATTORNEY'S OFFICE?
MENZA MENZA-- BUILDINGS ARE INEXPLICABLY CRUMBLING-- LAWSUITS ARE PILING UP, AND I CAN'T FIGURE OUT WHAT'S HAPPENING! HOW'S ALANNA?
SHE'S FINE-- MAYBE A LITTLE OVERWORKED, BUT WHAT ELSE IS NEW?
I PLAN TO MEET UP WITH HER AS SOON AS I FINISH HERE . . .
LICENSES
I'M GOING TO "CRASH" AN AOP MEETING SHE'S ATTENDING . . . I'M NOT A MEMBER, BUT AHEM MY GIRLFRIEND IS THE CHAPTER PRESIDENT!
YOU'RE DATING HARRIET BERYL? MY OFFICE CLASHES WITH HER AT CONSUMER AFFAIRS ALL THE TIME! YOU'RE A BRAVE MAN, JEFF BYRD!
GOT TIME FOR A QUICK BITE? YOU PROBABLY HEAR THAT FROM YOUR CLIENTS ALL THE TIME! HAW!
WELL, I--
WHOOM!
WHAT WAS THAT?!
THAT'S PROBABLY JUST SOME STEAM BLOWING OFF A MANHOLE COVER!
C'MON-- THERE'S A DINER ACROSS THE STREET-- MY TREAT!
SIR? I SAID, ARE YOU FINISHED FILLING OUT YOUR APPLICATION?
LICENSES
OH--SORRY! NOT YET! I JUST SAW SOMEONE I SHOULD . . . NEVER MIND! OH, DEAR . . .

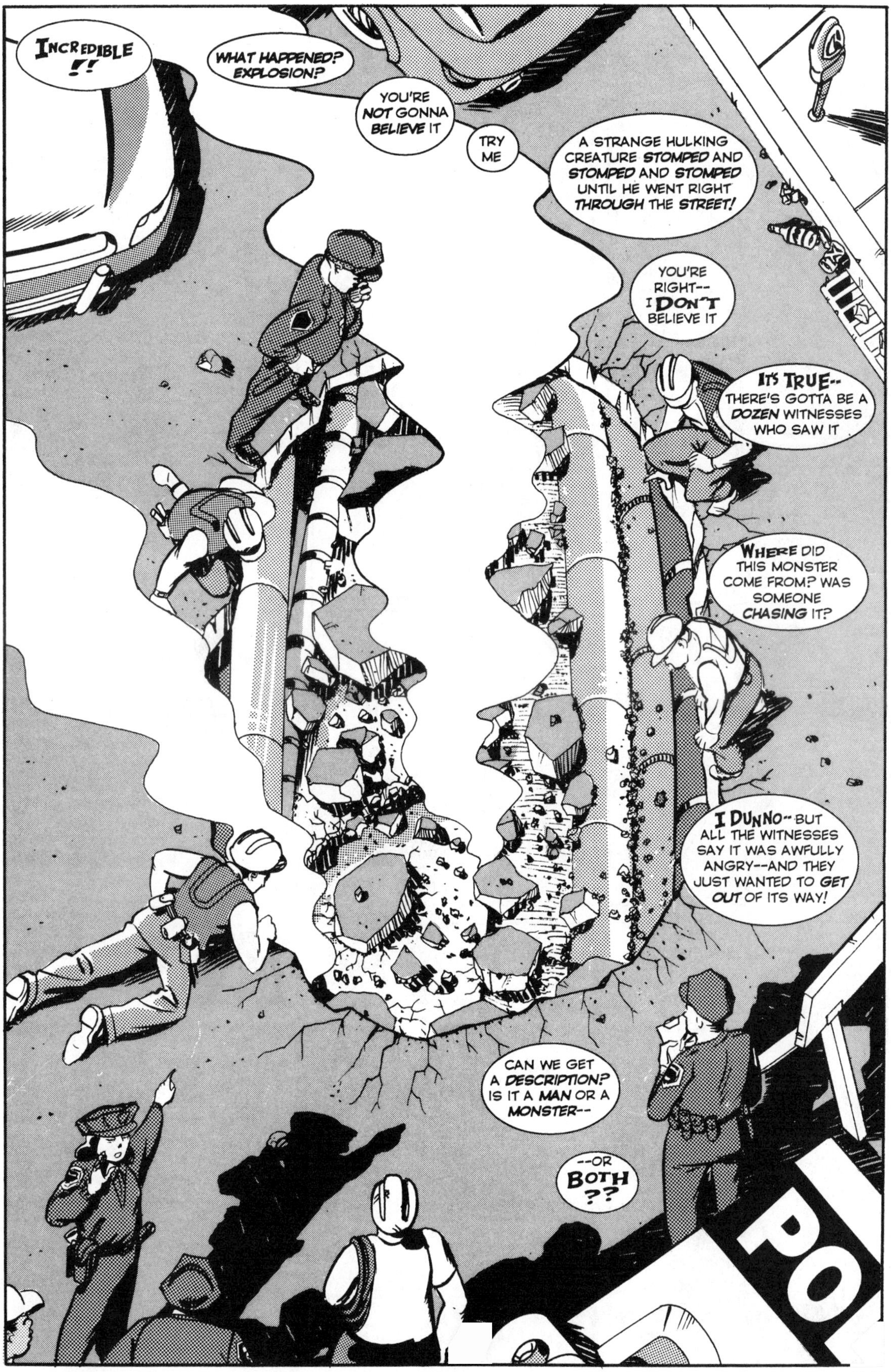
INCREDIBLE !!
WHAT HAPPENED? EXPLOSION?
YOU'RE NOT GONNA BELIEVE IT
TRY ME
A STRANGE HULKING CREATURE STOMPED AND STOMPED AND STOMPED UNTIL HE WENT RIGHT THROUGH THE STREET!
YOU'RE RIGHT-- I DON'T BELIEVE IT
IT'S TRUE-- THERE'S GOTTA BE A DOZEN WITNESSES WHO SAW IT
WHERE DID THIS MONSTER COME FROM? WAS SOMEONE CHASING IT?
I DUNNO-- BUT ALL THE WITNESSES SAY IT WAS AWFULLY ANGRY--AND THEY JUST WANTED TO GET OUT OF ITS WAY!
CAN WE GET A DESCRIPTION? IS IT A MAN OR A MONSTER--
--OR BOTH ??
PO

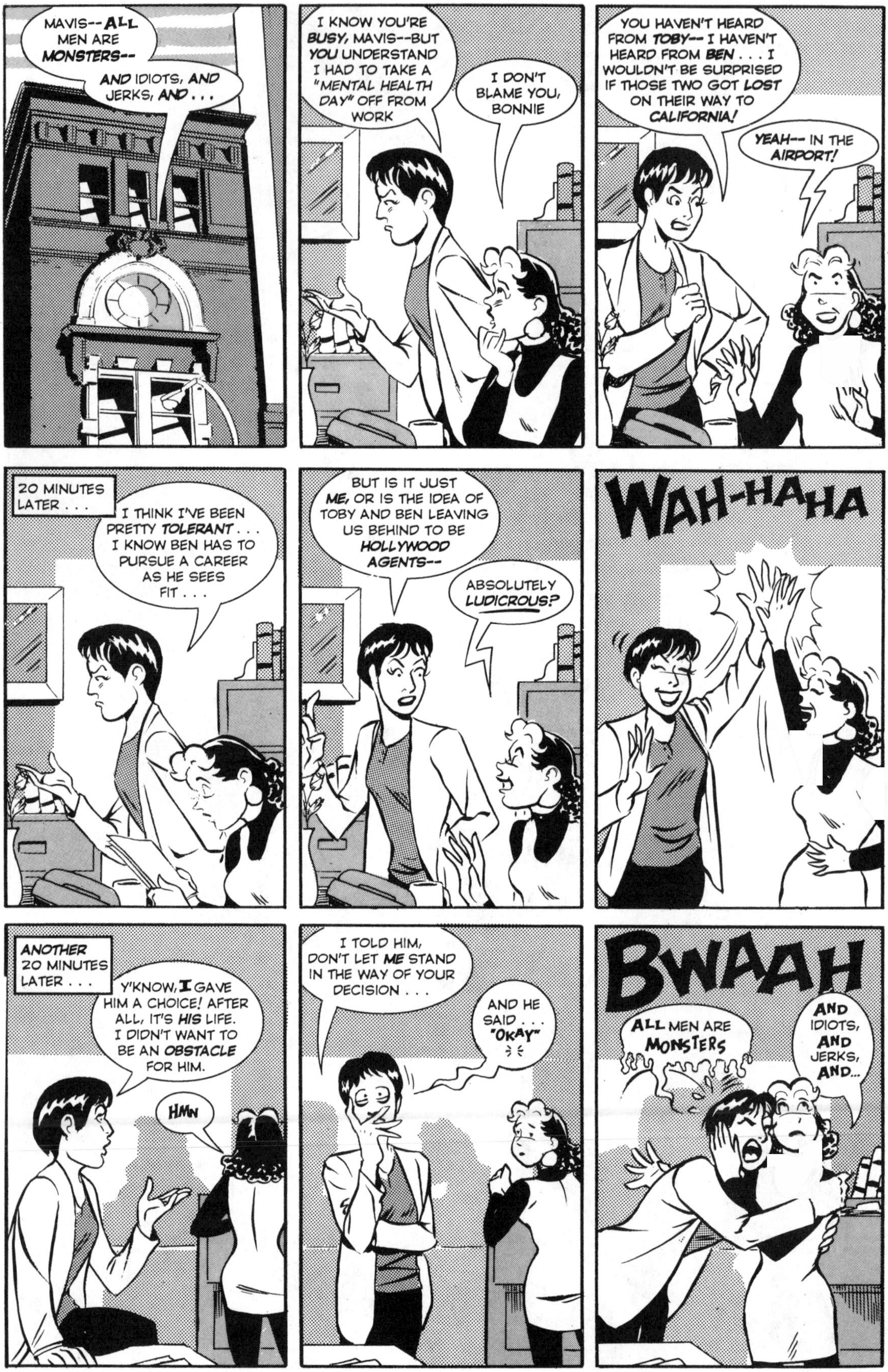

MAVIS--ALL MEN ARE MONSTERS--
AND IDIOTS, AND JERKS, AND . . .
I KNOW YOU'RE BUSY, MAVIS--BUT YOU UNDERSTAND I HAD TO TAKE A "MENTAL HEALTH DAY" OFF FROM WORK
I DON'T BLAME YOU, BONNIE
YOU HAVEN'T HEARD FROM TOBY-- I HAVEN'T HEARD FROM BEN . . . I WOULDN'T BE SURPRISED IF THOSE TWO GOT LOST ON THEIR WAY TO CALIFORNIA!
YEAH-- IN THE AIRPORT!
20 MINUTES LATER . . .
I THINK I'VE BEEN PRETTY TOLERANT . . . I KNOW BEN HAS TO PURSUE A CAREER AS HE SEES FIT . . .
BUT IS IT JUST ME, OR IS THE IDEA OF TOBY AND BEN LEAVING US BEHIND TO BE HOLLYWOOD AGENTS--
ABSOLUTELY LUDICROUS?
WAH-HAHA
ANOTHER 20 MINUTES LATER . . .
Y'KNOW, I GAVE HIM A CHOICE! AFTER ALL, IT'S HIS LIFE. I DIDN'T WANT TO BE AN OBSTACLE FOR HIM.
HMN
I TOLD HIM, DON'T LET ME STAND IN THE WAY OF YOUR DECISION . . .
AND HE SAID . . . "OKAY"
BWAAH
ALL MEN ARE MONSTERS
AND IDIOTS, AND JERKS, AND...

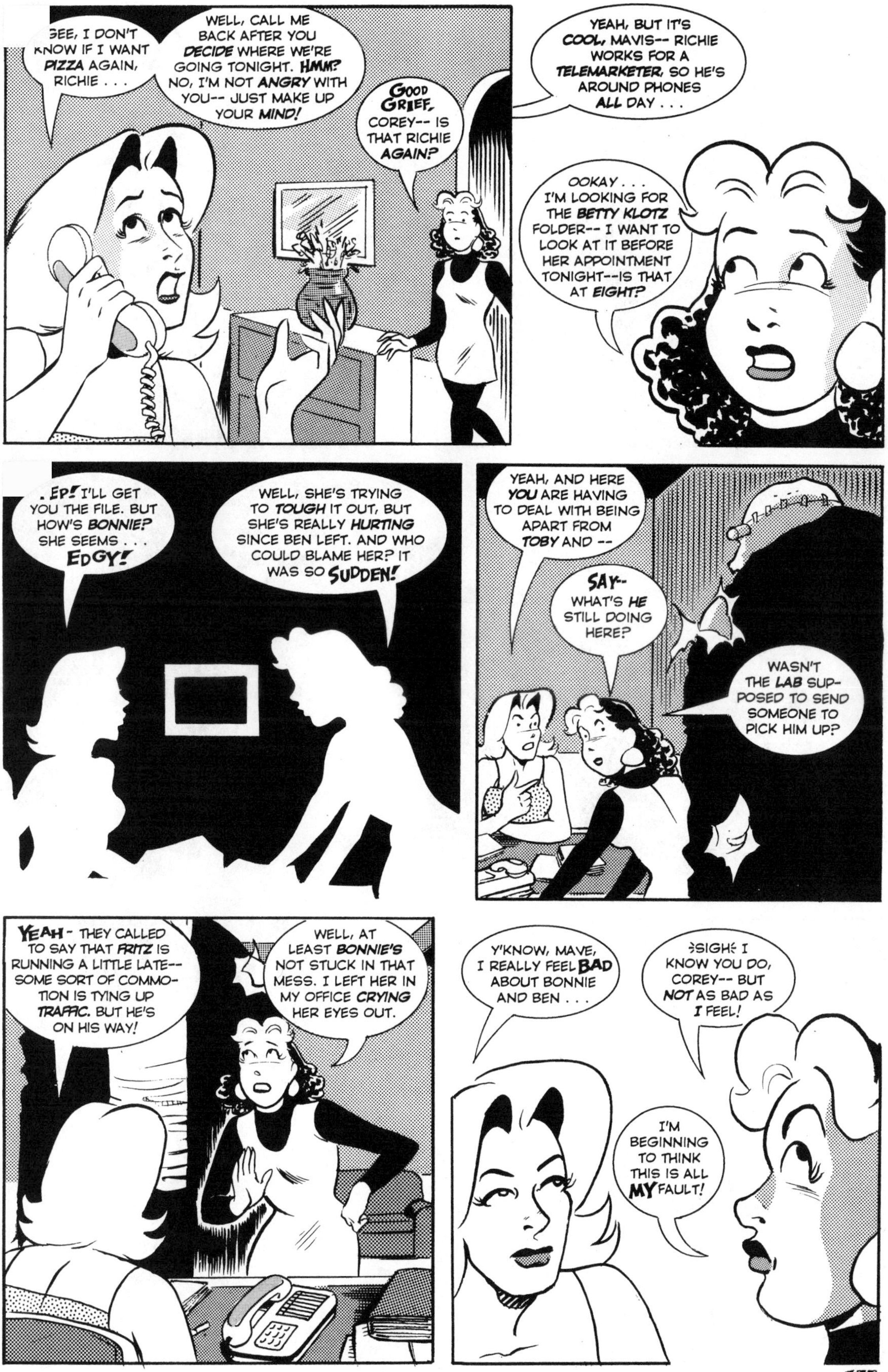
GEE, I DON'T KNOW IF I WANT PIZZA AGAIN, RICHIE . . .
WELL, CALL ME BACK AFTER YOU DECIDE WHERE WE'RE GOING TONIGHT. HMM? NO, I'M NOT ANGRY WITH YOU-- JUST MAKE UP YOUR MIND!
GOOD GRIEF, COREY-- IS THAT RICHIE AGAIN?
YEAH, BUT IT'S COOL, MAVIS-- RICHIE WORKS FOR A TELEMARKETER, SO HE'S AROUND PHONES ALL DAY . . .
OOKAY . . . I'M LOOKING FOR THE BETTY KLOTZ FOLDER-- I WANT TO LOOK AT IT BEFORE HER APPOINTMENT TONIGHT--IS THAT AT EIGHT?
. EP! I'LL GET YOU THE FILE. BUT HOW'S BONNIE? SHE SEEMS . . . EDGY!
WELL, SHE'S TRYING TO TOUGH IT OUT, BUT SHE'S REALLY HURTING SINCE BEN LEFT. AND WHO COULD BLAME HER? IT WAS SO SUDDEN!
YEAH, AND HERE YOU ARE HAVING TO DEAL WITH BEING APART FROM TOBY AND --
SAY-- WHAT'S HE STILL DOING HERE?
WASN'T THE LAB SUPPOSED TO SEND SOMEONE TO PICK HIM UP?
YEAH - THEY CALLED TO SAY THAT FRITZ IS RUNNING A LITTLE LATE-- SOME SORT OF COMMOTION IS TYING UP TRAFFIC. BUT HE'S ON HIS WAY!
WELL, AT LEAST BONNIE'S NOT STUCK IN THAT MESS. I LEFT HER IN MY OFFICE CRYING HER EYES OUT.
Y'KNOW, MAVE, I REALLY FEEL BAD ABOUT BONNIE AND BEN . . .
SIGH I KNOW YOU DO, COREY-- BUT NOT AS BAD AS I FEEL!
I'M BEGINNING TO THINK THIS IS ALL MY FAULT!

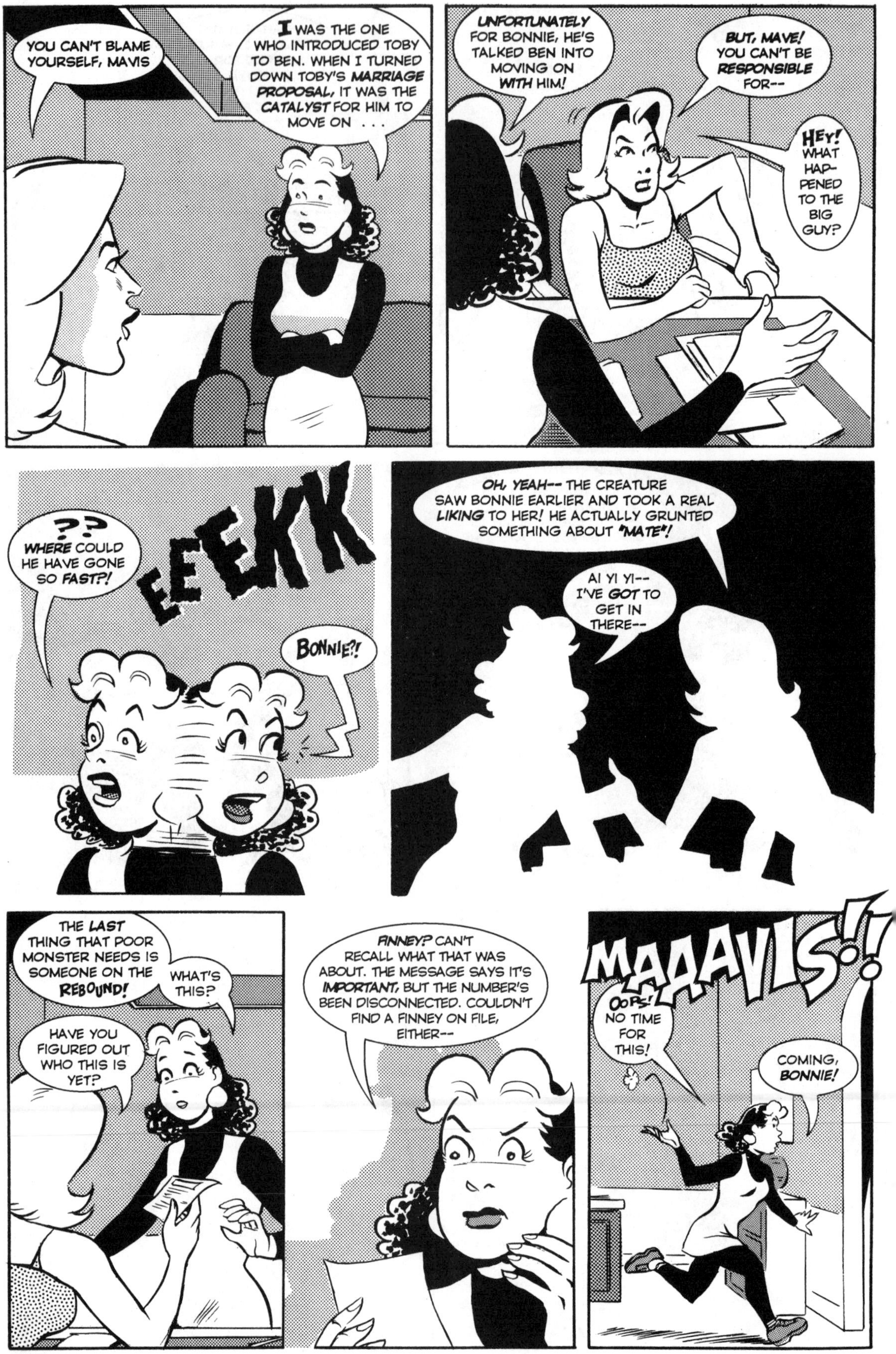

YOU CAN'T BLAME YOURSELF, MAVIS
I WAS THE ONE WHO INTRODUCED TOBY TO BEN. WHEN I TURNED DOWN TOBY'S MARRIAGE PROPOSAL, IT WAS THE CATALYST FOR HIM TO MOVE ON . . .
UNFORTUNATELY FOR BONNIE, HE'S TALKED BEN INTO MOVING ON WITH HIM!
BUT, MAVE! YOU CAN'T BE RESPONSIBLE FOR--
HEY! WHAT HAP-PENED TO THE BIG GUY?
?? WHERE COULD HE HAVE GONE SO FAST?!
EEEKK
BONNIE?!
OH, YEAH-- THE CREATURE SAW BONNIE EARLIER AND TOOK A REAL LIKING TO HER! HE ACTUALLY GRUNTED SOMETHING ABOUT "MATE"!
AI YI YI-- I'VE GOT TO GET IN THERE--
THE LAST THING THAT POOR MONSTER NEEDS IS SOMEONE ON THE REBOUND!
WHAT'S THIS?
HAVE YOU FIGURED OUT WHO THIS IS YET?
FINNEY? CAN'T RECALL WHAT THAT WAS ABOUT. THE MESSAGE SAYS IT'S IMPORTANT, BUT THE NUMBER'S BEEN DISCONNECTED. COULDN'T FIND A FINNEY ON FILE, EITHER--
MAAAVIS!!
OOPS! NO TIME FOR THIS!
COMING, BONNIE!

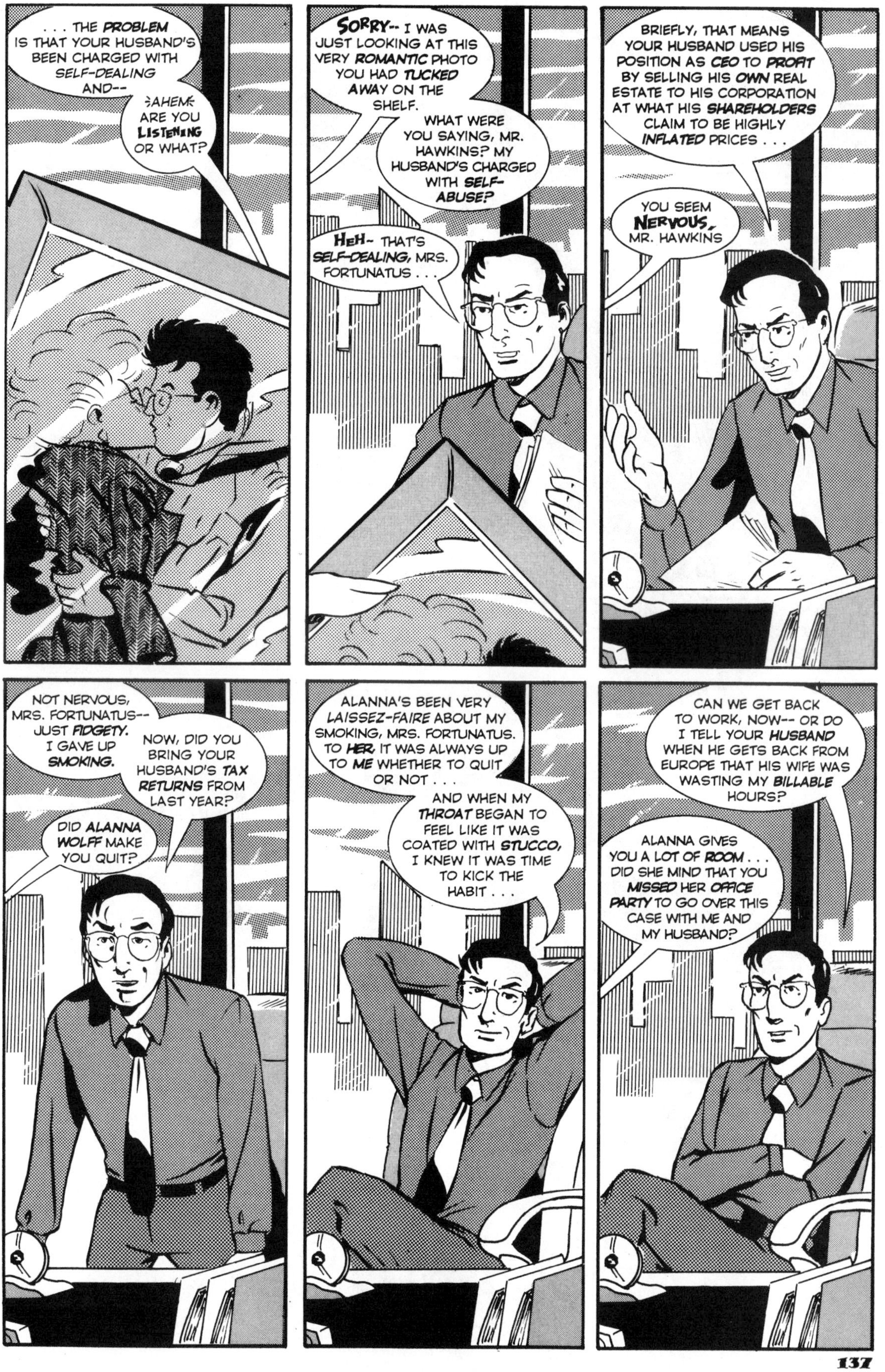
. . . THE PROBLEM IS THAT YOUR HUSBAND'S BEEN CHARGED WITH SELF-DEALING AND--
AHEM. ARE YOU LISTENING OR WHAT?
SORRY-- I WAS JUST LOOKING AT THIS VERY ROMANTIC PHOTO YOU HAD TUCKED AWAY ON THE SHELF.
WHAT WERE YOU SAYING, MR. HAWKINS? MY HUSBAND'S CHARGED WITH SELF-ABUSE?
HEH- THAT'S SELF-DEALING, MRS. FORTUNATUS . . .
BRIEFLY, THAT MEANS YOUR HUSBAND USED HIS POSITION AS CEO TO PROFIT BY SELLING HIS OWN REAL ESTATE TO HIS CORPORATION AT WHAT HIS SHAREHOLDERS CLAIM TO BE HIGHLY INFLATED PRICES . . .
YOU SEEM NERVOUS, MR. HAWKINS
NOT NERVOUS, MRS. FORTUNATUS-- JUST FIDGETY. I GAVE UP SMOKING.
NOW, DID YOU BRING YOUR HUSBAND'S TAX RETURNS FROM LAST YEAR?
DID ALANNA WOLFF MAKE YOU QUIT?
ALANNA'S BEEN VERY LAISSEZ-FAIRE ABOUT MY SMOKING, MRS. FORTUNATUS. TO HER, IT WAS ALWAYS UP TO ME WHETHER TO QUIT OR NOT . . .
AND WHEN MY THROAT BEGAN TO FEEL LIKE IT WAS COATED WITH STUCCO, I KNEW IT WAS TIME TO KICK THE HABIT . . .
CAN WE GET BACK TO WORK, NOW-- OR DO I TELL YOUR HUSBAND WHEN HE GETS BACK FROM EUROPE THAT HIS WIFE WAS WASTING MY BILLABLE HOURS?
ALANNA GIVES YOU A LOT OF ROOM . . . DID SHE MIND THAT YOU MISSED HER OFFICE PARTY TO GO OVER THIS CASE WITH ME AND MY HUSBAND?

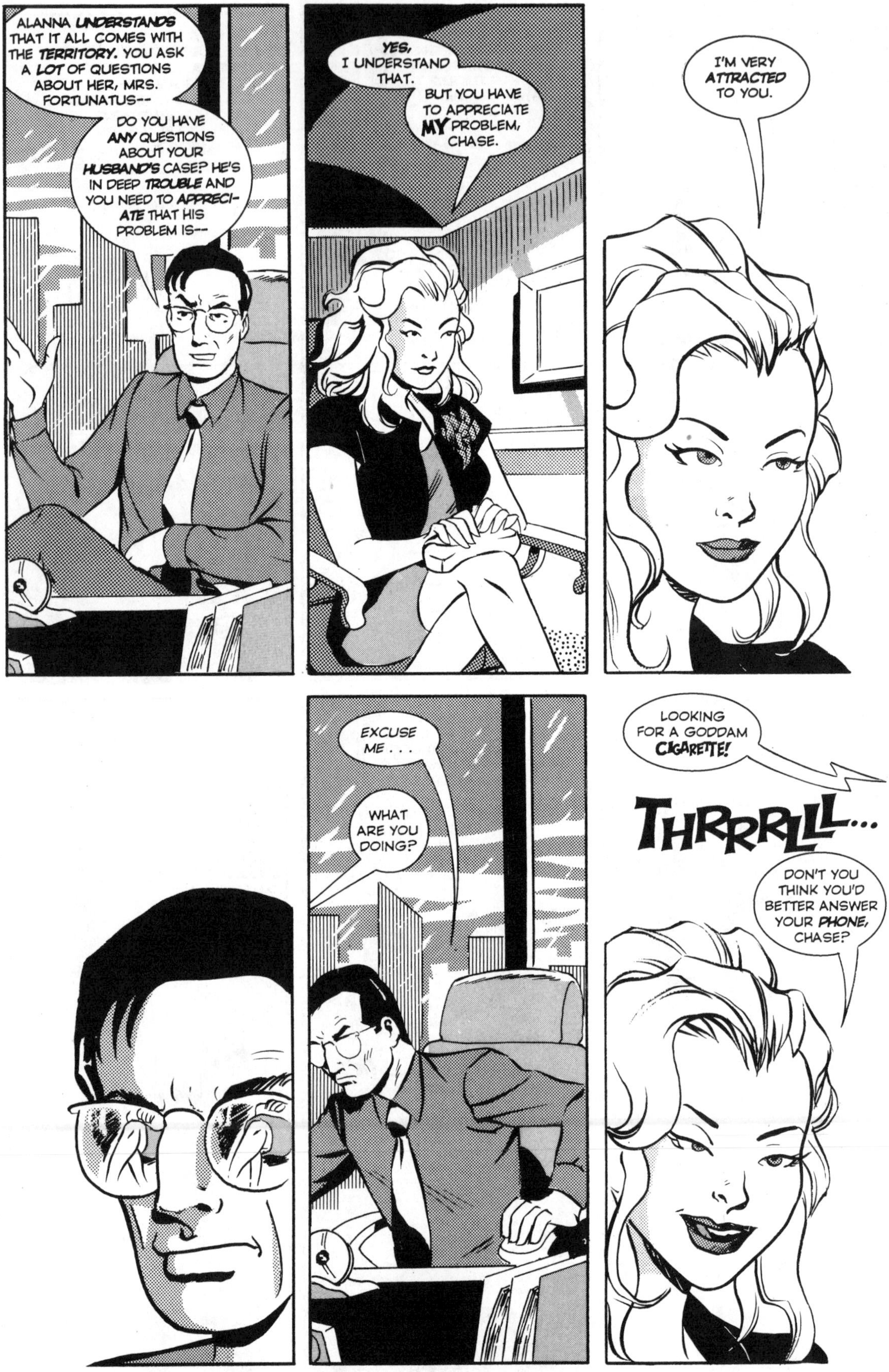
ALANNA UNDERSTANDS THAT IT ALL COMES WITH THE TERRITORY. YOU ASK A LOT OF QUESTIONS ABOUT HER, MRS. FORTUNATUS--
DO YOU HAVE ANY QUESTIONS ABOUT YOUR HUSBAND'S CASE? HE'S IN DEEP TROUBLE AND YOU NEED TO APPRECIATE THAT HIS PROBLEM IS--
YES, I UNDERSTAND THAT.
BUT YOU HAVE TO APPRECIATE MY PROBLEM, CHASE.
I'M VERY ATTRACTED TO YOU.
EXCUSE ME . . .
WHAT ARE YOU DOING?
LOOKING FOR A GODDAM CIGARETTE!
THRRRLLL...
DON'T YOU THINK YOU'D BETTER ANSWER YOUR PHONE, CHASE?

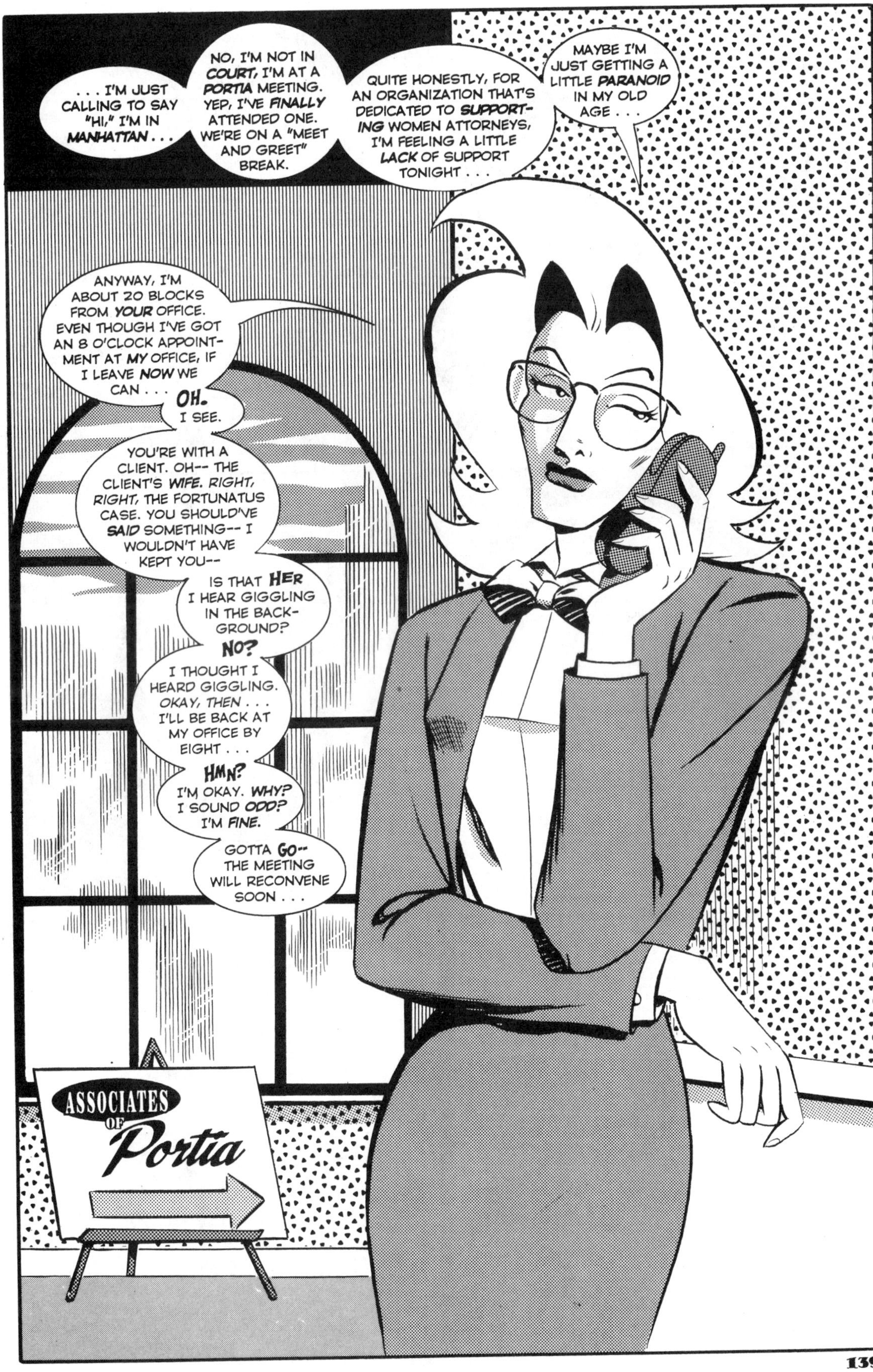
. . . I'M JUST CALLING TO SAY "HI," I'M IN MANHATTAN . . .
NO, I'M NOT IN COURT, I'M AT A PORTIA MEETING. YEP, I'VE FINALLY ATTENDED ONE. WE'RE ON A "MEET AND GREET" BREAK.
QUITE HONESTLY, FOR AN ORGANIZATION THAT'S DEDICATED TO SUPPORTING WOMEN ATTORNEYS, I'M FEELING A LITTLE LACK OF SUPPORT TONIGHT . . .
MAYBE I'M JUST GETTING A LITTLE PARANOID IN MY OLD AGE . . .
ANYWAY, I'M ABOUT 20 BLOCKS FROM YOUR OFFICE. EVEN THOUGH I'VE GOT AN 8 O'CLOCK APPOINTMENT AT MY OFFICE, IF I LEAVE NOW WE CAN . . .
OH. I SEE.
YOU'RE WITH A CLIENT. OH-- THE CLIENT'S WIFE. RIGHT, RIGHT, THE FORTUNATUS CASE. YOU SHOULD'VE SAID SOMETHING-- I WOULDN'T HAVE KEPT YOU--
IS THAT HER I HEAR GIGGLING IN THE BACKGROUND?
NO?
I THOUGHT I HEARD GIGGLING. OKAY, THEN . . . I'LL BE BACK AT MY OFFICE BY EIGHT . . .
HMN?
I'M OKAY. WHY? I SOUND ODD? I'M FINE.
GOTTA GO-- THE MEETING WILL RECONVENE SOON . . .
ASSOCIATES OF Portia

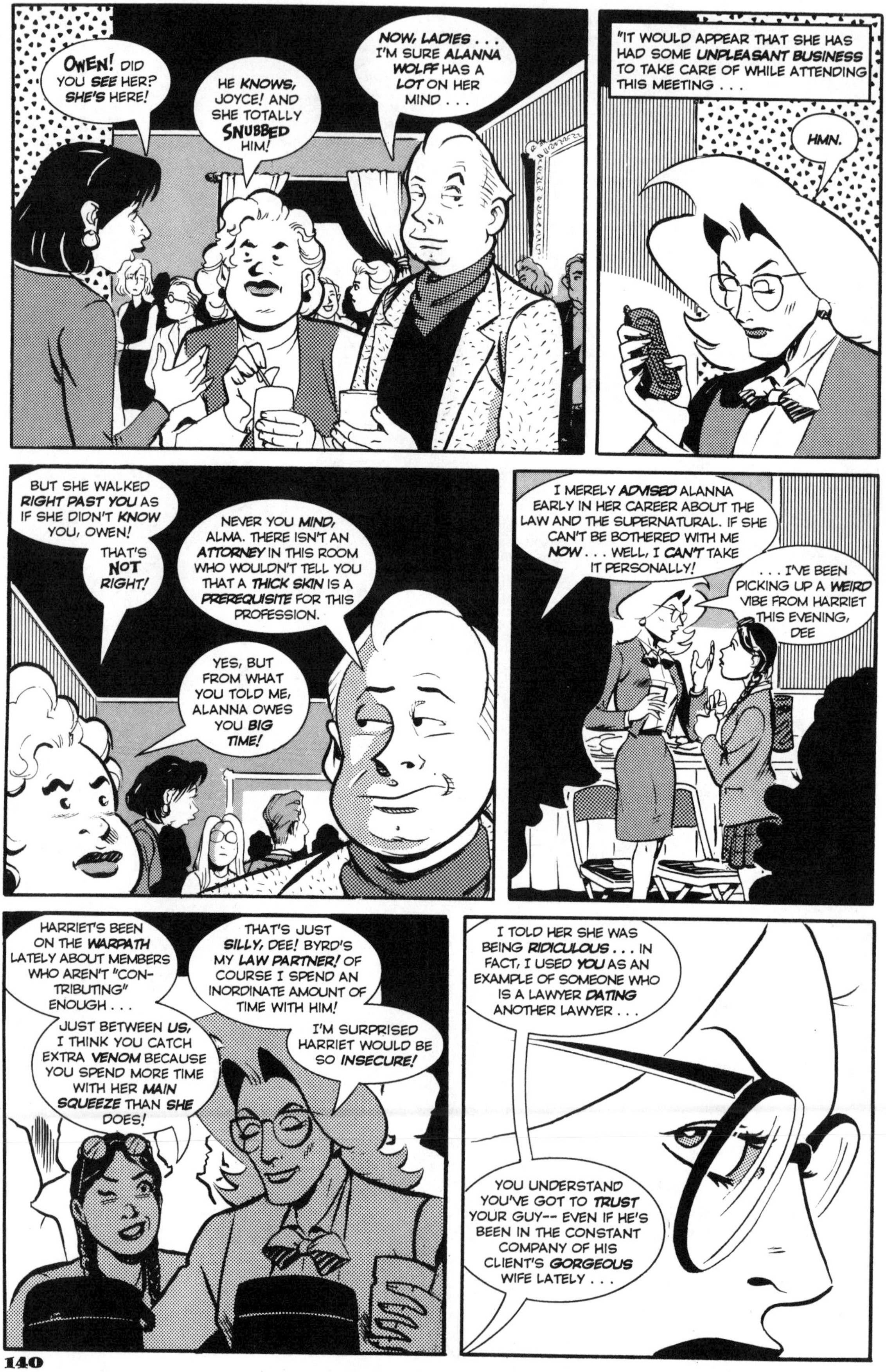
OWEN! DID YOU SEE HER? SHE'S HERE!
HE KNOWS, JOYCE! AND SHE TOTALLY SNUBBED HIM!
NOW, LADIES . . . I'M SURE ALANNA WOLFF HAS A LOT ON HER MIND . . .
"IT WOULD APPEAR THAT SHE HAS HAD SOME UNPLEASANT BUSINESS TO TAKE CARE OF WHILE ATTENDING THIS MEETING . . .
HMN.
BUT SHE WALKED RIGHT PAST YOU AS IF SHE DIDN'T KNOW YOU, OWEN!
THAT'S NOT RIGHT!
NEVER YOU MIND, ALMA. THERE ISN'T AN ATTORNEY IN THIS ROOM WHO WOULDN'T TELL YOU THAT A THICK SKIN IS A PREREQUISITE FOR THIS PROFESSION.
YES, BUT FROM WHAT YOU TOLD ME, ALANNA OWES YOU BIG TIME!
I MERELY ADVISED ALANNA EARLY IN HER CAREER ABOUT THE LAW AND THE SUPERNATURAL. IF SHE CAN'T BE BOTHERED WITH ME NOW . . . WELL, I CAN'T TAKE IT PERSONALLY!
. . . I'VE BEEN PICKING UP A WEIRD VIBE FROM HARRIET THIS EVENING, DEE
HARRIET'S BEEN ON THE WARPATH LATELY ABOUT MEMBERS WHO AREN'T "CONTRIBUTING" ENOUGH . . .
JUST BETWEEN US, I THINK YOU CATCH EXTRA VENOM BECAUSE YOU SPEND MORE TIME WITH HER MAIN SQUEEZE THAN SHE DOES!
THAT'S JUST SILLY, DEE! BYRD'S MY LAW PARTNER! OF COURSE I SPEND AN INORDINATE AMOUNT OF TIME WITH HIM!
I'M SURPRISED HARRIET WOULD BE SO INSECURE!
I TOLD HER SHE WAS BEING RIDICULOUS . . . IN FACT, I USED YOU AS AN EXAMPLE OF SOMEONE WHO IS A LAWYER DATING ANOTHER LAWYER . . .
YOU UNDERSTAND YOU'VE GOT TO TRUST YOUR GUY-- EVEN IF HE'S BEEN IN THE CONSTANT COMPANY OF HIS CLIENT'S GORGEOUS WIFE LATELY . . .

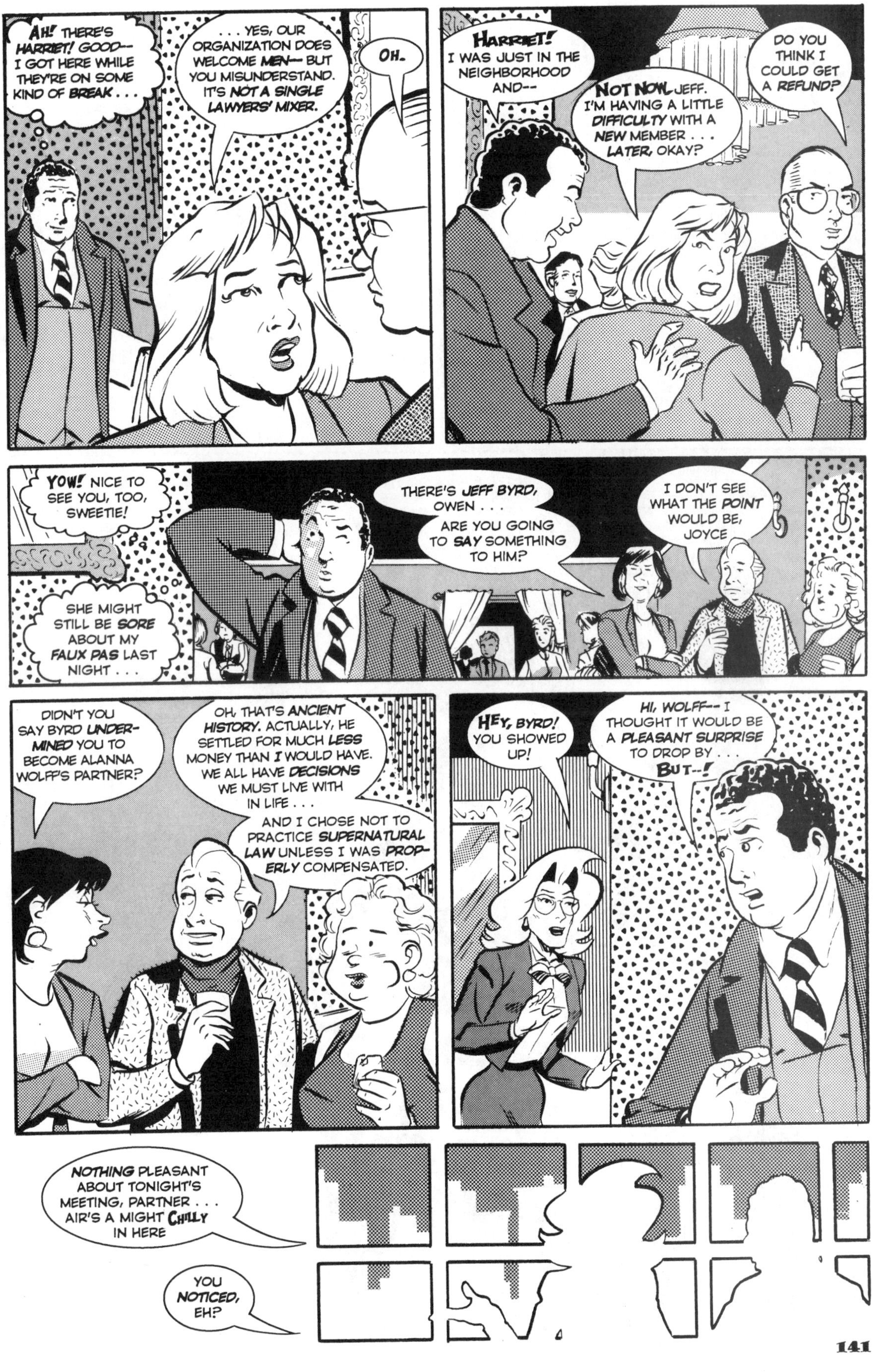

AH! THERE'S HARRIET! GOOD-- I GOT HERE WHILE THEY'RE ON SOME KIND OF BREAK . . .
. . . YES, OUR ORGANIZATION DOES WELCOME MEN-- BUT YOU MISUNDERSTAND. IT'S NOT A SINGLE LAWYERS' MIXER.
OH.
HARRIET! I WAS JUST IN THE NEIGHBORHOOD AND--
NOT NOW, JEFF. I'M HAVING A LITTLE DIFFICULTY WITH A NEW MEMBER . . . LATER, OKAY?
DO YOU THINK I COULD GET A REFUND?
YOW! NICE TO SEE YOU, TOO, SWEETIE!
SHE MIGHT STILL BE SORE ABOUT MY FAUX PAS LAST NIGHT . . .
THERE'S JEFF BYRD, OWEN . . .
ARE YOU GOING TO SAY SOMETHING TO HIM?
I DON'T SEE WHAT THE POINT WOULD BE, JOYCE
DIDN'T YOU SAY BYRD UNDERMINED YOU TO BECOME ALANNA WOLFF'S PARTNER?
OH, THAT'S ANCIENT HISTORY. ACTUALLY, HE SETTLED FOR MUCH LESS MONEY THAN I WOULD HAVE. WE ALL HAVE DECISIONS WE MUST LIVE WITH IN LIFE . . .
AND I CHOSE NOT TO PRACTICE SUPERNATURAL LAW UNLESS I WAS PROPERLY COMPENSATED.
HEY, BYRD! YOU SHOWED UP!
HI, WOLFF-- I THOUGHT IT WOULD BE A PLEASANT SURPRISE TO DROP BY . . .
BUT--!
NOTHING PLEASANT ABOUT TONIGHT'S MEETING, PARTNER . . . AIR'S A MIGHT CHILLY IN HERE
YOU NOTICED, EH?

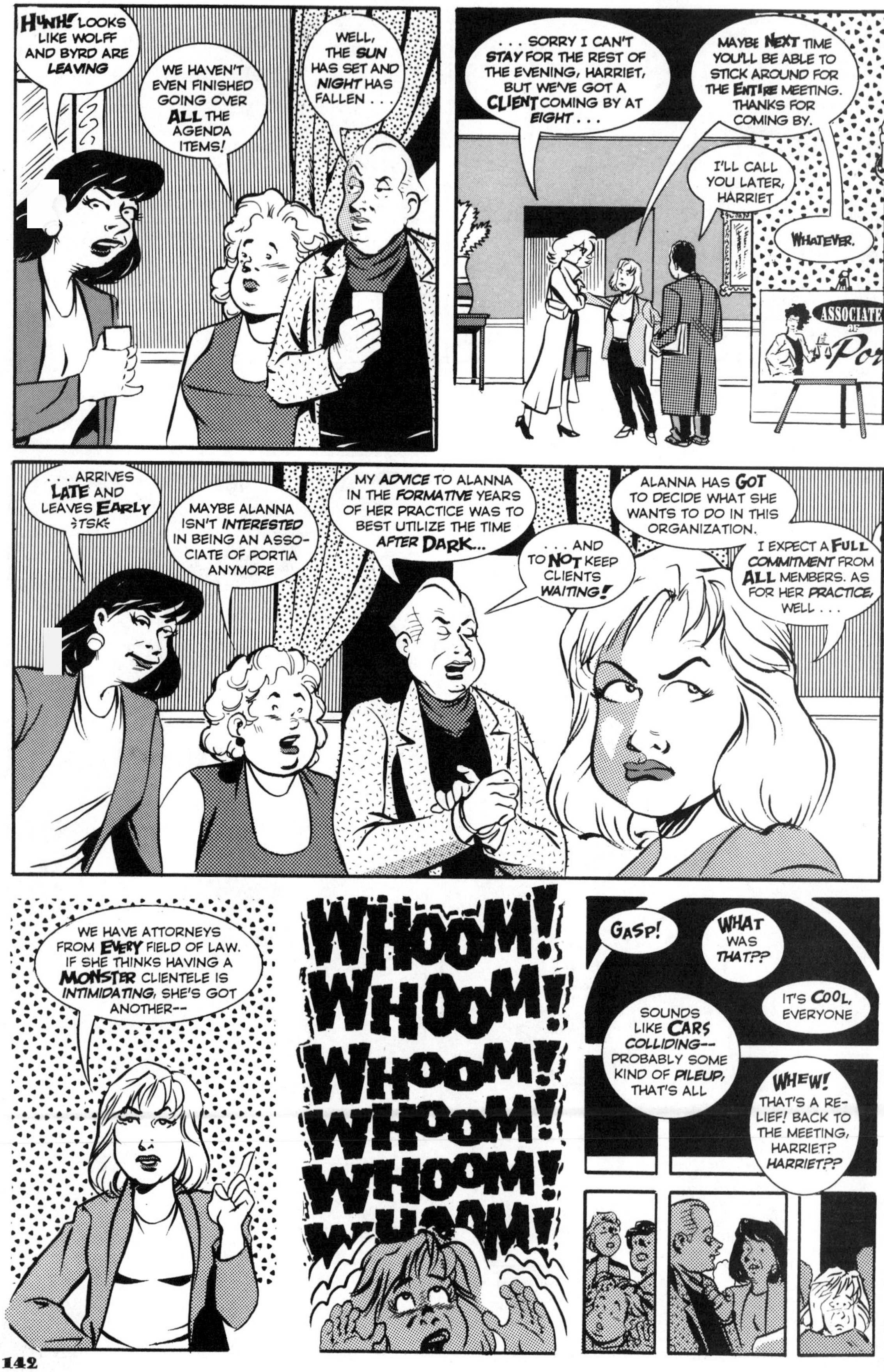
HUNH! LOOKS LIKE WOLFF AND BYRD ARE LEAVING
WE HAVEN'T EVEN FINISHED GOING OVER ALL THE AGENDA ITEMS!
WELL, THE SUN HAS SET AND NIGHT HAS FALLEN . . .
. . . SORRY I CAN'T STAY FOR THE REST OF THE EVENING, HARRIET, BUT WE'VE GOT A CLIENT COMING BY AT EIGHT . . .
MAYBE NEXT TIME YOU'LL BE ABLE TO STICK AROUND FOR THE ENTIRE MEETING. THANKS FOR COMING BY.
I'LL CALL YOU LATER, HARRIET
WHATEVER.
ASSOCIATE
OF
Por
. . . ARRIVES LATE AND LEAVES EARLY TSK
MAYBE ALANNA ISN'T INTERESTED IN BEING AN ASSOCIATE OF PORTIA ANYMORE
MY ADVICE TO ALANNA IN THE FORMATIVE YEARS OF HER PRACTICE WAS TO BEST UTILIZE THE TIME AFTER DARK...
. . . AND TO NOT KEEP CLIENTS WAITING!
ALANNA HAS GOT TO DECIDE WHAT SHE WANTS TO DO IN THIS ORGANIZATION.
I EXPECT A FULL COMMITMENT FROM ALL MEMBERS. AS FOR HER PRACTICE, WELL . . .
WE HAVE ATTORNEYS FROM EVERY FIELD OF LAW. IF SHE THINKS HAVING A MONSTER CLIENTELE IS INTIMIDATING, SHE'S GOT ANOTHER--
WHOOM!
WHOOM!
WHOOM!
WHOOM!
WHOOM!
GASP!
WHAT WAS THAT??
IT'S COOL, EVERYONE
SOUNDS LIKE CARS COLLIDING-- PROBABLY SOME KIND OF PILEUP, THAT'S ALL
WHEW! THAT'S A RELIEF! BACK TO THE MEETING, HARRIET? HARRIET??

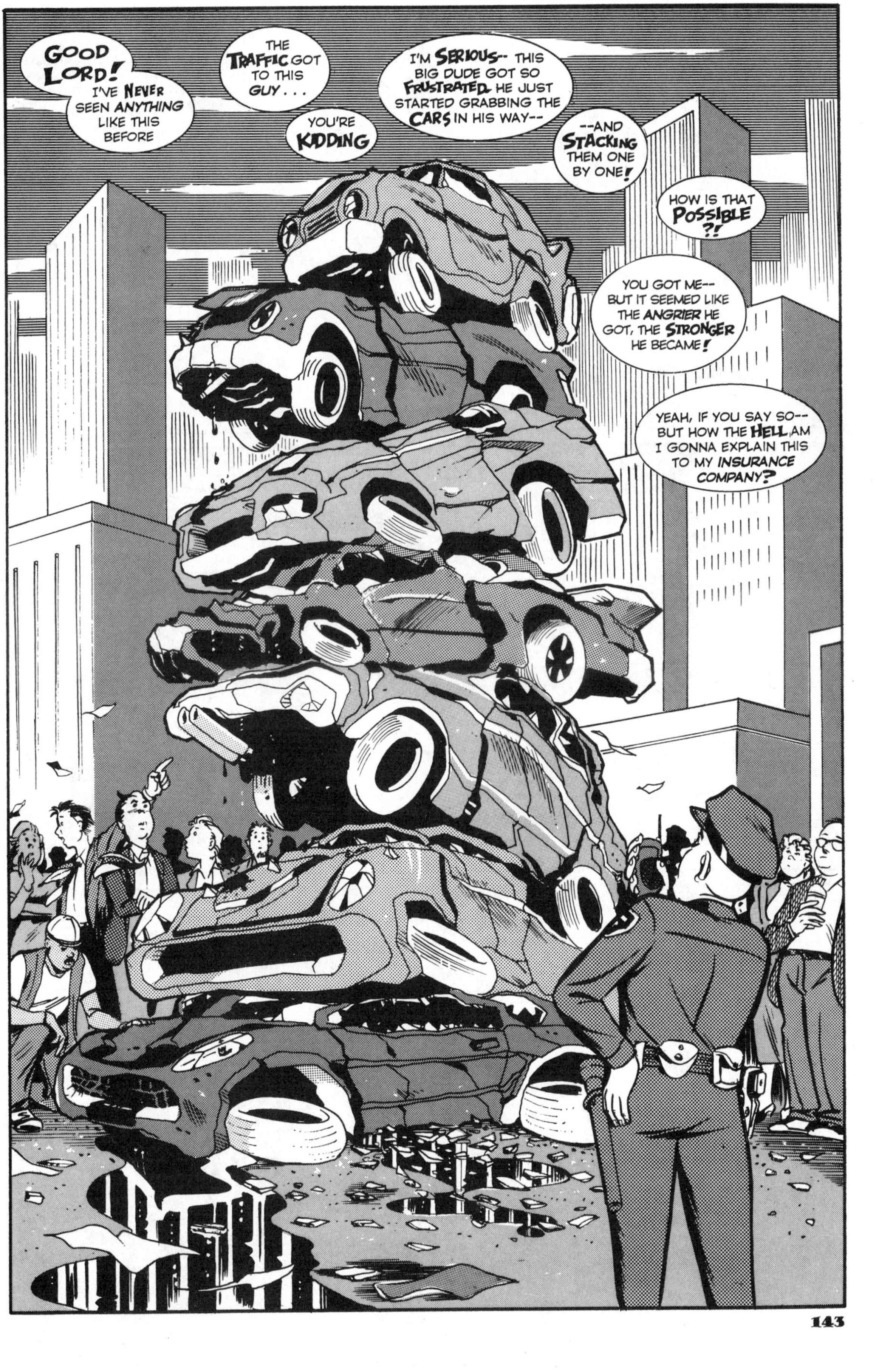
GOOD LORD! I'VE NEVER SEEN ANYTHING LIKE THIS BEFORE
THE TRAFFIC GOT TO THIS GUY . . .
YOU'RE KIDDING
I'M SERIOUS-- THIS BIG DUDE GOT SO FRUSTRATED HE JUST STARTED GRABBING THE CARS IN HIS WAY--
--AND STACKING THEM ONE BY ONE!
HOW IS THAT POSSIBLE?!
YOU GOT ME-- BUT IT SEEMED LIKE THE ANGRIER HE GOT, THE STRONGER HE BECAME!
YEAH, IF YOU SAY SO-- BUT HOW THE HELL AM I GONNA EXPLAIN THIS TO MY INSURANCE COMPANY?

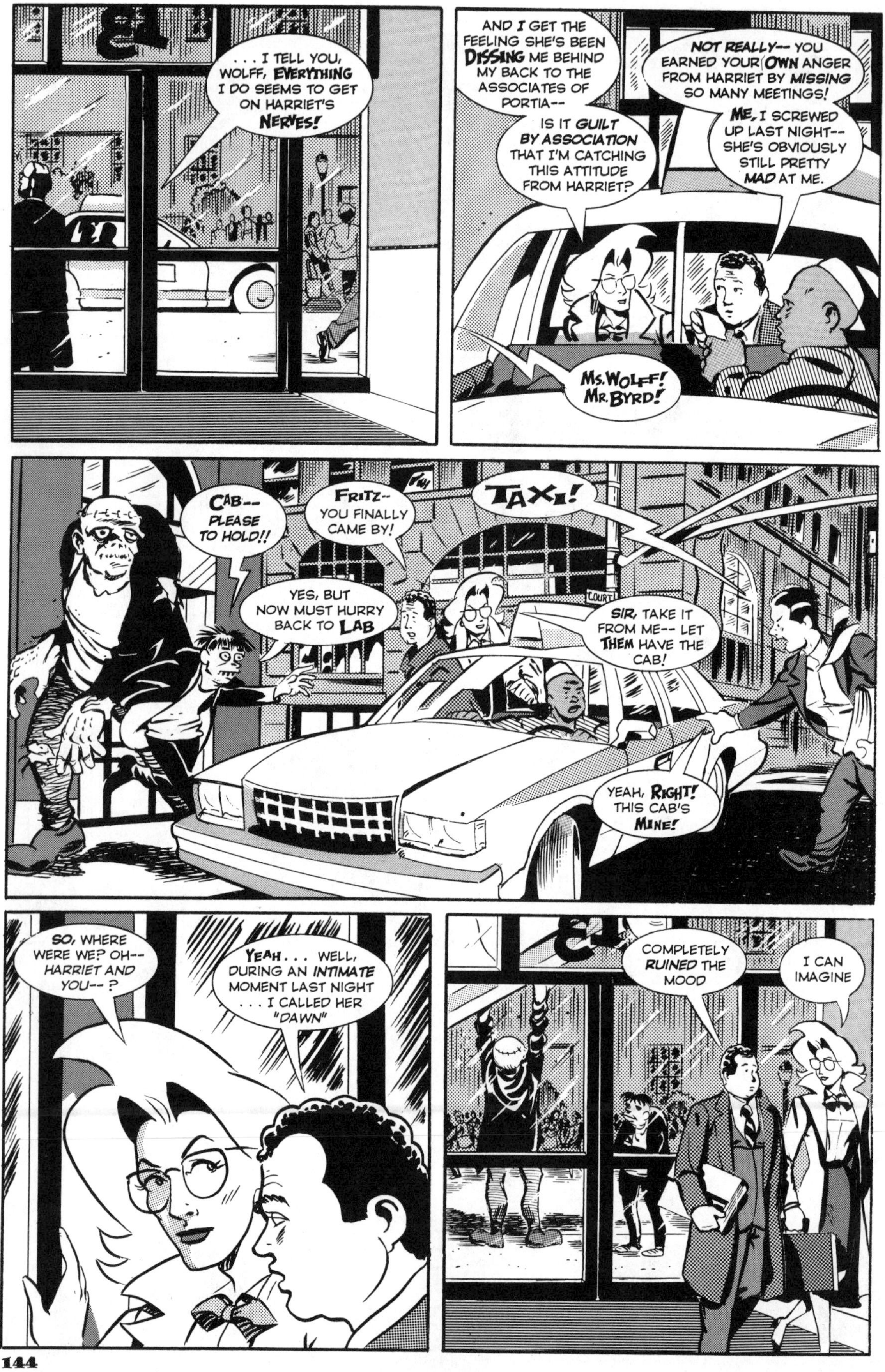

. . . I TELL YOU, WOLFF, EVERYTHING I DO SEEMS TO GET ON HARRIET'S NERVES!
AND I GET THE FEELING SHE'S BEEN DISSING ME BEHIND MY BACK TO THE ASSOCIATES OF PORTIA--
IS IT GUILT BY ASSOCIATION THAT I'M CATCHING THIS ATTITUDE FROM HARRIET?
NOT REALLY-- YOU EARNED YOUR OWN ANGER FROM HARRIET BY MISSING SO MANY MEETINGS!
ME, I SCREWED UP LAST NIGHT-- SHE'S OBVIOUSLY STILL PRETTY MAD AT ME.
MS. WOLFF! MR. BYRD!
CAB-- PLEASE TO HOLD!!
FRITZ-- YOU FINALLY CAME BY!
TAXI!
YES, BUT NOW MUST HURRY BACK TO LAB
COURT
SIR, TAKE IT FROM ME-- LET THEM HAVE THE CAB!
YEAH, RIGHT! THIS CAB'S MINE!
SO, WHERE WERE WE? OH-- HARRIET AND YOU-- ?
YEAH . . . WELL, DURING AN INTIMATE MOMENT LAST NIGHT . . . I CALLED HER "DAWN"
COMPLETELY RUINED THE MOOD
I CAN IMAGINE

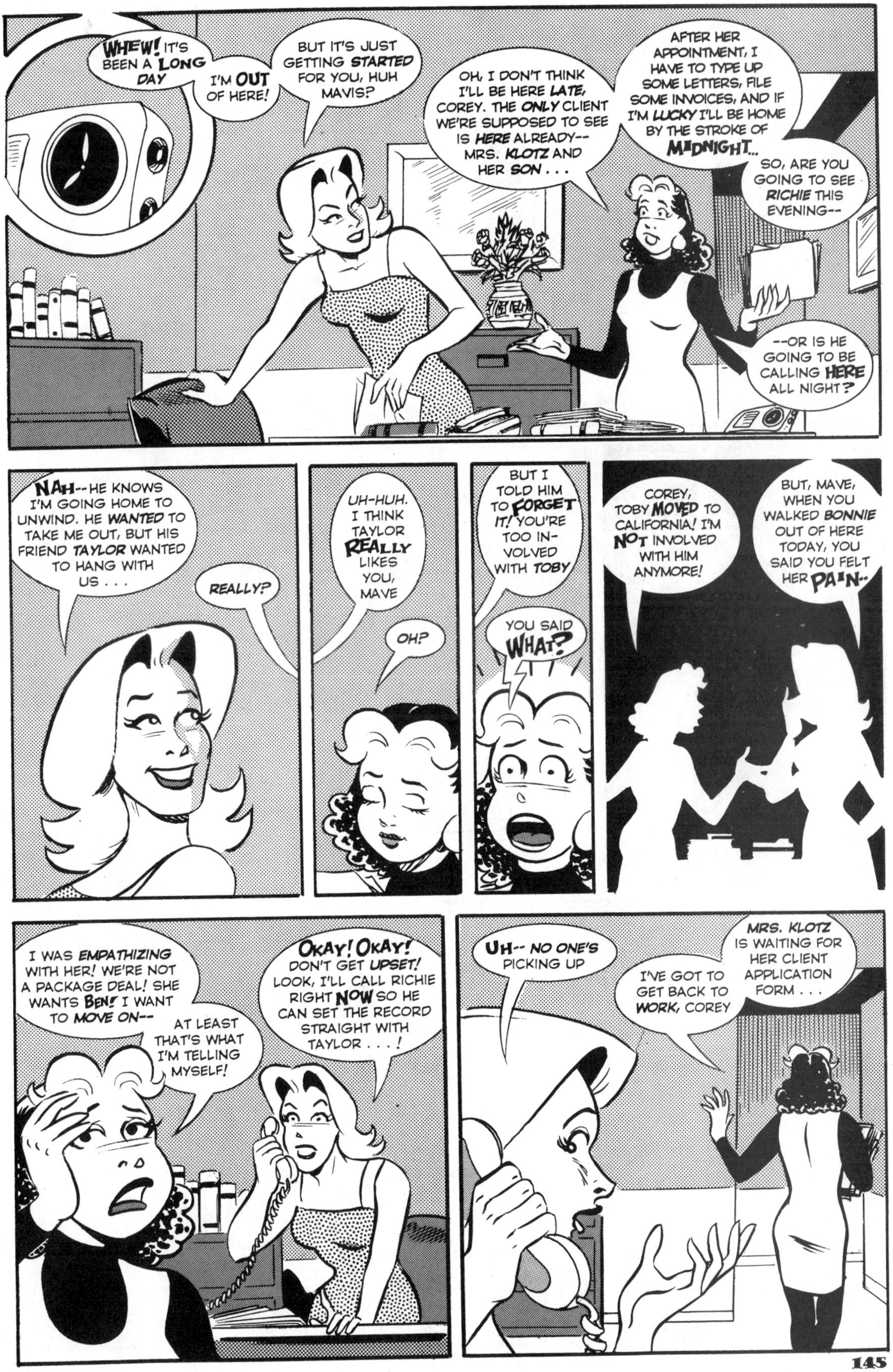
WHEW! IT'S BEEN A LONG DAY
I'M OUT OF HERE!
BUT IT'S JUST GETTING STARTED FOR YOU, HUH MAVIS?
OH, I DON'T THINK I'LL BE HERE LATE, COREY. THE ONLY CLIENT WE'RE SUPPOSED TO SEE IS HERE ALREADY-- MRS. KLOTZ AND HER SON . . .
AFTER HER APPOINTMENT, I HAVE TO TYPE UP SOME LETTERS, FILE SOME INVOICES, AND IF I'M LUCKY I'LL BE HOME BY THE STROKE OF MIDNIGHT...
SO, ARE YOU GOING TO SEE RICHIE THIS EVENING--
--OR IS HE GOING TO BE CALLING HERE ALL NIGHT?
NAH-- HE KNOWS I'M GOING HOME TO UNWIND. HE WANTED TO TAKE ME OUT, BUT HIS FRIEND TAYLOR WANTED TO HANG WITH US . . .
REALLY?
UH-HUH. I THINK TAYLOR REALLY LIKES YOU, MAVE
OH?
BUT I TOLD HIM TO FORGET IT! YOU'RE TOO IN-VOLVED WITH TOBY
YOU SAID WHAT?
COREY, TOBY MOVED TO CALIFORNIA! I'M NOT INVOLVED WITH HIM ANYMORE!
BUT, MAVE, WHEN YOU WALKED BONNIE OUT OF HERE TODAY, YOU SAID YOU FELT HER PAIN..
I WAS EMPATHIZING WITH HER! WE'RE NOT A PACKAGE DEAL! SHE WANTS BEN! I WANT TO MOVE ON--
AT LEAST THAT'S WHAT I'M TELLING MYSELF!
OKAY! OKAY! DON'T GET UPSET! LOOK, I'LL CALL RICHIE RIGHT NOW SO HE CAN SET THE RECORD STRAIGHT WITH TAYLOR . . . !
UH-- NO ONE'S PICKING UP
I'VE GOT TO GET BACK TO WORK, COREY
MRS. KLOTZ IS WAITING FOR HER CLIENT APPLICATION FORM . . .

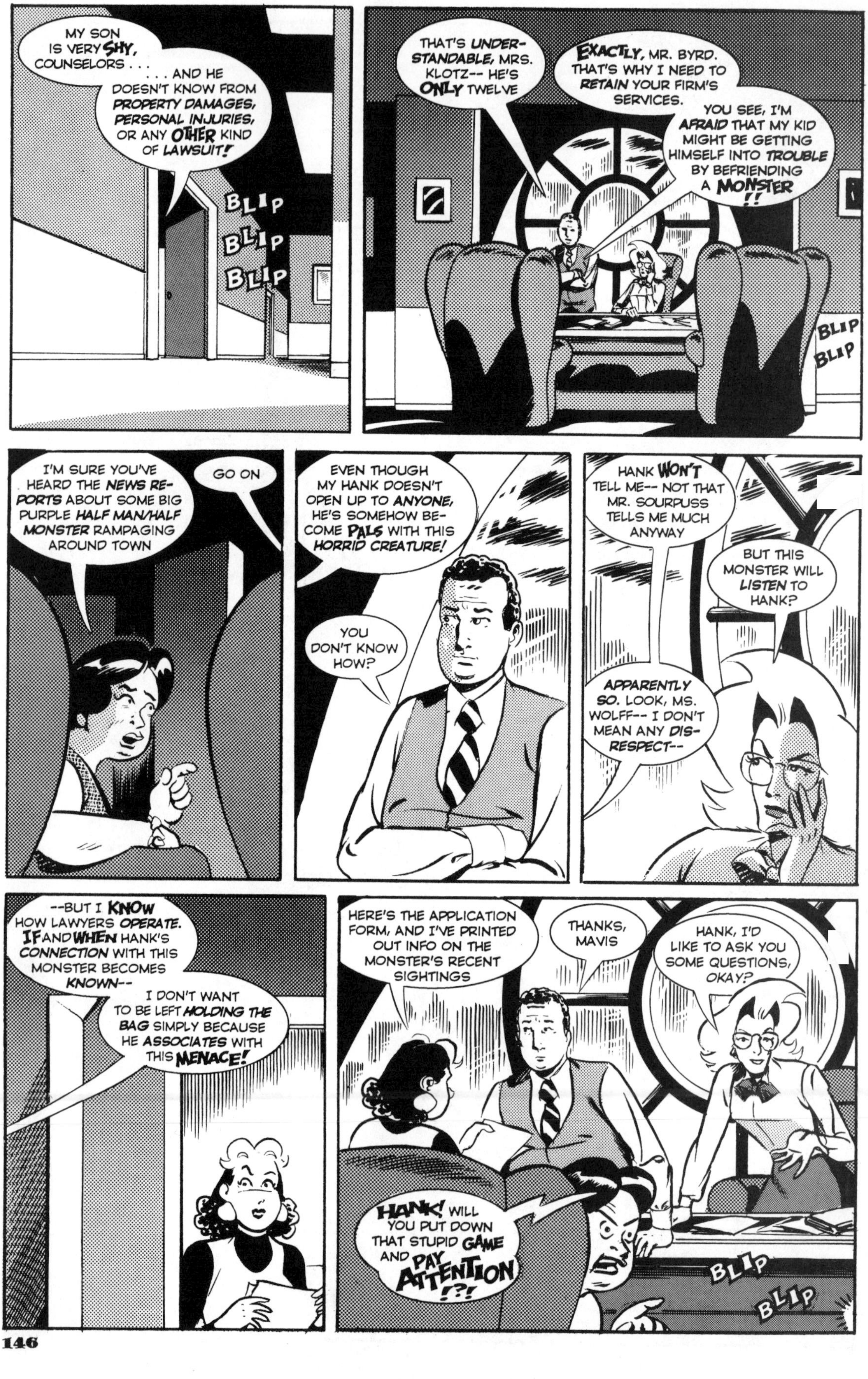
MY SON IS VERY SHY, COUNSELORS . . .
. . . AND HE DOESN'T KNOW FROM PROPERTY DAMAGES, PERSONAL INJURIES, OR ANY OTHER KIND OF LAWSUIT!
BLIP BLIP BLIP
THAT'S UNDERSTANDABLE, MRS. KLOTZ-- HE'S ONLY TWELVE
EXACTLY, MR. BYRD. THAT'S WHY I NEED TO RETAIN YOUR FIRM'S SERVICES.
YOU SEE, I'M AFRAID THAT MY KID MIGHT BE GETTING HIMSELF INTO TROUBLE BY BEFRIENDING A MONSTER!!
BLIP BLIP
I'M SURE YOU'VE HEARD THE NEWS REPORTS ABOUT SOME BIG PURPLE HALF MAN/HALF MONSTER RAMPAGING AROUND TOWN
GO ON
EVEN THOUGH MY HANK DOESN'T OPEN UP TO ANYONE, HE'S SOMEHOW BECOME PALS WITH THIS HORRID CREATURE!
YOU DON'T KNOW HOW?
HANK WON'T TELL ME-- NOT THAT MR. SOURPUSS TELLS ME MUCH ANYWAY
BUT THIS MONSTER WILL LISTEN TO HANK?
APPARENTLY SO. LOOK, MS. WOLFF-- I DON'T MEAN ANY DISRESPECT--
--BUT I KNOW HOW LAWYERS OPERATE. IF AND WHEN HANK'S CONNECTION WITH THIS MONSTER BECOMES KNOWN--
I DON'T WANT TO BE LEFT HOLDING THE BAG SIMPLY BECAUSE HE ASSOCIATES WITH THIS MENACE!
HERE'S THE APPLICATION FORM, AND I'VE PRINTED OUT INFO ON THE MONSTER'S RECENT SIGHTINGS
THANKS, MAVIS
HANK, I'D LIKE TO ASK YOU SOME QUESTIONS, OKAY?
HANK! WILL YOU PUT DOWN THAT STUPID GAME AND PAY ATTENTION!?!
BLIP BLIP

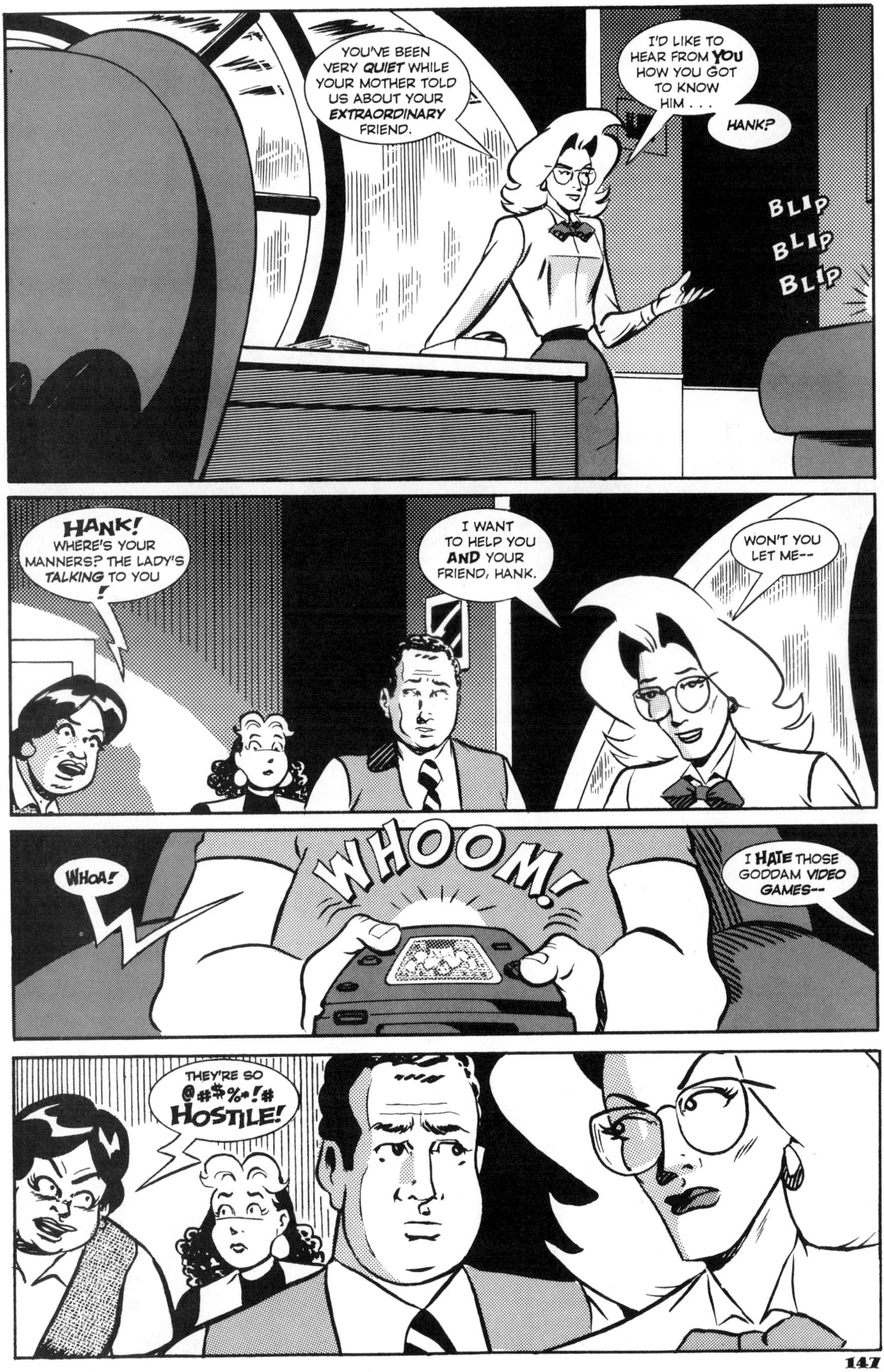
YOU'VE BEEN VERY QUIET WHILE YOUR MOTHER TOLD US ABOUT YOUR EXTRAORDINARY FRIEND.
I'D LIKE TO HEAR FROM YOU HOW YOU GOT TO KNOW HIM . . .
HANK?
BLIP
BLIP
BLIP
HANK! WHERE'S YOUR MANNERS? THE LADY'S TALKING TO YOU!
I WANT TO HELP YOU AND YOUR FRIEND, HANK.
WON'T YOU LET ME--
WHOA!
WHOOM!
I HATE THOSE GODDAM VIDEO GAMES--
THEY'RE SO @#$%*!# HOSTILE!

ONE WEEK LATER . . .

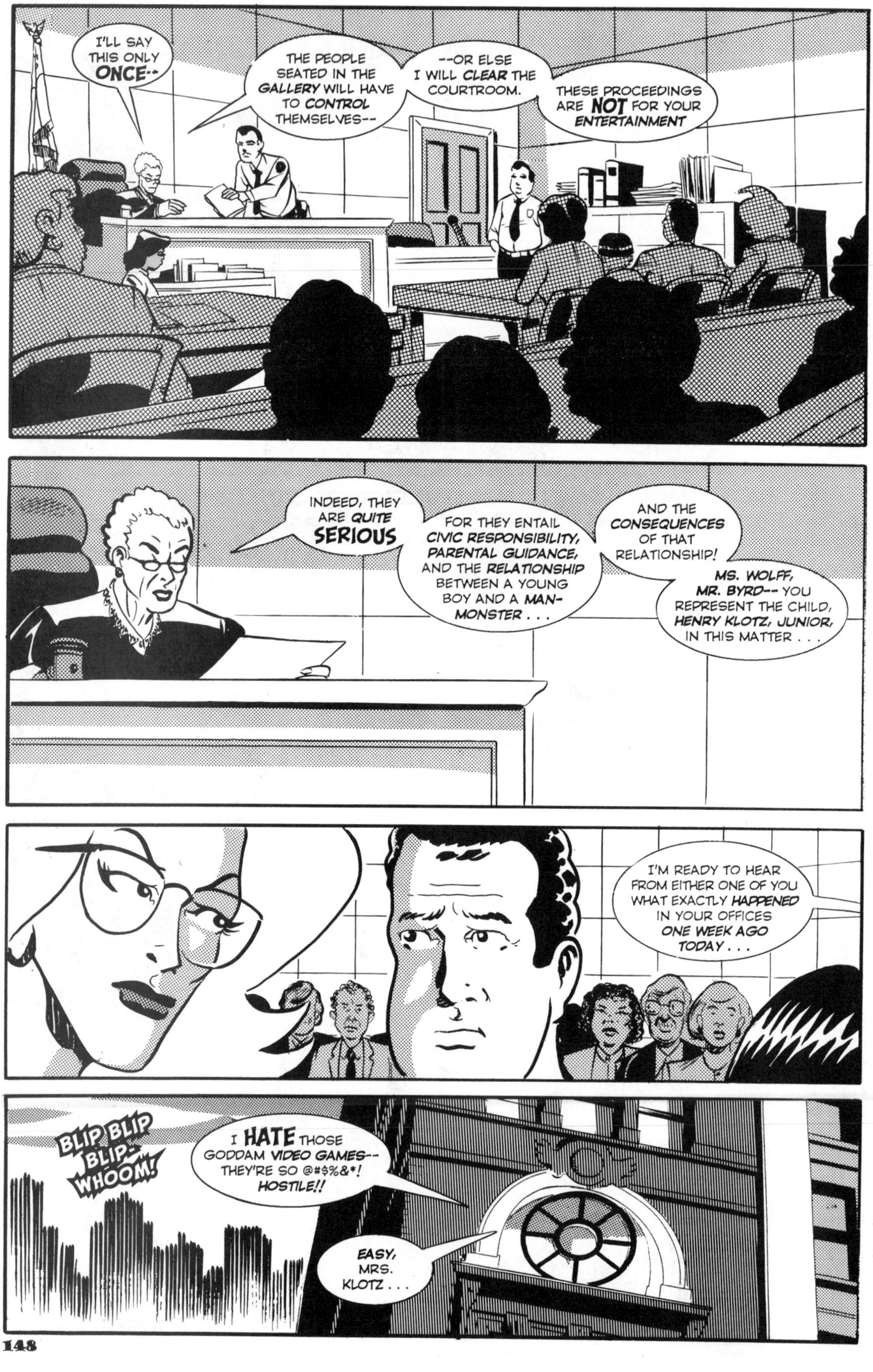

I'LL SAY THIS ONLY ONCE--
THE PEOPLE SEATED IN THE GALLERY WILL HAVE TO CONTROL THEMSELVES--
--OR ELSE I WILL CLEAR THE COURTROOM.
THESE PROCEEDINGS ARE NOT FOR YOUR ENTERTAINMENT
INDEED, THEY ARE QUITE SERIOUS
FOR THEY ENTAIL CIVIC RESPONSIBILITY, PARENTAL GUIDANCE, AND THE RELATIONSHIP BETWEEN A YOUNG BOY AND A MAN-MONSTER . . .
AND THE CONSEQUENCES OF THAT RELATIONSHIP!
MS. WOLFF, MR. BYRD-- YOU REPRESENT THE CHILD, HENRY KLOTZ, JUNIOR, IN THIS MATTER . . .
I'M READY TO HEAR FROM EITHER ONE OF YOU WHAT EXACTLY HAPPENED IN YOUR OFFICES ONE WEEK AGO TODAY . . .
BLIP BLIP BLIP-WHOOM!
I HATE THOSE GODDAM VIDEO GAMES-- THEY'RE SO @#$%&*! HOSTILE!!
EASY, MRS. KLOTZ . . .

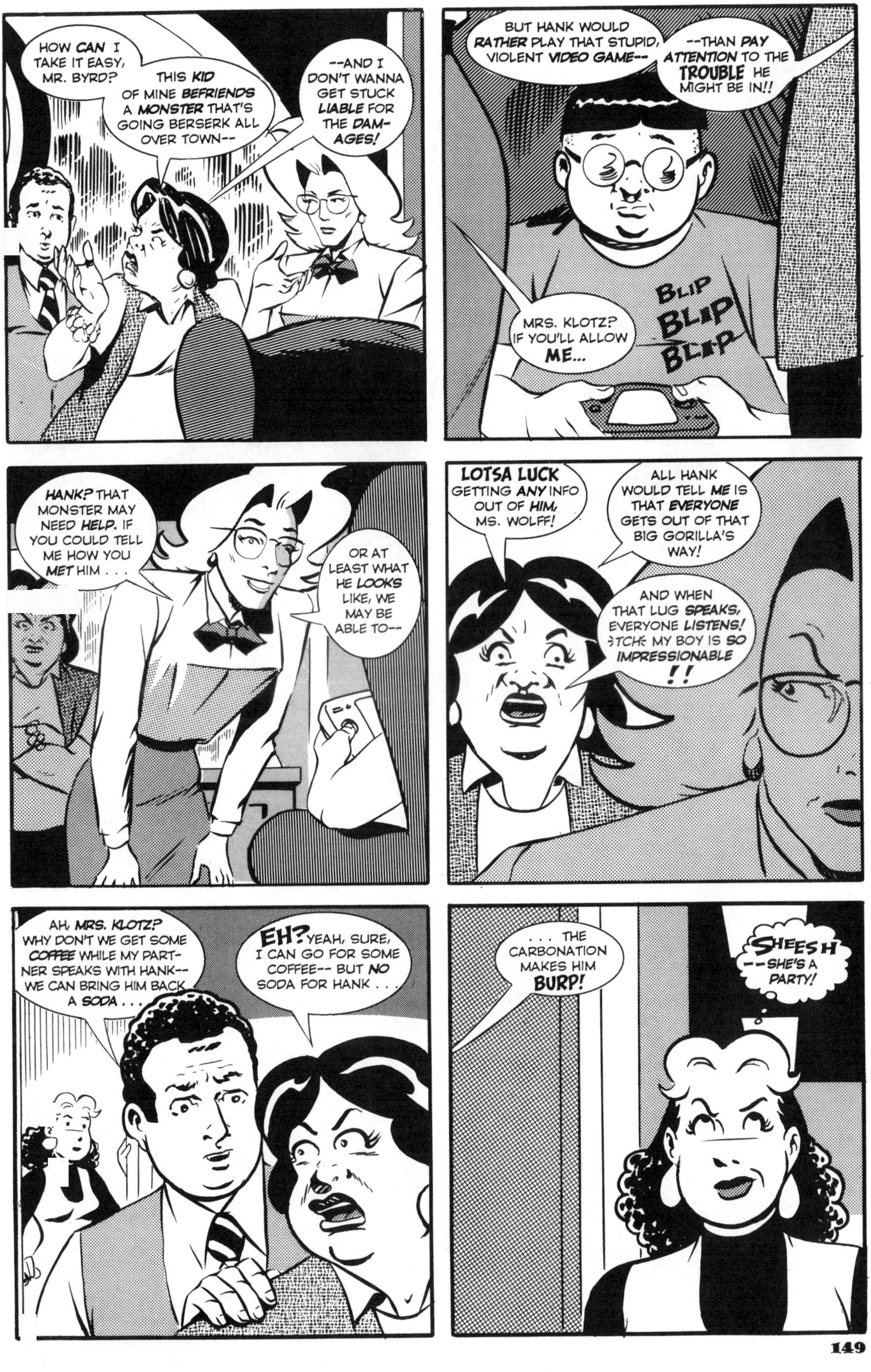
HOW CAN I TAKE IT EASY, MR. BYRD?
THIS KID OF MINE BEFRIENDS A MONSTER THAT'S GOING BERSERK ALL OVER TOWN--
--AND I DON'T WANNA GET STUCK LIABLE FOR THE DAMAGES!
BUT HANK WOULD RATHER PLAY THAT STUPID, VIOLENT VIDEO GAME--
--THAN PAY ATTENTION TO THE TROUBLE HE MIGHT BE IN!!
BLIP BLIP BLIP
MRS. KLOTZ? IF YOU'LL ALLOW ME...
HANK? THAT MONSTER MAY NEED HELP. IF YOU COULD TELL ME HOW YOU MET HIM . . .
OR AT LEAST WHAT HE LOOKS LIKE, WE MAY BE ABLE TO--
LOTSA LUCK GETTING ANY INFO OUT OF HIM, MS. WOLFF!
ALL HANK WOULD TELL ME IS THAT EVERYONE GETS OUT OF THAT BIG GORILLA'S WAY!
AND WHEN THAT LUG SPEAKS, EVERYONE LISTENS! *TCH* MY BOY IS SO IMPRESSIONABLE!!
AH, MRS. KLOTZ? WHY DON'T WE GET SOME COFFEE WHILE MY PARTNER SPEAKS WITH HANK-- WE CAN BRING HIM BACK A SODA . . .
EH? YEAH, SURE, I CAN GO FOR SOME COFFEE-- BUT NO SODA FOR HANK . . .
. . . THE CARBONATION MAKES HIM BURP!
SHEESH --SHE'S A PARTY!

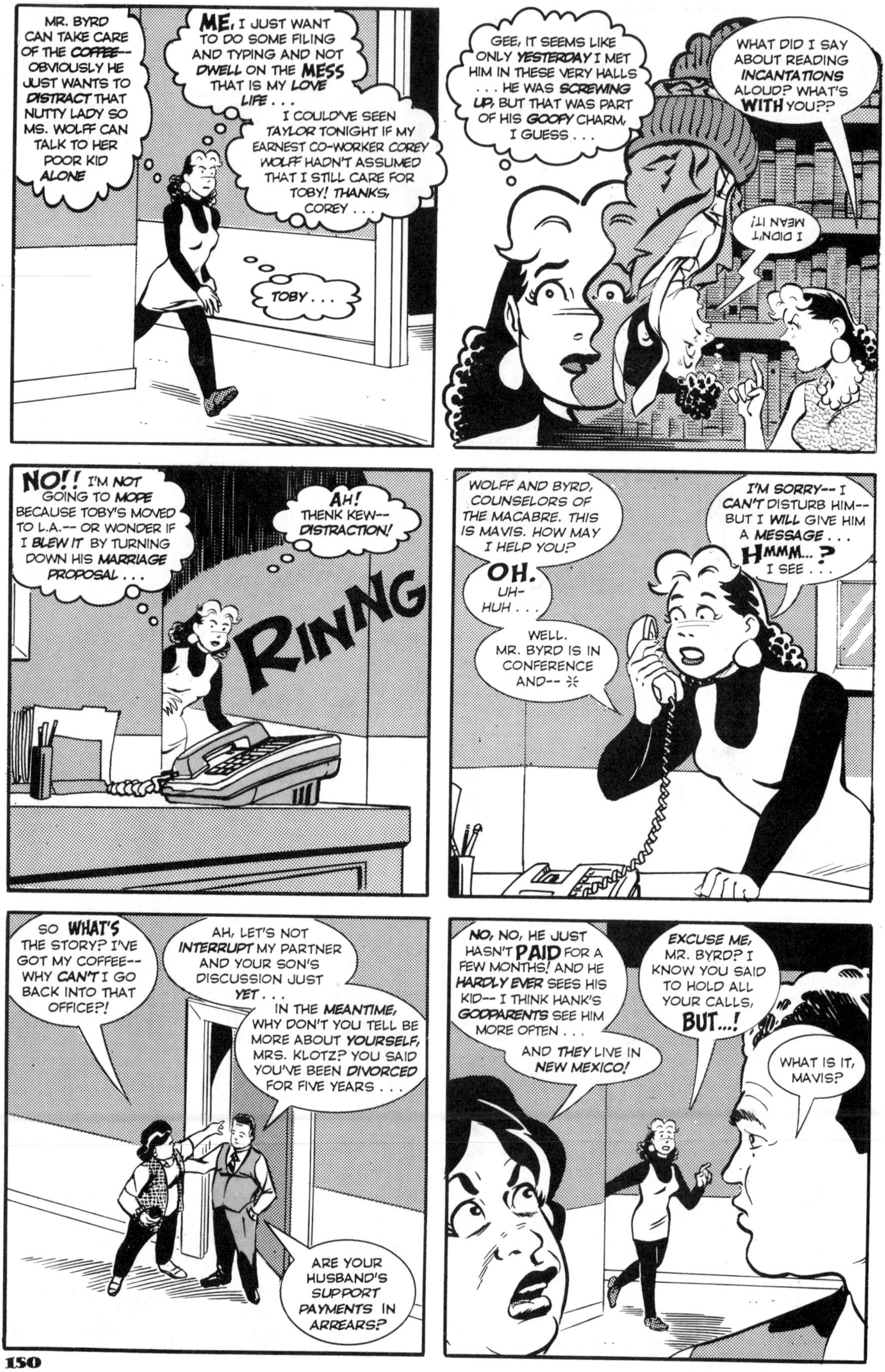
MR. BYRD CAN TAKE CARE OF THE COFFEE-- OBVIOUSLY HE JUST WANTS TO DISTRACT THAT NUTTY LADY SO MS. WOLFF CAN TALK TO HER POOR KID ALONE
ME, I JUST WANT TO DO SOME FILING AND TYPING AND NOT DWELL ON THE MESS THAT IS MY LOVE LIFE . . .
I COULD'VE SEEN TAYLOR TONIGHT IF MY EARNEST CO-WORKER COREY WOLFF HADN'T ASSUMED THAT I STILL CARE FOR TOBY! THANKS, COREY . . .
TOBY . . .
GEE, IT SEEMS LIKE ONLY YESTERDAY I MET HIM IN THESE VERY HALLS . . . HE WAS SCREWING UP, BUT THAT WAS PART OF HIS GOOFY CHARM, I GUESS . . .
WHAT DID I SAY ABOUT READING INCANTATIONS ALOUD? WHAT'S WITH YOU??
I DIDN'T MEAN IT!
NO!! I'M NOT GOING TO MOPE BECAUSE TOBY'S MOVED TO L.A.-- OR WONDER IF I BLEW IT BY TURNING DOWN HIS MARRIAGE PROPOSAL . . .
AH! THENK KEW-- DISTRACTION!
RINNG
WOLFF AND BYRD, COUNSELORS OF THE MACABRE. THIS IS MAVIS. HOW MAY I HELP YOU?
OH.
UH-HUH . . .
WELL. MR. BYRD IS IN CONFERENCE AND--
I'M SORRY-- I CAN'T DISTURB HIM-- BUT I WILL GIVE HIM A MESSAGE . . . HMMM...? I SEE . . .
SO WHAT'S THE STORY? I'VE GOT MY COFFEE-- WHY CAN'T I GO BACK INTO THAT OFFICE?!
AH, LET'S NOT INTERRUPT MY PARTNER AND YOUR SON'S DISCUSSION JUST YET . . .
IN THE MEANTIME, WHY DON'T YOU TELL BE MORE ABOUT YOURSELF, MRS. KLOTZ? YOU SAID YOU'VE BEEN DIVORCED FOR FIVE YEARS . . .
ARE YOUR HUSBAND'S SUPPORT PAYMENTS IN ARREARS?
NO, NO, HE JUST HASN'T PAID FOR A FEW MONTHS! AND HE HARDLY EVER SEES HIS KID-- I THINK HANK'S GODPARENTS SEE HIM MORE OFTEN . . .
AND THEY LIVE IN NEW MEXICO!
EXCUSE ME, MR. BYRD? I KNOW YOU SAID TO HOLD ALL YOUR CALLS, BUT...!
WHAT IS IT, MAVIS?

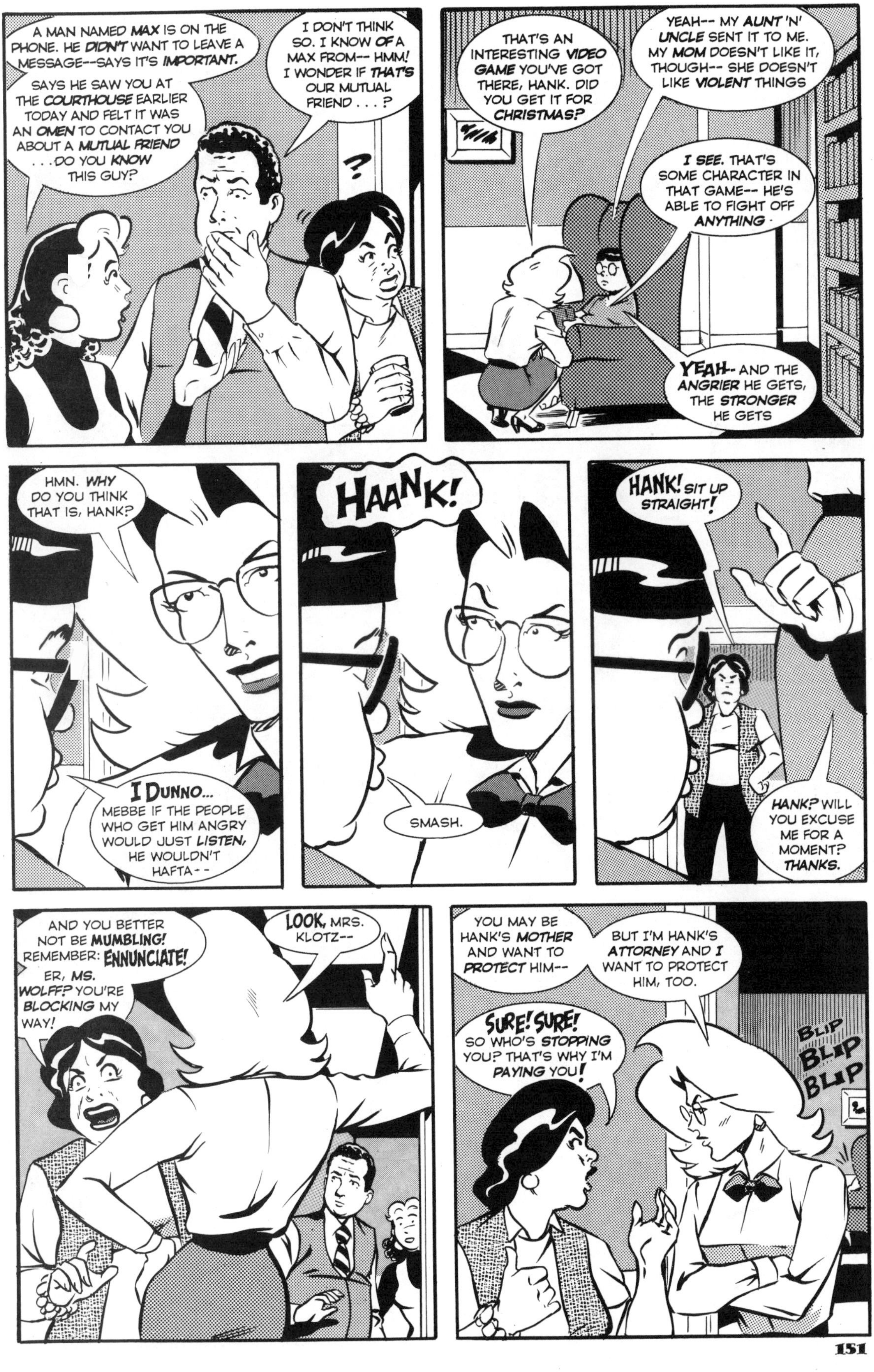
A MAN NAMED MAX IS ON THE PHONE. HE DIDN'T WANT TO LEAVE A MESSAGE--SAYS IT'S IMPORTANT.
SAYS HE SAW YOU AT THE COURTHOUSE EARLIER TODAY AND FELT IT WAS AN OMEN TO CONTACT YOU ABOUT A MUTUAL FRIEND . . . DO YOU KNOW THIS GUY?
I DON'T THINK SO. I KNOW OF A MAX FROM-- HMM! I WONDER IF THAT'S OUR MUTUAL FRIEND . . . ?
?
THAT'S AN INTERESTING VIDEO GAME YOU'VE GOT THERE, HANK. DID YOU GET IT FOR CHRISTMAS?
YEAH-- MY AUNT 'N' UNCLE SENT IT TO ME. MY MOM DOESN'T LIKE IT, THOUGH-- SHE DOESN'T LIKE VIOLENT THINGS
I SEE. THAT'S SOME CHARACTER IN THAT GAME-- HE'S ABLE TO FIGHT OFF ANYTHING -
YEAH-- AND THE ANGRIER HE GETS, THE STRONGER HE GETS
HMN. WHY DO YOU THINK THAT IS, HANK?
I DUNNO... MEBBE IF THE PEOPLE WHO GET HIM ANGRY WOULD JUST LISTEN, HE WOULDN'T HAFTA - -
HAANK!
SMASH.
HANK! SIT UP STRAIGHT!
HANK? WILL YOU EXCUSE ME FOR A MOMENT? THANKS.
AND YOU BETTER NOT BE MUMBLING! REMEMBER: ENNUNCIATE!
ER, MS. WOLFF? YOU'RE BLOCKING MY WAY!
LOOK, MRS. KLOTZ--
YOU MAY BE HANK'S MOTHER AND WANT TO PROTECT HIM--
BUT I'M HANK'S ATTORNEY AND I WANT TO PROTECT HIM, TOO.
SURE! SURE! SO WHO'S STOPPING YOU? THAT'S WHY I'M PAYING YOU!
BLIP BLIP BLIP

YOUR SON MAY HAVE TO *TESTIFY* IN COURT. I NEED TO HEAR, IN HIS *OWN* WORDS, WHAT HIS *RELATIONSHIP* IS WITH THAT CREATURE.

SO? WHAT'S YOUR POINT? *ASK HIM!* I'M JUST HERE FOR *MORAL SUPPORT!* YOU SEE MY KID--I COULD SWEAR HE'S PRACTICALLY *AUTISTIC*--

HANK *DOESN'T* HAVE A POSITIVE *MALE* ROLE MODEL AT HOME. IT'S UP TO *ME* TO LOOK AFTER HIM. HE--

BLIP
BLIP BLIP

FER CHRISSAKE'S, HANK!! ENOUGH, HANH?!

MRS. KLOTZ--!

BACK OFF, MS. WOLFF! DON'T TELL ME HOW TO HANDLE *MY* KID!

BLIP BLIP BLIP BLIP BLIP

BLIP

IT'S *TOUGH* ENOUGH TRYING TO RAISE A TWELVE-YEAR-OLD AS A *SINGLE* PARENT--

BLIP BLIP BLIP BLIP

BLIP

--WITHOUT LETTING *OTHERS* WHO THINK THEY *KNOW* BETTER *INDULGE* HIS EVERY WHIM!

BLIP BLIP BLIP BLIP

REMEMBER-- I HIRED YOU TO BE HANK'S *LAWYER,* NOT HIS *SHRINK!*

MRS. KLOTZ, YOU MAY HAVE EN- GAGED MY SERVICES, BUT YOUR *SON* IS MY *CLIENT*--

--AND IT'S *HIS* BEST INTERESTS I HAVE TO LOOK AFTER

YEOW!

BLIP BLIP BLIP

GOOD LORD!

WHAT HAS THAT-- THAT *BRUTE* DONE TO MY BOY??

MRS. KLOTZ, BRACE YOUR- SELF--

THAT *IS* YOUR BOY! HE HAS BECOME--

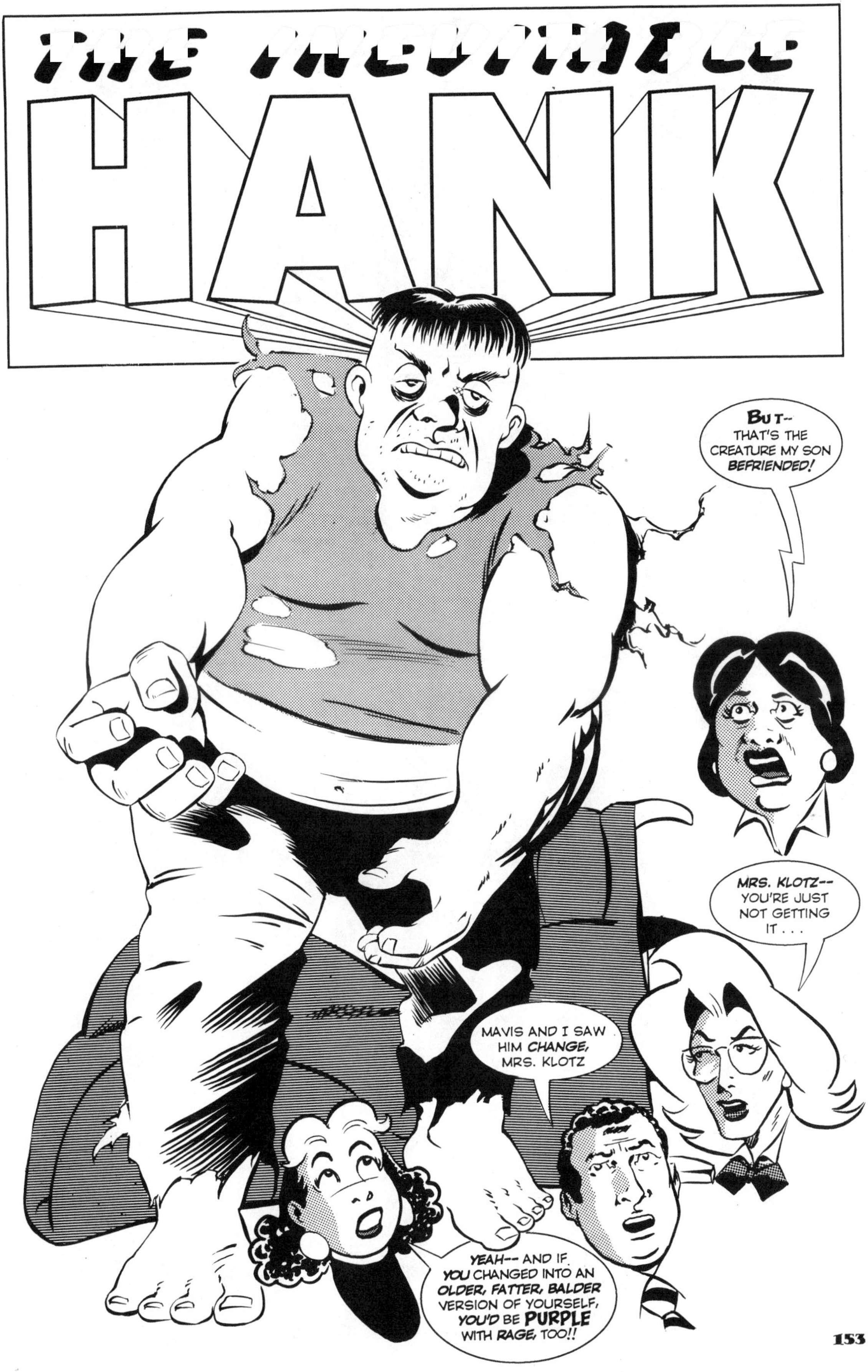
HANK
BUT-- THAT'S THE CREATURE MY SON BEFRIENDED!
MRS. KLOTZ-- YOU'RE JUST NOT GETTING IT . . .
MAVIS AND I SAW HIM CHANGE, MRS. KLOTZ
YEAH-- AND IF YOU CHANGED INTO AN OLDER, FATTER, BALDER VERSION OF YOURSELF, YOU'D BE PURPLE WITH RAGE, TOO!!

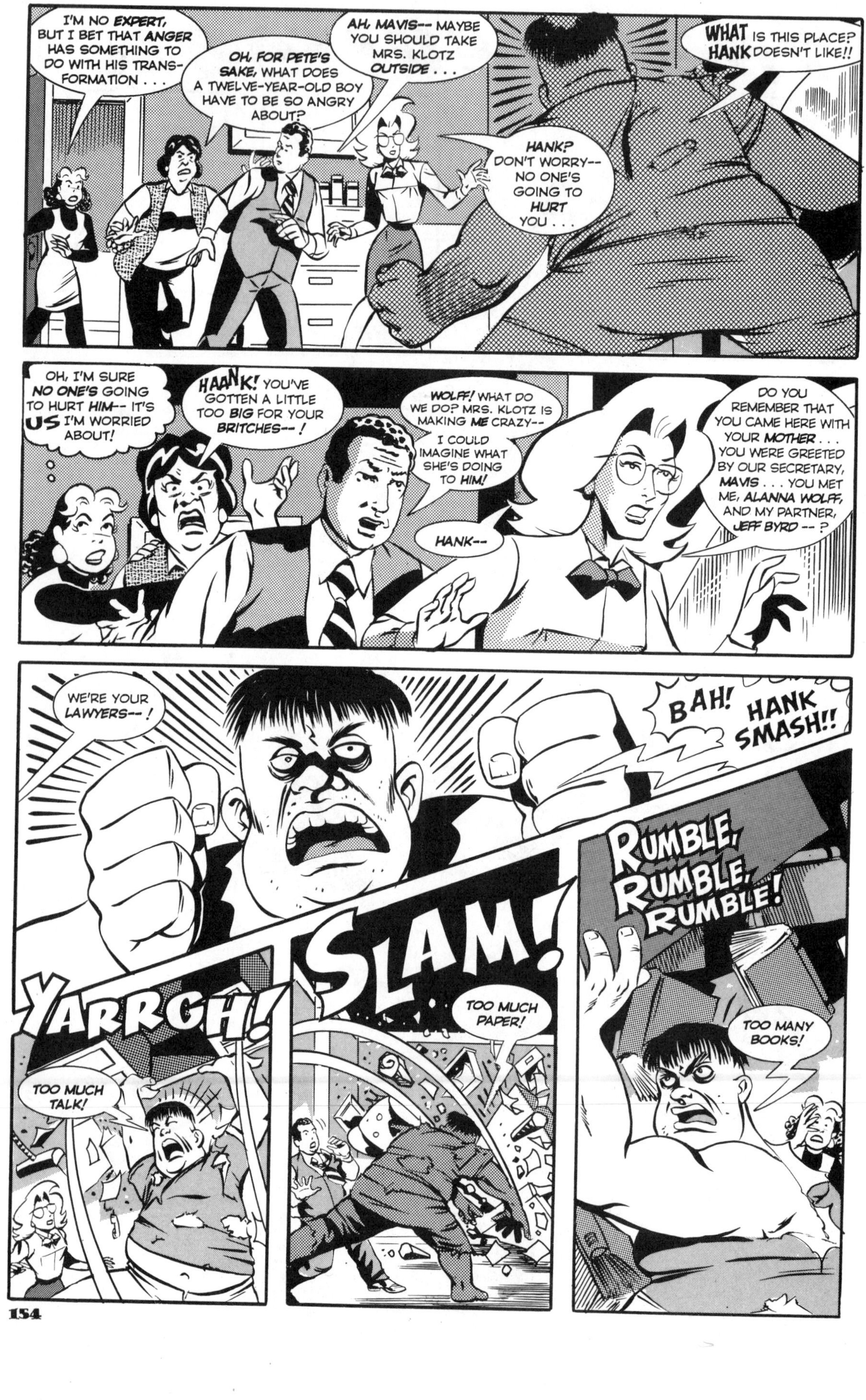
I'M NO EXPERT, BUT I BET THAT ANGER HAS SOMETHING TO DO WITH HIS TRANSFORMATION . . .
OH, FOR PETE'S SAKE, WHAT DOES A TWELVE-YEAR-OLD BOY HAVE TO BE SO ANGRY ABOUT?
AH, MAVIS-- MAYBE YOU SHOULD TAKE MRS. KLOTZ OUTSIDE . . .
WHAT IS THIS PLACE? WHAT HANK DOESN'T LIKE!!
HANK? DON'T WORRY-- NO ONE'S GOING TO HURT YOU . . .
OH, I'M SURE NO ONE'S GOING TO HURT HIM-- IT'S US I'M WORRIED ABOUT!
HAANK! YOU'VE GOTTEN A LITTLE TOO BIG FOR YOUR BRITCHES-- !
WOLFF! WHAT DO WE DO? MRS. KLOTZ IS MAKING ME CRAZY--
I COULD IMAGINE WHAT SHE'S DOING TO HIM!
HANK--
DO YOU REMEMBER THAT YOU CAME HERE WITH YOUR MOTHER . . . YOU WERE GREETED BY OUR SECRETARY, MAVIS . . . YOU MET ME, ALANNA WOLFF, AND MY PARTNER, JEFF BYRD -- ?
WE'RE YOUR LAWYERS-- !
BAH! HANK SMASH!!
YARRGH!
TOO MUCH TALK!
SLAM!
TOO MUCH PAPER!
RUMBLE, RUMBLE, RUMBLE!
TOO MANY BOOKS!

GET MRS. KLOTZ OUT OF HERE-- *NOW!*

USE THE *STAIRS* TO--

WHOOM!

I'M *NOT* LEAVING UNTIL I FIND OUT WHAT HANK IS TRYING TO *PROVE . . .!*

"BUT IT QUICKLY BECAME APPARENT THAT THE *RAMPAGING HANK* HAD NO *REAL* AGENDA-- HE WAS SIMPLY *VENTING . . .* AN ADOLESCENT *TEMPER TANTRUM* IN A MIDDLE-AGED BODY. UNFORTUNATELY, OUR OFFICE BUILDING CAUGHT THE *BRUNT* OF HIS *RAGE . . .*

BTAM!

RRRUMBLE

STOMP

STOMP

STOMP

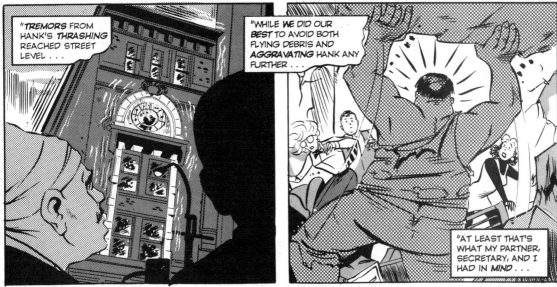

"*TREMORS* FROM HANK'S *THRASHING* REACHED STREET LEVEL . . .

"WHILE *WE* DID OUR *BEST* TO AVOID BOTH FLYING DEBRIS AND *AGGRAVATING* HANK ANY FURTHER . . .

"AT LEAST THAT'S WHAT MY PARTNER, SECRETARY, AND I HAD IN *MIND . . .*

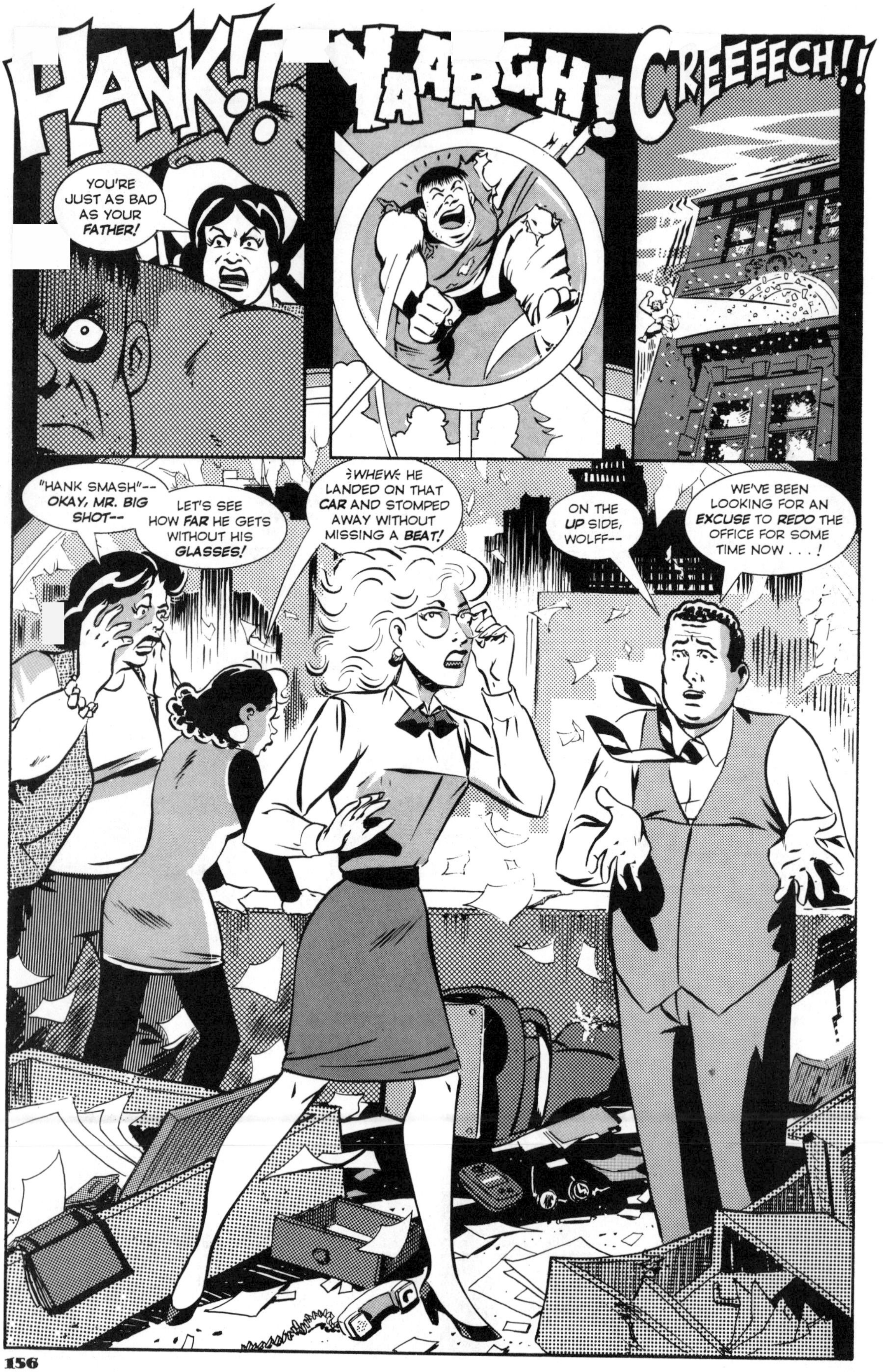
HANK!!
YOU'RE JUST AS BAD AS YOUR FATHER!
YAARGH!
CREEEECH!!
"HANK SMASH"-- OKAY, MR. BIG SHOT--
LET'S SEE HOW FAR HE GETS WITHOUT HIS GLASSES!
WHEW HE LANDED ON THAT CAR AND STOMPED AWAY WITHOUT MISSING A BEAT!
ON THE UP SIDE, WOLFF--
WE'VE BEEN LOOKING FOR AN EXCUSE TO REDO THE OFFICE FOR SOME TIME NOW . . . !

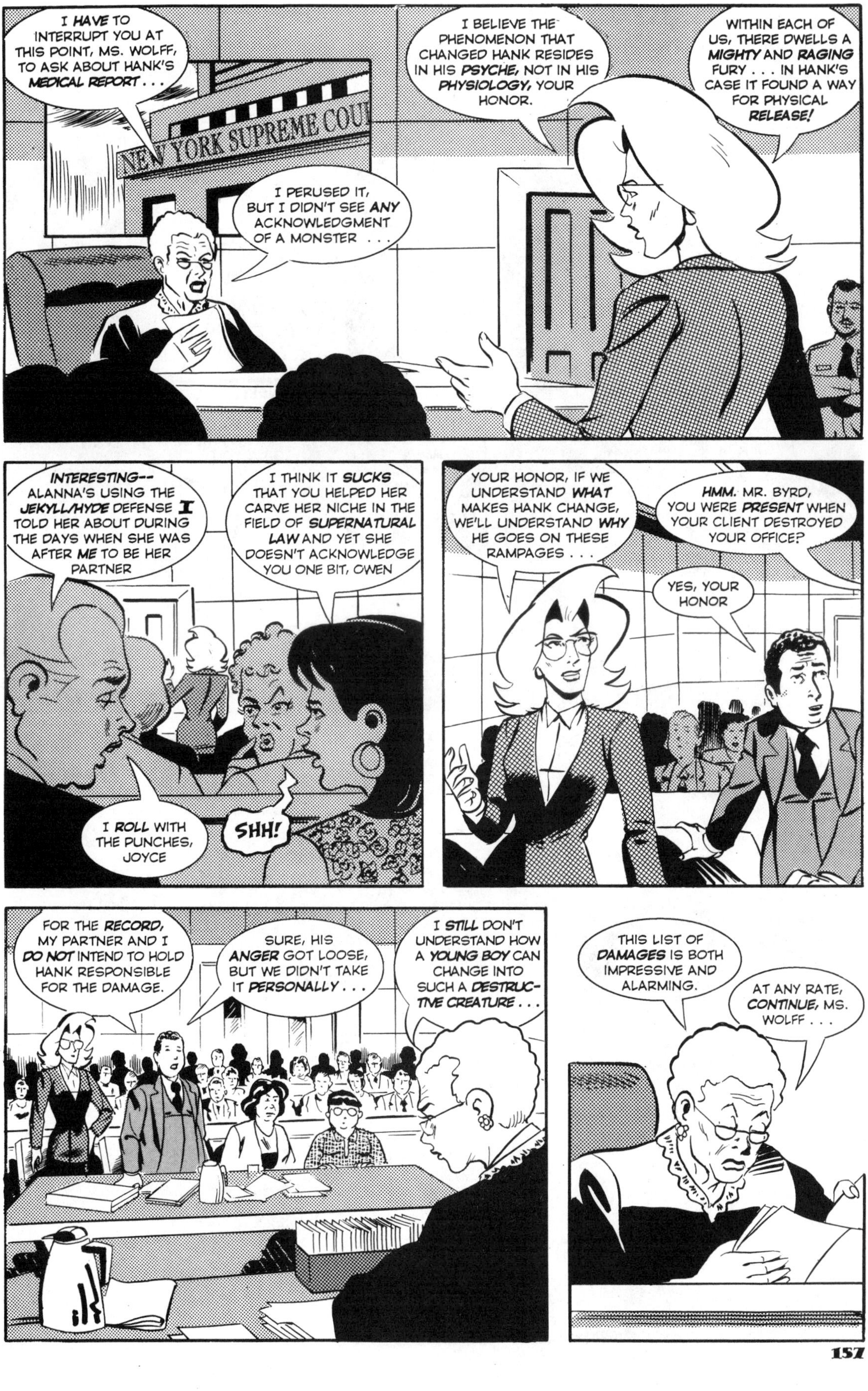

I HAVE TO INTERRUPT YOU AT THIS POINT, MS. WOLFF, TO ASK ABOUT HANK'S MEDICAL REPORT . . .
NEW YORK SUPREME COU
I PERUSED IT, BUT I DIDN'T SEE ANY ACKNOWLEDGMENT OF A MONSTER . . .
I BELIEVE THE PHENOMENON THAT CHANGED HANK RESIDES IN HIS PSYCHE, NOT IN HIS PHYSIOLOGY, YOUR HONOR.
WITHIN EACH OF US, THERE DWELLS A MIGHTY AND RAGING FURY . . . IN HANK'S CASE IT FOUND A WAY FOR PHYSICAL RELEASE!
INTERESTING-- ALANNA'S USING THE JEKYLL/HYDE DEFENSE I TOLD HER ABOUT DURING THE DAYS WHEN SHE WAS AFTER ME TO BE HER PARTNER
I THINK IT SUCKS THAT YOU HELPED HER CARVE HER NICHE IN THE FIELD OF SUPERNATURAL LAW AND YET SHE DOESN'T ACKNOWLEDGE YOU ONE BIT, OWEN
I ROLL WITH THE PUNCHES, JOYCE
SHH!
YOUR HONOR, IF WE UNDERSTAND WHAT MAKES HANK CHANGE, WE'LL UNDERSTAND WHY HE GOES ON THESE RAMPAGES . . .
HMM. MR. BYRD, YOU WERE PRESENT WHEN YOUR CLIENT DESTROYED YOUR OFFICE?
YES, YOUR HONOR
FOR THE RECORD, MY PARTNER AND I DO NOT INTEND TO HOLD HANK RESPONSIBLE FOR THE DAMAGE.
SURE, HIS ANGER GOT LOOSE, BUT WE DIDN'T TAKE IT PERSONALLY . . .
I STILL DON'T UNDERSTAND HOW A YOUNG BOY CAN CHANGE INTO SUCH A DESTRUCTIVE CREATURE . . .
THIS LIST OF DAMAGES IS BOTH IMPRESSIVE AND ALARMING.
AT ANY RATE, CONTINUE, MS. WOLFF . . .

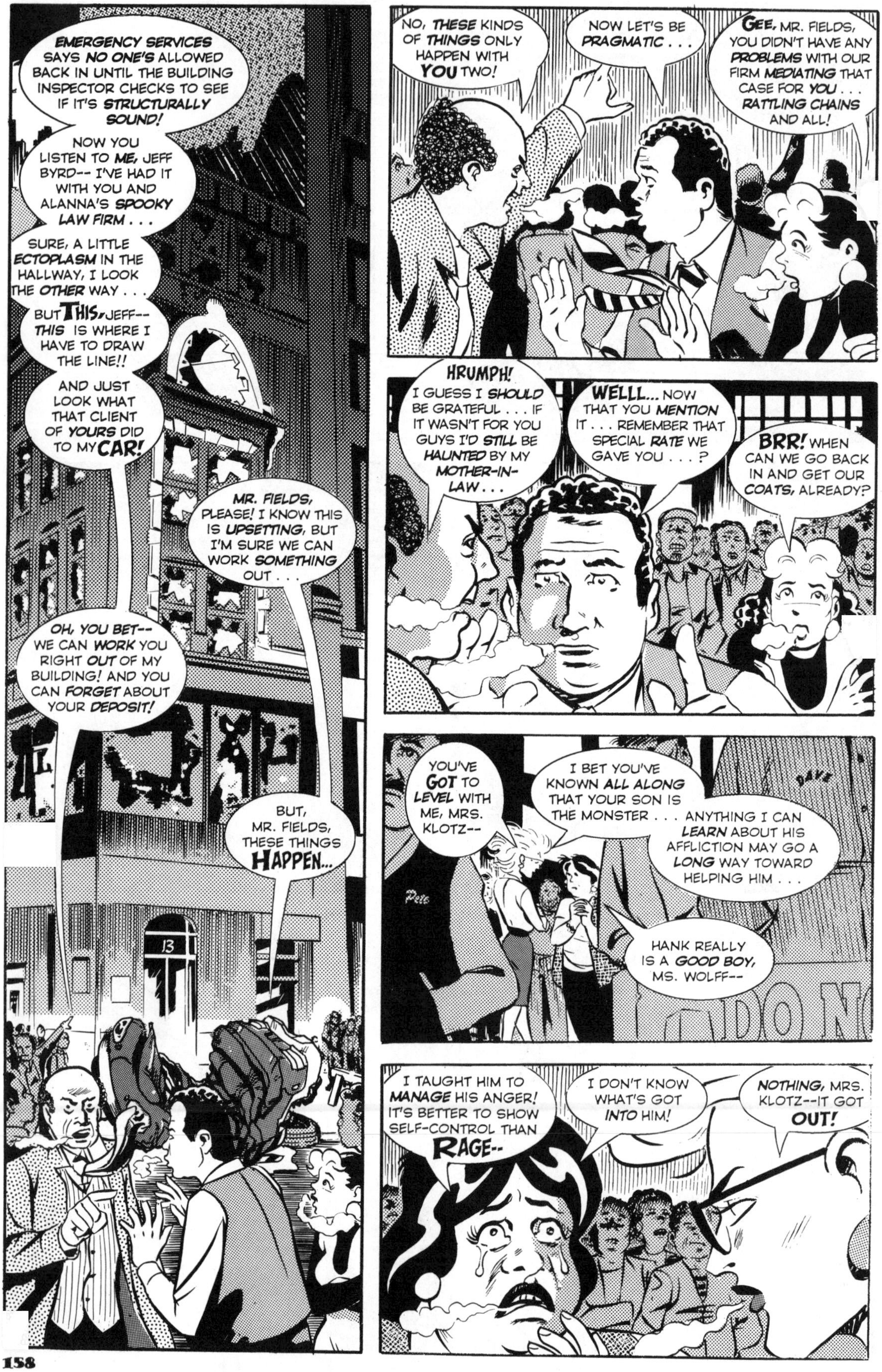
EMERGENCY SERVICES SAYS NO ONE'S ALLOWED BACK IN UNTIL THE BUILDING INSPECTOR CHECKS TO SEE IF IT'S STRUCTURALLY SOUND!
NOW YOU LISTEN TO ME, JEFF BYRD-- I'VE HAD IT WITH YOU AND ALANNA'S SPOOKY LAW FIRM . . .
SURE, A LITTLE ECTOPLASM IN THE HALLWAY, I LOOK THE OTHER WAY . . .
BUT THIS, JEFF-- THIS IS WHERE I HAVE TO DRAW THE LINE!!
AND JUST LOOK WHAT THAT CLIENT OF YOURS DID TO MY CAR!
MR. FIELDS, PLEASE! I KNOW THIS IS UPSETTING, BUT I'M SURE WE CAN WORK SOMETHING OUT . . .
OH, YOU BET-- WE CAN WORK YOU RIGHT OUT OF MY BUILDING! AND YOU CAN FORGET ABOUT YOUR DEPOSIT!
BUT, MR. FIELDS, THESE THINGS HAPPEN...
13
NO, THESE KINDS OF THINGS ONLY HAPPEN WITH YOU TWO!
NOW LET'S BE PRAGMATIC . . .
GEE, MR. FIELDS, YOU DIDN'T HAVE ANY PROBLEMS WITH OUR FIRM MEDIATING THAT CASE FOR YOU . . . RATTLING CHAINS AND ALL!
HRUMPH! I GUESS I SHOULD BE GRATEFUL . . . IF IT WASN'T FOR YOU GUYS I'D STILL BE HAUNTED BY MY MOTHER-IN-LAW . . .
WELLL... NOW THAT YOU MENTION IT . . . REMEMBER THAT SPECIAL RATE WE GAVE YOU . . . ?
BRR! WHEN CAN WE GO BACK IN AND GET OUR COATS, ALREADY?
YOU'VE GOT TO LEVEL WITH ME, MRS. KLOTZ--
I BET YOU'VE KNOWN ALL ALONG THAT YOUR SON IS THE MONSTER . . . ANYTHING I CAN LEARN ABOUT HIS AFFLICTION MAY GO A LONG WAY TOWARD HELPING HIM . . .
DAVE
PETE
HANK REALLY IS A GOOD BOY, MS. WOLFF--
DO N
I TAUGHT HIM TO MANAGE HIS ANGER! IT'S BETTER TO SHOW SELF-CONTROL THAN RAGE--
I DON'T KNOW WHAT'S GOT INTO HIM!
NOTHING, MRS. KLOTZ--IT GOT OUT!

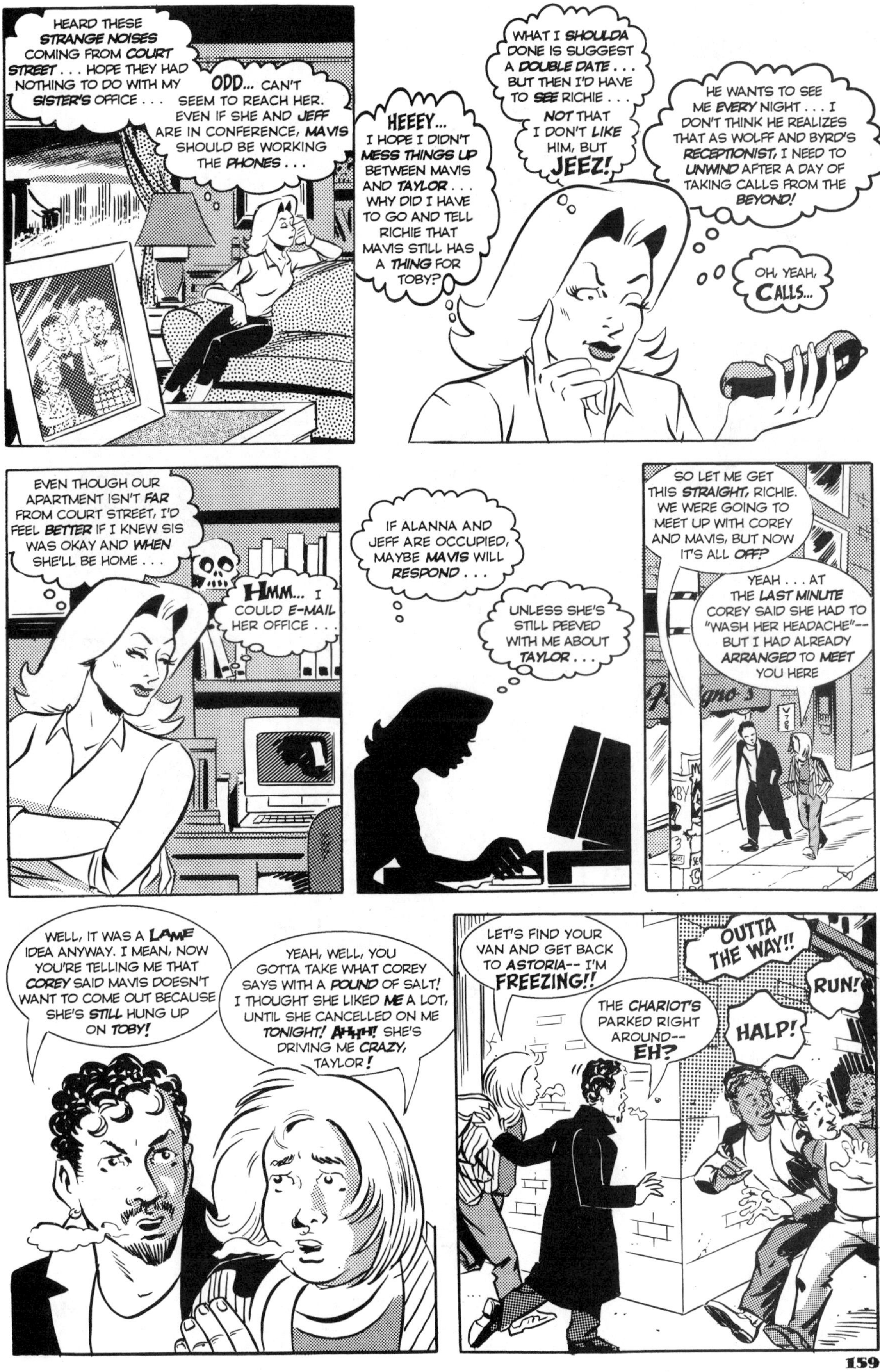
HEARD THESE STRANGE NOISES COMING FROM COURT STREET . . . HOPE THEY HAD NOTHING TO DO WITH MY SISTER'S OFFICE . . .
ODD... CAN'T SEEM TO REACH HER. EVEN IF SHE AND JEFF ARE IN CONFERENCE, MAVIS SHOULD BE WORKING THE PHONES . . .
HEEEY... I HOPE I DIDN'T MESS THINGS UP BETWEEN MAVIS AND TAYLOR . . . WHY DID I HAVE TO GO AND TELL RICHIE THAT MAVIS STILL HAS A THING FOR TOBY?
WHAT I SHOULDA DONE IS SUGGEST A DOUBLE DATE . . . BUT THEN I'D HAVE TO SEE RICHIE . . .
NOT THAT I DON'T LIKE HIM, BUT JEEZ!
HE WANTS TO SEE ME EVERY NIGHT . . . I DON'T THINK HE REALIZES THAT AS WOLFF AND BYRD'S RECEPTIONIST, I NEED TO UNWIND AFTER A DAY OF TAKING CALLS FROM THE BEYOND!
OH, YEAH, CALLS...
EVEN THOUGH OUR APARTMENT ISN'T FAR FROM COURT STREET, I'D FEEL BETTER IF I KNEW SIS WAS OKAY AND WHEN SHE'LL BE HOME . . .
HMM... I COULD E-MAIL HER OFFICE . . .
IF ALANNA AND JEFF ARE OCCUPIED, MAYBE MAVIS WILL RESPOND . . .
UNLESS SHE'S STILL PEEVED WITH ME ABOUT TAYLOR . . .
SO LET ME GET THIS STRAIGHT, RICHIE. WE WERE GOING TO MEET UP WITH COREY AND MAVIS, BUT NOW IT'S ALL OFF?
YEAH . . . AT THE LAST MINUTE COREY SAID SHE HAD TO "WASH HER HEADACHE"-- BUT I HAD ALREADY ARRANGED TO MEET YOU HERE
WELL, IT WAS A LAME IDEA ANYWAY. I MEAN, NOW YOU'RE TELLING ME THAT COREY SAID MAVIS DOESN'T WANT TO COME OUT BECAUSE SHE'S STILL HUNG UP ON TOBY!
YEAH, WELL, YOU GOTTA TAKE WHAT COREY SAYS WITH A POUND OF SALT! I THOUGHT SHE LIKED ME A LOT, UNTIL SHE CANCELLED ON ME TONIGHT! AHHH! SHE'S DRIVING ME CRAZY, TAYLOR!
LET'S FIND YOUR VAN AND GET BACK TO ASTORIA-- I'M FREEZING!!
THE CHARIOT'S PARKED RIGHT AROUND-- EH?
OUTTA THE WAY!!
RUN!
HALP!

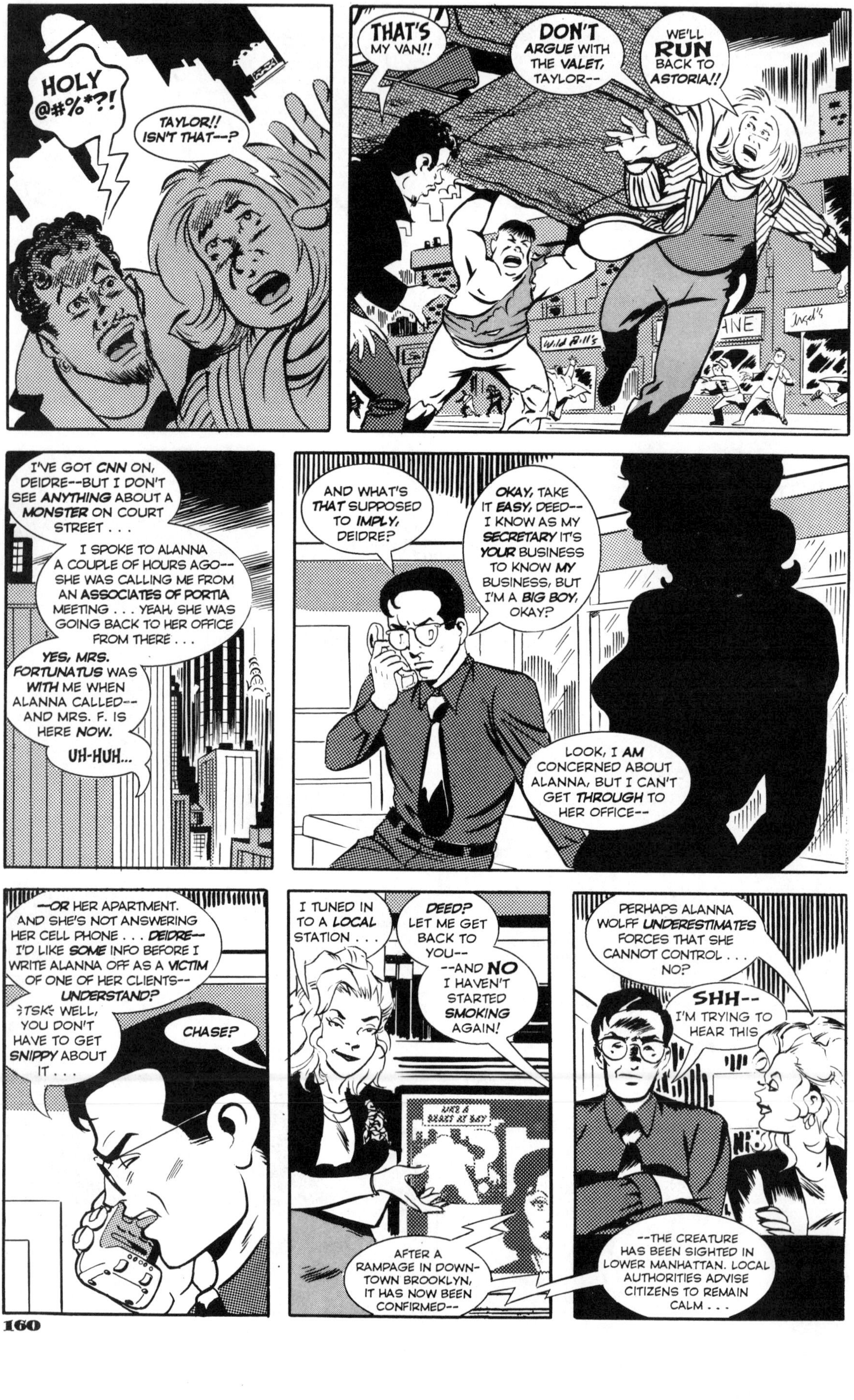
HOLY @#%*?!
TAYLOR!! ISN'T THAT--?
THAT'S MY VAN!!
DON'T ARGUE WITH THE VALET, TAYLOR--
WE'LL RUN BACK TO ASTORIA!!
I'VE GOT CNN ON, DEIDRE--BUT I DON'T SEE ANYTHING ABOUT A MONSTER ON COURT STREET . . .
I SPOKE TO ALANNA A COUPLE OF HOURS AGO--SHE WAS CALLING ME FROM AN ASSOCIATES OF PORTIA MEETING . . . YEAH, SHE WAS GOING BACK TO HER OFFICE FROM THERE . . .
YES, MRS. FORTUNATUS WAS WITH ME WHEN ALANNA CALLED--AND MRS. F. IS HERE NOW.
UH-HUH...
AND WHAT'S THAT SUPPOSED TO IMPLY, DEIDRE?
OKAY, TAKE IT EASY, DEED--I KNOW AS MY SECRETARY IT'S YOUR BUSINESS TO KNOW MY BUSINESS, BUT I'M A BIG BOY, OKAY?
LOOK, I AM CONCERNED ABOUT ALANNA, BUT I CAN'T GET THROUGH TO HER OFFICE--
--OR HER APARTMENT. AND SHE'S NOT ANSWERING HER CELL PHONE . . . DEIDRE--I'D LIKE SOME INFO BEFORE I WRITE ALANNA OFF AS A VICTIM OF ONE OF HER CLIENTS--UNDERSTAND?
TSK WELL, YOU DON'T HAVE TO GET SNIPPY ABOUT IT . . .
CHASE?
I TUNED IN TO A LOCAL STATION . . .
DEED? LET ME GET BACK TO YOU----AND NO I HAVEN'T STARTED SMOKING AGAIN!
AFTER A RAMPAGE IN DOWN-TOWN BROOKLYN, IT HAS NOW BEEN CONFIRMED--
PERHAPS ALANNA WOLFF UNDERESTIMATES FORCES THAT SHE CANNOT CONTROL . . . NO?
SHH--I'M TRYING TO HEAR THIS
--THE CREATURE HAS BEEN SIGHTED IN LOWER MANHATTAN. LOCAL AUTHORITIES ADVISE CITIZENS TO REMAIN CALM . . .

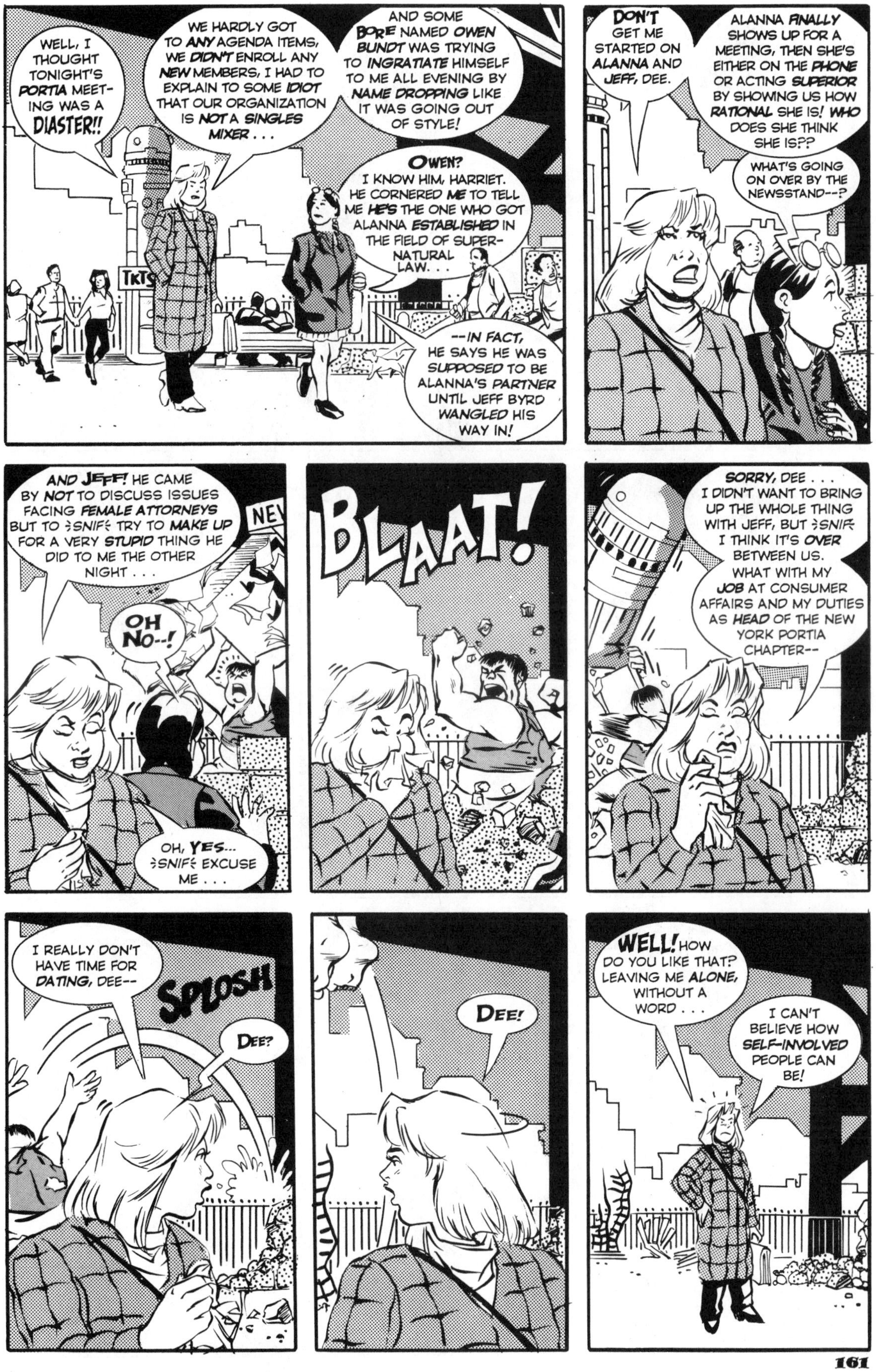
WELL, I THOUGHT TONIGHT'S PORTIA MEETING WAS A DIASTER!!
WE HARDLY GOT TO ANY AGENDA ITEMS, WE DIDN'T ENROLL ANY NEW MEMBERS, I HAD TO EXPLAIN TO SOME IDIOT THAT OUR ORGANIZATION IS NOT A SINGLES MIXER . . .
AND SOME BORE NAMED OWEN BUNDT WAS TRYING TO INGRATIATE HIMSELF TO ME ALL EVENING BY NAME DROPPING LIKE IT WAS GOING OUT OF STYLE!
OWEN? I KNOW HIM, HARRIET. HE CORNERED ME TO TELL ME HE'S THE ONE WHO GOT ALANNA ESTABLISHED IN THE FIELD OF SUPER-NATURAL LAW. . .
--IN FACT, HE SAYS HE WAS SUPPOSED TO BE ALANNA'S PARTNER UNTIL JEFF BYRD WANGLED HIS WAY IN!
TKTS
DON'T GET ME STARTED ON ALANNA AND JEFF, DEE.
ALANNA FINALLY SHOWS UP FOR A MEETING, THEN SHE'S EITHER ON THE PHONE OR ACTING SUPERIOR BY SHOWING US HOW RATIONAL SHE IS! WHO DOES SHE THINK SHE IS??
WHAT'S GOING ON OVER BY THE NEWSSTAND--?
AND JEFF! HE CAME BY NOT TO DISCUSS ISSUES FACING FEMALE ATTORNEYS BUT TO ⸗SNIF⸗ TRY TO MAKE UP FOR A VERY STUPID THING HE DID TO ME THE OTHER NIGHT . . .
NEW
OH NO--!
OH, YES... ⸗SNIF⸗ EXCUSE ME . . .
BLAAT!
SORRY, DEE . . . I DIDN'T WANT TO BRING UP THE WHOLE THING WITH JEFF, BUT ⸗SNIF⸗ I THINK IT'S OVER BETWEEN US. WHAT WITH MY JOB AT CONSUMER AFFAIRS AND MY DUTIES AS HEAD OF THE NEW YORK PORTIA CHAPTER--
I REALLY DON'T HAVE TIME FOR DATING, DEE--
SPLOSH
DEE?
DEE!
WELL! HOW DO YOU LIKE THAT? LEAVING ME ALONE, WITHOUT A WORD . . .
I CAN'T BELIEVE HOW SELF-INVOLVED PEOPLE CAN BE!

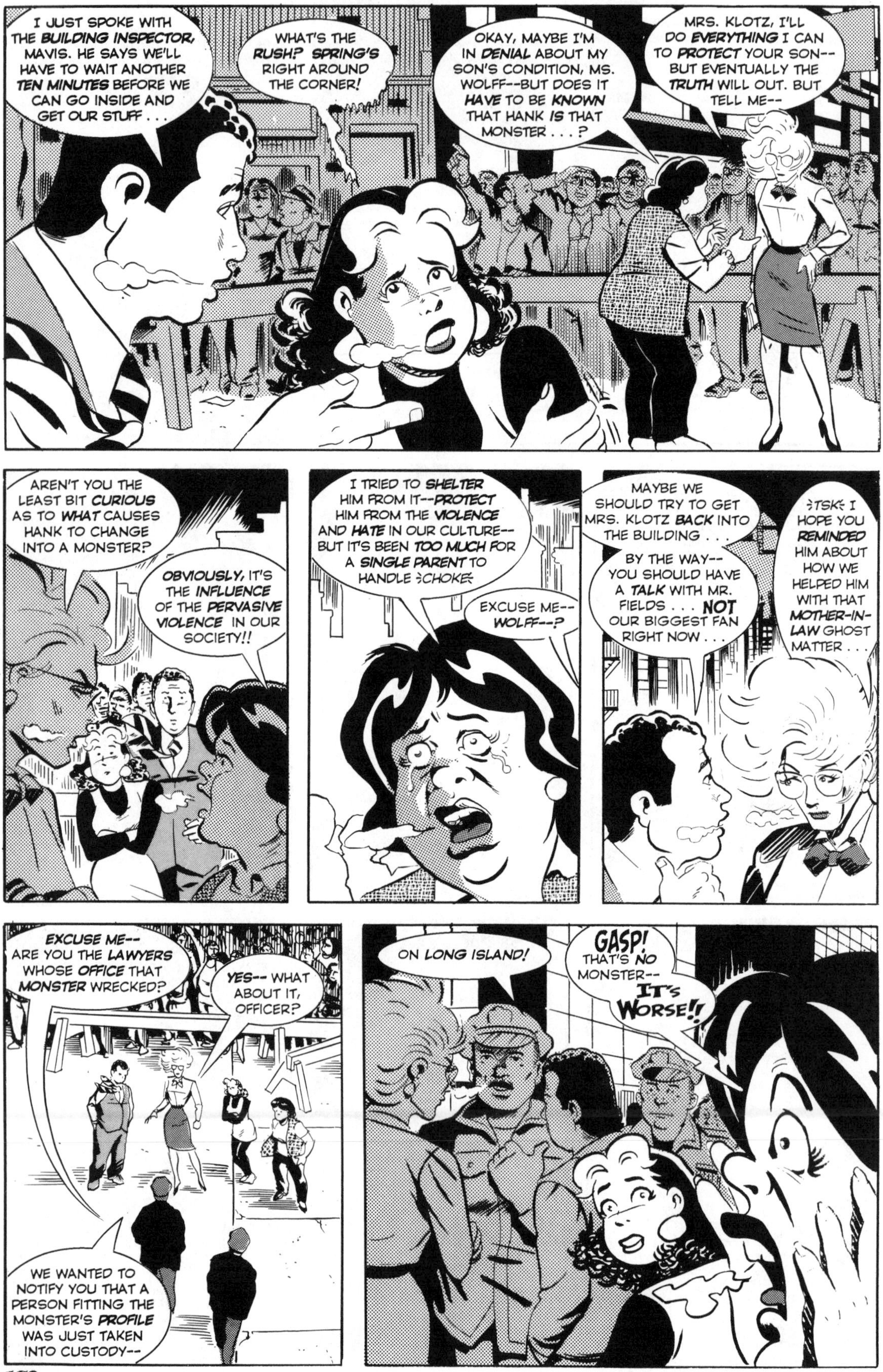
I JUST SPOKE WITH THE BUILDING INSPECTOR, MAVIS. HE SAYS WE'LL HAVE TO WAIT ANOTHER TEN MINUTES BEFORE WE CAN GO INSIDE AND GET OUR STUFF . . .
WHAT'S THE RUSH? SPRING'S RIGHT AROUND THE CORNER!
OKAY, MAYBE I'M IN DENIAL ABOUT MY SON'S CONDITION, MS. WOLFF--BUT DOES IT HAVE TO BE KNOWN THAT HANK IS THAT MONSTER . . . ?
MRS. KLOTZ, I'LL DO EVERYTHING I CAN TO PROTECT YOUR SON--BUT EVENTUALLY THE TRUTH WILL OUT. BUT TELL ME--
AREN'T YOU THE LEAST BIT CURIOUS AS TO WHAT CAUSES HANK TO CHANGE INTO A MONSTER?
OBVIOUSLY, IT'S THE INFLUENCE OF THE PERVASIVE VIOLENCE IN OUR SOCIETY!!
I TRIED TO SHELTER HIM FROM IT--PROTECT HIM FROM THE VIOLENCE AND HATE IN OUR CULTURE--BUT IT'S BEEN TOO MUCH FOR A SINGLE PARENT TO HANDLE *CHOKE*
EXCUSE ME--WOLFF--?
MAYBE WE SHOULD TRY TO GET MRS. KLOTZ BACK INTO THE BUILDING . . .
BY THE WAY--YOU SHOULD HAVE A TALK WITH MR. FIELDS . . . NOT OUR BIGGEST FAN RIGHT NOW . . .
TSK I HOPE YOU REMINDED HIM ABOUT HOW WE HELPED HIM WITH THAT MOTHER-IN-LAW GHOST MATTER . . .
EXCUSE ME--ARE YOU THE LAWYERS WHOSE OFFICE THAT MONSTER WRECKED?
YES-- WHAT ABOUT IT, OFFICER?
WE WANTED TO NOTIFY YOU THAT A PERSON FITTING THE MONSTER'S PROFILE WAS JUST TAKEN INTO CUSTODY--
ON LONG ISLAND!
GASP! THAT'S NO MONSTER--IT'S WORSE!!

"THE HEARING BEGINS TODAY FOR HANK KLOTZ, JUNIOR, THE ***BOY-TURNED-MONSTER*** WHO WREAKED ***HAVOC*** IN BROOKLN AND LOWER MANHATTAN LAST WEEK. BASED ON A SKETCHY DESCRIPTION, POLICE ORIGINALLY ARRESTED THE ***PROPRIETOR*** OF THIS REPAIR SHOP IN BAYPORT, LONG ISLAND, HANK KLOTZ, ***SENIOR.***

"THE SENIOR KLOTZ WAS SOON RELEASED, HOWEVER, WHEN WORD CAME IN THAT THE HANK MONSTER HAD BEEN ***APPREHENDED*** IN THE BATTERY PARK AREA. HANK SENIOR HAS BEEN ***SUBPOENAED*** TO APPEAR AT HIS SON'S HEARING . . .

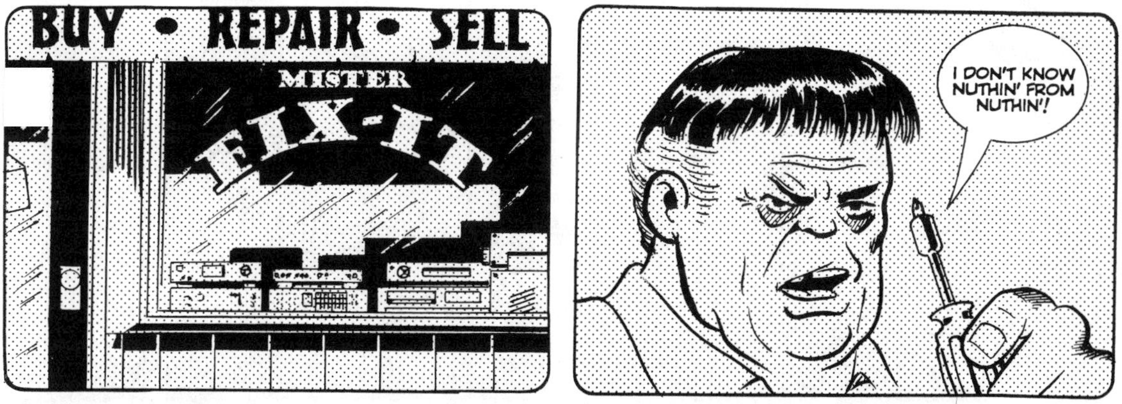
BUY • REPAIR • SELL
MISTER
FIX-IT
I DON'T KNOW NUTHIN' FROM NUTHIN'!

"THE INCREDIBLE HANK'S MINDLESS RAMPAGE HAD COME TO AN ***END*** IN A JOLLY KING ***FAST FOOD*** RESTAURANT, WHERE THE CREATURE HAD GORGED ITSELF ON SHAKES AND FRIES. A ***SECURITY CAMERA*** CAPTURED THE BRUTE SLEEPING OFF HIS HIGH-CARB SNACK . . .

"THE VIDEOTAPE, WHICH WE'VE SPEEDED UP, SHOWS THE ***AMAZING TRANSFORMATION*** OF THE PAUNCHY PURPLE POWERHOUSE INTO A PUDGY, PASTY-FACE PREPUBESCENT . . .

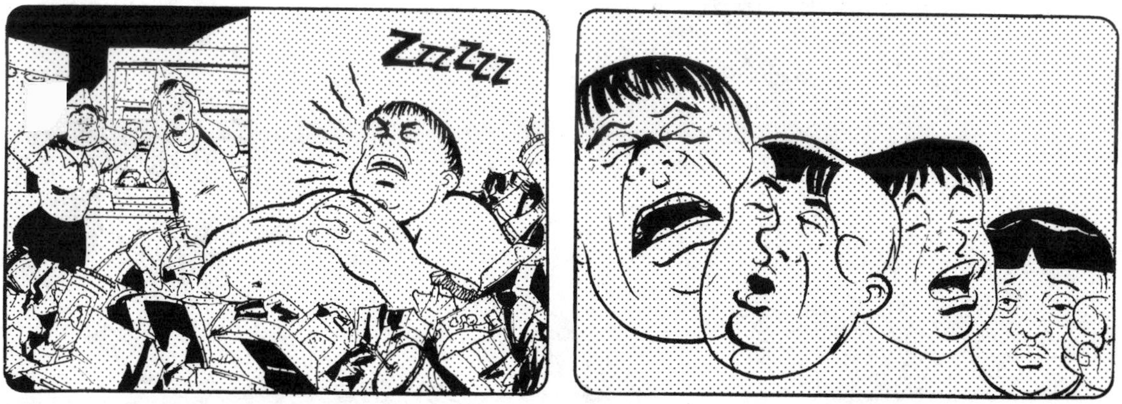
ZZZZZZ

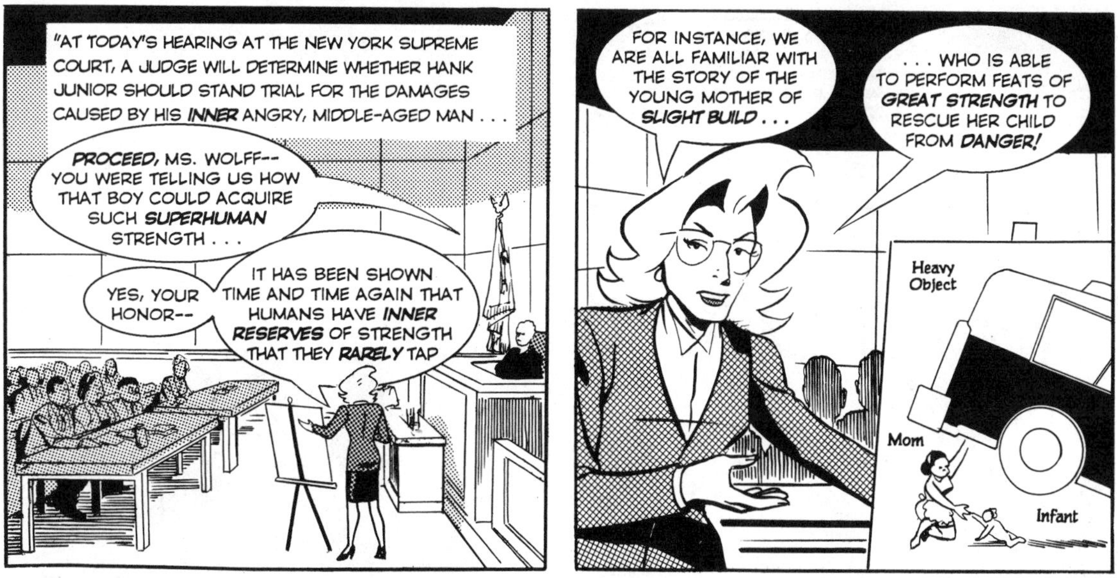
"AT TODAY'S HEARING AT THE NEW YORK SUPREME COURT, A JUDGE WILL DETERMINE WHETHER HANK JUNIOR SHOULD STAND TRIAL FOR THE DAMAGES CAUSED BY HIS INNER ANGRY, MIDDLE-AGED MAN . . .
PROCEED, MS. WOLFF-- YOU WERE TELLING US HOW THAT BOY COULD ACQUIRE SUCH SUPERHUMAN STRENGTH . . .
YES, YOUR HONOR--
IT HAS BEEN SHOWN TIME AND TIME AGAIN THAT HUMANS HAVE INNER RESERVES OF STRENGTH THAT THEY RARELY TAP
FOR INSTANCE, WE ARE ALL FAMILIAR WITH THE STORY OF THE YOUNG MOTHER OF SLIGHT BUILD . . .
. . . WHO IS ABLE TO PERFORM FEATS OF GREAT STRENGTH TO RESCUE HER CHILD FROM DANGER!
Heavy Object
Mom
Infant

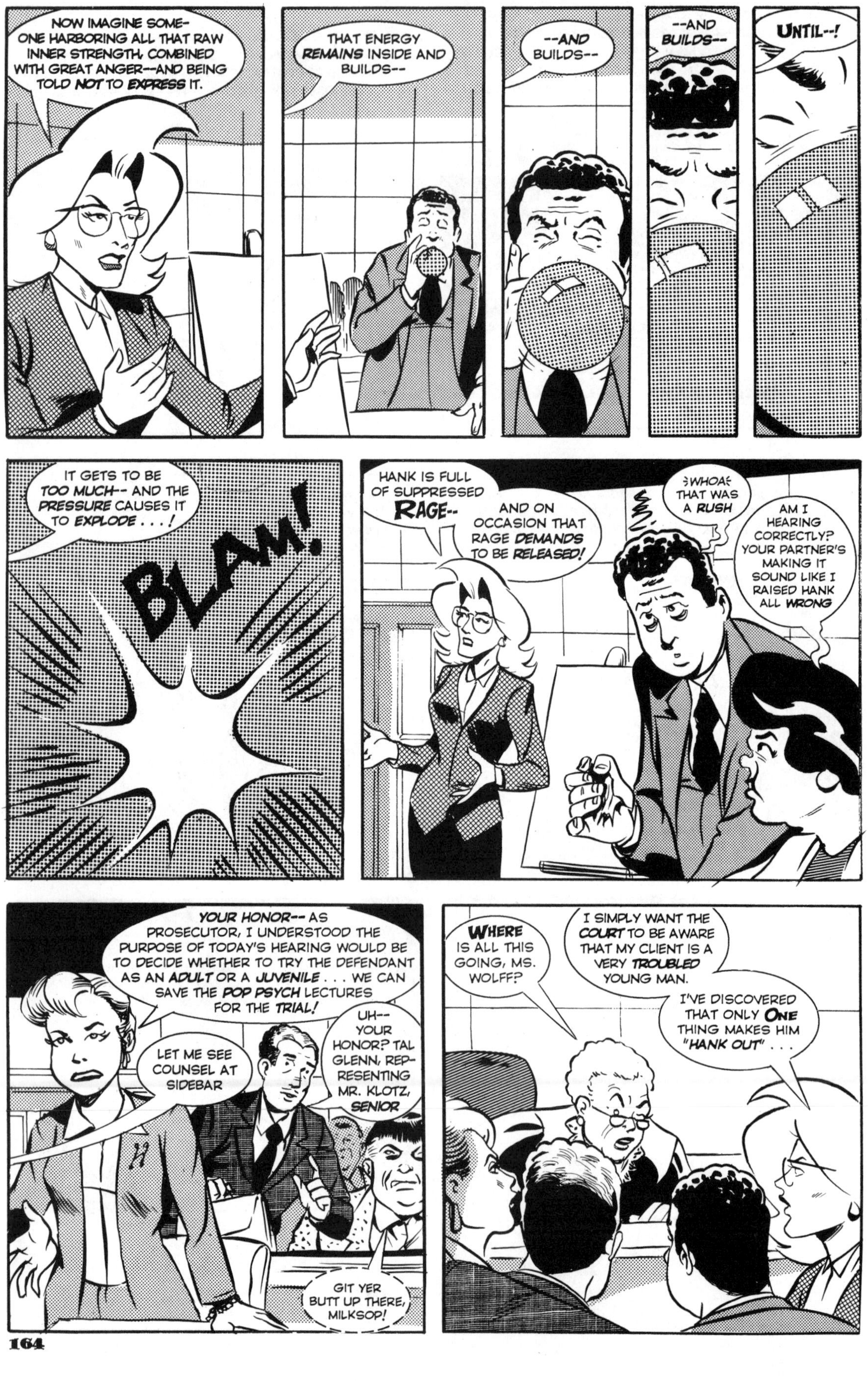
NOW IMAGINE SOME-ONE HARBORING ALL THAT RAW INNER STRENGTH, COMBINED WITH GREAT ANGER--AND BEING TOLD NOT TO EXPRESS IT.
THAT ENERGY REMAINS INSIDE AND BUILDS--
--AND BUILDS--
--AND BUILDS--
UNTIL--!
IT GETS TO BE TOO MUCH-- AND THE PRESSURE CAUSES IT TO EXPLODE . . . !
BLAM!
HANK IS FULL OF SUPPRESSED RAGE--
AND ON OCCASION THAT RAGE DEMANDS TO BE RELEASED!
WHOA! THAT WAS A RUSH
AM I HEARING CORRECTLY? YOUR PARTNER'S MAKING IT SOUND LIKE I RAISED HANK ALL WRONG
YOUR HONOR-- AS PROSECUTOR, I UNDERSTOOD THE PURPOSE OF TODAY'S HEARING WOULD BE TO DECIDE WHETHER TO TRY THE DEFENDANT AS AN ADULT OR A JUVENILE . . . WE CAN SAVE THE POP PSYCH LECTURES FOR THE TRIAL!
UH-- YOUR HONOR? TAL GLENN, REP-RESENTING MR. KLOTZ, SENIOR
LET ME SEE COUNSEL AT SIDEBAR
GIT YER BUTT UP THERE, MILKSOP!
WHERE IS ALL THIS GOING, MS. WOLFF?
I SIMPLY WANT THE COURT TO BE AWARE THAT MY CLIENT IS A VERY TROUBLED YOUNG MAN.
I'VE DISCOVERED THAT ONLY ONE THING MAKES HIM "HANK OUT" . . .

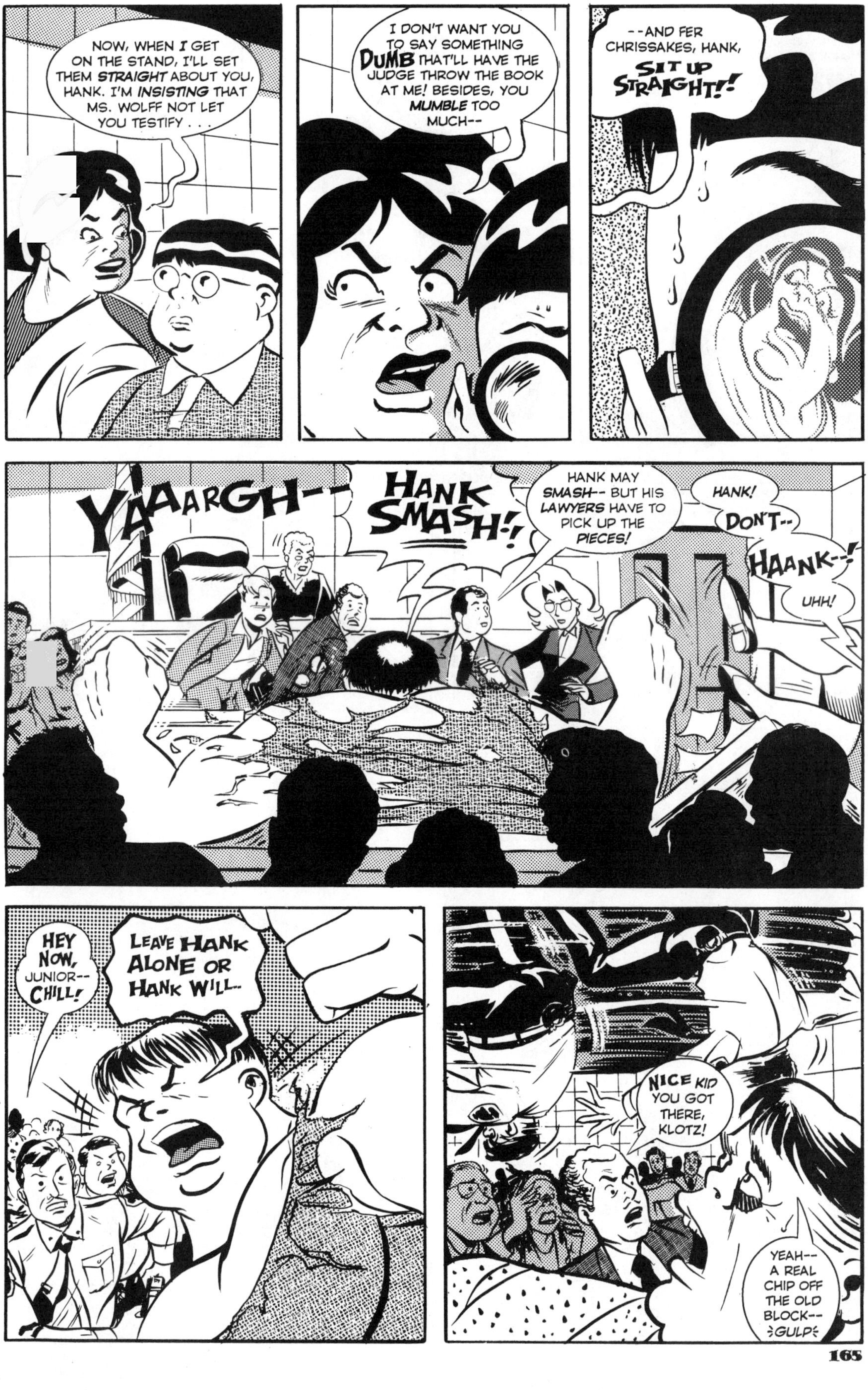
NOW, WHEN I GET ON THE STAND, I'LL SET THEM STRAIGHT ABOUT YOU, HANK. I'M INSISTING THAT MS. WOLFF NOT LET YOU TESTIFY . . .
I DON'T WANT YOU TO SAY SOMETHING DUMB THAT'LL HAVE THE JUDGE THROW THE BOOK AT ME! BESIDES, YOU MUMBLE TOO MUCH--
--AND FER CHRISSAKES, HANK,
SIT UP STRAIGHT!!
YAAARGH--
HANK SMASH!!
HANK MAY SMASH-- BUT HIS LAWYERS HAVE TO PICK UP THE PIECES!
HANK!
DON'T--
HAANK--!
UHH!
HEY NOW, JUNIOR-- CHILL!
LEAVE HANK ALONE OR HANK WILL..
NICE KID YOU GOT THERE, KLOTZ!
YEAH-- A REAL CHIP OFF THE OLD BLOCK--
GULP

YOU THINK *HE'S* ANGRY, COUNSELOR, WAIT'LL YOU SEE HOW PERTURBED *I'LL* GET IF YOU DON'T *RESTRAIN* YOUR CLIENT!

OF COURSE, YOUR HONOR--BUT YOU'VE SEEN A *SMALL* SAMPLE OF HANK'S INCREDIBLE RAGE *UNLEASHED.* EXCUSE ME . . .

HANK--? *NO* SMASH . . .

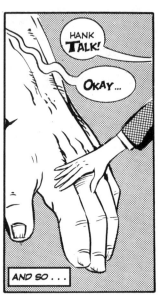

HANK *TALK!*

OKAY . . .

AND SO . . .

HANK, TELL THE COURT IN *YOUR OWN WORDS* WHY YOU WANT TO SMASH *PUNY HUMANS* . . .

GO AHEAD-- EVERYONE *HAS* TO BE *QUIET* AND *LISTEN* TO YOU-- RIGHT, JUDGE?

I OUGHT TO HAVE MY HEAD EXAMINED FOR *ALLOWING* THIS--

--BUT IN *MY* COURT, EVEN A PERSON WITH PURPLE SKIN AND A PETULANT PERSONALITY CAN *SPEAK* ON HIS OWN BEHALF.

PROCEED . . .

UMM . . . HANK NOT KNOW WHERE TO *START* . . .

ALL HANK KNOW IS THAT MOTHER AND FATHER ALWAYS *FIGHT...*

THEY NEVER *LIKE* EACH OTHER

HEARD THEM SAY HANK WAS *ACCIDENT*

MOTHER NOT WANT HANK TO *TURN OUT* LIKE FATHER

MUST BE *HANK'S* FAULT . . .

SHE JUST WANT TO *PROTECT* HANK-- OVERDID IT!

SHE WOULDN'T LET HANK WATCH *TV* OR PLAY *SPORTS* OR ANYTHING

BUT THEN SHE STARTED COMPLAINING THAT I WAS TURNING INTO A "BIG FAT NOTHING" . . .

I WANTED TO *PLEASE* MOM . . .

. . . SO I DIDN'T DO *ANYTHING* AT ALL!

JUST LIKE *DAD!*

WOULD YOU LIKE YOUR *GLASSES,* HANK?

THANKS-- BUT I THINK I CAN SEE PRETTY CLEARLY NOW . . .

WEEKS LATER . . .

. . . AND I'M GOING TO SEE MY *GODPARENTS* IN NEW MEXICO! THEY'RE GONNA TAKE ME *HIKING* AND *HORSEBACK RIDING* AND ALL *SORTS* OF STUFF . . . !

SOUNDS LIKE *FUN!* TELL YOU WHAT-- PLANE'S GETTING READY FOR *TAKEOFF,* BUT I'LL COME BACK AND WE'LL TALK SOME MORE, OKAY?

SWEET!

BONDING WITH THE *V.I.P.,* BETTY?

HE'S A GOOD KID, BOB-- HARD TO BELIEVE HE ONCE WAS ABLE TO TURN INTO A *MONSTER* . . .

I'VE READ *ALL ABOUT* HIS CASE. APPARENTLY HANK'S INNER MONSTER *NEVER* EMERGED AGAIN AFTER HE LET IT ALL *OUT* ON THE STAND!

IN FACT, THE JUDGE TURNED OUT TO BE PRETTY SYMPATHETIC. CRIMINAL CHARGES WERE DISMISSED-- EVEN THOUGH LOTS OF *LAWSUITS* ARE STILL PENDING!

HANK'S ATTORNEYS CONVINCED THE COURT THAT IT WAS THE BOY'S *MOTHER* WHO DID THINGS TO TRIGGER HANK'S "SPELLS" . . .

THE LAWYERS SUGGESTED THAT *THERAPY* AND *MEDICATION* MIGHT BE THE ANSWER!

SO THE KID'S *SEDATED?*

NO-- THE MOTHER IS! THE JUDGE ORDERED THAT SHE SEEK *PSYCHIATRIC* HELP . . . DOCTORS PRESCRIBED TRANQUILIZERS *AND* AN *OUTLET* FOR *HER* TO VENT HER ANGER . . .

BOY, I CAN'T *WAIT* TO SEE UNCLE HERB AND AUNT MARIE!

I'M GLAD YOU'RE *EXCITED,* DEAR . . .

WHAT HAPPENED TO THE *FATHER?*

I READ HE'S IN *HOT WATER* FOR *DELINQUENT* ALIMONY AND CHILD SUPPORT PAYMENTS . . .

BETTY--?

CAN YOU SEE IF ANY *PASSENGER* IS USING AN *ELECTRONIC DEVICE?* THERE SEEMS TO BE SOME *INTERFERENCE* WITH THE INSTRUMENTS . . .

I'LL CHECK, CAPTAIN ROSS

AH. MRS. KLOTZ? WE CAN'T TAKE OFF UNTIL YOU *TURN* THAT *OFF,* OKAY?

OH, YES, *YES* . . . OF COURSE . . .

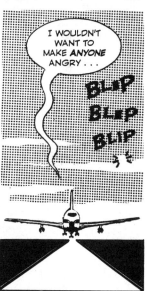

I WOULDN'T WANT TO MAKE *ANYONE* ANGRY . . .

BLIP BLIP BLIP

About the Author

Batton Lash was born and raised in Brooklyn, New York, where he attended James Madison High School. He went on to study cartooning and graphic arts at the School of Visual Arts in Manhattan, where his instructors included the legendary cartoonists Will Eisner and Harvey Kurtzman.

After graduating he took on various art-related jobs, including doing copywriting for an ad agency and serving as comic book artist Howard Chaykin's first assistant. As a freelance illustrator, Lash did drawings for *Garbage* magazine, a children's workbook, the book *Rock 'n' Roll Confidential,* the Murder to Go participatory theater group, a reconstructive surgery firm, and other projects.

In 1979 Brooklyn Paper Publications asked him to create a comic strip. Lash came up with "Wolff & Byrd, Counselors of the Macabre," which ran in *The Brooklyn Paper* until 1996 and in *The National Law Journal* from 1983 to 1997. He also did editorial cartoons for *The Brooklyn Paper* off and on for a 12-year period, prepared courtroom graphics for two cases, and prepared charts for *The New York Daily News* advertising department for sales meetings and in-house presentations.

In the 1980s and early 1990s Lash drew W&B stories for such publications as TSR's *Polyhedron, American Fantasy,* and *Monster Scene.* Original Wolff & Byrd stories have also appeared in a number of comic books and anthologies, including *Satan's Six, Mr. Monster, Munden's Bar, Frankie's Frightmare, Crack-a-Boom, The Big Bigfoot Book,* and *Murder By Crowquill.*

Lash's non-W&B work includes art for Hamilton Comics' short-lived horror line (*Grave Tales, Dread of Night,* etc.) and for *The Big Book of Death, The Big Book of Weirdos, The Big Book of Urban Legends,* and *The Big Book of Thugs* for Paradox Press. He wrote the notorious *Archie Meets The Punisher,* the 1994 crossover between Archie Comics and Marvel Comics, as well as a 4-part Archie story, "The House of Riverdale," in the fall of 1995. More recently, he has been writing the quarterly *Radioactive Man* series for Bongo Comics (publishers of *The Simpsons*).

Since May 1994, Wolff & Byrd have held court in their own bimonthly comic book, now titled *Supernatural Law,* from Exhibit A Press, which Lash established with his wife, Jackie Estrada. The comic book is currently under option at Universal, where it is being developed as a major live-action film.

Exhibit A Press co-publisher and editor **Jackie Estrada** wears many other hats, including convention organizer, book editor, and administrator of the Will Eisner Comic Industry Awards.

A San Diego resident since the 1950s, Jackie got involved in helping to put on the San Diego Comic-Con (now called Comic-Con International: San Diego) in the mid-1970s. In the years since then she has served on the Comic-Con's board of directors, edited ten of the souvenir program books, produced the at-show *Events Guide,* and chaired the guest and awards committees. She became administrator of the Eisner Awards (the "Oscars" of the comics industry) in 1990. As part of her commitment to the comics artform, she also served five years as president of Friends of Lulu, a national nonprofit organization devoted to getting more women and girls involved in comics.

As a professional editor for over 30 years, Jackie has edited hundreds of books and other publications. One of her favorite projects was editing *Comics: Between the Panels,* a lavish four-color coffeetable book from Dark Horse Comics. The book features more than 100 of her photos, taken of various comics professionals over the past 20-plus years. Jackie was also one of the founders of the San Diego Professional Editors' Network (SD/PEN) and has taught editing at the University of California, San Diego.

For Exhibit A Press, Jackie edits all of the company's comics and books, does the principal lettering for the comic book, and handles the marketing and public relations.

Want More?

If you enjoyed these cases and would like to read more Wolff & Byrd (and Mavis!) stories, you've got lots to choose from. Exhibit A Press has published over 30 issues of *Supernatural Law* (aka *Wolff & Byrd, Counselors of the Macabre*) comic books and three issues of *Mavis.* Many of these issues are still in print and are available from Exhibit A. In addition, Exhibit has published *Sonovawitch! And Other Tales of Supernatural Law* in the same format as *The Vampire Brat.* Like this book, *Sonovawitch!* is 176 pages and comprises six issues of the W&B comic (numbers 17–22, which immediately precede the stories in this collection), plus the first issue of *Mavis.*

In this collection, Wolff & Byrd's clients include:

- **"Dr. Life,"** a physician dedicated to reviving the dead
- **"Bugsy" Renfield,** a vampire member of the Nosferatu crime cartel
- **Ygor,** a hunchback charged with having taught Satanism to preschool children
- **Martin Woodhull,** accused of "hexual harassment" when his mom, a witch, puts a love spell on one of his co-workers
- **Dekoo Kei,** a Japanese holy man, guardian to a jewel that can unleash the power of a giant reptilian monster: the **Gormagon**
- **Barry Hopper,** a nice guy whose soul has accidentally possessed the body of the demon **Wasistlos**—and the demon is none too happy to have to deal with its "inner human"

PLUS: Wolff and Byrd's secretary, **Mavis,** has an adventure all her own. The self-proclaimed "World's Greatest Secretary" has no problem dealing with ghosts and ghouls in the office; what scares her is her private life, including her family and her boyfriend!

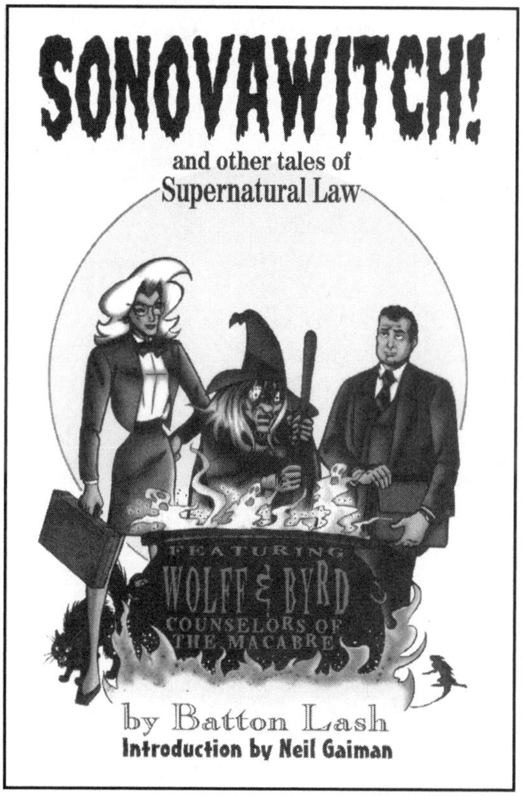
SONOVAWITCH!
and other tales of
Supernatural Law
FEATURING
WOLFF & BYRD
COUNSELORS OF THE MACABRE
by Batton Lash
Introduction by Neil Gaiman

ISBN: 0-9633954-6-7 $14.95

"Batton Lash's delicious Wolff and Byrd tales are the finest funny supernatural fictions ever created, and (as you will see as the tales in this book unfold) one of the best legal soap operas out there."

—From the Introduction by Neil Gaiman, award-winning author of *American Gods, Neverwhere, Sandman: The Dream Hunters,* and numerous graphic novels

All publications are available from **Exhibit A Press,** 4657 Cajon Way, San Diego, CA 92115 (if ordering by mail, include $4.00 per trade paperback for postage and handling) and online from **www.exhibitapress.com.** You can also ask for them at fine bookstores and comics emporiums everywhere. Visit the Exhibit A web site for a full catalogue of Wolff & Byrd/Supernatural Law products, along with news about Batton Lash, a photo gallery, and information about the *Supernatural Law* live-action motion picture.